S0-FMK-393

Dramatics for Creative Teaching

Samuel J. Citron

Dramatics for Creative Teaching

United Synagogue Commission on Jewish Education
New York, 1961-5721

Designed by Marilyn Marcus

Copyright 1961 by The United Synagogue of America

All rights reserved. No part of this book may be reproduced in any form
without permission in writing from the publisher
except by a reviewer who may quote brief passages in a review
to be printed in a magazine or newspaper.

Printed in the United States of America

296.68
C498d

10-9-78

To the memory of four whose essence of being has colored this work:

my father, Oved,
whose *N'shamah Y'terah* was in drama and song;

my mother, Sarah Peninah,
who found beauty in every aspect of creation;

my father-in-law, Aaron Shimon Shpall,
to whom every pupil was a precious vessel containing Israel's destiny;

my mother-in-law, Shulamith,
who, with love, accepted alike the bad and the good as life's gifts.

יהא זכרם ברוך

FUNDERBURG LIBRARY
c. 1
MANCHESTER COLLEGE

Preface

It took a long time to write this book.

My dear friend, Dr. Abraham E. Millgram, Educational Director of the United Synagogue of America, would say that it took more than a decade. As long ago as 1950 he asked me to write a book on dramatics for teaching. Ever since then he guided, encouraged, and urged me on with warm sympathy and understanding. I am deeply indebted to him.

The teachers who have been my students in the educational dramatics workshops which I have conducted at the Jewish Education Committee of New York would say that it took more than fifteen years. Since 1945 I have had the co-operation of hundreds of teachers and principals who attended these workshops. They tried out many of the techniques in their classrooms, offered suggestions for changes and different approaches, and generally helped refine the methodology to meet the practical needs of classroom situations. To all of them, and especially to Jacob Greenberg, I am very grateful.

My family would say that I have been involved with this book for at least twenty-five years. My wife has worked very closely with me in the development of many of the techniques, drawing on her experience as teacher and principal. My children, Aaron and Sharon, served as "subjects" during their childhood and more recently as constructive critics of many parts of the completed manuscript. I am grateful to them and to the Almighty for them.

Some of my dear friends would say that it all goes back even further. Esther Sommerstein Zweig would fix the date at 1929 when she involved me in my first educational dramatic venture in a Jewish school, and Leah Kleiman Leshefsky would pick the same year when she "tricked" me into writing my first dramatic script for Jewish children.

Were my parents alive, they would say that it all began when I was less than four years old. I am inclined to think that this is so. They took me to see a performance of Goldfadden's *Bar Kokhba* by a wandering Yiddish theatrical group that came for a one night stand to our tiny hamlet, Racionz in Poland. For months after, the Jewish homes re-echoed the songs of the operetta. Forever after I have been caught in drama's emotional net. The memory of its effect on me goaded me on to seek ways of utilizing it to enrich the lives of other children whose development was entrusted to me as their teacher.

There are many others to whom I am deeply indebted. I am grateful to my friend and colleague, Dr. Azriel Eisenberg, who first suggested that I write this book and encouraged me when the going became rough at times; to my colleagues, Dr. Leon Feldman, Yudel Mark, Frances Morgenlander, Jack Noskowitz, and Israel Weisberger who read sections of the manuscript and offered valuable suggestions; to Elhanan Indelman for his help with some of the Hebrew Choral Reading arrangements; to my former assistants, Edya Signer Arzt and Doris Einstein, who helped greatly in preliminary research; to my sister, Laura Citron Carper, a gifted drama teacher, who gave valuable suggestions in the formulation of the section dealing with Dramatization Readiness; to Bella Kulak, librarian of the Jewish Education Committee of New York, for her assistance in the use of the library facilities; and to Minnie Dight, Linda Napolin Katz, Jane Mincho, Niusia Shimrat, and Mildred Wenger who assisted in typing and preparing the manuscript.

I am grateful to the many teachers and principals whose schools and classes served as laboratories for my personal experiments with many of the techniques in this book. Especially noteworthy are the following New York City schools: Bialik School, Congregation B'nai Jeshurun, East Midwood Jewish Center, Forest Hills Jewish Center, Glory of Israel Talmud Torah, Hillcrest Jewish Center, Jewish Communal Center of Flatbush, Little Neck Jewish Center, Rego Park Jewish Center, Temple Gates of Prayer in Flushing, and Yeshiva of Flatbush.

I am deeply grateful to the Jewish Education Committee of New York. My work as the Director of its School Dramatics Department has provided me with rich opportunities for experimentation in creative approaches to teaching with dramatics.

My thanks go also to the United Synagogue Commission on Jewish Education, Rabbi Jack J. Cohen, Chairman, and its Committee on Textbook Publications, Mr. Henry R. Goldberg, Chairman.

I am greatly indebted to the Readers—Leah Jaffa, Consultant on Programming With the Arts, National Jewish Welfare Board, Dr. Paul Kozelko, Professor of Education, Teachers College, Columbia University, Dr. Norman Schanin, Educational Director, The Forest Hills Jewish Center, and Dr. Grace M. Stanistreet, Director, Children's Center for Creative Arts, Adelphi College—for their many helpful suggestions.

Samuel J. Citron

Flushing, New York, April, 1961

Contents

Indexes

Introduction

■ This is a book of dramatic methods and techniques for teaching the subject matter of the curriculum. Most of the procedures described may be applied to the teaching process in any school—religious or secular, Jewish or general. Many of the techniques are especially suited to the teaching of Social Studies and the Language Arts in elementary and junior high schools. However, as developed here, they are specifically aimed for application to the subject matter of the Jewish school curriculum. Some modification and adaptation, generally of a minor nature, will have to be made by the teacher in many of the procedures if they are to be applied to the teaching of subject matter of the general school curriculum.

Many of the techniques offered here are suitable for immediate and direct application in the classroom. They have been developed in a step-by-step fashion and highlighted by numerous illustrations of possible classroom procedures based on actual school uses. Teachers will find them useful in helping to solve immediate teaching problems. Their real value, however, lies in the fact that by means of these approaches the teacher is able actively to involve the willing participation of the pupils in the learning process as a whole and to maintain an emotionally stimulating and intellectually challenging educative climate in the classroom. Consequently, these approaches are offered as guides and stimulation for further experimentation on the part of the teacher in the use of these and other approaches to creative teaching and not as panaceas to solve all teaching problems or as models to be slavishly followed. After many years of experimenting under actual classroom conditions I am convinced that these techniques are good tools. But even the finest of tools require skillful use to achieve their fullest potential!

■ BASIC ASSUMPTIONS

In developing these teaching techniques I have been guided by several underlying assumptions:

1. The task of the Jewish school is to teach *Torah. Torah,* as I understand it, is the totality of Jewish knowledge as expressed in the Jewish sacred writings, laws and customs, language and prayer, history and literature, ethics and folkways—in short, every aspect of Jewish creativity which guides the life and conduct of the individual Jew, and serves to bind and unite him with Judaism and the Jewish people.
2. Teaching and learning are a continuum. The learner must be as active as the teacher in an effective educational experience. The student is not to be thought of as a passive receptacle for knowledge poured out by the teacher. Both teacher and student must contribute of their creative resources to the educative process if it is to be truly effective.
3. Learning is particularly effective when it proceeds from experiences. This is true in all areas and especially in relation to the so-called "skill subjects." The child who is curious about the signs on stores often learns to read without undue effort.

The pupil who is allowed to shop for his parents at the local grocery or stationery store generally finds it easier to assimilate the elements of arithmetic. In like manner, an understanding of the social scene as well as desirable attitudes and action-patterns are more easily acquired, assimilated, and retained by the learner when they derive from reality experiences.

4. Learning gains in effectiveness when it leads to use, to action. In Jewish tradition, study and practice are a unity. Rabban Gamaliel the son of Rabbi Yehudah Hanasi states in *Ethics of the Fathers*, II:2: "*V'khol torah sh'eyn immah m'lakhah sofah b'teylah*—All study of the Torah without accompanying activity must in the end come to naught." The Jew's affirmation of the unity of the Almighty, the *Sh'ma*, which is recited several times daily, is preceded in the Morning Service by a prayer for wisdom and understanding. This prayer reaches its climax with the plea: "*V'ha'eyr eynenu b'toratekha, v'dabek libenu b'mitzvotekha*—Deepen our insight in Thy Torah, and make our hearts cleave to Thy commandments." Learning and observance are spoken of in one breath, one leading directly to the other and both being interrelated.
5. At the same time it is to be recognized that not all learning can be or, for that matter, should be immediately applied and put into practice. A meaningful educational experience, more often than not, opens vistas of new and distant goals, holding out a promise of heights to be scaled, obstacles to be overcome, problems to be solved, and provides the emotional charge to propel the learner in that direction.
6. Both emotion and intellect are vital to the learning process. A learning experience generally gains in effectiveness when it is infused with emotion. Conduct is modified and value-patterns are established more easily and become more permanently fixed when the emotions of the learner are deeply involved in the educative process.

Proceeding from these basic assumptions, the teacher would strive, whenever possible, to create learning situations which revolve about reality experiences which are emotionally charged—experiences that call for problem solving on a level that is meaningful for the learner; that require him to draw on his intellectual faculties and emotional resources; that impel him to search for solutions willingly and actively; that are related to the value-patterns of his social environment; and that open up vistas toward newer goals which are meaningful, clearly discernible to, and desirable for the learner himself.

■ DRAMATICS FOR TEACHING

The list of reality situations to be found within the social environment or which can be established within the school and its orbit to lend vitality to the teaching process is quite long but definitely not inexhaustible. In a large measure, dramatics utilized as a technique in teaching offers us substantial help in this direction. It is by no means the complete answer to our teaching problems. It is certainly not to be considered as the sole or even the major teaching technique to be used. The textbook, lecture, discussion, question and answer, and other familiar techniques are continued to be used to their fullest potential. However, along with these, dramatics helps us to involve the students in educative reality situations in certain subject areas.

Through dramatization we are able to *simulate* reality situations that are distant from the here and now, provide for experiences which would otherwise not be possible, and invest with personal meaning problems and issues that are seemingly academic and abstract. By means of a dramatization the student can vicariously relive the experiences, and feel the emotions which motivated the actions of the historic figures. Through re-enactment of a story, Hebrew language becomes related to life. Through creative dramatization of parallel situations in modern settings, the moral lessons of the Bible can become guiding forces in the life of the learner. Similar applications are possible for nearly all areas of the curriculum.

Dramatization, when properly used as an educational technique, completely involves the student in an active learning process. It makes demands upon him—demands which he meets willingly, eagerly, because of his interest in the task at hand. It draws on his creative impulses, on his imagination, on his innermost intellectual and emotional resources. He is not merely being taught, receiving passively the knowledge transmitted to him by the teacher. He is an active partner in the learning process. He engages in research, he plans, he devotes out-of-school time, he draws on the precious resources of his innermost self.

These are tangible, obvious benefits of utilizing dramatics as an aid in teaching the subjects in the curriculum. There are other, intangible benefits accruing from its uses which, though less obvious, are equally important in the educative process.

Dramatization, for example, provides excellent opportunities for experiences in democratic living. The participants are involved in a common task. They work together for a common goal. They all help in planning the dramatization, doing the research, creating the dialogue. Guided by the teacher, they learn to evaluate their own work and the work of their classmates. They become habituated to respect the efforts of their colleagues and to have confidence in their own abilities. They learn when to compromise and when to defend their position. In short, since dramatics is by its very nature a social activity, it provides the students valuable experiences in social living within a democracy.

Dramatics is usually an activity which is willingly undertaken. There is almost a natural tendency on the part of everyone to dramatize. Children at play are constantly dramatizing. Adults, too, are not immune. Witness in this regard the growth of community theatres, amateur theatrical groups, synagogue and organizational dramatics for programs or fund raising, or the occasional tendency we all have to imitate the manner and rate of speech of the leading character after seeing a movie. The teacher, who skillfully puts to use this natural tendency to dramatize, will often see learning results far beyond normal expectations.

The school is primarily a place for learning—not for "having fun." However, it is generally agreed that we usually tend to remember pleasant experiences and we more readily forget the unpleasant ones. Dramatics infuses the learning process with an emotional quality which takes the subject matter studied out of the realm of the humdrum. It makes study a joy, learning an adventure, the classroom a place of enchantment, each lesson an eagerly sought experience. It fills the learning process with a spirit of life. Passive learning becomes active striving and leads to meaningful achievement.

Jewish educators have long been sensitive to the potential of dramatics in education. They have used dramatics as an aid to better learning and better retention as well as a means of adding beauty, romance, and emotional appeal to Jewish school life. Holiday celebrations, assembly programs, observance of community and historical events depend in large measure on the use of dramatics to make them meaningful and appealing. In the eighteen-nineties Bloch Publishing Company was already distributing plays for Jewish school use. Old-timers in the Jewish education profession still speak with nostaglia of the touching dramatization of the Hebrew lullaby, "*Numah Perah*," which was staged as far back as 1910 in Girls Prep School Number One, one of the very first modern Jewish schools established in New York City.

In the course of time the emphasis has shifted toward the use of dramatics as a teaching technique in the classroom. Nearly every curriculum, almost every syllabus suggests the use of dramatics both as an activity for its own sake and as a teaching technique. The question which concerns Jewish educators is not *whether* to use dramatics but *how* to use it. Teachers are eager to find new techniques and new applications of accepted dramatic techniques to the teaching process.

This book has been developed to meet the requirements of the teacher who subscribes to the desirability of using dramatics but needs help in applying its techniques to the teaching process. Many of the approaches given here were developed in the course of more than fifteen years in the educational dramatics workshops and in-service courses which this writer has conducted under the auspices of the Jewish Education Committee of New York. Many procedures and devices were hammered out in the give-and-take of class discussion. Others have been suggested by teachers in term papers. The bulk of them have been tested by the writer and his teacher-students under actual classroom conditions. Only those which stood the test were included in this volume.

In many instances, the different steps involved in the utilization of the techniques and the devices given here are illustrated by examples of teacher-student dialogue. Obviously these dialogues are not given as "scripts" to be used verbatim by the teacher. *They are offered merely as guides for the teacher* in order to make clear what is essential to be brought out in the course of the class discussion and to suggest ways how the teacher may stimulate the students to develop the lesson through their creative contributions. The actual dialogue, and quite often the very process itself, will of course vary greatly from class to class and from day to day.

Similarly, each device is illustrated with examples of actual dramatizations. These too are not offered as scripts to be memorized or read and used directly. *They are models, samples.* They are intended to indicate to the teacher what is possible and what is the aim in each given device. To use them as scripts would be to defeat the very purpose of utilizing dramatics for teaching—creative participation by the students in the entire process: research, planning, dialogue, presentation, discussion, evaluation. Every aspect that contributes to the process is the students' own creation under the stimulation and guidance of the teacher. Therein lies the greatest value of dramatics as a teaching tool. The creative teacher will make use of this tool to the fullest extent possible. In using it, he will be wary not to dull this tool by imposing curbs on the creative participation of the students in the full process of developing a teaching-learning dramatization.

CHAPTER 1

Games for Teaching and for Developing Dramatization Readiness

■ THE NEED FOR DRAMATIZATION READINESS

The concept of Reading Readiness is by now well understood and generally accepted in educational circles. Similarly, in relation to participation in creative dramatization there is the need of a state of mind which we will call Dramatization Readiness, without which it is extremely difficult, if not impossible, for the learner to derive the benefits inherent in this form of learning activity.

Reading Readiness is generally attained when the learner achieves a certain stage of maturity which usually comes with age and experience. Contrariwise, Dramatization Readiness is generally lost with maturity and can only be recaptured with deliberate effort. The teacher who plans to utilize creative dramatization as a learning experience must be aware of this and must be prepared to exert considerable effort to help his students toward Dramatization Readiness, where this quality is lacking, before proceeding to use dramatization itself.

What Is Dramatization Readiness?

The most precious ingredients of the classroom dramatization process are the elements of spontaneity, the free and untrammeled creative participation of the students in the planning of the dramatization, of its development and its enactment. In very young children the element of spontaneity, the ability to disregard the outside world and immerse themselves in make-believe is present. While at play they dramatize freely. Their imaginations soar. Household furniture becomes castles, trains, automobiles or whatever else is needed for the game. Inanimate objects become horses and cows. Dolls come to life. The children themselves assume characterizations and discard them at will. They create situations and dialogue easily, spontaneously. They move in and out of reality to make-believe freely, without self-consciousness.

As children grow older, as they are gradually projected into the adult-guided world and its growing tempest of "do's" and "don'ts," they begin to lose their spontaneity and the freedom of expression. More of this dramatization readiness is lost after they begin school. The formal atmosphere generally pervading most classrooms is not conducive to spontaneous expression. The authority image of the teacher serves as a brake on the children's freedom of action.

There are of course schools and teachers that consciously encourage free creative expression by the children. Many utilize dramatics in teaching and their students have numerous opportunities for experiences with this technique. Such students, when they come into the Jewish school, are quite ready for dramatization. With them, the teacher may proceed directly to dramatization without preliminary preparation. The large mass of students, however, have no such experiences in their secular schools. Generally, by the time they are old enough to attend the Jewish school they have built up walls of reserve which mitigate against their free expression in a dramatization. They are not ready to use dramatization without preliminary efforts on the part of the teacher to break down these walls built about the students by time and social pressure.

Nearly every teacher who has tried to dramatize a lesson in class has had this experience: The class has studied a lesson in Bible or history—let us say, the story of Abraham and Lot and their difficulties over pasture lands. The teacher decides that a dramatization of the story will be helpful. After some preliminaries the teacher selects two children to enact the story, one to play the role of Abraham, the other to portray Lot. They are asked to come to the front of the room. They come up. They are told to begin. There is an awkward silence. Teacher tries to help out and turns to the pupil who is to portray the Patriarch Abraham, "You are the Patriarch and older than Lot, suppose you begin, Abraham." Silence. Teacher urges some more, "Well, Abraham?" Continued silence while "Abraham's" face changes from red to white to red in rhythmic waves and "Lot" giggles self-consciously. The teacher continues to prod, "You're the Patriarch, Lot's uncle. Tell him it is wrong for your shepherds to fight over pastures." Our Abraham swallows hard, takes a deep breath and plunges in, repeating hurriedly, "Lot, it is wrong for our shepherds to fight over pastures." Now the teacher turns to Lot in this "creative" dramatization, "Well, Lot?" He stops giggling and turns to the teacher for help, "What shall I say?" Teacher: "Tell him that your shepherds don't listen to you." Lot: "My shepherds don't listen to me." And so it goes—dull, dragged-out, uninspired and uninspiring, until finally the teacher gives up in despair coming to the conclusion that "dramatization" may be a progressive term that looks good in a syllabus and in the lesson-plan, but in the classroom is sheer waste of time.

Dramatization Readiness Must Be Fostered

Of course this is not so at all. The trouble is not in the technique, but in its application. These children are just too frozen with reserve and inhibitions to disregard the eyes of their classmates that are focused on them, the rigidly lined up rows of desks, the teacher that is impatiently prodding for "results." These are the children who have, in the course of time, lost their Dramatization Readiness. We will have to help them to get it back before dramatization can help us to teach these children. Before these students can dramatize creatively, inventing their own situations, characterizations and dialogue in connection with a story or historical incident, they must be freed of self-consciousness. They must be conditioned to feel free and unfettered within the classroom environment, and in the presence of their teacher and classmates. They must be given experiences—gradually, slowly, step-by-step—in the use of the various elements which go into the making of a creative dramatization: plot, action, pantomime, dialogue and imagination harnessed to a purposeful task.

Developing Dramatization Readiness While Teaching Content

This process of preparation can not be sidestepped with the vast majority of children. The time that it will take will, of course, vary greatly with each group. With some pupils Dramatization Readiness will be achieved within several days. With others, it may take several weeks or even months.

Ordinarily this would be a luxury which the teacher in any school, and especially in a supplementary Jewish school, could ill afford in view of the limited time available. Despite the great value of dramatization as a teaching aid, the teacher could not devote the time necessary to engage in the elaborate processes of improvisation needed to break down the children's restraints and provide them with the basic elementary skills needed for dramatization. Fortunately, it is possible to achieve our purpose while teaching the regular subject matter of the curriculum. The teacher helps the students acquire Dramatization Readiness by means of a series of games, games that help to create a free atmosphere in the classroom, that give children experiences in pantomime and dialogue, that help them develop their imaginations and aid them in the creation of plot, situation and character. At the very same time, these games have the added function of being useful for direct teaching purposes—for motivation, for drill, for review and for testing in such subjects as Hebrew language, *Humash*, Festivals, History, etc. In fact, many of these games are so effective as teaching aids that the teacher will want to continue using them for that purpose long after their original object has been achieved and the pupils participate in dramatization freely and spontaneously.

The process of developing Dramatization Readiness utilizes a progression of steps. Each of these has a distinct function. However, there is a good deal of overlapping of purpose between them. Also, the emphasis given to each step individually will vary with the needs of each class. In some, a great deal of emphasis will be given to each step. In others, certain steps may be given only cursory attention or eliminated altogether.

■ A. TEACHING-GAMES TO ESTABLISH A PERMISSIVE ATMOSPHERE

The first step in developing Dramatization Readiness for the children individually and for the class as a whole is to loosen up the tight, formal atmosphere of the classroom and to establish a permissive climate in which the pupils will feel psychologically free to speak out, to express themselves under conditions of "having fun" while learning. All of the games offered under this heading have this as their basic purpose. In addition, each game has another, direct teaching value which will be indicated for each one individually.

1. Concentration

PURPOSES: *For testing:* to give the teacher an idea of how much the students remember about a festival from the previous year; what words they remember from a Hebrew lesson; what facts they recall from a lesson in Jewish history, Community, Current Events, etc.

For motivation: to orient them to the new matter to be taught by connecting it with previously learned material.

For drill or review: when used in connection with subject matter connected with facts or skills.

SUBJECT AREAS: Language; Jewish Life and Observance; History; Current History; Community; Israel; etc.

MANNER OF PLAYING: The teacher announces a theme about which the game will be played. For example: Hanukah; The story of Joseph and his brothers; the Hebrew story just concluded; etc. It is also possible to use as the theme a broad subject area such as: Festivals; Sabbath services; Israel; Hebrew words; etc.

All in the class, on a given signal, clap their knees with the palms of their hands, then they clap their hands together, then they snap their fingers, then the first pupil gives a word dealing with the theme. The steps of clap knees, clap hands, snap fingers, are repeated and the next student gives a word related to the theme. This goes on, the clapping and snapping being done rhythmically, by all the pupils together. If a pupil fails to give a word, or gives a word that is not connected with the theme, or repeats a word already given, he is out of the game. As the game continues, the teacher, who participates actively with the pupils, might increase the tempo so as to make the game more difficult. The last remaining in the game is the winner.

EXAMPLE: Assuming the theme is *High Holy Days,* the game would proceed as follows:

Clap knees	Clap hands	Snap fingers	Shofar
Clap knees	Clap hands	Snap fingers	Fasting
Clap knees	Clap hands	Snap fingers	Kol Nidrei
Clap knees	Etc. . . .		

2. The Lost Word

PURPOSES: To help concentrate the children's attention on new material being presented. For review and drill.

SUBJECT AREAS: Hebrew Language; Bible; History; etc. It is best suited for use in connection with material involving story elements.

MANNER OF PLAYING: The teacher tells a story—from history, Bible, a new Hebrew lesson, etc. On every key word in the story the teacher claps her hands and the pupils join her in clapping their hands. This continues until the story is concluded.

Thereafter, the teacher tells the story again, either during the same lesson or on a later occasion. At each key word, teacher and pupils clap their hands, while the teacher omits the word. It is given instead by the pupils in turn. If a pupil misses or gives the wrong word, he is out. The last one remaining in the game is the winner.

EXAMPLES: *Bible story*

Step 1: TEACHER: "When Abraham's servant Eliezer *(Clap)* arrived in Haran *(Clap)* he went directly to the well *(Clap)*. It was toward evening when the women *(Clap)* go out to draw water *(Clap)* at the well *(Clap)*. Eliezer raised his eyes to heaven and prayed

(Clap): 'Lord, God of my master Abraham' *(Clap)* . . ." (and so on until the end of the story)

Step 2: TEACHER: "When Abraham's servant . . . *(Clap)* arrived in . . . *(Clap)*, he went directly to the . . . *(Clap)*. It was toward evening when the . . . *(Clap)* go out to draw . . . *(Clap)* at the . . . *(Clap)*. Eliezer raised his eyes to heaven and . . . *(Clap)*: 'Lord, God of my master . . .' *(Clap)*, etc." This time, when teacher and pupils clap hands, pupils fill in the blanks, taking turns in doing so.

Hebrew lesson

Step 1: TEACHER: "*Horef. Yom kar* (Clap). *Bayit ham* (Clap). *Hamishpahah yoshevet baheder* (Clap) *hagadol. Al hakir t'munah* (Clap) *yafah*, etc."

Step 2: TEACHER: "*Horef. Yom* . . . (Clap)
STUDENT 1: *Kar.*
TEACHER: *Bayit* . . . (Clap)
STUDENT 2: *ham.*
TEACHER: *Hamishpahah yoshevet ba* . . . (Clap)
STUDENT 3: *baheder*
TEACHER: *hagadol. Al hakir* . . . (Clap)
STUDENT 4: *t'munah*
TEACHER: *yafah*, etc. . . .

3. *Double Up*

This is a variant of "Lost Word." Although it may be played in connection with any story, it is particularly suitable for Hebrew Language.

MANNER OF PLAYING:

1. After a new Hebrew lesson has been learned, each child selects a new Hebrew word as his very own.

2. The new story is told or read aloud.

3. Each time a new word is read aloud by the teacher or another student, the pupil who selected that word rises quickly and repeats it aloud.

4. A pupil who misses repeating, or "doubling up" his word is out of the game. The last remaining pupil is the winner.

4. *Ani*

This is a variant of "Double Up." Instead of repeating his word, the pupil jumps up and says, "Ani," each time his word is read or said.

5. *Alert*

This is another variant of "Double Up." It is helpful for Hebrew language review.

MANNER OF PLAYING: Each student is assigned one or more Hebrew words which they have previously studied. The teacher, or a student who has been chosen as Leader, begins a story in English. Each time that the story teller mentions a word that has been assigned to one of the students, that student stands, repeats the word in Hebrew and sits down. A student who fails to give his Hebrew word is out of the game.

6. *Animal Farm*

PURPOSES: Review. Testing.

SUBJECT: Language study.

MANNER OF PLAYING: This game is particularly suitable for a class of young children. One pupil is selected to be the Leader. (The teacher might be Leader when the game is first played.) The Leader mentions an animal and states what the animal does, viz: "Cow goes 'Moo.'" The pupils repeat, "Moo." At times the Leader fools them by saying the wrong thing, viz: "Cat goes 'bow, wow.'" If that happens, the pupils remain silent. Whoever is fooled into repeating the sound is out. The last remaining one becomes the Leader.

EXAMPLE:
LEADER: *Parah goah,* Moo.
CLASS: Moo.
LEADER: *Hatul m'yalel,* M'yau.
CLASS: M'yau.
LEADER: *Kelev nove'ah,* Meh.
CLASS: *(Remains silent. Whoever repeats "Meh" is out)*

7. *Sounds I Hear*

This is a variant of "Animal Farm." The sounds are not restricted to animals. The game may be structured around "Sounds I hear in the city" (automobile, airplane, telephone, child, etc.); "Sounds I hear in the country" (the brook, the trees, the cow, etc.); or any other place such as the class, the kitchen, etc. The game may also deal with sounds in general without restricting them to a particular place, so that all sounds may be used.

EXAMPLE: Using "Sounds I Hear" without limiting locale or source.
LEADER: *Hatelephone m'tzaltzel,* ring-a-ling
CLASS: Ring-a-ling
LEADER: *Hatinok bokheh,* ma-ma-ma
CLASS: Ma-ma-ma
LEADER: *Hamotor m'tarter,* bow-wow
CLASS: *(Remains silent)*
LEADER: etc., etc.

8. Shimon Omer (Simon Says)

This game is familiar to most teachers and is very popular with the children.

PURPOSES: Drill, review, testing.

SUBJECT: Language study.

MANNER OF PLAYING: A pupil is chosen as Leader. He gives commands to the class such as: "Simon says, stand." The class stands. "Simon says, sit." The class sits.

Whenever the Leader gives a command without prefacing it with the words, "Simon says . . .", the command is ignored by the class. Any one who obeys such a command is out of the game. Any one who disobeys a command properly prefaced with "Simon says . . ." or who does the wrong thing, is also out. The last one remaining becomes the Leader.

EXAMPLE:

LEADER: *"Shimon omer, imdu."*
CLASS: Stands.
LEADER: *"Shimon omer, yadayim al harosh."*
CLASS: Places hands on head. *(Those who do wrong things are out)*
LEADER: *Yadayim l'matah.*
CLASS: Ignores the command. *(It was not prefaced by the formula, "Shimon omer . . ." Anyone who does obey such a command is out)*

9. Bankers

PURPOSES: Drill, review, testing.

SUBJECT: Language study.

MANNER OF PLAYING: This game is usually applied to teaching numbers, although, like "Lost Word" it may be used in connection with any Hebrew words studied.

Each student is assigned one or more numbers in Hebrew.

A pupil is selected as Leader. The Leader calls out a number.

The pupil whose number has been called, jumps up, quickly raises his hands above his head, claps three times, repeats the number and sits down.

If anyone misses, he is out. The last remaining becomes the Leader.

VARIANTS: The game may be complicated by playing it with addition, subtraction, multiplication, division or combinations of these. Example: Leader says, "Three and four." Pupil who has number seven jumps up. Leader says, "Two from six." Pupil who has number four jumps up.

10. Dreidle Grab

This is a variant of "Bankers" and serves the same purpose. It may be used in connection with numbers, the Hebrew names of the months, the Hebrew names of the alphabet, or similar topics.

MANNER OF PLAYING: Each pupil is assigned one or more items from the topic.

A pupil is selected as the Leader. The Leader takes a dreidle and goes to the teacher's desk.

The Leader spins the dreidle (Hanukah top) and calls a word from the topic.

The student whose word has been called stands up and repeats the word. He then runs to the desk and tries to grab the dreidle before it stops spinning. If he succeeds he becomes the Leader. If he fails he is out of the game.

VARIANTS: As with "Bankers," variants may be introduced to complicate the game. For example:

If numbers are used, Leader may give addition, subtraction, etc., of the numbers.

If months are used, Leader may give the name of a holiday and pupil in whose month the holiday occurs is obliged to respond.

11. Numbers Change

This game is similar to "Marching to Jerusalem."

It is also similar in purpose and subject to "Bankers" and "Dreidle Grab."

MANNER OF PLAYING: In a classroom where the seats are not affixed to the floor, the seats are arranged in a semicircle. All the children are seated with the exception of one pupil who is "It."

Each of the seated pupils is assigned a number.

The Leader calls out a pair of numbers, like "three and five."

The pupils whose numbers have been called, rise and repeat their numbers and then run and change places with each other.

While the two are running to change places, "It" tries to take the place of one of the pupils. If he succeeds, he assumes that pupil's number and the one who lost a seat now becomes "It."

The game is over when the teacher feels it has gone on long enough.

VARIANTS: The game may also be used by pairing months, colors, male and female, and other classes of words which the class has been studying.

12. Catastrophe

PURPOSES: Presenting new lesson. Drill. Review. Testing.

SUBJECT: Language study. May also be applied to other areas such as history, festivals, etc., with slight variation.

MANNER OF PLAYING: A student is selected as Leader. (Teacher may be the Leader the first few times the game is played.)

The game is structured about a theme such as: House, Family, Class, etc.

Each student is given an item from the theme. For example, if the theme is "House," pupils would be: wall, ceiling, floor, chair, etc.

All the pupils, with the exception of one who becomes "It," are seated.

"It" has no seat, nor is he assigned a word.

The Leader begins to tell a story in Hebrew which deals with the selected theme. During the telling of the story "It" stands in front of the class, near the Leader. As the Leader tells the story and mentions an item assigned to a student, that student rises, turns around and sits down. Example: "The house had four *walls* (student who has the word *walls* rises, turns around and sits down) and a wooden *floor* (*floor* rises, turns around and sits down).

When the leader mentions a pair like: *wall* and *ceiling* or *table* and *chair*, both rise, turn around and then run and change places. As this happens, "It" tries to get one of the seats momentarily vacated. If "It" succeeds in capturing a seat, the pupil who is now without a seat becomes "It" and the previous "It" takes over his word.

When the Leader mentions the catastrophe previously agreed upon, such as: "The house collapsed" or "The family ran away" or "The class was dismissed," etc., all the pupils get up and change places, while "It" also tries to get a seat. The one remaining without a seat becomes "It."

The game ends at will. If desired, it may be agreed upon that the student who has never been "It" during the game, is to be the Leader the next time the game is played.

EXAMPLE:

LEADER: *"Li yesh bayit. Babayit sheli yesh ritzpah . . ."*
RITZPAH: *(Rises, turns around and sits down)*
LEADER: *"Al haritzpah . . ."*
RITZPAH: *(Rises again, turns around, and sits down)*
LEADER: *". . . yesh shulhan v'kisey."*
SHULHAN AND KISEY: *(Both rise, turn around and run to change places while "It" tries to take one of the places vacated temporarily)*
LEADER: *"Sarah yoshevet al hakisey . . ."*
KISEY: *(Rises, turns around and sits down)*

LEADER: . . . *v'ohelet. Pitom, kol habayit nofel!"*

ALL: *(On hearing the "catastrophe" phrase, "kol habayit nofel," all rise and scramble to change places. The one left out in the end is "It.")*

13. Down You Go

This is not, strictly speaking, a dramatic game. But it is helpful in developing a free atmosphere and is, of course, useful as an aid to teaching. The game is familiar to the pupils, being the hub of a popular television program.

PURPOSES: To help teach the Hebrew alphabet. Practice in writing and spelling.

SUBJECT: Language.

MANNER OF PLAYING: A student is chosen as Leader or teacher acts as Leader.

The class is divided into two teams—Whites and Blues, or similarly designated.

The Leader picks a word or a phrase in Hebrew. For every letter in each word he puts a dash on the blackboard, leaving a space between each word.

Members of each team take turns in calling out Hebrew letters. The letters must be called by name such as: *Bet, Yod, Tet,* etc., and not by their sounds, as the pupils first learned to know them when they began to read. In this way the pupils get practice not only in learning the names of the letters in the alphabet but also in the differences in use between like-sounding letters such as: *Vav-Vet, Kaf-Koof, Het-Khaf,* etc.

As a letter is called, the Leader puts it in its proper place over the dash in the word or phrase on the blackboard. This continues until the full word or phrase is written out with the letters suggested by the pupils, with each team taking turns in calling out letters.

If a student calls a letter that is not in the word or phrase on the blackboard, the Leader says: "Down you go!" and that student is out of the game.

The team which calls the most correct letters wins the round. One of its members becomes the Leader and a new round is begun.

The final winner is the team that has won the most rounds or remains with the most members still in the game at the end of the playing period.

■ B. GAMES TO DEVELOP USE OF IMAGINATION

Helping the pupils to use their imagination is part of the process of getting them ready for creative dramatization. The games offered here have as their purpose to awaken the latent creative powers of the pupils, to guide them to respond to stimuli and to enlarge upon them, to help them to see beyond the immediate and practical, to give wing to their thoughts, and to express their thoughts freely and imaginatively.

1. How, When, Why

PURPOSES: *To elicit information* on the extent of the pupil's knowledge prior to teaching a new lesson.

To reinforce learning by providing opportunity for review.

SUBJECT AREAS: History; Current History; Festivals; Community. The game may also be used, with minor adaptations, in connection with Synagogue Practice, Prayers, and even Language.

MANNER OF PLAYING: The teacher announces a theme for the game such as: *Humash*, Jewish history, etc. At times it might be advisable to narrow down the theme even further, for example: the Patriarchs, the Second Temple, Sabbath, etc.

A pupil is chosen to be "It." The teacher whispers to "It" the name of something connected with the theme. Examples: *Humash*—Moses' basket; History—Judah Maccabee; Festivals—Hanukah latkes.

The pupils, taking turns, try to guess the secret item by asking "It" one question. The questions may only be: "How do you like it?" "When do you like it?" and "Why do you like it?" asked in that order.

As soon as a pupil thinks he knows the answer, he raises his hand and, on being recognized, gives his answer. If he is right, he becomes "It." If he is wrong, he is out of the game.

The last pupil remaining is the winner.

"It" answers the questions as if he were the secret item, assuming, as it were, the personality of the item.

EXAMPLE: *The theme is:* Bible.
The secret item is: Moses' rod.

Q: How do you like it? A: Long and straight.
Q: When do you like it? A: When I am thrown on the ground.
Q: Where do you like it? A: On the palace floor.
Q: How do you like it? A: When I can wriggle.
Q: When do you like it? A: When I can swallow others.
Q: Where do you like it? A: In the land of Egypt.
Etc.

2. Close Your Eyes and See

This is a very good stimulant for emotional recall.

PURPOSE: To give teacher an idea of past learning and retention. To motivate a new lesson. To reinterpret past experiences within the framework of new knowledge.

SUBJECT AREA: Jewish life and practices.

MANNER OF PLAYING: The teacher calls a student to the front of the room. Selecting a word or sentence which would stimulate recall of sights, sounds, smells, etc. The teacher tells the pupil: "Close your eyes and see . . ." adding the stimulating word or sentence.

The pupil, keeping his eyes closed, recalls the sights, sounds, etc., associated in his memory with the given word or sentence, and relates them to the class.

A point is awarded for each item recalled. The pupil with the most points is the winner.

EXAMPLE:

TEACHER: Close your eyes and see the first night of Hanukah.
PUPIL: The Menorah on the window sill.
The smell of burning oil from the kitchen.
The red ribbon around the package mother is holding.
My sister trying to sing "Rock of Ages."
Etc.

POSSIBLE STIMULANTS:

Close your eyes and see. . . .
Friday night in your home.
Your first day in Hebrew School.
The end of Yom Kippur in the synagogue.
Lulav and *Etrog*.
Matzah.
Etc.

3. Story Chain-Reaction

PURPOSES: Drill and review.

SUBJECTS: History, Hebrew language, *Humash*, etc.

MANNER OF PLAYING: The teacher provides himself with a small bell and a bean-bag. He begins to tell a story which the children have learned—a historical incident, a section of the Bible in English or in Hebrew, a Hebrew story recently learned, etc.

At a given point in the story the teacher stops, rings his bell and throws the bean-bag to one of the pupils.

The pupil catches the bean-bag and immediately continues with the story where the teacher left off.

The teacher permits this pupil to tell the story for a little while and then rings the bell.

When the bell is rung, the pupil stops talking and throws the bean-bag to another pupil who now continues with the story until the bell is rung again.

This goes on until the story ends.

A pupil who cannot continue with the story, or relates the story incorrectly, is out of the game.

4. Original Story Chain-Reaction

This is a variant of the previous game. It is used with more advanced pupils.

MANNER OF PLAYING: The teacher structures a locale and occasion, such as:
Simhat Torah in Williamsburg, Brooklyn.
Yom Kippur eve in a small East European town.
Shabbat morning.
Near the walls of the Old City in Jerusalem.

The teacher begins to relate an original story centering about the structured locale and occasion. As the bean-bag is thrown to each pupil he adds a little to the story, making it up as he goes along.

EXAMPLE: *Locale and occasion:* Yom Kippur eve in a small town in Eastern Europe.

TEACHER: *(Begins the story)* This is a story that might have happened in a small town in Eastern Europe on Yom Kippur eve. The synagogue was crowded with worshippers. The scrolls of the Torah had been taken out of the holy ark. *Kol Nidrey* was about to be chanted. Everyone was waiting for the cantor to begin. The cantor, wrapped in his *Talit*, was preparing himself for the great moment. He was recalling his sins of the preceding year and softly pleading to the Almighty for forgiveness. Suddenly he remembered something. He threw off his *Talit* and quickly walked out of the synagogue. . . . *(Teacher throws bean-bag to pupil 1 and rings the bell)*

PUPIL 1: *(Continues with the story)* Everybody was very excited. Everybody was asking, "Why did the cantor leave just before *Kol Nidrey?*" The rabbi quieted them down and sent the *shamash* to follow the cantor. The *shamash* ran out and saw the cantor walking toward . . .

(Teacher rings the bell. Pupil 1 stops and throws the bean-bag to pupil 2.)

PUPIL 2: *(Continues with the story)* . . . and saw the cantor walking toward a small peasant hut on the outskirts of the town. The *shamash* followed the cantor. The cantor knocked on the door of the hut. A peasant voice asked him to come in . . .

(Teacher rings bell again. The bag is thrown to pupil 3. The story continues, being taken up by pupil after pupil until it reaches a logical conclusion or the teacher decides to call a halt. Such a story might later serve as a basis for a creative dramatization by the class.)

■ C. TO PROVIDE PRACTICE IN PANTOMIME

Pantomime, the expressive use of the body, is an important component of dramatization. A lift of the eyebrow, a shrug of the shoulder, a hand movement, often speak more effectively than speech itself. The position of the body, the manner in which a character walks, sits, or moves about often expresses his basic characteristics.

Practice in pantomime is particularly helpful to children in preparing them for dramatization. It is the bridge between games and actual dramatization. Physical activity is natural to children. Often, when a child feels the eyes of his classmates upon him, he may tend to shy away from expressing himself vocally but will feel less hesitant to do so through action. Experience in dramatizing through action habituates the children to stand up in front of their classmates to portray character and incident, overcoming their shyness and their fear of doing the wrong thing, of "making fools" of themselves.

The following games and exercises offer practice in pantomime. They will help the students to dramatize freely and effectively while at the same time serving direct teaching purposes. They arc divided into two sections: group pantomime and solo pantomime.

Group Pantomime

In the beginning the students feel more secure if they participate in pantomime as part of a group. Consequently, the teacher will begin with group pantomimes. Only after the pupils have had several opportunities to pantomime as members of a group are they exposed to solo pantomimes. Also, working with group pantomimes they learn to plan together and execute their roles as part of a team. This will stand them in good stead later, when they are called upon to develop and enact original dramatizations.

Captains are essential for all group games or activities. They act as chairmen during the planning, seeing that all are given opportunities to contribute ideas and that the discussions do not go off on tangents. In case of disagreement the captain makes the final decision. Generally, the teacher will select the natural leaders of the class as group captains. The captains choose their own teams. They alternate in making their choices of team members. In that way all pupils have an opportunity to be chosen.

1. Trades

This game can only be used in a classroom in which the seats are not fixed to the floor. The seats are moved out of the way so that there is a large, clear space in the room.

PURPOSE: To reinforce learning.

SUBJECTS: History, Current History, Jewish Life and Practices, Israel, etc.

MANNER OF PLAYING: The class is divided into two teams. The teams are given names, such as "Blue" and "White." Goals are set at either end of the room. Each team takes up a position behind its goal.

The teacher announces a theme for the game such as a holiday, history, Bible, the synagogue, etc.

The teams then alternate in pantomiming an act or an object connected with the theme. Each team decides for itself what it will pantomime and each member of the team pantomimes the same thing, but in whatever manner he chooses to do so. The first team, the "Blues" for example, having met in a huddle behind their goal and decided what to act out, the game proceeds as follows:

BLUES: *(Call out in unison)* Here we come!

BLUES AND WHITES: *(Advance and face each other in the center of the room. They sing to each other as follows:)*

WHITES: From where do you hail?

BLUES: Yisrael.

WHITES: What will you be?

BLUES: Watch and see.

BLUES: *(Every member of the team pantomimes the act or object which has been decided upon. Examples: Mother lighting candles, blowing Shofar, turning gregger for Haman, Solomon judging the case of the women, Hebrews walking around the walls of Jericho, Joseph in his coat of many colors, etc.)*

WHITES: *(Try to guess the subject of the pantomime. As soon as they guess, the captain of the Blue team calls out,* "That's our trade!")

(As soon as their captain calls out "That's our trade!" *all the members of the Blue team turn around and run for their goal. The members of the Whites try to tag as many Blues as possible. All Blues who are tagged are out of the game and take seats while the game continues. When a Blue gets behind his goal he is safe from being tagged and remains in the game.)*

(The White team now chooses an object or act to pantomime. The game continues, with each team alternating in pantomiming, until one of the teams is left without members and is "annihilated.")

2. *In the Manner of the Word*

PURPOSE: Drill, review.

SUBJECT: Language study.

MANNER OF PLAYING: A pupil is selected to be "It." He leaves the room.

The teacher gives the class a descriptive Hebrew word or phrase like: *b'simhah, k'mo tinok, b'kaas,* etc.

"It" is called back into the room. He tries to guess the word or phrase by asking different pupils in turn to do different things in the manner of the word or phrase. For example, he may tell the pupils to read, walk, talk, etc.

Each pupil called upon by "It" does what he has been asked to do in the manner of the word or phrase chosen. Thus he may walk, sing, talk, read, etc., *b'simhah*—joyfully, *k'mo tinok*—like a baby, *b'kaas*—angrily, etc.

"It" has to guess the Hebrew word or phrase from the manner in which the pupil pantomimes or acts.

When "It" guesses correctly, the player who was last to act becomes "It." Synonyms are acceptable.

3. *Pairs*

PURPOSE: To reinforce learning.

SUBJECTS: History, Bible, Current Jewish life, etc.

MANNER OF PLAYING: The teacher prepares a number of slips of paper on which he writes the names of famous or well-known pairs such as: Cain and Abel, Eliezer and Rebecca, Jacob and Rachel, Mattathias and the Traitor, Antiochus and Hannah's youngest son, etc.

Two pupils are selected. They are given one of the slips of paper. They leave the room for several moments so that they may consult and decide how to pantomime the pair that is mentioned on their slip of paper.

They return and pantomime some action that is representative of the pair they have been assigned.

The pupils try to guess who the pair is.

The pupil who guesses is the winner. He may now choose another pupil to be his partner. They are given a slip of paper with a pair. The game continues as outlined before.

4. Narrated Story-Pantomime

This is not a competitive game but rather a dramatic activity very similar in many ways to the games outlined above. After some experience with the competitive pantomime games, the students are ready for this form of story dramatization.

PURPOSE: To reinforce learning.

SUBJECTS: Language, History, Bible, etc.

MANNER OF PLAYING: A story is chosen from the subject matter currently being studied by the class.

The class determines through discussion what characters are needed to enact the story. Thus, the story of Jacob's first meeting with Rachel would call for Rachel, Jacob, and an indeterminate number of shepherds.

A Leader is selected. He will also serve as narrator. Students are selected to fill the necessary parts. They may be chosen by the Leader, the class, or by volunteering for selection by the teacher.

The Leader and the group are given a few minutes to decide how they will interpret the story.

The group returns to the room. The Leader tells the story or reads it from the text. The students pantomime the story as it is being told or read.

5. Story-Pantomime

This is similar to "Narrated Story-Pantomime" except that the narrator is eliminated. After having had some experience of dramatizing a story in pantomime with the emotional support of a narration, the students are ready to dispense with this prop.

Solo Pantomime

At this point, the students may have virtually overcome the emotional strictures which prevented them earlier from dramatizing creatively. Just a few steps more and they are quite ready to use creative dramatization freely and imaginatively. One of these steps is practice in solo pantomime, where the pupil is left to his own creative invention without the support of a group.

6. I Met

PURPOSE: To reinforce learning.

SUBJECTS: History, Bible, etc.

MANNER OF PLAYING: The teacher announces the theme of the game—a particular festival, a story, a historical period.

A pupil is chosen to be "It."

Teacher whispers to the pupil the name of the character he is to portray and the action of the character he is to pantomime. Examples: Rebecca at the well giving drink to Eliezer, Isaac feeling Jacob while blessing him, Moses before Pharoah.

"It" faces his classmates and recites:

On my way
To school today
I met ______

He then pantomimes the action of the character. The pupils try to guess whom he "met." The first one to guess becomes "It." If no one guesses, the teacher selects another pupil to be "It."

7. *I Did It*

This game is similar to "I Met."

PURPOSE: Reality practice, review.

SUBJECT: Jewish life and practices.

MANNER OF PLAYING: The game is played exactly as "I Met," except that instead of portraying a character, "It" pantomimes an action connected with Jewish customs or festival observance. Examples: lighting Sabbath candles, lighting Hanukah menorah, *kiddush*, using the *lulav* and *etrog*, taking out the Torah from the ark, etc. The pupils try to guess what he is doing and the occasion on which it is done.

8. *Detective*

PURPOSE: Practice in the use of Hebrew language.

SUBJECT: Language study.

MANNER OF PLAYING: "It," prepared in advance, enters the room dressed in all kinds of accessories that are mentioned in the lesson or carrying a tray with items from the lesson such as fruit, household utensils, etc.

"It" now pantomimes the action of the lesson such as taking a chair, sitting down, eating, etc.

His pantomime concluded, "It" leaves the room.

As quickly as possible, "It" divests himself of the props and returns to the room.

In the meantime pupils are given an opportunity to describe in Hebrew what they observed—what "It" wore, what he carried, what he did, etc.

The child with the biggest correct list is declared the best detective and wins the game.

If desired, the teacher might have the pupils write their lists instead of giving them orally.

9. Conflict Pantomime

In solo pantomime too, a point is eventually reached where the pupils are ready to enact a dramatic situation. This form of pantomime requires a series of pantomimic actions to play out the story.

PURPOSES: To motivate a new lesson, review.

SUBJECTS: History, Bible, Language.

MANNER OF PLAYING: A pupil is chosen "It." Teacher gives him a slip on which is a sentence or phrase which is the climax of a familiar conflict situation. Examples: "Am I my brother's keeper?" "Let my people go!" "Who is for the Lord? Follow me!"

"It" pantomimes the incident leading to the climatic phrase.

The class tries to guess the phrase. The first one to guess correctly becomes "It."

If necessary, the teacher may give some hints such as: "It happened in Egypt . . . A prince said it . . . etc."

■ D. TO PROVIDE PRACTICE WITH DIALOGUE

The following group of games affords the pupils opportunities for experiences in the use of dramatic dialogue, as distinguished from narrative or descriptive speech.

1. Who Am I?

PURPOSES: Drill, review.

SUBJECTS: History, Current History, Bible, Festivals, etc.

MANNER OF PLAYING: Teacher announces a theme for the game.

A pupil is selected to begin the game.

He rises and gives a line of dialogue—not a description but actual speech that would be characteristic of a person in history, Bible, or other area which has been selected as the theme for the game.

The pupils try to guess the character from the line of dialogue. The first one to guess is the next one to interpret a character with a line of dialogue.

EXAMPLES: The big idol did it! Who am I? —Abraham
Won't you give me a drink? Who am I? —Eliezer
What a lovely coat! Thank you, father. Who am I? —Joseph

2. *Speaking Pairs*

This is the same game as "Pairs" described under Pantomime except, as now played, the players use dialogue, with or without pantomime, to portray the characters.

MANNER OF PLAYING: Two pupils are selected.

Teacher gives them a slip of paper on which are the names of a famous pair.

Players enact the pair by means of two lines of dialogue.

Class tries to guess the identity of the pair. The first one to guess may pick a partner and the new pair of players now enacts a famous pair.

EXAMPLES: *Jacob and Esau:*
1. I am hungry. Feed me!
2. Not unless you sell me your birthright.

Elijah and Jezebel:
1. Why did you stop the rain from falling?
2. Because you worship idols and do evil things.

3. *Guess the Name*

PURPOSES: Motivation of new lesson. Review.

SUBJECTS: History, Community, Current History.

MANNER OF PLAYING: "It" is given the name of a character he is to portray and the place with which the character is associated.

"It" proceeds with this dialogue: "*Shalom Yeladim.* I come from America and my name begins with A."

The pupils try to guess his identity. This is done by means of the following questions and answers:

Q: Are you a prophet?
A: No, I am not Amos.
Note: if the answer is "No," "It" must give the name of a person in that category whose name begins with the letter announced.

Q: Are you a warrior?
A: No, I am not Antiochus.

Q: Are you a patriarch?
A: No, I am not Abraham.

Q: Are you a king?
A: No, I am not Ahab.

This questioning continues until some one guesses and becomes "It." He is given a new character to portray.

During the questioning, if the questioner guesses the occupation of the character, "It" answers "Yes." The questioner then indicates the name of the character. If he is right, he becomes "It." If he is wrong, he is out and the game continues with more questions.

As indicated above, to each question calling for a "No" the answer must include a personality in that category whose name begins with the same letter as the one announced, as indicated in the example given above. If "It" cannot think of a name, then he answers by divulging his identity. For example:

Q: Are you a general?
A: *("It" does not know the name of a general in Jewish history whose name begins with A. He therefore answers as follows:)* No, I am not a general, but my name is Asher Levy.

Q: *(The pupil who caused "It" to stumble now continues by asking:)* What did you do?
A: I fought for equal rights.

"It" has answered correctly. He sits down and the pupil who caused him to stumble now becomes "It." However, if "It" does not know the answer to the question "What did you do?" he is out of the game.

■ NOW WE ARE READY

The teacher continues to use these and similar games until such time as he feels that the pupils are ready to dramatize spontaneously, freely and creatively. When the teacher feels that this end has been achieved, he is ready to tie together all the elements—spontaneity, creative imagination, experience with pantomime, dialogue and characterization, and put them to work in utilizing various dramatic techniques as aids to teaching and learning. For, now the walls are down. Now we will no longer have the self-conscious giggling, the stammering and stumbling, and "what shall I say next?" Now the students are ready to dramatize and the teacher is in a position to help them reap the educational benefits which accrue from utilizing this creative aid to teaching.

CHAPTER 2

Story Telling

■ Most often classroom dramatizations proceed from stories. The pupils will dramatize Bible stories, Jewish folk tales, stories from Jewish history, the little stories they learn in Hebrew language study and the like. Consequently, the quality of the story determines in large measure the educational benefits to be derived from the dramatization. Similarly, the manner in which the teacher first told the story to the children will often determine the course and the fate of the dramatization.

A story properly told will almost invariably stimulate dramatization in a class that is at home with this technique. Moreover, a story well told is of itself an important teaching tool. In the younger classes where the textbook is seldom used, story telling is the most important medium for Jewish teaching. In the older classes the story provides color and content, enriches subject matter, and adds an emotional quality to learning.

In ancient days story telling was practically the sole medium used for teaching history, literature and kindred subjects. The Bible gives a vivid picture in Genesis IV: 23-24 of the ancient story teller spinning his tale, while the women about him listen eagerly:

> And Lamekh said to his women:
> "Adah and Zillah, hear my voice.
> Lamekhite women, listen to my words."

Thus the story teller calls his audience to attention. We can well imagine how, having quieted down somewhat the gossiping women, he proceeds directly to involve the interest of his listeners in the tale he is about to relate—a saga of the Lamkhites' early history that is enshrined in the race-memories of the tribe. To do this he uses the technique of the "teaser" which is so well known to us from the movies and television dramas. He begins with a climactic moment in the tale, and without actually giving away the story he hints at the exciting events he is about to relate. He throws himself into his subject, as a good story teller should, to the point where he begins to feel himself an actual participant in the events which he is about to relate. And so, he introduces his story with:

> For I have slain a man for wounding me,
> And a young man for bruising me;
> If Cain shall be avenged sevenfold,
> Truly Lamekh seventy and sevenfold.

The Bible stops at this point. The rest of the narrative is lost to us. But, in our imagination we can reconstruct the scene how, after this "teaser" opening, the Lamkhite bard goes on to spin out a tale of tribal heroes and great adventures which affected the destiny of the tribe.

Story and parable were teaching tools for the prophets of Israel, the sages of the Talmud, and the many anonymous teachers whose tales are enshrined in the *Midrashim*. The Hasidic rabbis used the story, more than any other technique, as a means for teaching basic ethical values to their disciples. Consider the way the Messenger in An-sky's folk drama of Hasidic life, *The Dybbuk,* teaches Sender Brinitzer by way of the Parable of the Mirror about the pitfalls attendant upon the acquisition of wealth:

> One day a Hasid came to the Rabbi. The Hasid was rich, but a great miser. The Rabbi took him by the hand and brought him over to the window. "Look out there," the Rabbi said. The rich man looked into the street. "What do you see?" the Rabbi asked. "People," the rich man answered. Once more the Rabbi took him by the hand. He led him to the mirror. "What do you see now?" the Rabbi asked. "Now I see myself," the rich man answered. Then the Rabbi said to him: "See? In the window there is glass and in the mirror there is glass. But the glass of the mirror is covered with a little silver, and no sooner is the silver added than you no longer see others but see only yourself."

Among Hasidic rabbis, Rabbi Mendel of Kotzk is known as the rationalist, the proponent of the supremacy of the intellect. Despite this, when asked how he became a Hasid, he replied: "I became a Hasid because in the town where I lived there was an old man who told stories about *Tzadikim* (Hasidic rabbis). He told what he knew, and I learned what I needed."

The great emphasis placed by the Hasidic rabbis on story telling as a teaching aid was undoubtedly due to the fact that they were trying to educate the masses—the simple folk who were short on learning and sophistication. In that respect their pupils were not unlike the pupils in the elementary Jewish school who arrive there young and impressionable, to whom much of Jewish life and values is unfamiliar and unexplored territory. One of the great Hasidic teachers, Rabbi Nahman of Bratslav took full advantage of the didactic possibilities inherent in the story. He spun fanciful tales and told them to his disciples, who in turn retold them to their own eager pupils. Each of these stories, however, was also a shell surrounding kernels of great truths which Rabbi Nahman brought to the fore by means of the story. These tales were so valued that it was said of them that "the tales of Rabbi Nahman of Bratslav are so filled with both hidden and visible holiness, that they may be recited as prayers in the synagogue."

Traditionally then, the story has always been an important vehicle for education in general and for Jewish education in particular. The more effective use the teacher is able to make of the story, the more effective his teaching will be. This section, therefore, will explore the possibilities of this medium and indicate guides for the teacher toward its effective utilization.

■ VALUES OF STORY TELLING

Provides a Meaningful Art Experience

The story is, first and foremost, an expression of the creative spirit. It is a work of art which, in the reading or telling provides an emotional art experience to its readers or hearers. Therein lies the basic reason for its use in the school whose task it is to furnish as many varied experiences as possible to contribute to the emotional and intellectual growth of its students. The Jewish story, expressive of

Jewish culture, is its own reason for telling in the Jewish school. It provides the pupils with an art experience which quickens their spirits and vibrates their emotions in harmony with Jewish cultural values. It surrounds Jewish life and living with an aura of romance and wraps it in the nostalgic mantle of "once upon a time." It sensitizes the students to the idealized experiences of their people. Above all it brings joy and pleasure to the learning process which, all too often, is seriously purposeful and at times rather grim in many of our schools. Over and above this basic function of story telling, there are a number of adjunct values which substantially increase its importance for the teacher.

Establishes Bond Between Teacher and Pupils

The teacher who frequently tells stories establishes a bond with the pupils that is based on shared spiritual joys. They soon learn that there, up in the front of the room, sits not a drillmaster, but a source of wonder and romance. Eagerly and avidly they listen to the teacher's tales. Some of this eagerness is carried over to other areas of learning which, although more prosaic, are nevertheless important for their Jewish education.

Helps Eliminate Discipline Problem

It would certainly be most incongruous to label story telling as an aid to classroom discipline. It does, however, indirectly contribute to the elimination of the problem of class discipline by helping the pupils to establish the habit of concentration. To clarify this, we need but recall the timeworn device of the after-dinner speaker, lecturer, or sermonizer: "which reminds me of a story." It is their open sesame to capture the attention of their audience and the net with which to draw back their hearers when their minds begin to wander. For the teacher too, the story is a most effective device for helping his students to concentrate, for getting and holding their attention. An unruly class will quickly come to attention when teacher begins an interesting story—speaking softly, intently, so that at first only those pupils closest to him can hear; concentration flowing from them in waves, as it were, to those further back, until all are quietly and absorbedly listening to the tale being spun by the teacher.

Enlarges Pupil Experience

Story telling expands the experiences of the pupils, bringing them near to distant times and far-off places. It helps them to develop sympathy and understanding of the problems and acts of others by bringing them imaginatively within the orbit of the motivations of the story's characters. The little girl in Chicago yearns with her counterpart in an Israeli co-operative settlement for a flock of goslings all her own. The adolescent from a sheltered home in the suburbs feels the anxieties of the immigrant boy who yearns to rise above the grime and sordidness of his surroundings. The American child who lacks for nothing in physical comforts feels the bitter-sweet joy of the habitually hungry East European boy who for once eats his fill from the rewards he receives for carrying Purim gifts for the town's householders.

Motivates to Action

The story often motivates the listeners to action in emulation of the tale's heroes. Nathan Hale's "My only regret is that I have but one life to give for my country" inspired many American boys when called upon to defend their land. The tales of Bar Kokhba, Judah Maccabee, or Joseph Trumpeldor motivated many who rushed to help Israel to gain independence in 1948. For, in listening to a story, the student often becomes part of the story, reliving vicariously the events which the story relates. He himself is the hero of the tale, feeling, if only fleetingly, the emotions of the story's personality. This feeling, which may disappear almost completely the moment the tale is told, nevertheless leaves a residue on the personality of the pupil. It is on this residue which he draws when the call comes to meet his obligations to society.

Is Basis for Creative Dramatization

All of these values and many more are inherent in the well-constructed, well-told story. Story telling is therefore a most worthwhile classroom activity for its own sake. The creative teacher is aware of this and will constantly seek to find more and better stories for telling and will improve his technique in telling them. However, the values of story telling are greatly enhanced or even multiplied when the story becomes the basis for a creative dramatization. Whereas the story only tells about happenings, in the dramatization they actually happen; in the story the pupil hears about the deeds of heroes, in the dramatization he is the hero and he performs the deeds; in the story he hears about life, in the dramatization he lives it. Consequently, both for the sake of the telling itself and for the sake of the dramatic activity which may follow, the choice of story material and the manner in which it is presented by the teacher are of critical importance.

■ WHAT STORIES TO TELL TO WHOM

There are two major factors which will influence the teacher's choice of story material: The purpose for which the story is to be used, and the tastes and capacities of the students.

Goal Influences Choice

Often the teacher tells a story purely for the pleasure of it, for the joy and relaxation it will afford the students, or as an interlude in the formal class routine. In that case subject is not nearly as important as suitability for the group of listeners. Generally, however, the teacher tells a story with a definite didactic purpose is mind—to enrich the subject being taught, to provide background knowledge, to teach specific moral values, etc. If that is the purpose for telling the story, the teacher must exercise great care in its selection. All too often teachers follow the course which the Dubner Maggid claimed to have followed in his sermons.

The Preacher of Dubno was famous for his use of story and parable to illustrate his moral preachments. Once, he was asked how he was able to find a story to illustrate every moral he tried to teach, every point he wanted to make. The Maggid smiled and replied as follows:

"I will answer your question with a story. Once, an army officer came to an inn. He led his horse toward the stable where he saw a most amazing sight. On the wall of the stable were painted a number of targets and right in the very middle of each target there was a bullet hole. The astonished officer called for the innkeeper. 'Tell me,' the officer said, 'who is this wonderful marksman who consistently shoots only bull's-eyes?' The innkeeper smiled and went into his house. A moment later he returned, leading his seven year old son by the hand. 'Here is the marksman,' the innkeeper told the army officer. Now the officer was even more astonished. 'This little boy?' he asked. 'Yes,' replied the innkeeper. 'My seven year old son. He is the one who shot all the bull's-eyes.' 'But, I don't understand,' the officer said. 'How is it possible?' 'Quite simple,' the innkeeper replied. 'First he shoots off the gun. Then he draws a target around the bullet-hole.' That's exactly what I do. First I tell the story, then I find a moral to fit it."

Judging by the success of the Dubner Maggid as a popular teacher, we can only assume that this anecdote was told in jest. Planless, haphazard teaching can lead only to haphazard and often indifferent results. The teacher generally starts out by deciding what he wants to teach. He then proceeds to find suitable story material which will help to teach the particular lesson.

Source of Stories

To help him in this task, the teacher will find many sources of Jewish stories. To mention only a few, there are: Ginzberg's *Legends of the Jews,* Goldin's *Jewish Legends,* Belth's *World Over Story Book,* Eisenberg's *Modern Jewish Life in Literature* and such classic children's favorites as Weilerstein's *K'tonton,* Sholom Aleichem's *Mottel,* and Simon's *Helm Stories.* These are but a few of the sources. The teacher will do well to become familiar with them and others that are readily available.

Children's magazines are a good source of stories. *World Over, Young Israel* and *Young Judaean* are rich mines for Jewish stories suitable for children. Some schools keep files of back numbers of these and similar publications as do the reference divisions of some public libraries.

In Hebrew, *Hadoar Lanoar* which is published in America, *Davar Liy'ladim* and other children's magazines published in Israel are a good source of stories. There are also many books of children's stories in Hebrew as well as Yiddish books and publications like *Kinderwelt* and *Pedagogisher Bulletin.*

To make a proper selection and to find quickly a suitable story when needed, the teacher should maintain a constantly expanding card file of stories he has read. Each story is synopsized briefly and indexed according to subject as well as to the age of the pupils for whom it is suitable. In that manner the teacher is able readily to put his hands on the proper story as and when it is needed. The teacher will also gain considerable help from the classified index by Kastle, *658 Stories,* published by the Jewish Education Committee of New York.

CRITERIA FOR SELECTING STORIES

Children Like Action

Often, the chief value of a story is its beautiful language while it has very little action. Generally speaking, the teacher should use this type of story rather sparingly in the elementary grades. If used at all, it is suited only for telling and should not be used as a basis for dramatization. A story with a good plot, a meaningful conflict situation, and continuously rising action leading to a strong climax, is usually preferred by children. In addition, if it is to be the basis of a dramatization, it is desirable that it contain a good deal of dialogue.

Living Characters

In all instances, the story gains in effectiveness if its characters are presented as human beings who can evoke our interest and involve us emotionally in their problems. Often, deficiencies in this regard may be overcome by minor adaptations. Little human touches will change a stereotype into a sympathetic, recognizable human being. The general who stubs his toe and has to limp all the way to his tent, the Patriarch who stops to straighten his robe before leaving his tent to face the royal messenger, the mother who plays with her baby's toes until he stops crying before she puts him in the basket, become warm human personalities who mean something to us, and we care about what happens to them. Such human touches can usually be added to the heroes of history without doing violence to historical truths.

Language Not Too Difficult

In choosing a story the teacher will, of course, not select one in which the language is so difficult that it will interfere with its understanding and appreciation by the pupils. This does not mean that the story is to be devoid of literary quality. On the contrary, good writing style enhances the effectiveness of a story. But the teacher is to take care that there be no unduly involved sentence structure nor too many words which the children of that particular age cannot understand. This not only interferes with the pleasurable appreciation of the story by the children but also leads to a feeling of frustration and annoyance on the part of the listeners, thus defeating the very purpose for which the story has been used. However, the teacher need not hesitate to use occasional unfamiliar words if the children will understand them in the context of the story. This has a distinct advantage in that it helps to enlarge the children's vocabulary, enabling them to listen to more complex material in the course of time.

Interests the Children on Their Level

Teachers are greatly concerned with the problem of what is suitable for each particular age group. In regard to story telling there is no hard and fast rule as to what type of story to tell for each particular group. As teachers generally know, there is a good deal of overlapping of mental development and sense of appreciation between each age. Furthermore, exposure to television, radio, and the movies gives the modern youngster a greater degree of sophistication than his parent had at the same age. The outside world of reality and of make-believe has been brought into their living room. Repeated exposures to electronically conveyed experiences has sharpened their perceptions, widened their interests, and developed their tastes—often, unfortunately, in a negative manner. It would be foolhardy, therefore, to set down rigid rules about what kind of story a child will like at what age. Nevertheless, as a result of our observation of the tastes of children during many story telling sessions, we may permit ourselves some generalized rules of thumb. But we should constantly bear in mind that they are not to be followed too rigidly.

The child up to age seven

Children up to the age of seven usually love to imitate. They have a deep interest in the everyday things that happen all around them. They are constantly discovering new things at home, on the street and in their school. They are eager to savor the new experiences, to test them, to try them out for themselves.

In stories, children of this age group are generally interested in those which deal with everyday life, with family relationships, with those things with which they can identify themselves most readily. This is the age when children most persistently ask for tales of mother when she was a little girl and they want their favorite episodes repeated over and over again. They relish humor and action, but the humor is of the slapstick variety and the action clear-cut, strong and repetitive.

The teacher will find that biblical stories dealing with characters near their age, appeals to these children. The story of "Moses in the Bullrushes" is a prime favorite. "The Boy Samuel," "David the Shepherd Boy," and "Abram in the Idol Shop" hold their interest. They listen eagerly to tales like "Joel's Seder," in which a little boy puts pepper in his *Hagadah* so as to sneeze and stay awake until the end of the *Seder*. Animals that act like human beings have a particular fascination for them. When somewhat simplified by the story teller they enjoy listening to such legends as "King Solomon and the Bee," "The Pious Cow," and Solomon Simon's "Rabbi Meir Bear."

Seven to nine

Many of the stories suitable for younger children are often enjoyed also by children between seven and nine years of age. At this age they are most eager listeners to fairy tales, to stories of ancient kingdoms, and handsome princes and beautiful princesses. In general literature this is the age for Cinderella or Snow White.

In the Jewish school the teacher will tell the children such biblical stories as "Noah's Ark," "David Before Saul," "Joseph and His Brothers," and similar tales which appeal to the imagination. Sadie Rose Weilerstein's *K'tonton* is greatly loved by children of this age. They will enjoy the legends in Bialik's *And It Came to Pass* and his retelling of "Genesis," the story of the boy who was saved because of his attachment to the book of Genesis.

Magical adventures appeal greatly to children of this age. Judah Steinberg's "The Magic Top" and Peretz's Jewish Cinderella story "The Golden Slippers" are representative of this type of story.

Nine to twelve

This is the age when, in his imagination, one storms the battlements of the castle, defies the dragon, or roams the Spanish Main with Kidd and Lafite. This is the heroic age, when children like to think of themselves in impossible situations in which they perform great deeds of heroism. The child of nine to twelve loves stories of adventure, of physical courage, of pioneering, of struggling against the elements and against great odds.

At this age they are moved by stories of the Maccabees, Bar Kokhba, David, Samson, and the like. They are eager for stories like "Joseph Who Honored the Sabbath," "Beyond the Sambatyon," "King Solomon and Ashmedai," "The Princess in the Tower," and "Ariel the Lion." Although they still like tales of imagination, they delight in such modern heroic tales as "My Cousin Avigdor," adventure stories like "The Hermit of Lag B'Omer Hill," and Hasidic tales such as "Why the Tzadik Laughed."

Everyone, no matter what his age may be, enjoys stories which tell how the supposedly simple person outsmarts the reputedly clever one. Such tales are special favorites with children in this age group. "*Eineni Yode'a*," the story of a coachman who wins a disputation by asking his adversaries to give the meaning of the Hebrew words *Eineni Yode'a*, "The Rabbi and the Coachman," and "Napoleon and the Tailor" are stories of this genre.

The stories of *The Wise Men of Helm* and Solomon Simon's *The Wandering Beggar* are greatly enjoyed by children of this age. This may be due to the fact that, having had an opportunity to feel some of the hardships of life, the children at this age begin to become sensitive to the plight of the unfavored of humanity. This may perhaps explain their particular liking for such stories as "The Boy Who Whistled," "The Seven Good Years," and "The Two Brothers."

Twelve and up

At this age, when adolescence starts, the child begins to feel vague stirrings within him. He is moved by a snatch of song, a flower bending to the wind, clouds scudding across a winter sky. This is the age of romanticism when life is idealized, when we are drawn to the imaginative, the fanciful and the sentimental. This is the age when "causes" become the hub of life and the soul is stirred with a longing for serving and sacrificing.

Joseph Trumpeldor stirs the young romantic. Tales of the early pioneers of modern Israel and of the *Shomrim* inspire yearnings to emulate their deeds. The martyrdom of Rabbi Akiba and the travails of the heroes of Sholem Ash's *Kiddush Hashem* assume personal significance.

It is for this age group that the teacher uses such stories as Peretz's "Three Gifts" or "Bontshe Schweig." Tales of spiritual heroism such as "If Not Higher," or Zweig's *The Buried Candelabrum* have a special appeal. "The Magician," "The Woman Who Sued the Wind," "The Bar Mitzvah of Private Cohen," and "Miracle on the Sea," are the type of romantic story which, although suitable for younger groups as well, are particularly effective with the early adolescent.

■ ADAPTING THE STORY

To Tell All or to Adapt?

Are we to tell the stories as we find them, or shall we adapt them for telling? That depends on the story and on our purpose for using it. If the story is a recognized literary creation and the purpose in presenting it is both to expose the students to the content of the story and to the literary style of the author, the teacher will change nothing or very little from the original. However, where content and not style is of paramount importance, as is generally the case in class story telling, the teacher will adapt the story so that it will be suitable for the particular purpose and group for which it is to be used.

In adapting a story, the teacher may be called upon to delete extraneous material, to excise incidents which complicate the story too much, and to eliminate characters which have no significant function in advancing the thread of the story. At times the teacher may find that the story presents a significant idea and plot, but is too meager in incident and action. In this case the teacher adapts the story by adding incidents, rounding out characterizations, and adding new characters where necessary. Of course, if the story is such that more has to be created than is actually there to begin with, the teacher may find it more advisable to abandon it altogether and look for another and better story.

Avoid Distortion of Facts

The teacher must be very careful in adapting historical incidents chosen for story telling. Certainly nothing is to be done which will distort the historical event or change historical facts no matter how much the story may gain thereby in interest or drama. However, much can be added to the facts as they are known to us in a historical tale which will add to its interest; and such additions will not only not distort history but will help to present it in proper perspective. A good example of this is the possible treatment of the biographical tale.

Adding Supplemental Characters

Undoubtedly, the biographical story is one of the easiest kind to handle. It usually presents a unified plot and because it deals with an identifiable personality, it exerts a dramatic appeal on the emotions of the listeners. However, since we do not want to give the students a distorted picture of history, we cannot place all the concentration on the "hero." The pupils must also be given a conception of the part played by the masses in the development of great historical events. Furthermore, the history book, because of limitations of space, deals only with the leading figures and does not mention collateral characters which, no doubt, functioned in the leading character's environment. This is particularly true of the way the Bible relates its stories.

The teacher, however, would not be true to the facts if he were to convey the impression that the historical and biblical characters lived in a vacuum. We know that David had brothers. Surely he also had cousins and neighbors who were concerned with his rise. Surely Yokhebed and Amram had neighbors who were slaves to Pharaoh and lost their children in the waters of the Nile. Surely the village of Modin had children, one of whom, perhaps, might have been the first to notice the arrival of the Syrians with their idol.

Enlarging on Social Environment

It is through characters such as these that collateral situations may be developed which heighten the drama of the story and recreate the environment within which the historical or biblical characters functioned, and which influenced their actions. To invent such collateral characters and situations is a proper function of adaptation for story telling. This is not falsifying history but bringing it to life and giving it a sense of immediacy and reality. An illustration will best make clear this point. Here are two ways in which the teacher might tell the opening section of the biographical tale of the leader of the last Judaean revolt against Rome, Shimon Bar Kokhba. The first, relates the story as the teacher finds it:

> Even as a little boy Shimon Bar Kokhba made up his mind that some day he would bring freedom to his people in Judaea. He saw how the Roman conquerors oppressed his people. The Romans did not permit the Jews to observe their religion or to study their Torah. He made up his mind that some day, when he would grow up, he would raise an army and drive the Romans out of Palestine.

Here is another way of telling the same story:

> Many, many hundreds of years ago, there lived in the Land of Israel a little boy whose name was Shimon. Shimon's father lived in a small village and, like all the people of the village he had a small house of his own, a field and some sheep. Although Shimon was only a little boy, not quite six years old, his father let him take care of the sheep, lead them out to the hills for pasture in the morning, and bring them back to the barn toward evening.
>
> One evening, right after Shimon had brought back the sheep and put them into the barn, his father called him into the house. "Sit down, Shimon," his father said to him. "I have something important to tell you."
>
> Shimon sat down quietly on the mat near the fireplace. "Why is father bolting the door?" Shimon wondered. But he was too well-mannered to ask. He remained silent even while his father covered the only window in the room with a heavy cloth.
>
> Now the room was completely dark except for the flickering light from the fire on the hearth. Shimon's father walked over to the wall. He pushed very hard at one of the stones in the wall. Slowly, very slowly the stone began to turn and right behind it Shimon saw a dark hole in the wall. Out of this hole his father took a large scroll. Then he sat down on the mat next to Shimon.
>
> "My son," his father began, "you are now six years old. The time has come for you to begin the study of the Torah. I will teach you to read the word of God from this scroll. We will have to be very careful, my son. You must not tell anyone that you are studying the Torah."

"But why, father?"

"The Romans," his father answered. "If they catch us, they will kill us both. It is forbidden to study the Torah. That is their law."

"But father," Shimon cried out. "The Land of Israel is our land. What right have they to pass laws like . . . ?"

"Shimon!" his father interrupted. "The Romans rule this land. They are stronger than we are. They do as they please. There is nothing we can do. Promise me you will never say anything about your studies."

Shimon promised. Shimon also made a promise to himself. "Some day," he said, "I will raise an army that will be stronger than the Romans. We will drive them out of our land. Then, no one will be afraid to study the Torah."

In the first version we have a straightforward, meager recital of the historical facts. In the second version we have adapted the skeletal story and enlarged upon it, without doing violence to the historical truth as it is known to us. We have dramatized the facts and recreated a picture of home life in ancient Israel, which, although different from ours, nevertheless has something of the familiar about it which helps the students to understand the background and characters and to identify themselves with the story itself.

The Element of Conflict

Conflict is important to a story, particularly if it is later to serve as a vehicle for creative dramatization. Often this element may be latent in the story and the teacher is called upon to bring it out and to emphasize it.

By *conflict,* as used here, we mean the struggle of two opposing forces which involves our interest in the outcome. This does not necessarily imply violent action. It may be a physical conflict or one of the spirit. Will the baby Moses be drowned in the Nile or will he be saved? Will the boy give his dime to Keren Ami or will he buy himself some candy? Each is a conflict of an entirely different kind. However, about each of these a complete story may be built. Without such a conflict, our story is extremely weak. More often than not it is better left untold, unless the teacher succeeds in weaving in such a meaningful conflict.

Driving for the Climax

The story should be made up of a series of clear-cut events, leading directly, one into the other, and each one in turn advancing the story to its final climax and conclusion. Generally, a story with long descriptive passages needs editing. Children grow restless and irritated when the action of the plot is halted for the sake of describing locale, social climate, and the like. Where such descriptions are absolutely essential they should be made as brief as possible. Much more will be gained if this type of information is woven into the narrative so that it comes out as part of the action.

Not this way:

> Noam, the Israeli boy, and William, his American cousin, started out on their two-day hike into the mountains of Judaea. All around were the brown mountains sloping upward toward the sky. There was little vegetation for, during the summer, it does not rain in this part of the world. Over toward the right could be seen a large, dark green patch along the rolling backs of the mountains. This was a Jewish National Fund forest which had been planted ten years earlier. The money for that forest project had been provided by children in Jewish schools in America. . . .

But this way:

> Noam and William started out on their two-day hike into the mountains of Judaea. They climbed up and up along the backs of the brown hills sloping toward the sky. Suddenly William stopped.
>
> "Say, Noam," he said. "I forgot to pack my raincoat."
>
> Noam smiled. "It's easy to see you're an American, William. Had you been born in Israel as I was . . ."
>
> "What's that got to do with it?" William interrupted, annoyed. "Do you always have to rub it in that you are a *Sabra,* born in Israel, and I'm only a tourist from America?"
>
> "Come on," Noam spoke soothingly, "I didn't mean anything like that. It's just that not being an Israeli you couldn't be expected to know everything about Israel like, for instance, that it never rains here during the summer."
>
> "Never?" William asked, surprised.
>
> "Well, I've lived here all my life and I never saw it rain in the summer time. So you see, we won't need any raincoats."
>
> "So that's why everything is so dry and brown here," William mused.
>
> "Exactly."
>
> The boys continued their climb until they reached the crest of a hill.
>
> "What's that green patch over there to the right, Noam?" William asked.
>
> "A Jewish National Fund forest," Noam answered. "It was planted ten years ago . . . Just little saplings . . . Now they are big trees." Noam chuckled, "See, William? The *Sabras* didn't do everything in Israel."
>
> "What do you mean?" William asked, puzzled.
>
> "Well," Noam replied, "take that forest for instance. You and kids like you in America planted it."
>
> "How do you mean . . . ?"
>
> "Well, you brought in pennies and dimes and quarters and dollars for J.N.F. to your schools. Then the J.N.F. used the money for planting this forest. So it's really you Americans who planted it. See?"

Noam grinned at William. William smiled back. Now he was no longer irritated and angry.

"This will be some hike, Noam."

"It sure will," Noam answered . . .

Back Tracking to Be Avoided

A story is easily spoiled when the teacher begins to go backward in telling it. The teacher should be so familiar with the story that he will not have to revert in the chronology of the story to fill in some detail which may have been left out. This will only irritate the listeners and their attention may be lost. They want to be carried along in a straight path with the story's action and not zigzag back and forth. A notable exception to this is the story that deals with different events which occur simultaneously in different places. It is in this type of story that the so-called "Cliff-hanger" technique is used with telling effect. A segment of the action taking place in one locale is related and brought to a suspenseful moment. It is then broken off, while the narrator shifts his tale to the events taking place at the other locale.

For example:

> . . . William shouted frantically. There was no answer except from the hills echoing back his calls. The sun was setting. Night was falling rapidly. William looked about him. He was growing frightened. If he had only had the sense to take along some matches he could build a signal fire after dark. Maybe Noam would see it. He called out again, "Noam! Noam!" The hills of Judaea answered back, "Noam! Noam!"
>
> Meanwhile, only a short distance away, on the other side of the mountain, Noam was frantically searching the dry, hard ground. He was looking for a clue, some tracks that would lead him to his lost cousin. He knew how frightened William must be in these wild mountains with night coming on. . . .

Desirable Elements of Climax

The climax of the story is its ultimate goal. All the happenings in the story have been leading toward it. A strong, meaningful climax gives the listeners a sense of satisfaction, a vicarious feeling of accomplishment. An anemic, inconclusive climax substantially weakens the story and generally spoils the listeners' pleasure. As far as possible there should be an element of surprise to the climax. However, the surprise must be such that, after hearing it, the listener is left with the feeling that the result was logical, fitting, almost inevitable in the light of what had happened up to that point. An illogical, unmotivated climactic surprise only serves to leave the listener with a feeling of frustration, of having been "taken." Thus, when at the end of a mystery story, the Arab who had lived in the neighboring village before Israel's War of Independence proves to be the one who set fire to the fields of the Kibbutz, the result is accepted as surprising but inevitable, logical. The listener is, as it were, saying to himself, "Now why didn't I think of that?" If, however, a brand new character is brought in at the climax, who had nothing to do with the events related up to this point, and he proves to be the incendiary, the listener is annoyed and feels cheated, imposed upon.

After the climax it is best to bring the story to an end as quickly as possible. Having discovered the resolution of the conflict, the listeners will be attentive for a short time while the loose strands of the tale are tied up. However, their attention will begin to wander if the story continues long after the climax.

Don't Moralize!

A good teacher is rarely dogmatic about anything. As a rule he expresses his thinking and teaching through such words as "generally," "usually," "rarely," "often," etc. He avoids "never," "always," and other absolutes. There is one exception which teachers will do well to permit themselves: *Never* moralize at the end of a story! If the story is well built and well told, there will be no need for the teacher to point out the moral at the end of the story. The moral will emerge from the story itself. When, at the end of a story, the listener says to himself, "The boy in the story was selfish. I would never refuse to help the blind man as he did," the story teller has touched his heart. The story has left an imprint of lasting potential. When the teacher says at the end of a story, "This story teaches us not to be selfish," he is talking to the pupil's mind. If the story itself has not brought this out, the teacher's admonition will probably not register and will only tend to irritate the listener.

When You Come to the End, Stop!

Listening to a story is a pleasurable experience. It is often spoiled by teachers who will not leave well enough alone when the story is done. It is good to bear in mind the advice which the King of Hearts gave to the White Rabbit in *Alice in Wonderland:* "Begin at the beginning, and go on till you come to the end: then stop." Asking questions about the story often spoils it for the listener. There are better, more effective ways to discover whether the pupils have assimilated the story, or to fix the facts of the story in the minds of the listeners. On another occasion, one of the students might be asked to retell the story to the class. Children like retelling and rehearing stories which they have enjoyed. The students will be quick to correct the student-narrator if he leaves out anything important or makes a factual mistake. Follow-up activities such as scrapbook, art work or dramatization will further help in fixing the story in the minds of the students.

■ HOW TO TELL A STORY

Become Involved in It

The very first requisite in story telling is that the teacher become emotionally and intellectually involved in the story. The teacher must visualize the action and the characters before he can hope to bring the story to life for the listeners. It is necessary that the emotions, feelings, and motivations of the story's cast of characters become real to the teller before he can project them for the listeners with a semblance of reality. In short, to tell a story, one must feel it and become part of it.

The Hasidim who valued story telling as an educational medium laid great stress on the teller's emotional involvement in the tale. It is related of a Hassidic rabbi whose grandfather had been one of the Besht's disciples, that he was a master story teller. His tales never failed to capture the imagination of his listeners so that they almost believed that the incidents of the story were happening before their very eyes. Once this rabbi was asked for his secret in story telling. "A story," the rabbi said, "has to be told in such a way that it helps both the listeners and the story teller himself. I will illustrate: My grandfather, who had been one of the holy Besht's disciples, had been lame for some years. Once he was asked to tell a story about his teacher. My grandfather began to relate how the holy Besht, of blessed memory, was in the habit of swaying and hopping and dancing while he prayed. As my grandfather was telling his story he was so carried away with it that he rose and began to hop and dance just as his teacher used to do. He completely forgot about his lameness while telling the story and from that time on he was cured of his infirmity. That's the way a story should be told!"

To Memorize or to Read?

Unless the purpose in bringing the story to the class is to give them an appreciation of the literary style of the author, it is generally preferable that the story be told orally. Learning the story by heart and then relating it to the children helps establish a direct contact with the listeners without the intervening distraction of the book.

It is not necessary, nor even desirable, that the story be memorized word for word. Doing so will generally result in a stilted presentation. Instead, the story teller reads the story a number of times until he is familiar with the sequence of events and can visualize the action of each sequence. If necessary, he notes down on a card each incident in its proper sequence so that he can refresh his recollection with a glance at the card, thus avoiding the risk of leaving out some important action due to a lapse of memory. Telling a story orally after having become familiar with it to the extent that the story teller can actually visualize mentally its flow of action, results in a feeling of warmth and spontaneity which helps immeasurably in involving the emotional and intellectual participation of the listeners.

Rehearse the Story

The story teller should treat his material as if he were an actor preparing for a part. Thorough familiarity with the material as a result of full rehearsal helps the actor to project the feeling to the audience that they are witnessing an event that is actually taking place, as it were, before their very eyes; that the words of the character are being said now for the very first time. That element of spontaneity and projection of on-the-spot-creation can similarly be achieved by the story teller as a result of thorough rehearsal. For, he too is an actor who is bringing life to events that are imagined or have long passed by. But, he is even more than that. He is the scenic and costume designer who sets the stage and fixes the period. He is the director who moves his characters about for greatest effectiveness and establishes the mood to capture the heart and mind of his audience. This complex role can be properly played by most story tellers only with thorough advance rehearsal.

If at all possible, the story teller rehearses by telling the story to a member of his family or a friend. They will point out the flaws in the narrative which the story teller may be able to correct before bringing it to his audience. Also, by seeing the reactions of his "preview" audience, he will know what to leave out as dull and superfluous and what to emphasize and enlarge upon. If sympathetic rehearsal listeners are not available, the story teller relates his narrative aloud to the walls of his room. Either way, the story is to be rehearsed as many times as needed for the story teller to become so familiar with it that there will be practically no possibility of telling it haltingly, or forgetting important details.

Impersonate and Interpret

As indicated previously, the story teller is like an actor. He plays all the parts in the story. Consequently a certain amount of impersonation of each character in the story adds to the effectiveness of the narration. This does not mean that the story teller must act out each part to the hilt. The effect is achieved by much simpler means. A slight change in voice for each character's speech will do it. Using lighter tones for a woman, heavier for a man, gruff or oily, as the case may be, for a villainous character, loud and blustering speech for the bully, thinner tones for children, and so on, will help to characterize the figures of the story, giving each a distinct individuality.

Special Effects for Story Telling

First and foremost, the story teller must speak in clear tones at a level that is loud enough for everyone to hear him. That is not to say that the story is to be shouted at the listeners. On the contrary, a story told softly often gains in effectiveness in the establishment of the proper mood. Proper projection, clear enunciation, slight pauses for breath between phrases, and putting energy and drive behind the spoken words make it possible for the story teller to be heard in the farthest corners of the room even while he is using a normal voice level, only slightly louder than in ordinary conversation.

Monotonous voice tones can spoil even a very good story. It is helpful for the story teller consciously to practice voice modulation, varying the tones of his voice —speaking sometimes louder and sometimes softer, raising the inflection of his voice for questions or exclamations, lowering the pitch for describing sad moments, etc.

The tempo in which the words are spoken helps greatly to set the mood of the story. For example, exciting events will be narrated in quick tempo, increasing as the excitement mounts. Sad or lyrical moments will be narrated in slower tempo, the voice growing softer and softer.

Contrasts in speech are used for dramatic effect. The intense whisper helps establish mystery or excitement. This mood is also heightened by drawing out the words and spacing them as: "Slow—ly ever so slow——ly the steps grew lou-der and louder . . ."

The slight pause before a crucial part is a useful mood-setting device. Example: "And then *(Pause for a beat, then speak very quickly)* they threw him into the pit!"

Weaving in occasional songs or snatches of song add to the interest and effectiveness of a story. For example:

Not: "The scouts climbed upward on the winding road, singing 'On Hill, in Vale.' Suddenly they heard a shout. . . ."

But: "The scouts climbed upward on the winding road, singing: *(Story teller sings)*

On hill, in vale
Let each his fellow hail,
Hurrah, hurrah resounding.
We shout, we sing,
We let our voices . . .

(Breaks off song and picks up narration) Suddenly they heard a shout. . . ."

Physical Arrangements

The story teller takes a position in front and in the center of the group so that every listener has a clear view of the story teller's face. This helps to maintain contact between teller and listener. Also, this position is helpful in making it possible for all to hear the narrator.

In a room where there are no fixed seats, the seats are arranged in a semicircle, or the children are seated in a semicircle on the floor. The story teller takes a position in front of them and in the center, facing the open semicircle.

Some story tellers prefer to stand during their narration, so that they can move about somewhat as they feel impelled to do by the flow of the story. Generally, the story teller finds it more helpful to be seated so that the attention of everyone in the listening group may be focused in one direction. If the story teller is seated, it is helpful, if at all possible, that his seat be somewhat raised above the level of the seats of the listeners. This is particularly important when the listeners facing him are seated in several rows behind each other. By being slightly raised, the story teller's face is not hidden from the children in back by the heads of the children in the row in front of them.

To Summarize:

Choose a story that will not be too difficult for the listeners, nor too simple for them, both in language and in content.

Be sure the story has a well defined and meaningful conflict.

All events should lead directly one into the other so that there will be no need for backtracking.

Embellish the story with additional incidents and extra characters where necessary to recreate the social environment within which the chief characters functioned.

Adapt the story to your needs, but beware not to do violence to the story by distorting known or accepted historical facts.

Do not moralize or ask questions about the story at the conclusion.

Learn the story. Rehearse the story. Tell it orally.

Dramatize the story by including conversation and changing your voice to suit the different characters when they speak.

These are but a few guideposts to effective story telling. Carefully followed, they will help most teachers to utilize stories effectively. The teacher's story telling technique will generally improve with actual use. Story telling techniques come very naturally with some. Others may have to exert real effort in mastering them. The effort will seem eminently worthwhile as the teacher sees the effect on the children when he uses story telling properly, both as an end in itself and as a basis for creative dramatization.

CHAPTER 3

Story Dramatization

FUNDERBURG LIBRARY
c. 1
MANCHESTER COLLEGE

■ Nearly all dramatization techniques, from the simplest to the most complex, may be considered as forms of story dramatization. The techniques may differ considerably in complexity, development and application. Basically, however, they dramatize a story, which may be a single incident, an involved tale, an original story of which plot and action were created by the pupils, a familiar folk-tale, or a literary creation by an established author. Consequently, an understanding of the steps that are involved in the process of story dramatization must be considered as basic to the effective use of dramatization of any type as an aid to teaching.

The Process Step by Step

The emphasis which is given to each of the steps in the process will vary considerably with every single use, depending on the material and its teaching application, as well as the personality of the teacher, the composition of the class, and other variables. Generally, however, story dramatization involves the following steps:

■ BREAK DOWN INTO SCENES

Stimulated and guided by the teacher, the class discusses the story to be dramatized, breaking it down into scenes. In this context, each important block of action is considered to be a separate scene. The teacher may well take as a model for this purpose the German or French form of dramaturgy where each entrance or exit of an important character indicates a new scene. Further subdivision is advisable where new blocks of action occur while the same characters are still on the scene. Thus, even a story such as "Abraham and the Angels" which takes place in a single setting and in one segment of time (so that during the final enactment it will be played as one continuous scene) requires a preliminary breaking down into separate blocks of action, such as:

1. The angels arrive and Abraham greets them.
2. The angels are seated and Abraham orders food.
3. The food is served and the angels ask him about his family life.
4. The angels bless him and Sarah laughs.
5. The angels scold Sarah, repeat their promise and depart.

By dividing the story into individual blocks of action, the task of creating the dramatization, with its action and dialogue, becomes very much easier for the students. Furthermore, by exposing, as it were, the bare skeleton of the story through this type of scene division, the students become aware of the need for creating additional plot and action to round out the story, to give it body and substance. For, to dramatize a story means much, much more than simply to put it into dialogue form. To get the full benefit from classroom dramatization the students must be guided by the teacher to build upon the basic story; to develop situations which bring to the fore social background, characterization, and action motivation. If in the process of doing so the students become aware of their inadequacies, if they begin to realize that they lack sufficient information about the historical background of the story and about the forces which may have been at work to motivate its characters in their actions, so much the better. The need of this information for the development of the dramatization will be a strong motivation for the students to go to sources and do research to find such material, thus adding to their knowledge by their own efforts willingly undertaken.

It goes without saying that a more involved story which takes place in a number of different locales and during several time periods, will of necessity have to be divided into scenes. In that type of story each incident becomes a scene and each scene is further divided into sub-scenes for each major segment of action. Consider for example the Peretz narrative of the *Aggadah*, "The Seven Good Years." At first the story is divided into major scenes as follows:

1. The porter Toivyoh meets the "German."
2. Toivyoh consults his wife Serel.
3. Toivyoh announces his decision.
4. Toivyoh meets the "German" seven years later.
5. Serel and the "German."

These major scenes will need further breaking down into sub-scenes. For example:

SCENE 1

The porter Toivyoh meets the "German"

In this scene we want to bring out the general background of the story, the personality of Toivyoh, his need, the strangeness of a "German" in the East European market setting, the offer made to Toivyoh, and Toivyoh's reliance on his wife's good sense. Consequently, Scene 1 would have the following blocks of action or subscenes:

a. Toivyoh approaches several passersby, asks them for work, is refused, pleads his need to earn for the Sabbath.

b. A woman shopper who has been confronted by Toivyoh notices the "German." She and Toivyoh comment on the strangeness of his attire. The "German" approaches and the woman shopper leaves.

c. The "German" addresses Toivyoh. He draws the porter into conversation, eliciting information about his family—seven children, no money to pay for their schooling, etc.

This sub-scene might continue to the end of the scene since it is a continuous dialogue between the porter and the "German." However, unless the students have had a good deal of experience in creative dramatization, the teacher will find it advisable to make of the following a separate sub-scene:

d. The "German" offers the porter seven good years with a choice as to whether he will take it now or at the end of his lifetime. Toivyoh is in a dilemma. (For comic element he might change his mind several times, and in the end, finally . . .) He suggests he will ask his wife Serel. "German" agrees. Toivyoh hurries off.

Scene 2 offers us further opportunities to enlarge on the East European background of the story as well as on the characters of Toivyoh and Serel.

SCENE 2

Toivyoh consults his wife Serel

a. Several of Toivyoh's children are playing. They call their mother and ask for food. There is nothing in the house. Perhaps papa will earn something.

b. Oldest boy arrives. Mother asks why he left *Heder*. He tells her he didn't go that morning since he was ashamed to go without tuition money.

c. Toivyoh arrives. All confront him, hoping he had earned money. He tells them about the "German's" offer. Serel tells him to take the seven good years immediately.

SCENE 3

Toivyoh announces his decision

Toivyoh's announcement to the "German" of Serel's decision might be treated as a separate scene. It is that in the Peretz narrative—the porter going back to the marketplace to inform the "German." However, a multiplicity of scenes, shifting the action from one locale to another, tends to diffuse the concentration of interest and is to be avoided—particularly when the individual scene would be very brief. In this instance, Scene 3 can easily be combined with Scene 2 by the simple expedient of having the "German" come to Toivyoh's house for his decision. Consequently the rest would be sub-scenes of Scene 2, as follows:

d. "German" arrives and asks for decision. Toivyoh tells him. "German" tries to dissuade him. Porter and wife insist. "German" gives in.

e. Commotion from children. They found gold in sand. "German" disappears during excitement. Parents thank the Almighty. Children dance with joy.

SCENE 4

Toivyoh meets the "German" seven years later

a. Toivyoh trying to get work from passersby.

b. "German" arrives. Wonders why Toivyoh is working as porter. Toivyoh tells him it's his trade. "German" announces end of seven good years. Toivyoh is indifferent. Tells "German" to go tell this to his wife. Both leave.

SCENE 5

Serel and the "German"

a. Scene shows changes: everything is the same, except that oldest son now sits and studies Talmud. Serel comes out and asks for other children. They are all still in their various *Hadarim*. Serel beams—her children are growing up to be scholars.

c. Several committees as well as needy individuals come for help. Serel gives gladly. They bless her.

d. Toivyoh and "German" appear. "German" announces end of seven good years. Serel informs him that they used gold only to help poor and to school the children. "German" decides to leave gold with them as most deserving.

As indicated, this subdivision not only makes it easier for the students to develop the dramatization by allowing them to concentrate on brief episodes but also helps enrich the dramatization. As Peretz tells it, a knowledge of East European life on the part of the reader is assumed. As developed here, this background information comes through by means of the additional incidents which are included to round out each block of action. The dramatization might be further enriched by the inclusion of folk-ways, sayings, anecdotes, songs, and other elements expressive of the time and the period. Thus: in the market scene we might have a cobbler at his bench singing a Yiddish cobbler's song, a magician performing for the crowd, peddlers crying their wares, etc. In the home scene we could show the children playing typical games, singing a Yiddish play-song, etc.

Although the inclusion of action and incident to enrich the background and round out the characterizations is very desirable, the teacher must be on the alert not to overdo this to the point where the story is lost because of the many extraneous elements. Furthermore, many stories require judicious pruning rather than expansion. Often an author introduces incidents which are interesting in themselves and even lend color to the tale. However, if allowed to be included in the dramatization they would only serve to distract attention from the main story line. Such incidents are eliminated during the development of the scenes and sub-scenes.

In working with the pupils the teacher will note a tendency to try to adhere rigidly to the story, to put in every detail whether or not it is important to the story. If allowed to proceed along these lines, a good deal of time would be lost in discussions about minute points and trivial details which add nothing of value to the dramatization. The teacher is therefore constantly on the alert to guide the students so that they move along with the task, without bogging down in such details and side issues.

To understand better the procedure of guiding the class in formulating a scene-by-scene dramatization of a story we will examine the actual process involved, utilizing the story of "Joseph-Who-Honors-the-Sabbath" by way of example.

JOSEPH-WHO-HONORS-THE-SABBATH

THE STORY

On the outskirts of Baghdad there lived a very poor man by the name of Joseph and his wife Deborah. Joseph and his wife were so poor that all week long they hardly ate enough to keep body and soul together. But Joseph spared no expense to buy the finest foods for his Sabbath table, thus earning the name "Joseph-Who-Honors-the Sabbath."

Joseph earned his meager livelihood by working for Ali ibn Ibrahim, a wealthy Arab landowner. His employer kept him at work from before sunrise until late in the evening, and paid him only a few coppers a day for all his labors.

When Ali found out that Joseph spent most of his earnings to buy food for the Sabbath, he was greatly annoyed. He called in Joseph and asked: "Is it true that you spend a great deal for food for your Sabbath table?"

"It is true," Joseph answered.

"Where do you get the money?"

"I save it. If I earn three coppers a day working for you, my master, I use one to buy what I need that day and put aside two with which to buy food for the Sabbath. With the money that I save up all week I buy fish and meat and *Hallah* and wine for *kiddush* and other good things for my Sabbath table."

"Oho!" said Ali, "It seems to me that I pay you too much for your work if you are able to put so much aside for food for your Sabbath. We will have to put a stop to this!"

"What do you mean, my master?" Joseph asked.

"It's very simple. From now on your wages will be reduced. Instead of three coppers a day you will get only one."

"But master," Joseph pleaded. "How will I buy food for Sabbath?"

"That's none of my affair," said the Arab. "You told me yourself that all you spend is one copper a day for food. If that's all you spend, that's all you need."

"But the rest is for the Sabbath. If I only get one copper a day how will I . . .?"

"That will be enough," the Arab master interrupted him. "Get out now and go about your work."

Ali turned away and Joseph, his head bowed, went back to work.

Late that night he came home and told his wife Deborah what had happened. His wife smiled at him and scolded gently: "Don't look so sad. The world isn't coming to an end. We will manage somehow."

"How, Deborah? How will we manage? I am not a skilled worker. I can't get another job and with one copper a day . . ."

"Never mind, my husband," Deborah interrupted. "We will eat less every day. Half a copper we will spend for food each day and half a copper we will put aside every day for our Sabbath food."

She smiled at her husband, and Joseph smiled back at her. They ate a piece of dry bread for their supper. Then they said their prayers and went to sleep.

Ali too had a conversation with his wife that night. "Can you imagine," he cried out angrily. "Just hear this Fatima! That Joseph, that pauper spends more for his meals than we do!"

His wife Fatima bowed low to her husband. "How is that possible?" she asked. "He is only one of your laborers. You only pay him three coppers a day."

"And he spends twelve coppers for one day's food. It is to honor his Sabbath, he said. The gall of this pauper! Twelve coppers for food!"

"It is unheard of," said Fatima. "You must do something about this, my husband."

"I already did," Ali answered. "From now on I will only pay him one copper a day."

"You did very wisely my husband," Fatima said, bowing low to her lord and master.

She motioned to her servants who brought in food and wine for their evening meal. First Ali ate, while his wife Fatima helped to serve him. When he had eaten his fill he motioned to Fatima to eat her evening meal from the food he had left over. Then Ali and his wife went to sleep.

During the night Ali had a terrible dream. An old man with a long, grey beard appeared to him and said: "Ali ibn Ibrahim, you have treated your laborer Joseph very badly. You have robbed him for a long time by paying him only three coppers a day for his hard work. Now you want to rob him still more. You will be punished. You will lose all your wealth. It will go to one who is more deserving than you are!" With that the old man disappeared.

Ali awoke, terribly frightened. He told Fatima about his dream. Fatima listened and then she gave him this advice:

"My husband, my lord and master," she said, "why don't you sell all your possessions. With the money you can buy one single jewel and always keep it on your person. In that way nobody will be able to take your wealth."

Ali thought this to be good advice. He did exactly what his wife had told him. He sold all his fields and houses and with the money he bought a great diamond. This diamond he sewed into his turban which he never took off from his head. Waking or sleeping, he always wore his turban on his head; and inside his turban was all his great wealth—the huge, sparkling diamond.

One day Ali was walking across the bridge when a great storm arose. Ali began to walk very fast, to get across the windy bridge quickly. Suddenly a fierce gust seized his turban and blew it off his head. Ali began to run after the turban. It kept rolling away, faster and faster. Ali ran faster still. Now he almost had it. He reached out for the turban. The wind seized it and blew it right into the river.

"My turban! My diamond! My fortune!" Ali cried. He dived into the river but the turban was now out of sight. The current had carried it away. Ali began to flounder and drown. Only the alertness of Joseph who happened to be passing by and dived in after him saved the Arab from drowning.

Ali was now even poorer than Joseph. All his fortune was in the diamond and the diamond was gone, sunk without a trace in the waters of the river. Ali was too ashamed to look for work in the city where every one had known him as a wealthy man. He took his wife Fatima and left Baghdad. No one ever heard of both of them again.

For Joseph things began to look up a little. With Ali gone, Joseph looked for other work. He soon found another job which was much easier than the one he had with Ali. The pay was better, too. He was getting five coppers a day for his work. He kept to his old custom of spending one copper daily for his and his wife's food. The rest he saved for the Sabbath meals.

A short time after Ali and Fatima had disappeared an exciting thing happened in the Bazaar of Baghdad. A fisherman arrived with a basket of fish for sale. Among them was a huge trout, one of the biggest that was ever seen in the Baghdad Bazaar. Everyone came to look at the huge fish but no one was ready to pay the price the fisherman asked for it.

The passersby began to tease the fisherman. "You had better make a party and serve the fish to your guests!" "Throw him back in the river before he spoils!" The fisherman just smiled and said nothing.

After he sold all his smaller fish he picked up the giant trout, slung him across his shoulder and started off.

"Where are you going with your giant fish?" the other merchants asked him.

"To Joseph's house. This is Friday. Joseph-Who-Honors-the-Sabbath will buy him for his Sabbath table."

Now the merchants understood why the fisherman listened so patiently to their teasing comments. Of course Joseph-Who-Honors-the-Sabbath would buy the fish! Nothing is too good for his Sabbath table! Sure enough, even though it took every copper he had saved, Joseph bought the giant fish for his wife to serve that Sabbath.

"Isn't it wonderful, Deborah?" he exclaimed. "Now we will be able to invite all our friends to eat with us and honor the Sabbath in our home. This fish is big enough to serve many, many people."

"It is a wonderous fish, my husband," Deborah answered.

"It was very expensive," Joseph commented. "But I am happy we were able to buy it. The holy Sabbath day deserves to be honored with the best we can get." With this, Joseph began to clean the huge fish.

Joseph scrubbed the scales on one side and his wife Deborah on the other. It took a long time. Finally all the scales were off and Joseph began to cut open the huge fish. Suddenly he shouted: "Look Deborah! Look in this fish's belly. Something glitters, like a diamond."

"Let me see," his wife called excitedly. Out of the fish's belly they took a huge, beautiful, glittering diamond. "See, my husband! The Good Lord rewards us for honoring the Sabbath!"

What a Sabbath they had that week! All the neighbors were invited. They sang Sabbath *Z'mirot* and gave praise to the Almighty for His great goodness. When Sabbath was ended, Joseph sold the diamond. For the rest of his life he was a wealthy man. He used his riches to help others in need. For himself he took nothing of his great wealth all week long. He lived on a few coppers a day. But for the Sabbath he used his wealth freely. Nothing was too good for the Sabbath table of Joseph-Who-Honored-the-Sabbath.

After telling the story, the teacher stimulates the class to dramatize it. Often the suggestion that the story be enacted will come from the students themselves, particularly if they have had adequate preparatory experiences leading to Dramatization Readiness. If the suggestion does not come from the pupils, the teacher proposes it with a simple statement such as, "Shall we make a play out of this story?" or "Wouldn't this story make a fine play? How would you like to play it?" Thereafter the teacher guides the pupils in the first step of the dramatization process—dividing the story into scenes—somewhat as follows:

TEACHER: Many things happen in our story. Each is a different episode or scene. It will be a lot easier for us to make a play out of our story if we work on each scene separately. Now, what do you think should be the first scene of our play?

STUDENT 1: We ought to show how Joseph buys things for the Sabbath.

STUDENT 2: I think we ought to show first how poor he is.

TEACHER: Maybe we can combine both ideas. Let's decide first where the opening scene should take place.

STUDENT 4: Why not in the Bazaar? It should be a lot of fun showing a Bazaar in Baghdad.

STUDENT 5: I think that's a crummy idea!

STUDENT 4: What's the matter with it?

STUDENT 5: It's just crummy, that's all.

TEACHER: You mean you don't like his suggestion?

STUDENT 5: No, I don't like it.

TEACHER: Why?

STUDENT 5: I just don't like it, that's all.

TEACHER: What would you suggest instead?

STUDENT 5: I don't know.

TEACHER: If you have no better suggestion to offer, I suppose we will just have to use the suggestion that the first scene be in the Bazaar. Does everyone agree with this?

STUDENT 6: I don't know. Maybe we shouldn't have a Bazaar?

TEACHER: Why?

STUDENT 6: It's sort of hard to have a Bazaar in class. We'd need lots of merchants and customers and that kind of thing.

TEACHER: Well, is there another way we can bring out that he was poor and he bought good things only for the Sabbath? Could we have it at his home perhaps?

STUDENT 6: We could.

TEACHER: How would we bring out this information? Does anyone have a suggestion? No one? How about combining the ideas of the Bazaar and the home? Suppose Joseph were coming home from the Bazaar with a fine chicken he bought and showed it to his wife? What do you think his wife might say to this?

STUDENT 7: She might say, "Are you sure we can afford it? You must have spent our last copper."

STUDENT 8: She might go on and say, "How will we eat all next week?" That would show how poor they are.

We can see from this teacher-student discussion that the teacher is confronted here with two problems that are fairly common, especially the first few times that something new is tried in class: 1. Destructive criticism which, if allowed to go unchecked, will choke off any creative contributions on the part of most students for fear of being made to look foolish. 2. A lack of suggestions and ideas coming from the students, either because of timidity, inexperience, lack of stimulation to creative thinking, or any other reason.

The first must be coped with as soon as it emerges for the very first time. Otherwise, it will become "the thing to do" to heckle the project. Here, the teacher immediately challenged the heckler to offer a better suggestion. Had he answered the challenge, the discussion would have continued in a constructive manner. Not being able to answer the challenge, the teacher just brushes it off so that the heckler, instead of gaining status with the other pupils, realizes that he would have done better if he had gotten attention by contributing in a positive way.

The second problem calls for positive guidance and often for actual help by the teacher. It would be naive to think that because this is a *creative* dramatization, reliance is to be placed solely on what may be forthcoming from the children and, if for some reason an impasse is reached, the teacher must under no circumstances "manipulate" the *creative* process. *Creatio ex nihilo* is not within the province of mortals. Human creativity comes as a result of stimuli. Sometimes these are massive in nature. Sometimes they are as evanescent as a strain of melody, a bird in flight, a ray of sunshine fragmentized through the prism of a raindrop, or the gurgle of a child's laughter. In the classroom too, creative contributions from the students may be stimulated at times by a title, a line of a poem, or a judicious question by the teacher. At other times, more massive stimulation is called for such as a leading question, or even a direct suggestion by the teacher to get things moving. This in turn stimulates the students to build on the teacher's contribution, adding suggestions of their own and keeping the creative process going. On the other hand, the teacher is careful not to monopolize the discussion or to impose himself on the students even though he is thoroughly convinced that his ideas are far superior to those offered by the students. In short, the knowing teacher does not consider himself the final arbiter. Nor does he see himself as a referee, standing aside, judging and evaluating the students' contributions, proclaiming the "game" is ended when, for one reason or another, the students stop contributing ideas of their own. He rather looks upon himself as a member of the team, a quarterback who does not dominate the play, but guides it along, and from time to time takes an active part in it.

The process of dividing the story into scenes and the development of the scenes continues:

TEACHER: Do you think it is a good idea to make Deborah a complaining wife? How does she appear in the story?
STUDENT 1: In the story Deborah is very devoted to Joseph. She encourages him to honor the Sabbath.
STUDENT 2: Why can't Joseph say this?
TEACHER: What do you mean?
STUDENT 2: Well, he comes home from the market and his wife says, "What a plump chicken!" Then Joseph says, "It cost a great deal. Now we won't have anything left for next week." Then the wife says, "Never mind, Joseph. As long as we can honor the Sabbath with this fine chicken."
TEACHER: What would Joseph say to that?
STUDENT 2: He might be worried about spending all their money.
STUDENT 3: That would be all wrong. Joseph is the one who loves to honor the Sabbath. He ought to say, "Of course. As long as we can honor the Sabbath I am ready to go hungry all week."
TEACHER: That's an excellent suggestion. Now, what should happen next?
STUDENT 4: That's all. The next scene should be in the Arab's house.
STUDENT 5: Maybe we ought to have a messenger come from Joseph's master asking him to come to see the Arab.
TEACHER: That's a first class suggestion! In this way we will tie scene 1 together with scene 2 very nicely.

The teacher is alert to notice which students are holding back from the discussion. Also, the teacher is sufficiently familiar with the students in the class to know which are naturally shy and retiring and will not generally participate in acting roles. Although these should gradually be encouraged to greater participation, they are not to be forced into situations which are painful for such children. Instead, they are to be given tasks which will draw them into the project in other ways. Thus:

TEACHER: That just about gives us our first scene. We will need a secretary to keep a record of our scenes. Jacob, will you please be our Scene Secretary? You will put down on the blackboard what we decided, so that we will not forget.
JACOB: All right.
TEACHER: You don't have to put down everything. Just the most important things. For instance: "Scene 1—Joseph's house. He brings chicken. They discuss finances. Messenger calls Joseph to Ali's house." Clear?
JACOB: All right.
TEACHER: Good. Now, what should be our second scene?
STUDENT 6: Ali's argument with Joseph.
TEACHER: That seems pretty clear. Put it down, please, Scene Secretary. How will you write it, Jacob?
JACOB: "Scene 2—Ali argues with Joseph. Cuts his salary."

TEACHER: That's very good, Jacob! I like this "cuts his salary." Put it down, please. Now, scene 3. Any suggestions?

STUDENT 7: Joseph tells his wife about his troubles.

TEACHER: That seems correct. It follows our story. Now for scene 4.

STUDENT 8: Ali tells Fatima about Joseph.

STUDENT 1: I think this should be scene 3.

TEACHER: Why?

STUDENT 1: Because why go back and forth all the time? Scene 2 is in Ali's house. Scene 3 should be in the same place.

TEACHER: Anybody think differently?

STUDENT 2: It isn't like in the story. There Joseph tells his wife first. Then Ali tells Fatima.

STUDENT 1: What difference does it make? It doesn't change the story any.

TEACHER: Well, let's vote on it. How many think the scene at Ali's should come before the scene at Joseph's? I see most of you think so. All right, Jacob. Put it down. "Scene 3. In Ali's house."

STUDENT 2: If that's the case, why do we need a new scene? Why can't we just have Fatima enter in scene 2, right after the argument and have Ali tell her what happened?

TEACHER: That's a very fine idea! The only thing is, it might be a little too much for us to work out all at once. Maybe we had better divide it after all.

STUDENT 2: Let's make it scene 2 and scene 2a. We can work them out separately and then, when we play them we can do them together.

TEACHER: That sounds reasonable. All right Jacob. Instead of scene 3, we will call this 2a. Scene 3 then is "Joseph tells Deborah his troubles with Ali." What's scene 4?

STUDENT 4: Scene 4 should be the dream.

STUDENT 5: I don't think it's such a good idea to show a dream. It's too much of the spooky stuff.

STUDENT 6: But the dream is important to the story.

STUDENT 5: Then why can't we just have Ali tell Fatima about it?

STUDENT 4: That's no fun. That's just a bunch of speeches.

TEACHER: You may be right. In a play we are supposed to *show* what happened rather than *tell* about it. Still, maybe it would be too spooky. We'll vote on it. How many think we should show the dream? How many feel Ali should tell Fatima about it? It looks as if most of you are for showing the dream. So, what will you write for scene 4, Jacob?

JACOB: "Scene 4, Ali's dream."

TEACHER: Fine. What's next?

STUDENT 7: Ali tells Fatima and she advises him to sell his possessions and buy a jewel.

TEACHER: Any other ideas?

STUDENT 8: This we can really combine! Why can't we show the dream, then have Ali wake up and call for his wife and tell her about it?

TEACHER: Why not, indeed? Does anybody have any objections to this suggestion? All right, Scene Secretary, add to Scene 4, "Ali tells Fatima about dream. Fatima advises to sell possessions and buy a jewel." What's next?

STUDENT 1: Scene 5 should be how he sells everything and buys a jewel.

TEACHER: Do we really need a scene for this? Can anyone think of a better way to bring this out? No ideas? Well, let's see—what would you show after he sold his possessions?

STUDENT 2: How he loses the jewel.

TEACHER: On the bridge?

STUDENT 2: Yes.

TEACHER: I know the story doesn't say it but does he have to be alone on the bridge?

STUDENT 3: He could be going with his wife.

TEACHER: He could. Then he would have someone to talk to. Does that give you an idea about scene 5?

STUDENT 4: I know. They could be walking. The wife says, "Are you sure you have the jewel?" and he says, "Don't worry. It's sewn into my turban. I watch it very carefully. It's our whole fortune."

TEACHER: Very good!

STUDENT 5: Then the wind grabs it. The wife shouts, "Don't jump in the river!" Then she calls for help and that's how we know he jumped in.

TEACHER: Now we're moving along. So, Scene 5 is on the bridge. What's scene 6?

STUDENT 6: How Joseph jumps in and saves him.

STUDENT 7: How are you going to show that?

STUDENT 6: I don't know. But it's in the story.

TEACHER: We don't really have to show it, do we? In the next scene Joseph could bring it out. How do you think we might do that?

STUDENT 8: Joseph could tell his wife how he saved Ali from drowning.

STUDENT 5: Then we could bring out in their talk that Ali and his wife disappeared.

TEACHER: Anyone think differently? No? All right, Jacob, put down "Scene 6, Joseph's house. They talk of rescue and Ali's disappearance." Now what's the next part of the story?

STUDENT 6: The big fish.

TEACHER: How shall we show it?

STUDENT 6: In the Bazaar.

STUDENT 5: I thought we decided not to have a Bazaar scene.

TEACHER: So we did. Can we show this also in Joseph's house?

STUDENT 3: Why not? As they talk about Ali's disappearance, the fisherman comes to sell them the big fish.

STUDENT 4: Sure. Then they buy it, open it, find the jewel, decide to make a big party.

TEACHER: All in one scene?

STUDENT 5: Why not? They could even agree not to use the money for themselves but only for buying food for the Sabbath.

TEACHER: So that the play would end in scene 6.

STUDENT 4: Sure.

TEACHER: I'm afraid this may be a little too much to work on all at once.

STUDENT 7: We could do the same as with scene 2. We could work first on the conversation between Joseph and his wife. Then with the fisherman. Then Joseph and wife again. When we play it in the end, we would do it as one scene.

TEACHER: That sounds very good. Put it down, please, Jacob: "Scene 6. In Joseph's house. Joseph and Deborah talk about Ali. Fisherman comes. They buy fish.

Find jewel. Decide what to do with their riches. End."

Now that the story has been divided into scenes, the process proceeds, from this point until the final enactment, on a scene-by-scene basis. Each scene is developed up to the point of the final enactment before proceeding to the following scene.

■ DETERMINE CHARACTERS

We now go back to the first scene of our dramatization. The class discusses the characters who are needed for the scene. Each character is developed as an individual, as a human being, in addition to his function as a figure in the story. One of the great values of dramatization is that the students learn to look at every single human being as a personality, not as a stereotype. The teacher guides the students in developing for each character individual traits, distinguishing characteristics which would make him different from other human beings. In the first few attempts at story dramatization, these characteristics will naturally be drawn in bold terms—is he tall or short, slow of speech or hurried, quick to anger or "slow-burning," etc.? In time, the students are guided to look for finer shadings of character so that they will learn to see the weaknesses which make a hero a human being instead of a cardboard figure, and the occasional good traits to be found even in a thoroughgoing villain.

TEACHER: Now that we have decided on our scenes and we have a sort of general blueprint of our play, we are ready to go ahead and make our dramatization itself.

At this point we have an opportunity to involve a number of additional shy and retiring pupils by giving them important but non-acting tasks.

TEACHER: We will go back now to our first scene. But, before we do anything else we must appoint some of you to several important jobs. Morris, you've been rather quiet today. I have a very special job for you. You will be our Stage Manager and Linda will be your assistant. You will not only be responsible for setting up any furniture which may be necessary for each scene, but you will also have to remember everything that we decide and watch out that we don't make any mistakes or leave out anything important. All right, let's begin. Morris, please read for us what Jacob, our Scene Secretary wrote on the blackboard for Scene 1.

MORRIS: *(Reads)* "Scene 1: Joseph's house. He brings chicken. They discuss finances. Messenger calls Joseph to Ali's house."

TEACHER: Thank you, Morris. Now, what characters do we need for the first scene? Esther, you will be our Characters Secretary. Please put down on the blackboard the names of the characters for each scene. Now, whom do we need here?

STUDENT 1: Joseph.

TEACHER: Of course. He's our main character. Write it down please, Esther. Put down "Scene 1" on top and underneath put down "Joseph." Who else?

STUDENT 2: Deborah.

TEACHER: Good. Put it down Esther, "Deborah, his wife." Who else?

STUDENT 3: Ali's Messenger.

TEACHER: Write it down please. Anyone else? What about some neighbors?

STUDENT 4: There are no neighbors in the story.

TEACHER: That's true. But do you think it would change our story if we had some neighbors come over to talk to Deborah before Joseph comes in?

STUDENT 4: Maybe it wouldn't change the story, but what do we need them for?

TEACHER: That's a very good point. Even if it would not change our story, we never introduce extra characters unless having them will help our dramatization. Can any one see how introducing neighbors, or people like the Rabbi of Baghdad would improve our play?

STUDENT 5: I think I have an idea. Why not have the Rabbi of Baghdad come to visit Deborah? He is worried that Joseph and his wife eat so little all week. Maybe he wants to tell them not to overdo it. In that way we find out about the family all we want to know.

TEACHER: That's an excellent idea! And maybe we can use the Rabbi later to tell them that it is all right for them to keep the jewel.

STUDENT 6: We could still have neighbors. Say two women come to see Deborah. They're going home from the market. They talk about the fact that it will soon be Sabbath and in that way bring out that Joseph is shopping and that everybody calls him Joseph-Who-Honors-the-Sabbath. Then one of them says "the Rabbi is coming," and we go on as Student 5 said.

TEACHER: Now we are really getting there! It isn't a very great accomplishment to just act out the story. What we're doing is giving it life and spirit. Very good! Put it down, Esther: "Rabbi, Neighbor 1, Neighbor 2."

STUDENT 7: Couldn't we give them names instead of numbers?

TEACHER: I don't see why not. What shall we call the neighbors?

STUDENT 8: Maybe we'll call them Jane and Joan—like twins sort of—and we could make them funny.

TEACHER: Aren't you forgetting? The play takes place in Baghdad not in America. Do you think they would call them by American names?

STUDENT 1: Scheherezade lived in Baghdad. We could call one Scheherezade. I like that!

STUDENT 2: But that's not a Jewish name. Why not call one Rachel and the other Leah, like Jacob's wives.

TEACHER: Good. Write them down, please, Esther. Now that we have our characters for the first scene, let us see what they are like.

MORRIS: Excuse me, please . . .

TEACHER: Yes, Morris?

MORRIS: We left out a character. Ali's Messenger.

TEACHER: Of course! Thank you, Morris. It seems we have a Stage Manager who is really wide awake. Put it down, Esther. Now, what kind of person is Joseph to be?

STUDENT 1: Kindly.

TEACHER: Yes.

STUDENT 2: Doesn't get angry quickly.

TEACHER: Would he speak slowly or rapidly?

STUDENT 3: Slowly.

TEACHER: Why?

STUDENT 3: Well, it sort of seems to fit him, if he is patient and kindly and a hard worker—like a peasant maybe.

TEACHER: What about that? Would you say that Joseph is learned or not too well educated.

STUDENT 4: I think he is educated.

TEACHER: Why?

STUDENT 4: Well, he's our hero—so he should be educated.

STUDENT 5: I think he shouldn't be at all educated. It makes it all the more important if he is a simple man but observes the Sabbath as he does.

TEACHER: We seem to have a real difference of opinion here. Would any one care to comment?

STUDENT 6: I think he's right. Plain people can be heroes too. If we make Joseph a plain, uneducated, hard-working man who obeys the law and honors the Sabbath, he will come out even more important than if he was a scholar.

STUDENT 7: Sure. That's why the Rabbi comes to him, to tell him that the law doesn't expect him to go hungry all week so he could feast in honor of the Sabbath. Then Joseph convinces the Rabbi that he is right and that makes Joseph even more important.

TEACHER: Anybody disagree? I guess our Joseph will be a simple, honest man, very pious but not too well learned in the law.

STUDENT 8: But I don't think he ought to be altogether ignorant.

TEACHER: You are probably right. Throughout the ages Jews valued learning and even the most simple knew the prayers, many of the laws, and even a little Bible. Joseph could be a man like that. What about Deborah? How old do you think she should be?

STUDENT 1: About thirty, maybe.

STUDENT 2: She should be older—around forty.

TEACHER: We'll compromise and make her thirty-five. How does she talk?

STUDENT 3: She should be excitable, talk quickly, flare up at the smallest thing.

TEACHER: Why?

STUDENT 3: Well, it's more interesting to make each character different.

TEACHER: Do you all agree with him?

STUDENT 4: I don't think so. She always comforts her husband in the story.

STUDENT 3: I didn't say she's got to be mean. She can be kind and comfort her husband and still talk quick and excited like.

TEACHER: Sounds reasonable. Any objections? All right. What about neighbor Rachel?

STUDENT 5: She can be an old woman, a granny like, talking a little squeaky maybe.

TEACHER: And Leah?

STUDENT 6: Let's make Leah young—Rachel's granddaughter.

TEACHER: The Rabbi?

STUDENT 7: He could be a very slow-speaking old man, full of dignity, respected by everybody.

TEACHER: Any other ideas? All right, our Rabbi will be old and dignified. Now the Messenger.

STUDENT 8: He should be like a soldier.

STUDENT 1: I think he should be Ali's foreman, a sort of . . . Oh, they have a name for them in old stories . . . you know, the man that's in charge of things . . .

TEACHER: The major domo?

STUDENT 1: That's right. Ali sends his major domo for Joseph.

TEACHER: What kind of man is he?

STUDENT 1: Oh, just anybody—a messenger, that's all. He's not too important.

TEACHER: In a play every character is important. And no human being is just anybody. We will have to do better than that.

STUDENT 2: Why can't he be the comedy in the play. We can make him fat, huffing and puffing, always running when Ali gives him an order, because he's anxious to do what the boss wants. Then he loses his breath.

STUDENT 3: Sure. We can make him even funnier if he will always repeat the last two words of every sentence. I once saw somebody like that in the movies. He was awfully funny.

STUDENT 4: He could try to talk very fast so that at the end of each sentence he loses his breath and begins to cough and Joseph has to slap him on the back so he can catch his breath.

TEACHER: I can see that you all agree that our Messenger is to be the major domo and should be a comic character. Now this gives us our cast of characters for Scene 1. I must say that you have made up a very interesting cast. We should have a very interesting play with such a group of people.

■ SELECT THE CAST

The cast is selected by asking for volunteers. In our hypothetical class that is ready for dramatization there would usually be no lack of volunteers for all parts. If anything, the teacher may have to re-assure the students that those who have not been chosen for parts in the first scene will get their chance in subsequent scenes.

There is no hard and fast rule as to whether the teacher is to fill first the minor or the major roles. Generally it adds importance to the minor roles if the teacher begins with them. On the other hand, the teacher may find that the abler students hold back from volunteering for these roles in the hope that they will get the leading parts and the more timid, not having the example of the more forward to follow, are afraid to volunteer altogether. It would seem that the teacher will have to feel his way in each instance, depending on the class and the temperament of the students.

The teacher is careful not to permit any students to monopolize the proceedings. In every class there are pupils who are eager to take a part and others who hold back. Regardless of their ability, the teacher sees to it that a pupil who plays the lead in one scene, will play a supporting role in another, while those who have played a minor character are given an opportunity to spread their wings and play the longer and more difficult roles. However, under no circumstance will the teacher force a student into accepting a part which is beyond his capabilities. This will only cause him embarrassment and put him in an uncomfortable position in relation to his fellow-students. The process of leading a student from very simple roles to more complex ones is to be gradual, carried out gently, almost imperceptibly. It is well to remember that despite all the efforts which a teacher may exert, some pupils will just never go beyond playing very minor roles while some will never assume any role at all and be very happy in their positions of stage manager, secretary, stage hand, research assistant, etc.

In asking for volunteers it is usually easier to involve the interest of the students if, instead of referring to the character, the teacher emphasizes a salient characteristic of the character to be cast. For example:

Not: Who would like to play the Messenger?
But: Who would like to be our fat, wheezing, coughing major domo?
Who likes to try to speak hurriedly and be very excited like our Deborah?
Who would enjoy being a dignified, slow-speaking old scholar?

After the entire cast for Scene 1 is selected in this manner, the teacher proceeds to develop the scene in detail through class discussion.

■ DISCUSS THE SCENE

The discussion of the scene in detail before its enactment not only helps to clarify it but serves to enlarge upon it, to add details of history, character, social environment etc. Furthermore, thorough discussion in advance makes it easier for the players to create the necessary dialogue during the enactment.

TEACHER: Now we are almost ready to play our first scene. Let's just go over it for a few minutes so that everything will be clear about it. How do we begin?
STUDENT 1: We can start with Deborah cleaning the house for Sabbath.
STUDENT 2: She can be singing a Sabbath song while she does it.
TEACHER: What song do you suggest?
STUDENT 1: How about "*Shabbat Shalom?*"
TEACHER: All right. Then what happens?
STUDENT 3: Rachel and her granddaughter Leah come by. They ask Deborah if she is ready for the Sabbath. She says, "not yet." She's waiting for her husband.
TEACHER: How would we bring out at this point that Joseph is called Joseph-Who-Honors-the-Sabbath?
STUDENT 4: Rachel could say, "Joseph is probably looking for the best food to buy for Sabbath." Then Deborah could say, "He always does that," and Leah could say, "That's why everybody calls him Joseph-Who-Honors-the-Sabbath, because nothing is too good for his Sabbath table."
TEACHER: Do you think we could now bring in the fact that he is poor?
STUDENT 5: Sure. Deborah could say something about having to go hungry all week.
STUDENT 6: I don't think it would be like Deborah to complain.
TEACHER: What would you suggest?
STUDENT 6: The old woman Rachel could say, "Sure, you go hungry all week so you could honor the Sabbath with fine food." Then Deborah could answer, "The Sabbath day is holy and we love to honor it, even if we go hungry all week."
TEACHER: And at this point the Rabbi would come in.
STUDENT 7: Leah could say, "There comes the Rabbi. I wonder why he is coming here."

TEACHER: What follows now?

STUDENT 1: The Rabbi comes in and tells Deborah that he came to talk to her about her husband. It isn't right to starve all week to honor the Sabbath. Then, before she could answer, Joseph comes in with the chicken.

STUDENT 2: Joseph would be all excited. He bought the biggest chicken in the Bazaar in honor of the Sabbath. Then the Rabbi interrupts him and tells him what he told Deborah.

TEACHER: What do you think Joseph answers?

STUDENT 3: He tells the Rabbi that honoring the Sabbath is his greatest pleasure in life.

TEACHER: Perhaps Joseph might give his reasons for doing this? What do you think they would be?

STUDENT 4: He could tell the Rabbi that the Sabbath is a holy day.

STUDENT 5: He could say that the Creator of the world rested on the Sabbath.

STUDENT 6: He could tell how hard he works all week and only on the Sabbath he rests and feels joy in everything.

TEACHER: How would he describe the Sabbath?

STUDENT 7: As a day of rest.

TEACHER: Can you think of a better description? We studied the Friday night hymn "*Lekha Dodi.*" Let's look at the English translation. Here, Philip, will you read it aloud, please.

PHILIP: *(Reads)* Come, my beloved, with chorus of praise. Welcome Bride Sabbath, the Queen of the days.

TEACHER: So, what is Sabbath called here?

STUDENT 7: A bride and the Queen of days.

TEACHER: Would Joseph call the Sabbath by these names?

STUDENT 8: Sure. We decided that he knew a little, that he could read the prayer book and so on.

TEACHER: Now what happens? Is the Rabbi convinced?

STUDENT 1: I think so.

STUDENT 2: Maybe he's not convinced but he sees how Joseph feels about things and understands.

TEACHER: That makes sense. What happens next?

STUDENT 3: The Messenger comes in puffing and tells Joseph that Ali wants to see him.

MORRIS: End of Scene 1.

TEACHER: Very good, Mr. Stage Manager. End of Scene 1.

■ ENACT THE SCENE

The teacher calls the students who have been selected to play Scene 1 for the first time to come up in front of the room and enact the scene, using their own words, making up the dialogue as they play the scene. Generally teachers find this to be the most difficult part of the process. However, if story dramatization will not be attempted in a class before its pupils have developed a certain amount of Dramatization Readiness, this step should proceed easily and spontaneously. Having had previous experience with dramatic games calling for simple dialogue, the students will normally have no difficulty at this point in improvising the speech of the characters, particularly if the situations have been carefully developed through discussion before the improvisation begins.

During the first enactment the teacher allows the scene to continue without interruption until the very end—this despite any mistakes which the players may make. Such errors can be rectified during the evaluation which will follow the enactment.

If the dramatization hits a snag and the players stop in the middle, the teacher may get the enactment moving again with a gentle reminder such as: "Leah, isn't this about the time when you notice that the Rabbi is coming?" "Deborah, do you agree with the Rabbi that your husband is wrong in spending most of his earnings for Sabbath food?" If the enactment bogs down to the point where such reminders are insufficient to get it moving again, or if the actors stop too often, at a loss as to what to do or say, the teacher stops the enactment with the remark, "It seems as if we didn't discuss this scene enough. We began to play it before we were really ready for it. Let's take our seats for a little while and talk about it some more." The teacher then leads the class in further discussion, working out the scene in more detail, particularly that part with which the players had difficulties.

The teacher bears in mind, however, that it is not to be expected that the players give a finished and smooth performance, certainly not the very first time a scene is tried, and not even at the very end, when the entire dramatization is enacted for the last time. The teacher never forgets that in classroom dramatics the educative *process* is of prime importance and not the performance itself. This does not mean that the teacher and the players are not to strive for good artistic standards. It is simply that classroom dramatizations have a different goal than formal plays which are prepared for showing to an outside audience. The teacher never forgets this and always keeps the true goal in sight.

The following is an example of what the first enactment of Scene 1 might be like:

SCENE *(Two chairs near a table. Deborah is straightening things out on the table, singing "Shabbat Shalom.")*

RACHEL: *(Enters with her granddaughter Leah)* Good afternoon, Deborah.

DEBORAH: Good afternoon Rachel. Good afternoon Leah. Where do you come from?

RACHEL: The Bazaar.

LEAH: You should see the nice fish we bought. Look, Deborah! *(She pantomimes showing a fish)*

DEBORAH: My, he is big!

RACHEL: He should be. He cost enough.

DEBORAH: But it's worth it. After all, it's for the Sabbath.

RACHEL: We're poor people. We can't all be like you and your husband Joseph.

DEBORAH: We're not rich, Rachel. You know how hard my Joseph works for Ali ibn Ibrahim and all that his Arab master pays him is three coppers a day.

RACHEL: I know. And you spend only one copper a day for food and you save two coppers to buy things for the Sabbath.

LEAH: Everybody knows this. That's why we call him Joseph-Who-Honors-the-Sabbath.

RACHEL: I think it's wrong to go hungry all week just so you could buy the best food for the Sabbath table.

LEAH: I think it's wonderful.

RACHEL: Nobody is asking you, granddaughter. Children should be seen, not heard.

LEAH: Look! Here comes the Rabbi.

RACHEL: He seems to be coming to you, Deborah.

RABBI: *(Enters)* Good afternoon, Deborah. Good afternoon, Rachel. Is this your granddaughter?

RACHEL: Yes, Rabbi.

RABBI: Where is your husband, Joseph?

DEBORAH: He didn't come back from the market yet.

RABBI: I want to talk to you about him. I heard that you both eat almost nothing all week so you could buy food for *Shabbat*.

JOSEPH: *(Enters, pantomiming carrying a big chicken)* Look at this big chicken I was able to buy for the Sabbath!

DEBORAH: Joseph, the Rabbi is here.

JOSEPH: Good afternoon Rabbi. Look what a big chicken I bought! In honor of the Sabbath, Rabbi.

RABBI: It must have cost a lot.

JOSEPH: Sure! Every copper I saved all week.

RABBI: That's what I came for, Joseph. It is not right to starve all week, even if it is to honor the Sabbath.

JOSEPH: But honoring the Sabbath is the greatest pleasure I have. It's the holiest day of the week. The Creator rested on the Sabbath day.

RABBI: I know, but to go hungry all week . . .

JOSEPH: All week I don't care. But on the Sabbath I rest, I am joyous. I sing songs for the Queen Sabbath and put food on the table that's the best . . .

RABBI: I don't know. Maybe you are right.

MESSENGER: *(Comes in puffing)* Joseph! Hurry up! The master wants to see you. He wants to see you.

JOSEPH: What for?

MESSENGER: I don't know. He's very angry . . . very angry.

JOSEPH: All right. I'm coming.

■ ANALYZE THE SCENE CRITICALLY

As soon as the players reach a point where the information has been brought out, the teacher stops the enactment. The scene is completed. The teacher thanks the players, praises their efforts, and opens the analysis by the students of the scene that was just played.

The teacher guides the discussion so that it concerns itself mainly with the content of the scene and not with the way it was acted by the pupils. At the same time he will permit some evaluation of the acting aspect also. The teacher will stimulate this by pointing out the good things that were done—how Leah took Joseph's part, how the grandmother lectured her, how Deborah reminded Joseph that he did not greet the Rabbi, etc. The pupils will be encouraged to express themselves in like manner. They will also be permitted, up to a point, to criticize omissions, wrong actions, etc.

Naturally, the teacher will be on guard not to permit the criticism to become vicious or vindictive. But, neither will the teacher become so overprotective as to choke off all negative criticism. Children must learn how to give criticism and how to accept it. Furthermore, it is a part of the educative process for pupils to learn how to view things analytically and critically. It is part of living in a democracy to become habituated not to accept every handout without question, no matter what the source may be. The right and the duty to look critically at the acts of our leaders and to voice our criticism—kindly, respectfully, but firmly, with conviction—is the very basis of a democratic society. It gains thereby in vitality and strength. By the same token, a dramatization gains in quality by the pupils' critical evaluation. At the same time, both players and critics gain in skill, knowledge, confidence and discrimination by the criticism they give and receive.

The critical analysis of Scene 1 might proceed somewhat as follows:

TEACHER: Thank you. This ends our first scene. You played it very well. You held our interest to the very end. You may go back to your seats now. Didn't they do really well? What did you like best about it, Class?

STUDENT 1: The way Rachel was grumpy and gruff.

STUDENT 2: I liked the way Rachel bawled Leah out for saying that she thought Joseph was wonderful.

TEACHER: Wasn't it nice though the way Leah said it? It made us all feel that almost everybody respects Joseph for what he does. What did you especially like about the whole scene?

STUDENT 3: The way they played it. It sounded for real.

STUDENT 4: They brought out everything.

STUDENT 5: Not everything. They never mentioned where the scene was taking place.

TEACHER: That's a very good observation. What could they have done to let us know that the scene took place in Baghdad?

STUDENT 5: When Leah said "everybody knows how Joseph saves his money to buy food for the Sabbath" she could have said "everybody in Baghdad knows . . ."

TEACHER: That's a very good suggestion. We must remember this the next time we do the scene. What else could we do to improve the scene?

STUDENT 6: I think we ought to get rid of Rachel and Leah when the Rabbi comes in.

TEACHER: Why?

STUDENT 6: Well, they don't say anything after the Rabbi comes in.

STUDENT 7: They don't have to say anything. They help the scene if they make out like they admire the chicken, or shake their heads as if they agree when the Rabbi says he shouldn't go hungry . . .

TEACHER: That's a very good point. The players don't always have to speak to help the scene along. They do it with pantomime, with movement, and sometimes they help to make the scene by just being there.

STUDENT 6: But isn't it sort of embarrassing to have the Rabbi speak in front of the neighbors about how poor Joseph is?

STUDENT 7: What's embarrassing about it? Everybody in Baghdad knows it.

STUDENT 8: Sure. That makes it even more important when he spends so much for Sabbath food.

TEACHER: These seem like good arguments. What do you say, Class? Shall we let them stay or have them leave when the Rabbi comes? How many think they should stay? How many think they should leave? I guess they stay. What other improvements can we make?

STUDENT 1: I don't think Joseph showed the Rabbi enough respect when he came in.

TEACHER: Why do you say that?

STUDENT 1: Well, he didn't greet him.

STUDENT 2: But he was excited about the chicken.

STUDENT 1: That's no excuse. Even if he was excited, he should have excused himself to the Rabbi afterwards.

TEACHER: That makes good sense. He could say, "Excuse me Rabbi. I am so excited that I didn't see you when I came in." Any other suggestions?

STUDENT 3: He didn't call the Sabbath a bride when he told the Rabbi why he honors it.

STUDENT 4: We could bring that out later, when he explains to Ali about the Sabbath.

TEACHER: That's a good suggestion. Well, it seems to me we have said a good deal about this scene. Now let's give the players a chance. If you had an opportunity to play the scene over again, how would you improve it?

DEBORAH: I would show Rachel and Leah some of the things I had prepared for the Sabbath like the fish and the *Hallah*. In that way we would bring out how much we really do for the Sabbath.

RACHEL: I think that I could have said something about how little Joseph gets from Ali and ask why he doesn't try to get another job.

TEACHER: How would that help the scene?

RACHEL: It would bring out how hard it is to get a new job and show that Joseph isn't just a dope for working for Ali.

TEACHER: What about you Leah?

LEAH: I don't think I could add anything.

TEACHER: Rabbi?

RABBI: Well, if I had a chance to look it up before I play the scene again, I would use some saying from the Rabbis in my argument with Joseph.

TEACHER: Why?

RABBI: Well, it would make me sound more like a Rabbi—you know, learned and all that. A saying from the Rabbis would help.

TEACHER: Like "*Pikuah nefesh doheh Shabbat*—saving a life in danger is greater than the Sabbath."

RABBI: Something like that.

TEACHER: That might be a good argument for the Rabbi. We Jews have always felt that human life is more important than most of the laws of the Torah. As a matter of fact there is another saying of the Rabbis, "He who saves one life, it is as if he had saved the entire world." I suppose that's why the Rabbi comes to Joseph. He's afraid that going hungry during the week may injure his health. How would you improve your part, Joseph?

JOSEPH: If I could do it over I would refuse to go to Ali.

STUDENT 5: That's not in the story.
JOSEPH: What difference does that make?
STUDENT 5: Well, you can't just go and change the story.
JOSEPH: Why not? It's only a story, not history. We can change it if it will make it better. Can't we?
TEACHER: I imagine we can—if it will make it better. Why would you refuse to go?
JOSEPH: Well. The way the story is now, Ali is just mean, without any reason.
STUDENT 6: But he *is* mean!
JOSEPH: Sure he is—but if we give him a reason for acting mean, he'll still be no good but he will be more real.
TEACHER: What do you suggest?
JOSEPH: I would say, "I'm sorry. It's almost Shabbat I can't go and see him now. I have to prepare a lot of things for the Sabbath." Then everybody tries to make me go . . .
LEAH: Not Leah. She'd say that you're right, that you ought to stand up to him.
STUDENT 7: See! I told you we shouldn't get rid of Rachel and Leah when the Rabbi comes in.
TEACHER: What do the rest of you think of this idea?
STUDENT 1: I like it. It also gives us a chance to see how much the Sabbath really means to Joseph if he takes a chance to get mean Ali angry.
TEACHER: Your analysis certainly shows that you're wide awake. I am sure that the next time we play this scene, it will come out even better than it was this time. Now, let us consider Scene 2. If you remember . . .

■ REPEAT WITH OTHER SCENES

The same process is now repeated with each of the scenes that follow—the class determines the characters needed; the cast is selected; the scene is discussed; the scene is enacted; the enactment is evaluated.

It is advisable to select a different cast for each scene. In that way as many pupils as possible are given an opportunity to participate in roles.

■ ENACT THE ENTIRE STORY

Ultimately the time comes to enact the entire story with a single cast, without interruption, as if it were a performance before an audience. This may come immediately after each scene has been played and discussed once. Sometimes the teacher may have the students play over certain scenes a number of times before the final enactment, either because gross errors need correction, the scene offers unusual learning opportunities, or other valid reason.

The story has grown by now beyond the restricted scope of the tale and has assumed living dimensions. The plot, the action, the characterizations and the playing itself have developed as a result of teacher stimulation, student research, discussion, improvisation, and critical analysis. The process has been both a creative, artistic experience for teacher and students as well as an intensive educational experience, involving student participation in a reality experience that is vital and meaningful to them. The final enactment too is part of this growth process. It is more than a culmination of an activity. It now provides the players with an opportunity for intellectual and emotional identification with the story, its characters, and its values. Though to a lesser degree, the viewers too participate in this emotional involvement, while at the same time they have another occasion for fixing in their minds the story, its facts and its values.

The following is a version on a twelve year old level of a final enactment of our story:

JOSEPH-WHO-HONORS-THE-SABBATH

THE DRAMATIZATION

SCENE 1

SCENE *(In the house of Joseph. A table and two chairs.)*

DEBORAH: *(Joseph's wife is straightening out things on the table. She sings "Shabbat Shalom" while she works.)*

RACHEL: *(An old woman, Deborah's neighbor, sticks her head in from the outside, through the window.)* You're home, Deborah?

DEBORAH: I'm home.

RACHEL: May I come in for a while?

DEBORAH: Sure, Rachel. Come in.

RACHEL: *(Enters with her granddaughter Leah)* This is my granddaughter Leah. You know her, don't you?

DEBORAH: I know her. Good afternoon, Leah.

LEAH: Good afternoon.

RACHEL: Look at the big fish I just bought in the Bazaar for *Shabbat!*

DEBORAH: It is big! Why, your fish is almost as big as the one my husband brought home last evening.

RACHEL: Oh no . . . Your Joseph always gets the biggest for his Sabbath table. The fishermen save the big ones for him. Not like us poor people . . .

DEBORAH: We're not rich, Rachel.

RACHEL: That's just what I said! Your Joseph works hard for Ali ibn Ibrahim from dawn to nightfall and all he gets is three coppers a day. And what does he do with it?

DEBORAH: He does what he thinks is right.

RACHEL: Sure. All week he starves. You too. He spends only one copper a day for food. Two coppers he saves every day. For what?

DEBORAH: For the Sabbath.

RACHEL: Exactly! I ask you, is this right?

DEBORAH: He honors the Sabbath.

LEAH: Everybody in Baghdad knows this. That's why we call him Joseph-Who-Honors-the-Sabbath.

RACHEL: So they call him that! So what! Meanwhile both of you nearly starve all week. I think it's terrible!

LEAH: I think it's wonderful!

RACHEL: Nobody is asking you, granddaughter. Children should be seen, not heard.

DEBORAH: The Sabbath is a holy day. We love to honor it by eating the best foods at a beautiful table. It's our greatest pleasure.

LEAH: Look! Here comes the Rabbi.

RACHEL: He's coming here, to see you.

RABBI: *(Enters)* Good afternoon.

WOMEN: Good afternoon, Rabbi.

RABBI: I have come to see your husband, Joseph. Is he home?

DEBORAH: No, Rabbi. He went to the Bazaar. Last night he couldn't find a chicken that he thought was good enough for our Sabbath table. He's looking for one now.

RABBI: I should have known that's where he would be. Nothing is good enough for him when it comes to honoring the Sabbath.

LEAH: That's why we call him Joseph-Who-Honors-the-Sabbath.

RACHEL: Leah! You said that once before.

RABBI: I have heard something that disturbs me . . .

JOSEPH: *(Comes in, excited. He pantomimes carrying a large chicken.)* Look, Deborah! Look at this fine chicken I was able to buy for the Sabbath.

DEBORAH: Joseph, the Rabbi is here.

JOSEPH: Excuse me, Rabbi. I'm so excited I didn't notice you. This is a great honor. Sit down, Rabbi, please . . .

RABBI: *(Sits down)* This is a fine chicken.

JOSEPH: The best they had!

RABBI: It must have cost a great deal.

JOSEPH: Nothing is too good for honoring the Sabbath.

RABBI: But all week you starve.

JOSEPH: Not exactly, Rabbi. We eat little so that we can save the money to buy things for the Sabbath.

RABBI: That's wrong, Joseph. You must take care of your health. The Bible says, "*Ush'martem et nafshotekhem*—ye shall guard your lives." It is a sin not to take care of your health.

JOSEPH: My health is all right, Rabbi. Honoring the holy Sabbath is my greatest pleasure. It's the holiest day of the week. The Creator Himself rested on it and made it holy.

RABBI: Of course, of course. But to go hungry all week . . .

JOSEPH: All week—who am I all week? Just a laborer for the Arab Ali ibn Ibrahim. But on the Sabbath—on the Sabbath I rest, I am joyous, I sing songs for the Sabbath Queen and honor her with fine food on my table, as fits a queen.

RABBI: Well . . . maybe you're right . . . maybe you know better. . . .

KASIM: *(Comes in puffing)* Joseph! Hurry up! Hurry up!

JOSEPH: What's the matter, Kasim?

KASIM: The master wants to see you! He wants to see you!

JOSEPH: What for?

KASIM: He needs you. Hurry up! Hurry up!

JOSEPH: I can't go, Kasim. This is Friday afternoon. I never work Friday afternoon. I have to get ready for the Sabbath.

KASIM: He wants you to grade the wheat and get it in bags. Right away! Right away!

JOSEPH: Why? We weren't going to do that until Sunday.

KASIM: He wants to bring it to the Bazaar to sell tomorrow. Come on! Come on!

JOSEPH: It will take hours to grade and bag the wheat. It will be way after dark by the time we finish. I can't go.

KASIM: You have to. The master wants you. He wants you.

JOSEPH: I can't go. Tonight the Sabbath begins. I won't work tonight.

KASIM: He'll be angry. You'll lose your job.

JOSEPH: Even if I lose my job, I can't go.

RACHEL: But you'll starve without a job.

JOSEPH: God will help me.

RABBI: Maybe you ought to work until dark and then . . .

JOSEPH: No, Rabbi. You don't know my master. Once I get there he'll make me work until I finish. And anyhow, I still have to do a lot to get ready for the Sabbath.

RABBI: Still, maybe you should try and see . . .

JOSEPH: Deborah, what do you say?

DEBORAH: You know best, my husband.

JOSEPH: Kasim, go and tell your master that I will work twice as hard on Sunday. But I cannot come now. I must get ready for the Sabbath.

KASIM: You'll be sorry! You'll be sorry, you will!

SCENE 2

SCENE *(In Ali's house. Ali is sitting down. Joseph is standing.)*

ALI: Well, Joseph, did you finish bagging the wheat?

JOSEPH: Yes, master.

ALI: Everything?

JOSEPH: Yes, master.

ALI: Are you hungry, Joseph?

JOSEPH: Yes, master. I worked since before sunrise without stopping to eat.

ALI: Good, good. It is two hours after sunset now. You haven't eaten then in fourteen hours.

JOSEPH: Well, I wanted to finish the work. You see, since I couldn't come on Friday like you asked me . . .

ALI: Yes. Yes. So you are good and hungry.

JOSEPH: Yes, master.

ALI: How much do I pay you, Joseph?

JOSEPH: Three coppers a day.

ALI: And I hear that you save two coppers every day.

JOSEPH: For the Sabbath, master.

ALI: You do a lot for the Sabbath, don't you?

JOSEPH: Yes, master. The Sabbath is holy. We Jews love the Sabbath. She is like a bride to us. We try to make everything in our house beautiful for the Sabbath Bride.

ALI: Even if it means disobeying me?
JOSEPH: I couldn't help it, master. I would have had to work on the Sabbath had I come when you sent for me.
ALI: So you didn't come.
JOSEPH: No, master.
ALI: You deliberately disobeyed me.
JOSEPH: I couldn't . . . really . . .
ALI: How much do you spend for food every day?
JOSEPH: One copper.
ALI: Good. From now on your wages will be one copper a day.
JOSEPH: One copper? How will we live?
ALI: You just told me you only spend a copper a day for food.
JOSEPH: But the rest I save to honor the Sabbath!
ALI: To honor the Sabbath, so you can disobey me, your master, so you can insult me, Ali ibn Ibrahim, the richest merchant, the biggest landowner in Baghdad. One copper a day, that's all you get. Now get out.
JOSEPH: But master . . .
ALI: I said, get out!
JOSEPH: Yes, master. *(He leaves)*
ALI: *(Shouts)* Fatima! Bring the food!
FATIMA: *(Enters, pantomiming carrying a tray of food)* Here it is, my husband.
ALI: Good. Good. Put it down here.
FATIMA: Yes, my husband. *(She pantomimes putting down the tray near Ali. He pantomimes eating as he talks. She remains standing.)*
ALI: That will teach him!
FATIMA: Who? Joseph?
ALI: Yes, Joseph-Who-Honors-the-Sabbath. Now he will know whom to honor, the Sabbath or me, his master.
FATIMA: What did you do?
ALI: I reduced his wages. Now he'll get only one copper a day instead of three. That will teach him.
FATIMA: Good for you. He was being paid too much anyhow.
ALI: You're a clever wife, Fatima. The less I pay out, the more I will have for myself. Here. I've eaten enough. Now you can eat.
FATIMA: Thank you, my husband and master.
ALI: That will teach him!

SCENE 3

SCENE *(In Joseph's house. Joseph and Deborah are talking.)*

DEBORAH: But how will we manage?
JOSEPH: We will have to. We will eat less all week.
DEBORAH: But even for a copper a day we nearly starved.
JOSEPH: We'll manage, Deborah. We will spend half a copper a day for food and save half a copper. That way we will have three coppers for food for Sabbath.
DEBORAH: Couldn't you get another job?

JOSEPH: Maybe. But I would have to leave my job with Ali ibn Ibrahim to look for other work. I'm afraid to take the chance.

DEBORAH: Why did he have to ask you to come just on Friday before *Shabbat?*

JOSEPH: That's the way Ali is. If he wants something he doesn't care about anybody else. Maybe God wanted to test us to see if we really honor the Sabbath even when it is very hard.

DEBORAH: But one copper a day! How could Ali do this?

JOSEPH: We'll manage. God will help us.

DEBORAH: You know best, my husband. All right, we'll manage on half a copper a day.

SCENE 4

SCENE *(In Ali's house. Ali is lying down, asleep.)*

OLD MAN: *(Enters and calls)* Ali! Ali ibn Ibrahim!

ALI: *(Sits up)* who are you?

OLD MAN: Never mind who I am. Why are you robbing Joseph-Who-Honors-the-Sabbath of his wages?

ALI: He disobeyed me, his master.

OLD MAN: He was obeying his real Master, the Creator of the world who said, "Remember the Sabbath day to keep it holy!"

ALI: But I am his master!

OLD MAN: You were always robbing him. Even when you paid him three coppers a day you robbed him. He worked for you faithfully and made you rich with his work and you kept everything for yourself and let him starve. Now you will receive your punishment.

ALI: Please, I'll give him three coppers again if you say so.

OLD MAN: Too late. You will lose all your fortune. It will be given to one who deserves it more than you.

ALI: Please . . . I'll pay him ten coppers . . . a hundred. . . .

OLD MAN: Too late, Ali ibn Ibrahim. *(He leaves)*

ALI: *(Falls back as if asleep, tossing about as in a nightmare and shouting)* A thousand! Ten thousand! Ten thousand!

FATIMA: Ali! Ali! what's the matter? *(She shakes him)* Wake up, Ali! You're having a nightmare. Wake up!

ALI: *(Wakes up, dazed)* Where am I?

FATIMA: You were having a dream, Ali.

ALI: A terrible dream, Fatima. An old man came to me and said I would lose all my fortune, that it would go to somebody more deserving.

FATIMA: It's nothing. It's something you ate that gave you this nightmare.

ALI: No Fatima. It's that Jew, Joseph. It's on account of him that I'll lose my fortune.

FATIMA: You really think this dream is true?

ALI: Of course it's true. What am I to do?

FATIMA: I have an idea. Sell all your houses, your farms, your merchandise, everything.

ALI: Yes. Sell everything. Then what?

FATIMA: Then, with the money, buy one big jewel.

ALI: What good will that do?

FATIMA: You will sew the jewel inside your turban. You will never take the turban off your head. Then the jewel will always be with you. Nobody can take it then.

ALI: Clever! Clever! That's just what I will do! I will sell everything. I will buy a jewel. I will sew it inside my turban. It will always be with me. I am really clever to have thought of this.

FATIMA: You thought of this. . . ? But it was I who . . .

ALI: *(Sternly)* Fatima!

FATIMA: Yes, my husband. Yes, my master. You thought of it. You're very clever, very clever.

ALI: That's better. We will see who is smarter, Ali ibn Ibrahim or the Old-Man-of-the-Dream.

SCENE 5

SCENE *(On the bridge. Ali and Fatima are walking.)*

FATIMA: It's awfully windy.

ALI: That's because we're on this bridge across the river. It's always windy here.

FATIMA: It's a beautiful jewel.

ALI: And I have it right here in my turban.

FATIMA: Be careful you don't lose it.

ALI: I won't. It's worth a fortune. All my possessions are in this jewel. Nobody will take it from me.

FATIMA: The wind is getting stronger. Ali! Look out!

ALI: My turban! The wind blew off my turban!

FATIMA: The jewel! Run Ali! The wind is blowing your turban toward the edge. It will fall into the river!

ALI: *(Running, trying to catch the turban)* My turban! My jewel! All my wealth!

FATIMA: It fell into the river! Don't, Ali! Don't jump! . . .

ALI: My jewel! My wealth! I'll get it! I'll get it!

FATIMA: Ali! Help! My husband is in the river. He's drowning. Help!

JOSEPH: *(Runs in)* Fatima! What's the matter?

FATIMA: Look there . . . in the river. . . . It's Ali. He jumped in after his turban. He's drowning.

JOSEPH: Don't worry. We'll get him out. Here . . . to the river bank . . . it's shallow here . . . I'll hold out a branch to him . . . come on. *(Both run off)*

SCENE 6

SCENE *(In Joseph's house. Joseph and Deborah are talking.)*

DEBORAH: And so you saved his life.

JOSEPH: The branch wasn't long enough so I had to go into the river after him.

DEBORAH: That's more than Ali deserved.

JOSEPH: Deborah! What are you saying? "He who saves one life, it is as if he saved the whole world." I couldn't let him drown.

DEBORAH: Of course not—even if he was mean to you.

JOSEPH: He's been punished. He lost everything he had.

DEBORAH: What will he do now?

JOSEPH: Look for work, I guess. He took his wife and left the city of Baghdad. He said he will not live as a common laborer in the city where everyone knew him as a rich man.

DEBORAH: Where did he go to?

JOSEPH: No one knows. He just disappeared with Fatima.

DEBORAH: For you it's a good thing you had to look for another job. Now you are getting three times as much as Ali ever paid you.

JOSEPH: Which reminds me, we have no fish for *Shabbat,* and here it is Friday again. I will go to the Bazaar.

DEBORAH: Maybe you don't have to. There's a man coming here and he is carrying a very big fish.

FISHERMAN: *(Enters)* Will you buy this fish, Joseph?

JOSEPH: It is very big. The biggest fish I have ever seen.

FISHERMAN: That's why I came to you. I caught him this morning in the river. I brought him to the Bazaar. I asked fifty coppers for him. Nobody wanted to spend that much.

JOSEPH: So you came to me?

FISHERMAN: Sure. I figured Joseph-Who-Honors-the-Sabbath will buy him if nobody else will.

JOSEPH: I would like to buy him for my Sabbath table. With a big fish like this I could invite all our neighbors to share our Sabbath food. But I don't have fifty coppers.

FISHERMAN: How much have you got?

JOSEPH: Nine.

FISHERMAN: I'll take that and trust you for the rest.

JOSEPH: It may take a few weeks.

FISHERMAN: I'm not worried. I'll trust you.

JOSEPH: Thank you.

FISHERMAN: Have a joyous Sabbath. *(He leaves)*

JOSEPH: With a fish like this, we will have a joyous Sabbath. All our neighbors will come to eat with us. We will sing Sabbath songs and be very joyful. Come Deborah. I will help you clean the fish.

DEBORAH: Good. You start on this side. I will work the other side. *(They pantomime scrubbing the scales.)*

JOSEPH: He's the biggest!

DEBORAH: We will be able to serve at least thirty people.

JOSEPH: This will be some Sabbath!

DEBORAH: The finest we ever had!

JOSEPH: The finest! *(He begins to sing a Sabbath song as they work. Deborah joins him.)* Now we will open him up and clean the insides. *(He pantomimes doing so, as they sing.)*

DEBORAH: Joseph, look!

JOSEPH: A jewel . . . inside the belly of the fish . . . *(He takes it out)* Look at it Deborah!

DEBORAH: It's the biggest jewel I ever saw.

JOSEPH: Look how it glitters! It must be worth a fortune.

DEBORAH: Joseph . . . Do you think maybe . . .

JOSEPH: Yes, Deborah . . . I think it is . . .

DEBORAH: Ali's jewel.
JOSEPH: Now what shall we do?
DEBORAH: I don't know.
JOSEPH: I must give it back to Ali. But how can I? He's disappeared. No one knows where he may be.
DEBORAH: Joseph, the Rabbi is coming this way. Let us ask him.
JOSEPH: We will ask the Rabbi. He will know what we should do.
RABBI: *(Enters)* Good afternoon Joseph . . . Deborah . . . It looks as if I always come to you on Friday afternoon.
JOSEPH: I am so glad you came, Rabbi. I have an important question to ask you.
RABBI: *(Smiling)* What to do with the jewel you found?
JOSEPH: You know, Rabbi?
RABBI: I know.
DEBORAH: But how, Rabbi? We just this minute found the jewel as we opened . . .
RABBI: . . . the belly of the fish.
JOSEPH: Yes.
DEBORAH: Yes. . . .
RABBI: I had a dream last night. An old man came to me and said, "Tomorrow, after midday, go to Joseph-Who-Honors-the-Sabbath. He will find a great jewel inside the belly of a fish. Tell him to keep this jewel. It belongs to him. He deserves it." I see now my dream did not fool me.
JOSEPH: But the jewel is Ali's. We can't keep it.
RABBI: The old man gave it to you. It is now yours.
DEBORAH: The Rabbi is right. You worked for Ali many years. He never paid you what you were worth. Now you are being paid all at once.
JOSEPH: This is too much. It is more than I deserve.
RABBI: It is to repay you for honoring the Sabbath.
JOSEPH: Oh no, Rabbi. Every time I honored the Sabbath I received my reward right then and there.
RABBI: How so, Joseph?
JOSEPH: In the joy I had, in the joy of the Sabbath.
RABBI: Even so, the jewel is now yours.
DEBORAH: Anyway, Ali has disappeared. You can never find him.
RABBI: It is the will of Heaven that you be rich.
JOSEPH: Rich? I need no riches. This is what I will do. I will go on working as before. But now, I will use all the money I earn to feed me and Deborah all week.
RABBI: And the jewel?
JOSEPH: I will sell the jewel. I will use the money to help the poor and the needy of Baghdad.
RABBI: And nothing for yourself?
JOSEPH: Oh, yes. I will use some of the jewel money to buy beautiful things for my Sabbath table—fine linens, silver candlesticks, and every Friday the best fish, meats, *Hallot* and wine. And I will always have many guests at my *Shabbat* table to help me to honor the Sabbath Queen, the Sabbath Bride.
RABBI: Blessed are the people Israel if it has sons like you, Joseph-Who-Honors-the-Sabbath.

■ EVALUATE THE DRAMATIZATION AND GENERALIZE

In evaluating the final enactment, the emphasis now is almost completely on the content of the dramatization rather than on the manner it was played. Now it is no longer, "how did you like the way the Rabbi argued with Joseph?" but rather, "what do you think of the Rabbi's arguments? Do you agree with him? Why?" Students are permitted to speculate on better ways of solving the moral dilemmas raised by the dramatization and are encouraged to put themselves in place of the characters.

As the evaluation of the enactment proceeds, the teacher gradually leads the pupils away from the specifics of the play to the general principles involved. They are guided to generalize and apply the same principles to other possible life situations with which they may be familiar.

The teacher opens the discussion with a few words of praise and then proceeds directly to deal with the content of the play:

TEACHER: Wasn't this a really fine play? You see how much we improved since we first started? What did you think of the way Joseph acted in the end? Why do you think he refused to use the jewel for himself?

STUDENT 1: Because he knew that the jewel belonged to Ali.

TEACHER: Do you think there may have been another reason?

STUDENT 2: Maybe he liked to live on his own earnings.

TEACHER: That's very possible. Many people go right on working no matter how rich they are. Do you know any one like that?

STUDENT 3: President Kennedy.

STUDENT 4: New York's Governor Rockefeller.

TEACHER: Why do you think they do that? They could just do nothing and enjoy themselves all the time. Why do you think they want to go on working?

STUDENT 5: They like it.

STUDENT 6: They would get bored if they did nothing.

TEACHER: That's true. People can get awfully tired not working. What about the fact that Ali couldn't be found? Should that have made a difference? What happens nowadays in a case like this?

STUDENT 7: The property belongs to the finder.

TEACHER: That's true. But the finder usually has to make an effort to locate the owner. How does he do that?

STUDENT 1: He asks people in the neighborhood if they lost something.

STUDENT 2: He advertises in the newspapers.

STUDENT 3: He brings it in to the police.

TEACHER: But in the end, if the owner cannot be found, it belongs to the finder. Do you think Joseph may have refused to keep it because he expected Ali to show up one day?

STUDENT 1: It's possible.

TEACHER: But he did use the money for charity and for the Sabbath. Why do you think he did that?

STUDENT 3: Because charity and honoring the Sabbath are things that God wants people to do.

TEACHER: But I am sure you wouldn't say that this should be done with other people's money. Why do you think Joseph felt he was right in doing it?

STUDENT 4: Because the Rabbi told him to keep it.

STUDENT 5: Because the old man said to keep it.

STUDENT 6: Is it possible that the fact that Ali had been cheating him all the time had something to do with it?

STUDENT 7: Sure. It must have.

TEACHER: But we don't usually go over and take things by ourselves from people who cheat us. What do we do in such a case?

STUDENT 8: We take them to court. The judge decides.

TEACHER: Exactly! Did Joseph do this?

STUDENT 9: The Rabbi told him to . . .

TEACHER: That's right. The Rabbi in olden times was the court of the Jewish community. He was the judge who decided cases for the Jews. Even today, people often bring their disputes to the Rabbi if they don't want to go to trial in a general court. So the Rabbi's opinion no doubt played a great part in Joseph's decision that he had a right to use the money for charity and the Sabbath.

■ RELATE TO PUPILS' EXPERIENCES

The evaluation and generalizing continue as long as time permits or as long as pupil participation in the discussion warrants it.

Generally a story offers opportunities to relate its lessons to the pupils' own, personal experiences. The teacher does not belabor this. In many instances the dramatization does not provide clear-cut possibilities, and twisting it to this purpose will only spoil whatever the teacher may have gained up to now. However, wherever this is possible, even to a limited degree, there is much to be gained in pupil identification with the story and its values.

Our current story offers a number of possibilities for correlation with pupil experiences. The following is the most obvious.

TEACHER: Joseph must have had quite a joyous Sabbath after he found the jewel. How do you think he celebrated?

STUDENT 1: He invited many guests.

STUDENT 2: They had a great feast.

STUDENT 3: They said the Sabbath prayers.

STUDENT 4: They sang songs.

TEACHER: We do many of these things nowadays too. How do you celebrate the Sabbath in your homes?

STUDENT 5: Mother lights the candles on Friday night.

STUDENT 6: We eat *Halloth.*

STUDENT 7: We eat *Gefilte fish.*

STUDENT 8: We sing songs.

STUDENT 1: We make *Kiddush.*

The discussion continues along these lines for a minute or so. After a little while, the teacher guides the discussion so that it becomes a jumping off point for learning new material with which the story and its dramatization may be correlated.

■ CORRELATE WITH NEW STUDIES

Most stories have within them elements which can serve as motivation for new studies of subject matter. Furthermore, the teacher will generally choose such stories for telling and dramatization as will permit correlation with other curricular studies.

Our current story, for example, can quite easily be tied in with study of the concept of charity, of social justice, of the Sabbath, and the like. We will consider as our example the area of Sabbath:

TEACHER: Joseph kept on calling the Sabbath a holy day, saying that God made it so. Have any of you any idea where we can find that God made the Sabbath holy?

STUDENT 1: In the Bible.

TEACHER: That's right. Do any of you know just where in the Bible we may find this?

STUDENT 2: In the story of creation.

TEACHER: Very good. Let's turn to our Bibles and see just how the event is described. You will find it in the Book of Genesis on page . . .

The teacher then goes on in the usual way to teach the Bible lesson. The dramatization might be correlated with Prayer, as:

TEACHER: Every Sabbath we declare the holiness of the day in a number of prayers. Can any of you think of such a prayer?

STUDENT 1: *Kiddush.*

TEACHER: Excellent. That is what *Kiddush* actually means—declaring the holiness of the day. (Let us turn to it. Or . . .) We also have such prayers in the *Kabbalat Shabbat,* the Friday night service of welcome for the Sabbath. If you will turn to the *Amidah,* the Silent Prayer, for Friday night, you will see such a declaration in the prayer *Atah Kidashtah.* You will find it in your Prayer Books on page . . .

Similarly, the dramatization of the story may be correlated with such subject areas as Customs and Ceremonies, Sabbath Music, Jewish Community, and others.

■ IN SUMMARY

A great deal of the subject matter which we teach in our schools involves the use of story elements. Bible, Jewish History, Current Events are basically a succession of stories. Much of the material in all other areas of the curriculum is possible of conveyance through the story medium and is usually so taught. It becomes readily apparent how a technique such as Story Dramatization, which calls forth intensive involvement on the part of the students, intellectually and emotionally, can help us greatly to achieve our educational objectives in many areas of the curriculum.

In the sections which follow, a number of areas of the curriculum will be considered separately, and the dramatic techniques which are particularly suitable for teaching them will be developed in detail. Story Dramatization is at the heart of most of these dramatic forms, although it undergoes many variations and transmutations. Consequently, a familiarity with Story Dramatization and the process leading to it is basic to the use of dramatics for teaching.

Finally, it must be pointed out that many of the techniques which are developed in detail under a particular subject area, can readily be applied to other areas of the curriculum—sometimes exactly as given, often with minor modification. The teacher will be well advised to become familiar with all of them so that he may be in a position to use them interchangeably wherever and whenever they will be most helpful in attaining the educational objectives of the moment.

CHAPTER 4

Dramatizing History

■ History is more than the record of past events. It is the study of a continuing pattern of a developing saga, within which the generations of the past and their experiences are linked and united with the men and women of today and with their problems. To be properly appreciated therefore, history must be studied as a living organism. In a sense, the student of history must constantly re-create through his imagination the life that has passed. Historic characters must be clothed with flesh and blood, infused with the breath of life and endowed with virtues and vices, hopes and problems, so that instead of being amorphous figures in a text—strange, vague and one-dimensional—they become human beings whom the student can recognize, with whom he can identify and feel a sense of kinship. Historic events must be given a sense of purpose and significance as well as a feeling of immediacy and relevance to the day-to-day life and problems of the student and the civilization of which he is a part.

Recognizing these imperatives, the effective teacher utilizes a variety of techniques for vitalizing the study of history. One of the most valuable of these is creative dramatization. While involved in the preparation of a dramatization of a moment in history, the student acquires a knowledge and understanding of historical characters and events far beyond that which is possible through textbook study alone. While participating in a dramatization, the student gains an insight into characters and events by assuming for the moment the personality of the figures and reliving vicariously the experiences of the moments in history that are the subjects of the enactment.

In this section we will deal with various dramatic techniques for bringing the study of history to life and infusing it with an emotional quality. We will begin with the most simple and proceed, step by step, to the highly complex. The teacher will do well to follow the same procedure, utilizing the simplest techniques at first and proceeding to the more difficult ones as the students gain experience in creative dramatization.

Before proceeding with techniques, however, it will be helpful to be aware of some underlying considerations.

■ HISTORY IN THE CURRICULUM

Jewish history is part of the curriculum of practically every Jewish school. Almost without exception Jewish educators affirm that the study of the Jewish past is an essential aspect of Jewish education. Theoretically Jewish history ranks in importance with Jewish language study (Hebrew or Yiddish), Prayer *(Siddur)*, Bible *(Humash)*, or Jewish Practices (Customs and Observances). However, in connection with history, as with a number of other subjects of the Jewish school curriculum, there is a wide gap between theoretical acceptance and classroom implementation.

In many schools the key position of the study of Jewish history in the Jewish education of our children is recognized and understood. Adequate time is allocated for its study. Much thought and ingenuity go into making the subject vital, alive, exciting, and meaningful for students.

Quite a few schools however, although officially conceding the importance of Jewish history, often neglect it. In some classrooms it is completely ignored. In others it is relegated to the position of "busy work," being utilized as a time filler between intensive sessions of *Siddur* reading and Hebrew language drill.

Then there are other schools that do devote a proportionate amount of time to Jewish history. The manner of instruction however, is pedestrian and uninspired. Consequently, history study in those schools lacks vitality and interest for the students and its residual benefits are practically negligible.

The basic ills besetting the study of history in many of our schools are an indifferent attitude and indifferent results. The first springs from ignorance of the role which a knowledge and appreciation of history may play in a people's survival, cultural development, and growth. The second is the result of poor transmission lines between teacher, student, and subject matter. The fact is that understanding the function of history study and improving the methodology for teaching the subject are interrelated. The proper methodology flows naturally out of a clear conception of the role and purpose of Jewish history study. Dramatics as a teacher's tool can play a crucial part in relation to both:

1. To place the subject on its proper level of importance.
2. To imbue its study with life and vitality, purpose and relevancy.

Why Teach History?

The time has long passed when history teaching meant the forced feeding of our children with dates, tables of events, catalogues of great figures, and important battles. True, recitals of facts and incidents are part of history, and the great figures of the past have made history. However, it is now generally conceded that in teaching history our aim is not merely the transmission of these facts or the identification of these figures. We teach history in order to develop in our children a sense of identification with their past, to learn from the past how to live in the present, to gain knowledge and inspiration for building a bright future.

Bruce Catton in his article, "The Wind in the Wires" voices the sentiments of many thoughtful educators relative to the function of history study. "History is the past speaking to the present. It tells about the future too, in a strange but effective way, for the inevitable changes that lie ahead always grow out of the things that men have been doing and saying and thinking in the years before. If we do not understand the past, we cannot understand the future either; we may hear strange sounds in the air, but the language will be unfamiliar and we will look in vain for an interpreter."

The past teaches us a great deal that is applicable to our daily lives. This in essence is the true purpose of the study of history! The fratricidal struggles in Jerusalem which contributed so much to the destruction of the Jewish state by the Romans serve as a warning to the political parties in the State of Israel today. The self-sacrifice of Eliezer the Hasmonean, the bravery of Shimon Bar Kokhba, the heroic death of Joseph Trumpledor, inspired those who fought for Israel's liberation in 1948. The unbelievable rise of Hitler which led to the holocaust of World War II and the martyrdom of six million Jews serve as a warning to us to take seriously even the most petty aspirants to the mantle of tyranny, to render them harmless before they gain in strength and do irreparable damage. This we realize: our forefathers did great and noble things—let us imitate them; they made mistakes—let us avoid them; they debased themselves—let us rise above them.

History Is Life

History means different things to different people. Cicero says that, "History is the witness of the ages, the light of truth, the life of memory, the messenger of antiquity." Oscar Wilde on the other hand felt that, "History is merely gossip." Whether we agree with the noble sentiments of Cicero or with the cynical aphorism of Wilde, the fact is that for both, *life* is at the core of history—and even "gossip" has much to teach us. Indeed, history is the record of *life* in times gone by. It is the record of deeds of people like ourselves, who once lived and walked this earth, who, like us, strived, hoped, dreamed and schemed. Like us, they suffered in adversity and rejoiced in good fortune, hungered in famine and splurged in prosperity. Like so many of us, they were small in great things and rose to great heights over small details. The Temple, legend has it, was destroyed "because of a rooster." Hannah's youngest son died rather than bow down to pick up the tyrant's ring.

Bring It to Life!

Many facets of life can be studied through dead records. To be properly understood, savored, and appreciated, life must be confronted in its living form. If, then, history is the record of *life*, we must somehow find the means of bringing it to life, of re-creating it so vividly that the student will actually live through—if only vicariously—the crucial moments of history. To understand the past the student must be helped to relive the past, and through emotional projection, to become an active participant in historical events. That is the meaning of the talmudic dictum, "In every generation each person must see himself as if he personally had participated in the exodus from Egypt."

Dramatics as the Means

There are those students who, merely by reading history, are able to project themselves into the past and to identify themselves with characters long dead. There are those inspiring teachers who, merely by the force of their personality, are able to breathe life into the pages of the textbook. In most classroom situations, however, history might well remain a dead record of a dead past unless some means is found to bring it to life, to re-create it, as it were. Dramatization is the method best able to do this, the most suitable medium for making the study of history into a vital, living experience, the best instrument to help us re-create the past in many of its nuances.

The students portraying historical characters in a dramatization are not only learning about them and what they did, but get to know them intimately, to understand them and the motivations which caused them to act the way they did. Furthermore, in assuming the role of a historical character, the student of today identifies emotionally with the character, developing a sense of kinship and closeness with his personality and his acts.

■ SPECIFIC BENEFITS OF DRAMATICS IN TEACHING HISTORY

The benefits listed above are basic in all uses of dramatizations in history teaching. In addition there are a number of specific educational benefits arising from the use of the technique. The following are some of them:

Minimizing Misconceptions

Teachers are well aware how easily misunderstanding may arise in the teaching process. We are often regaled with the so-called students' boners—the products of faulty learning resulting from a blocked transmission line between teacher and student. For example: teachers report that many students will give the Hebrew meaning of the word *hero* as *Sh'ma*—since they translate *Sh'ma Yisrael* as *Hero Israel* instead of *Hear O Israel*. Many translate the Hebrew word *b'vakashah—quiet!*—since many teachers, when the class becomes somewhat noisy will say *B'vakashah*—actually *please!* In the Pledge of Allegiance many children recite *for Richard's stand* in place of *for which it stands*. A little girl brought up on Hebrew as her first language for many years called parsley *yofi (beauty)* since when she asked "What's this?" on seeing parsley for the first time as it was being used to garnish a platter of food she was given the answer "*yofi*—beauty." The same little girl for a time called a motorcycle an *Eisenhower*. After the end of World War II she had been taken to see the victory parade featuring the return of General Eisenhower. As the motorcycle escort came into view with the Eisenhower car behind it, everyone began to shout "Eisenhower!"

In the same manner, learning history "by the book" alone may readily result in developing completely misleading images in the students' minds. What does a shepherd look like? Is he dressed as an Australian sheep herder or Western cowboy? How does he act? Is he hard drinking, quick to take an insult and get into a brawl like the stereotypes of the Westerns? How does this image measure up to the shepherd Moses whom the Almighty entrusted with the care of His flock, Israel? What images go through the mind of the student whose learning is confined to the textbook when he reads of the heroes of history? What misconceptions become fixed in his mind when his sole point of reference is the perforce frugal account in the text?

History is replete with instances of historical misconception. The oft-quoted, classic example is, of course, Michelangelo's heroic statue of Moses. The Lawgiver is depicted as sprouting horns from his forehead—a mistranslation of the biblical description "*Karan P'nei Moshe*, the face of Moses shone with bright rays." Instead of "*Karan*" (shone with bright rays), Michelangelo read the Vulgate translation of "*Keren*" (horn). Thus we have "the horns of Moses' forehead."

The many paintings of biblical scenes by medieval and Renaissance artists are another illustration of such misconceptions, resulting either from misunderstanding or ignorance. We see biblical characters portrayed as Dutch burghers functioning in water-logged Netherland countrysides; French nobles lolling about in Gothic towns; Italian princes and knights in Renaissance garb performing their tasks with castles and Tuscany hillsides as backgrounds. Beautiful as these paintings are, inspiring as these artistic creations may be, they are completely misleading from a historical point of view. Everything about them, the dress, the setting, the implements, is completely distorted. Many of them, it is true, were deliberately done in this fashion for a variety of reasons—in order to create a familiar relationship between the viewer and the subject, to feed the vanity of contemporary leading personalities or artists' patrons by including their portraits in biblical scenes, etc. In most instances, however, such misleading portrayals, such flagrant anachronisms and lack of authenticity were the results of ignorance of the period portrayed. This was to be expected since, in most instances, these artists relied primarily on texts for their knowledge of the biblical period without resorting to proper research. The effect of such disregard for authenticity of detail on the part of these artists was to convey a wholly erroneous conception of biblical times to the great masses for whom such pictures were often the sole source of biblical knowledge. Thus the evil was compounded—misconception breeding misconception.

The so-called Miracle Plays are another example of misconceptions arising from sole reliance on text without proper research. The dress, the decor, the manner of speech, the many details of life in the mis-en-scenes of such productions had little relation to the realities of the biblical scene.

Proper research helps us to avoid such misconceptions and in this regard, dramatization as a teaching tool is of great help. Since it requires careful research as a preparatory step in the process, the students who are at work developing a historical dramatization soon find that they must go beyond the confines of their textbook. Questions are constantly arising during the creative process:

> Would Rabbi Akiba pursue his studies in a printed book or a parchment scroll? Why?
>
> Would Jacob sit on a chair, a stool, or on the ground?
>
> Would Hagar speak to Sarah as to an equal, or would her speech be obsequious, servile? Would the situation change after she bore Ishmael? What was the relationship of mistress and hand-maid during that period?
>
> What kind of food would Joseph serve his brothers at the fateful banquet? How would it be served?
>
> What would be the nature of the "small talk" in which Abraham would engage while feeding his three visitors? Would they discuss the weather, the crops, the business situation? What is the nature of the weather in that part of the world? What crops did people raise in the Land of Canaan at that time? Would Abraham have raised crops at all? What were economic conditions at that period? etc.
>
> How would David Reubeni address the Pope? How did people generally greet the Pope and speak to him? Would Reubeni follow general usage? If not, why? Is it because it might be in violation of his religious principles? How would the Pope react to this departure from usage?

In finding the answers to such and similar questions, the students become involved in the quest for information regarding the proper dress, the correct household implements, the furnishings, the way of life of the characters which they are to portray. They discover that they must delve into the minute and seemingly unimportant facts of the story in order to create believable dialogue and an atmosphere of reality. In this, the encyclopedia, supplementary books, paintings, archeological finds, museum objects, all become the raw material for the students' recreation of the characters and the period that they seek to portray.

Understanding Social Climate

Students at work on a dramatization soon discover that treating the isolated incident in its bare form as given in their textbook is usually not satisfactory in a dramatization. They very quickly become aware that their historical characters did not exist in a vacuum. They had a function, not only in relation to the events of the historic incident described in the text, but also as part of a complete social cosmos. Again, the questions arising in the process of creating the dramatization bring about this result. For example:

> We are dramatizing the story of Joseph and the Coat of Many Colors. How shall we bring out the fact that his brothers were jealous of him and the reason for their jealousy. Shall we do it by means of a statement by one of the characters such as Jacob, a brother, Joseph himself? That might be dull. Perhaps we should open the scene on a conversation between two minor characters discussing the situation? That might be more interesting. Who are these characters to be? Slaves? Neighbors? Sisters? Did they have slaves? Did they live near enough to neighbors? Is it possible that sisters existed although they are not specifically mentioned in the Bible? Why might they not be mentioned? What was the attitude of the period to females? etc.
>
> Our dramatization deals with the Gaon of Vilna. We want to show the scene of the Gaon being offered the Rabbinate of Vilna and his refusal. Who would come to offer him the position? A merchant perhaps? What business would he be in that might affect his manner of speech? What businesses did Jews engage in at that time? Who else? Would it be a doctor? Did Jews practice medicine then? Would a working-man be in the delegation? What was the attitude of the community toward laborers? Were they held in high regard or were they looked down upon and therefore excluded from such important community functions? etc.

So, in seeking answers to such questions—questions that almost inevitably arise during the planning of a dramatization—the student soon discovers that, even though the story in the book centers about the leading figures of history, the acts of these figures were influenced by the social climate in which they lived and that their acts in turn exerted an influence on many people who were not unlike the student himself, his parents, teachers, neighbors, school friends, etc. They learn that the world of the historic heroes was filled with collateral characters such as merchants, farmers, teachers, beggars, etc.—characters which, although not mentioned in the history book, are nevertheless essential for an understanding of the forces motivating the actions of the major characters about whom the stories in the text revolve. And so, discovering what kind of collateral characters might be used under the social conditions of the period without doing violence to the facts and spirit of the story, the student creates them. He provides them with speech and actions which help round out the story, being careful at the same time to preserve its authenticity. Thus, the social climate in which the historical characters functioned is re-created in the dramatization. In re-creating this social climate, the history lesson acquires an inner life of its own far more meaningful and of much greater import than simply the skeletal story line of the book.

To demonstrate, let us contrast by actual examples the form in which a story might emerge as given in the textbook and as it develops through the use of dramatization. Note particularly the re-creation of social climate here referred to. In each instance, only fragments are given:

JOSEPH AND HIS BROTHERS

a. The Textbook

Jacob settled in the Vale of Hebron. He was now a well-to-do man. He owned great flocks of sheep and many tents. The sheep were cared for by ten of his sons. The other two, his children from his wife Rachel, he kept at home close to him. Benjamin was too young to be sent to the pastures. Joseph he loved too much to part from him. So, Joseph remained close to his father, the favorite of Jacob's twelve sons. When Joseph was seventeen years old he was considered the handsomest young man in the neighborhood. His father's greatest delight was to dress Joseph in beautiful clothes which showed off his handsome face and figure. The brothers did not like the special attention which their father paid to Joseph. One day Jacob bought for Joseph a very beautiful coat. It was striped and of many colors. When Joseph put it on he looked handsomer than ever. When his brothers returned from the field he ran out eagerly to show it to them. . . .

b. A Dramatization

Following is a sample dramatization of the same story. Note how this form provides many opportunities for development of social climate in a natural manner. Also, the characters come alive—their problems and their story being brought to the fore, not through the medium of narration but through meaningful action and dialogue that is natural to the environment. In the example which follows, the script is given in the left hand column. The right hand column, labeled "Analysis," is used to point out problems of research which had to be solved, instances of development of social climate, dialogue which tends to provide opportunities for conveying historical information, open up areas for future discussions, enrich the characterizations of the personalities, etc.

SCRIPT	ANALYSIS
SCENE *(Inside Jacob's tent. In a corner, a pile of cushions. Milkah, a young servant, is straightening up. Keturah, an old woman and chief of the household servants, enters.)*	The opening immediately characterizes the household as nomadic, tent dwelling. The sparse furnishings, the cushions for seating, are reminiscent of the Bedouin of today. Research was required to determine how the scene is to be set.

SCRIPT	ANALYSIS
KETURAH: Milkah! I've been looking for you.	The names of the characters are introduced at the earliest opportunity so that the audience will be able to identify them as individuals and not mere figures. "Jacob's tent" identifies the locale, particularly important in a classroom dramatization where no scenery is used.
MILKAH: Why, Keturah—I've been here in Master Jacob's tent all the time.	
KETURAH: Why does it take you so long? You've been at this since the noonday meal.	Role of Keturah as superior is established.
MILKAH: There is much to be done. Master Joseph never puts his things away.	By offering excuse, Milkah is established as the subservient. Joseph characteristic introduced as seen by others in household.
KETURAH: *(Angrily)* I won't have you talking disrespectfully about Master Joseph!	
MILKAH: *(Sullenly)* Well, it's true. Look at this cloak. Master Jacob bought it for him only a month ago. Now look at it—a rag.	In defending herself, a natural thing for her to do when under attack, Milkah further characterizes Joseph for us.
KETURAH: *(Sternly)* It's none of your affair, Milkah. Your task is to clean up and mind your own affairs. You're a servant, Milkah. Don't you forget that.	The position of Milkah is clearly established. Research was required to learn what type of characters might be utilized for the exposition. On discovering that servants were common at the time, they were chosen.
MILKAH: Yes. I'm a servant, but I'm not blind. Master Jacob never buys his other sons such fine things.	Such background information can often come out from dialogue of collateral characters discussing leading figures. Servants talking about their masters are very handy.
KETURAH: Well . . . Master Joseph is his favorite. Everybody knows that.	More about role of Joseph as father's favorite.
MILKAH: But why?	
KETURAH: Maybe it's because Master Joseph is the son of Rachel who was his favorite wife.	Milkah's natural curiosity and Keturah's reminiscing are for review of previously learned material: Jacob had more than one wife.
MILKAH: The servants always speak of Rachel. Did you know her in Padan Aram, Keturah?	Rachel was favorite. Rachel bore Joseph. Rachel came from Padan Aram. Rachel is dead.
KETURAH: I was a servant in her father Laban's house even before she was born. I served her until the day of her death. Beautiful, she was—and a fiery one . . . Why, once when her father, my master Laban, wanted to. . . .	Rachel's father was Laban. Rachel was very beautiful. Rachel was a woman of spirit. In reminiscing, Keturah also conveys to us her status as a servant—albeit an old and trusted one.

SCRIPT	ANALYSIS
MILKAH: How long is it since Rachel died?	The questioning of one curious servant of another offers further opportunity to develop the background for our story and at the same time provides the teacher an opportunity for review of the fact that Rachel is dead a long time. She died in childbirth. She had two sons, Joseph and Benjamin.
KETURAH: Oh—years and years. She died giving birth to her second son.	
MILKAH: Benjamin?	
KETURAH: Yes, Master Jacob's youngest. It was on the road near Bethlehem, when the Master came back to this Land of Canaan from Padan Aram. What a sad homecoming that was for Master Jacob!	She died on the road to Bethlehem. She died when Jacob came home. Also, we learn that the locale of our play is the Land of Canaan.
MILKAH: Poor Rachel—and poor infant Benjamin. How did the master manage to . . . ?	By now, enough background has been established and the play returns to its action —otherwise it might slow up to the point where interest will be lost. The device of the chief ordering the subordinate to go back to work is used to do this.
KETURAH: Questions! Questions! All the time questions and the work is still not finished. Enough of talk, Milkah. Finish your work!	
(Jacob enters. The servants bow.)	Form of greeting in use by servants to master requires research by students.
KETURAH: Welcome back, Master Jacob.	Her greeting identifies him for us at the very outset.
JACOB: Thank you, Keturah.	Courtesy to servants characterizes him immediately.
KETURAH: Did you have a good journey?	The fact that she questions him and he answers her about his acts, characterizes her privileged position.
JACOB: It wasn't easy. I bought a large flock of sheep in the market. The men had a lot of trouble driving them home. Where's Joseph?	More to establish the role of sheep as the basis of the household economy. In this society there is commerce, there are markets. Jacob is rich. His first thought is of his favorite Joseph.
KETURAH: Near the well in the courtyard.	Environment of home of the period—courtyard, well. Research!
JACOB: *(Sits on cushion)* I would like to see him.	Manner of sitting at period. Research!
KETURAH: Milkah—run and call Master Joseph. *(Milkah bows to Jacob and leaves)*	This is a device to get rid of Milkah who, having served her purpose in the exposition, is now no longer needed and might be in the way.
JACOB: Where are my other sons?	

SCRIPT	ANALYSIS
KETURAH: Benjamin is with his teacher. Your other ten sons have gone with the flocks to the field of Dothan.	This conversation is device to allow time for arrival of Joseph. It also serves to give us more review. Jacob had total of twelve sons. They tended sheep.
JOSEPH: *(Enters eagerly)* My father! Welcome home. *(He goes quickly and squats down near his father)*	
JACOB: *(Hugs him)* Joseph, my beloved son.	This clinches the relationship!
JOSEPH: Was the market very exciting?	This is a dramatization for teaching purposes. It is important to learn what a market was like at the time. However, we cannot have a character go into a descriptive speech. But what is more natural than a youth eagerly questioning his father about his trip? The father's reply provides us with the knowledge we seek to convey. The students had to do research to learn these facts about a market of the period.
JACOB: Very exciting.	
JOSEPH: What was it like?	
JACOB: There were large crowds—merchants shouting their wares, Ishmaelites selling spices, Canaanite chiefs bargaining for cloth and jewels and animals.	
JOSEPH: Were there jugglers?	These are the things that interest frivolous Joseph!
JACOB: Oh yes.	
JOSEPH: Were there fire eaters?	The father tolerates in Joseph his frivolity.
JACOB: *(Smiling tolerantly)* There were two of those.	
JOSEPH: And acrobats?	
JACOB: *(Laughs)* Many acrobats, to amuse the crowds.	
JOSEPH: *(Sulky)* Why didn't you take me with you?	
JACOB: *(Seriously)* I told you when I left. The journey to Hebron is a dangerous one. It isn't safe for you.	More to establish role of Joseph as favorite of father!
JOSEPH: But why? Am I not already grown?	Students readily identify with this complaint. It also offers opportunity to bring out Joseph's age.
JACOB: *(Smiling)* Of course. You are seventeen now.	
JOSEPH: Then why didn't you take me with you to the market?	

SCRIPT	ANALYSIS
JACOB: *(Earnestly)* Your mother Rachel died on a journey. I will not risk losing you. *(He rises, picks up a bundle he had brought in, takes a cloak from it. It is striped and colorful)* Look what I brought you.	This fact, planted in the servants' conversation, now plays an important role in motivating Jacob's acts. Research is required to determine what this important prop should be like.
JOSEPH: *(Excitedly)* What a beautiful cloak! Look at its stripes! Look at the many colors!	The climax to which we have been moving all along.
JACOB: Put it on.	
JOSEPH: *(Puts on cloak)* Does it fit me?	Vanity (?)
JACOB: It fits you very well.	
JOSEPH: *(Eagerly)* I must run and show it to my brothers. They should be coming back from the pasture now.	His is the innocent thoughtlessness of youth—sure that all would share his joy—that gets him into trouble.
JACOB: Joseph, maybe you had better not.	Jacob has a feeling that this may lead to trouble but does not forbid anything outright to his favorite.
JOSEPH: But why not? It's so lovely, I must show it to them. *(He runs off.)*	
KETURAH: I am worried, Master.	A foreboding!
JACOB: Why, Keturah?	
KETURAH: His brothers . . . they are jealous of Master Joseph.	Now it's out in the open (!)
JACOB: Nonsense! I treat all my sons alike. If I bring Joseph something special—you must admit he is handsome . . .	The blindness of the father who refuses to see the evil he is helping to create.

THE ROLE OF RABBI AKIBA IN THE BAR KOKHBA REVOLT

a. The Textbook

The yoke of Rome was heavy on the necks of the Judeans. Every day new Roman laws were proclaimed, each more oppressive than the previous. All over the land there was bitterness against the Romans. In secret meetings, in woods and in caves, urgings became more and more insistent to revolt against the Roman oppressors. Everyone waited only for word from the venerable sage, Rabbi Akiba. One word from him and the revolt would flare up. But Rabbi Akiba held back. He counselled patience. But the people's patience was nearly exhausted. Finally a new set of laws was announced by the Roman government: Henceforth, the study of the Torah, the observance of the Sabbath, and the rite of circumcision were to be forbidden. These laws threatened the very existence of the Jewish people. Now, even Rabbi Akiba's patience was at an end. Rabbi Akiba gave his blessing to the Bar Kokhba revolution against Rome.

b. A Dramatization

SCRIPT	ANALYSIS
SCENE *(Rabbi Akiba is seated on a low stool, studying from a scroll. Father enters and remains standing at the entrance.)*	Research is required to determine the manner of life of the period. Would the rabbi sit on a stool or chair? Would he read from a book or scroll?
FATHER: Rabbi Akiba, forgive me for disturbing you.	The attitude of the father indicates the high regard in which the sage is held.
AKIBA: What is it, my son?	The opening line characterizes the sage as fatherly, kindly.
FATHER: I have come to . . . *(He notices what Rabbi Akiba is doing. Surprised, he walks closer)* Rabbi! You are studying!	The shock of the father at seeing the sage studying hints that this is an extraordinary act. Why? Isn't it natural for a sage to study?
AKIBA: Of course.	
FATHER: The Torah?	
AKIBA: Naturally.	This indicates that Torah study was usual and to be expected.
FATHER: But, aren't you afraid?	The political situation is now about to be introduced.
AKIBA: Of whom?	
FATHER: The Romans. You know their law.	We learn that the country is under the rule of Rome.
AKIBA: It forbids the study of the Torah . . . ?	In a natural conversation, the details of the Roman oppressive measures are conveyed. Use of this device is preferred to convey necessary information which would otherwise only be conveyed thru narrative—a dull way. The repetition hints at the matter that is on his mind.
FATHER: *(Breaking in)* . . . and the observance of the Sabbath and the circumcising of our children—the circumcising of our children, Rabbi!	
AKIBA: *(Sadly)* I know.	
FATHER: And yet? You study the Torah?	
AKIBA: I will tell you a little story, my son. Once a fox passed the river bank and saw fish rush about in the water, frightened. "Of whom are you afraid?" the fox asked the fish. "Of the fishermen," they answered.	The famous parable is introduced in a natural manner, as part of the action of the play. The moral of the parable is conveyed to the audience without preachment. The audience is here given an opportunity to meet the sage in "action"—as a wise

SCRIPT	**ANALYSIS**
"Well now," said the fox, "Why not leave the water and come ashore to me?" The fish laughed and said, "We thought that you, fox, are the wisest of animals and yet you speak so foolishly. The water is the source of our life. Surely if we leave it we will have much more to fear than now." *(To father)* Do you understand me, son?	man, teacher, and leader of his people. The social climate of the time is brought to the fore, when the people looked to their sages and scholars for leadership, both spiritual and political.
FATHER: Yes, Rabbi.	
AKIBA: *(As if to himself)* The Torah is our life. If we leave it, we have much more to fear than the might of the Romans. *(To father)* But tell me, why have you come?	Back to the action! To dwell longer on exposition would destroy the interest.
FATHER: My wife gave birth to a son.	
AKIBA: I see . . .	A foreshadowing of the crucial problem.
FATHER: Eight days ago.	
AKIBA: *(With stress)* And today is the circumcision. . . .	Again, in a natural manner, as part of the action of the play an important fact of Jewish life is introduced. Research was needed here.
FATHER: I hope so.	
AKIBA: Then go and circumcise your son.	
FATHER: The Romans forbid it.	
AKIBA: *(Forcefully)* The Torah commands it!	Now we meet the other facet of the sage—force of personality—zealous for the basic principles of his faith.
FATHER: I am afraid, Rabbi.	
AKIBA: I know. Come. I will go with you.	Attributes of the leader: sympathy, understanding, does not ask of his followers to take risks he would shirk.
FATHER: The Romans have posted guards outside my house to prevent it.	
AKIBA: The child must be circumcised! We will drive away the guards.	No compromise with basic principle involved.
FATHER: They are armed.	The underlying causes which brought Akiba to the side of the Jewish rebels have been brought out, not by an expository statement but by a personalized problem which has the potential of involving the students in its development and solution.
AKIBA: We too can be armed. Come!	

Understanding Motivation

In the process of preparing a creative dramatization, the students of necessity gain an understanding of the motivations which determine the deeds of the historical characters. Nothing is done without a reason. The study of history becomes to a large extent a study of cause and effect. The students gain a deeper insight into the emotional currents running through history's manifestations.

Understanding motivation comes about as a result of learning many things, some of which we have already discussed in detail. By learning the social climate within which the characters functioned, the students become aware of the social pressures to which these characters were subjected. By knowing the economic conditions the students realize the temptations to which characters succumbed or which they have overcome. By knowing the spiritual currents of a given period the student arrives at a better understanding of the historical characters' reactions to ethical problems with which they were confronted. By investigating in the course of research the political conditions of a given time the student becomes aware of the forces contributing to the emergence of national heroes and conversely of national blackguards.

Naturally, the age and maturity of the students will determine the extent and complexity of this type of investigation. But even for the youngest groups, creative dramatization offers an opportunity for an awareness of motivation—an awareness which the teacher nurtures and fosters. For, while investigating and laying stress on ethical problems and their historic solutions, the student is helped to learn to be aware of such problems in his own life. He is guided to seek and to find socially acceptable and ethically right solutions.

The student's horizons are substantially widened when he learns to understand how much such factors motivate the actions of people. Conversely, the acts of heroism, of self-sacrifice, or of high moral principle on the part of historic characters become even more meaningful when viewed in the light of the pressures—social and cultural—which they had to resist and overcome. For example: knowing the environment in which historical characters functioned not only helps to clarify the "whys and wherefores" of the character's actions, but often helps us to understand their true measure of greatness.

Sir Leonard Wooley in his book, *Digging Up the Past,* makes this point clear. He describes how archeologists were able to work out the original appearance of a private home in Ur of the Chaldees in the time of Abraham. Recreating the physical environment he says, "supplies a new and unexpected background to a familiar figure, and challenges us to recast our judgment of him. . . . We had been accustomed to think of Abraham as a simple dweller in tents, and find him a possible occupant of a sophisticated brick house in a city . . ." How much more meaningful the lesson of *Lekh Lekha* now becomes! Because of our readings in legend and Midrash we had built up a mental image of Abraham as a villager in a primitive society. Even his very king, Nimrod, emerges as a primitive hunter, a man of the fields. It is comparatively easy for a person brought up under such conditions to abandon his early life at the command of the Almighty and become a nomad. Research—purposeful research which the students undertake, with little or no urging, in order to fill them in on the background of the character they are to portray—brings forth an altogether different image of Abraham, a nobler, more heroic, more self-denying figure. Abraham emerges as a man reared in an advanced civilization, in a city of great palaces, beautiful temples, luxurious homes—a product of comfort and luxury. All this he abandons without murmuring in obedience to the command of the Almighty, "Go forth out of your country, your homeland, and your father's house unto a land that I will show you." The research which the students undertake as a prerequisite for the creation of a dramatization has brought this image of Abraham to the fore.

Research into background to help understand motivation is not confined solely to scientific sources. Legendary sources, midrashic tales, often add new dimensions to our understanding of historical characters. The very tale of Abraham will serve to illustrate this. The biblical account of Abraham is very sparse when dealing with his early life. It sets forth his place of origin, his ancestry, and almost immediately proceeds to the ringing command: "Go forth . . . !" How did Abraham come to the recognition of monotheism? How did this lone believer in one God adjust to his polytheistic environment? How did his relatives and neighbors react to this religious rebel? What position, if any, did the civic authorities of a country, which like many states of the period was theocratic in nature, take to this individual who denied the existing order? The Bible is silent on these provocative questions. Legend—folk memory colored by folk creativity—comes forth with the answers. It projects a noble image of man who questions, who seeks after truth, who arrives at a truth that satisfies his searching spirit and who risks his very life in its defense. No, the teacher will definitely not neglect to send the students to legendary sources during their research. Moreover, when legend is not in contradiction to known facts, the teacher encourages that it be woven in as part of the fabric of the dramatization.

Finally the search into the factors which contribute to the understanding of motivation and the inclusion of these factors as part of the dramatization results in an enriched creation—interesting and vital. The material is exploited in collateral conflict situations which add to the students' knowledge and contribute emotional qualities which hold the students' attention, capture their imagination and involve them deeply in the unfolding tale.

The following examples will illustrate these observations:

RABBI ISRAEL BAAL SHEM TOV

a. The Textbook

From his earliest childhood, the young Israel who was later to be known by the name of Rabbi Israel Baal Shem Tov, was always thinking of God and the way to worship Him. He would wander through the fields and the woods of his native Carpathian mountains, watch with awe the growing trees, listen to the singing of the birds, look at the rushing brook—and in all these he saw the spirit of the Creator. His heart filled with love for his God. His greatest hope was that some day he might teach others to know God in the same way and to love Him. At times, his heart was so full that he burst forth in song and began to dance in ecstasy, worshipping his Creator.

He earned his bread by helping the teacher of the town where he lived to take care of the children. He had no home of his own, having been orphaned of both his parents in early childhood. The elders of the town permitted him to sleep in the synagogue. While there, he watched with pain the low state of the handworkers, the cobblers, the tailors, the water carriers, who were not learned in the Law. Every one treated them with contempt. Because they were not learned in the Torah, they were often kept at a distance from taking part in the worship and ceremonials of the Jewish religion. The boy Israel could not understand this. Every Jew, he felt, can worship God, whether he is learned or ignorant, as long as his worship comes from his heart. What he saw, influenced his thinking and later found expression in his teaching . . .

b. A Dramatization (A fragment)

SCENE *(A synagogue, Simhat Torah night, during Hakafot. At a table the Gabbai is calling the names of the people who are to come up, take a Torah scroll and walk with it in the procession in honor of the Law. Yankel the miller and Moishe the cobbler stand at the rear of the synagogue. Near them is a 12 year old boy, Israel—later to be konwn as Rabbi Israel Baal Shem Tov.)*

GABBAI: *(Calling with a chanting tone)* Reb Yitzhok b'reb Dovid, arise and honor the Torah! Reb Sholem b'reb Aaron, arise and honor the Torah!
(As each is called, he goes to the front and takes a Torah scroll.)

YANKEL: Look Moishe, they're almost finished with *hakofes.*

MOISHE: Do you think they'll call us?

YANKEL: They didn't last year. They didn't the year before.

MOISHE: *(With longing)* Once in my life—just once in my life I'd like to be up there in the procession, carry a Torah scroll like the rest and sing "*Oyzer Dalim, Hoysheeo No,*" with the others—like a somebody . . .

YANKEL: Maybe Zoreh the Gabbai just forgot. *(Determined)* I'm going up there to ask him. *(He walks over to the Gabbai)* Reb Zoreh . . . please. . . .

GABBAI: *(Annoyed)* What do you want, Yankel the Miller?

YANKEL: *(Confused, stammering)* A *Hakofe* . . . please. . . .

GABBAI: I see. You, Yankel the Miller want to carry a Torah.

YANKEL: *(Pleading)* Please, Reb Zoreh . . . it's Simhas Torah . . . I also want to honor the Torah . . . like every Jew . . . to carry it in procession. . . .

GABBAI: *(Sarcastic)* So . . . It's Simhas Torah and you want to honor the Torah?

YANKEL: *(Confused)* Well . . . I thought . . . I meant. . . .

GABBAI: *(Mimicking him)* I thought . . . I meant . . . Tell me, Yankel the Miller, do you study the Torah? Do you know what's written in the Torah?

YANKEL: I'm only a poor miller. I never learned.

GABBAI: And why not? Every Jew should study the Torah. Don't you know that?

YANKEL: We were always poor. When I was eight years old I went to work in the mill. I worked hard every day until late at night. I would get up before dawn. I'd go to sleep near midnight . . . all my life . . . always in the mill . . . trying to earn enough to feed my family. When could I learn? Always in the mill . . .

GABBAI: *(Sternly)* Then stick to the mill, Yankel the Miller! Leave honoring the Torah to those who studied the Torah.

YANKEL: But, Reb Zoreh . . . !

GABBAI: *(Angrily pushes him aside)* Out of the way, miller! You are disturbing the service. *(Continues his chanting call)* Reb Yehuda b'reb Zev, arise and honor the Torah. Reb Mordecai b'reb Shloimo, arise and . . . *(His voice fades).*

YANKEL: *(Crestfallen, returns to Moishe)*

MOISHE: See? I told you.

YANKEL: *(With bitterness)* Yes . . . You told me.

ISRAEL: *(The boy walks over to the two men, pulls Moishe by the sleeve)* Please Reb . . . Reb . . .

MOISHE: Never mind the "Reb," little boy. That title is only for scholars. I'm just plain Moishe—Moishe the Cobbler, and this is Yankel—Yankel the Miller. Understand?

ISRAEL: Yes, Reb Moishe.

MOISHE: Again "Reb"! Stubborn—aren't you? What do they call you, little boy?

ISRAEL: My name is Israel.

MOISHE: And who's your father?

ISRAEL: I'm an orphan. I help the teacher with the children. For that, kind people feed me every day.

MOISHE: And where do you sleep?

ISRAEL: In the synagogue.

MOISHE: Alone?

ISRAEL: *(Seriously, simply)* No. God is with me.

MOISHE: So . . . Still, aren't you afraid—alone in the synagogue?

ISRAEL: Why should I be? I told you, God is with me.

YANKEL: *(Laughs, amused)* I see. A privileged character . . .

ISRAEL: *(Simply, explains patiently)* No. God is with me in the synagogue. God is with you, Reb Yankel, in your mill. God is with Reb Moishe at his cobbler's bench. He is with everybody. He is everywhere . . . Why wouldn't the Gabbai give you a *Hakofe,* Reb Yankel?

YANKEL: *(Sullen)* You heard him, Israel. Because I'm ignorant. Because I never learned the Torah.

ISRAEL: Even so?

MOISHE: *(Bitter)* That's the way things are—wherever Jews are, that's the way it is. If you're a scholar, you're honored, you're respected. If you work hard for a living and can't spend your time studying, you're nobody. You just don't count. That's the way it is.

ISRAEL: Wherever Jews are?

MOISHE: Yes, everywhere—here in this little village in the Carpathian mountains or in the big cities like Kiev or Lemberg or Warsaw, in Russia or the Ukraine, in Lithuania, Rumania or Poland—all over—it's all the same.

ISRAEL: But why?

MOISHE: I just told you.

ISRAEL: I know you told me, Reb Moishe. But it's wrong, so wrong! Is it not written, "*Verahamov al kol maasov*—His mercy is for all His creatures?" All of us are children of our Heavenly Father. Ignorant or learned—all of us have a right to serve Him.

YANKEL: Oho! These are big words for a little boy. Be careful! If the *Balebatim* hear you, you may even lose your place to sleep in the synagogue. They don't like to hear such talk. Come, Moishe. Let's go. There's no use standing here. Next year on Simhas Torah I won't even bother to come to the services. Come on!

ANALYSIS

The scene dramatizes a moment in the life of Rabbi Israel Baal Shem Tov. By involving collateral characters which functioned in his millieu, who were part of the social climate in which he lived, we are able, in a living manner to make clear the motivations affecting his later development as the bearer of the ideal of the equality of all people in serving their Creator.

Broken down into details: The scene during *hakafot* emphasizes the centrality of religion in the life of the Jew in Eastern Europe at that time. Through Yankel and Moishe we learn about the economic conditions. On the one hand we have the *Balebatim,* with much time on their hands for study, and on the other hand we have the *Balmelokhe* who toils from dawn until midnight to earn a meager living. The social climate comes to the fore, in which the scholar is given prerogatives, whereas the ignorant person, no matter how eager and sincere, is not even permitted to participate properly in worship.

All of these forces are at work on this young boy Israel, who emerges as a sensitive child immersed in dreams of the Infinite, whose later philosophy is strongly affected by moments such as these. By understanding the motivation, the student is able to understand more clearly the crucial acts of the characters of history.

EMMA LAZARUS

a. The Textbook

Emma Lazarus was a descendant of Portugese Jews. She lived in New York City. During the 1870s and 1880s she was gaining a reputation as a fine poet, writing on classical themes such as nature, mythology, ancient Greece and so on. The problems of the Jews did not concern her until one day she paid a visit to the immigrants arriving from Russia. When she saw the Jews who were escaping from persecution, her whole outlook on life changed. She stopped writing about the myths of ancient Greece. From that day on she began writing beautiful and moving poetry on Jewish themes. It was at this time that she wrote the sonnet, "The New Colossus." Twenty years later this sonnet was inscribed in the pedestal of America's best known symbol of liberty—the Statue of Liberty.

b. A Dramatization (A fragment)

SCENE *(The Lazarus living room in their home on West 14th street in New York City, 1860. Moses Lazarus is seated on a chair, reading a newspaper. Hettie, his wife, is doing some needlework.)*

MOSES: Hettie . . .

HETTIE: Yes, Moses?

MOSES: Listen to this editorial by Mr. Horace Greely: "The Union has never been in greater danger. Vipers all over our land are raising their heads, seeking to destroy her. The vipers must be crushed . . ."

HETTIE: Mr. Greely uses strong language.

MOSES: Strong language is needed when the situation is desperate. The Slave States threaten to secede from the Union the very day after Election Day, if Abraham Lincoln is chosen President.

HETTIE: Do you think he will be elected, Moses?

MOSES: I earnestly hope so. Only Abraham Lincoln has the wisdom and the courage to preserve the Union. Just listen to this, Hettie. Mr. Greely goes on: "The very existence, the life of our nation is in . . ."

EMMA: *(Enters, excited)* Father. . . .

HETTIE: Please, Emma! You are disturbing your father.

EMMA: I am sorry, Mother. I just wanted to ask Father . . .

MOSES: It's all right, Emma. What is it you wanted to ask me?

EMMA: Are we true Americans, Father?

HETTIE: Now Emma Lazarus! What brought this on?

EMMA: Cook said that the Indians were the only true Americans. Is that right, Father?

MOSES: In a way.

EMMA: Aren't we true Americans?

HETTIE: What a foolish question, Emma! Of course we are true Americans!

EMMA: But, Mother . . . ! Father just said that Cook was right.

MOSES: I said that Cook was right in a way. The Indians were in America first. All white people came here afterwards from other places at one time or another. Many came from England. Others came from Holland and Sweden and Germany and a great many other countries.

EMMA: Where did we come from, Father?

MOSES: Portugal.

EMMA: Long ago?

MOSES: Oh yes. The Lazarus family has been in America more than two hundred years. Your mother's family, the Nathans, have been here even longer.

HETTIE: That's right. On my side of the family we are descended from Isaac Rodriguez who came here when New York was still New Amsterdam.

EMMA: Why did our family leave Portugal?

HETTIE: That's enough questions, Emma!

EMMA: Why did they leave Portugal, Father?

HETTIE: Emma!

EMMA: Why, Father?

MOSES: Another time, Emma.

EMMA: Don't you want to tell me, Father?

MOSES: Some questions, a girl of eleven like yourself, might leave unanswered until she's a little older. There's time to learn of the world's troubles when you have . . .

EMMA: Are we ashamed of our ancestors, Father?

MOSES: *(Taken aback)* Ashamed?

EMMA: Were they pirates, Father? Did they come here to hide out from the King's . . . ?

MOSES: *(Laughing)* What an idea! You sure can think up things! Of course they weren't pirates. They were respectable merchants, even as I am.

EMMA: Then why did they leave Portugal? Tell me, Father, why?

HETTIE: You had better tell her Moses. With our Emma time always comes a little early.

MOSES: Very well. They left Portugal because they were not wanted there. They came to America to find freedom and escape from persecution in Portugal.

EMMA: Why were they persecuted in Portugal?

MOSES: Because they were Jews, Emma.

EMMA: Even so . . . ?

MOSES: That's the way it is, Emma. But in America things are different. That is why so many come here seeking new homes. It has always been so.

EMMA: Always?

MOSES: From the day the first white men came here. The Jews, the Catholics, the Pilgrims came to escape religious persecution. The Irish escaped from famine. The Germans, the Hungarians, and the Poles fled from political oppression. They all came here and America threw open its doors for them and made them all welcome.

EMMA: Then nobody is really the first.

MOSES: Nobody, Emma. Nobody. . . .

ANALYSIS

The textbook conveys the impression that Emma Lazarus came to her Jewish consciousness in a flash. Seeing the miserable lot of the Jewish immigrants of the early eighties of the 19th Century became her "moment of spiritual awakening." From that day on she was a Jewish poet.

This may well have been so. However, such sudden conversions are rare. Usually a change in spiritual direction is the outgrowth of many experiences which act as propellents with the critical experience giving the final push in the new direction.

The educator is aware of this and consequently continues to add for the student experience upon experience in order finally to arrive at his educational destination. The teacher who keeps this in mind, encourages the students who are at work on a dramatization to search the background of the historic characters for possible motivating experiences which may have added their cumulative force to propel the character in the direction which he took, and consequently made him historically noteworthy. During this search, the students not only learn to understand the personality of the historic character but also acquire much information which is, of necessity, omitted from the textbook. Then, in planning the dramatization, the trivial is omitted and the crucial is developed into a scene or scenes which clarify the motivating forces at work on the historic characters to the class audience viewing the enactment.

Breaking this particular dramatization down into details: The opening of the scene introduces us to the family and home life of Emma Lazarus—financially well to do, cultured. We learn about the period—the question of slavery, Lincoln, etc. We find out that Emma is, even as a child a person who searches for answers, who has a will of her own, who will not be put off by flimsy avoidances. We see that her parents seek to shelter her from life's realities and troubles—We learn how the poet who gave expression to the American ideal of equality for all and welcome for the persecuted, came to think along these lines as a result of personal experience. We see how the lot of the persecuted Jew came to have personal meaning for her when connected with the experience of her ancestors. Dormant those experiences may have remained for many years—but they were there, nevertheless. Meeting the refugee Jews from Russia could then be properly understood as the spark which ignited the fuel placed within her by the earlier experience shown in the dramatization.

Develops Analytical Attitude

The student who frequently is called upon to take part in the task of preparing a history dramatization, soon develops an analytical attitude towards the manifestations of history. All too often history is taught with a "this is it" attitude. "This is what happened. This is when it happened. This is what caused it to happen." Only rarely are students, particularly in the elementary grades, taught the "why" of history. Even more rarely is the student encouraged critically to question the acts and facts of history.

If history is current events grown older, it might be expected that thinking habits which are developed in connection with the study of history will be carried over to the reading of the news of the day. A habit of taking the acts of historic characters for granted may have its carry-over in taking the acts of today's statesmen and political leaders for granted. This hardly helps in developing a sense of civic responsibility in the student. A citizen who accepts the acts of his representatives without questioning becomes easy game for corrupt politicians and political racketeers. Nor does this help in developing in the students a Jewish consciousness and a sense of responsibility to *K'lal Yisrael*—the Community of Israel. Accepting the dictum "Israel will never lack its poor" without questioning is certainly inimical to the development of Jewish social service. Had Herzl and others like him not questioned the wisdom of the great majority of their contemporary leaders, the ideal of Jewish political reconstruction in the Land of Israel might well have been stillborn.

Asking questions and seeking the answers is the basis of progress—scientific, economic, political, or what have you. Working on a dramatization in a history class develops this habit. For, just as a brick structure is raised by placing brick on brick, so is the dramatization created by adding answer to answer—each one the result of critical analysis, of searching for what, who, and why of historic events. In truth, questions are the bloodstream of a creative dramatization:

What happened?

Who caused it to happen?

What kind of person was he?

What did he try to do?

How did he go about doing it?

Why did he do it?

Who helped him? Why?

Who opposed him? Why?

What did he accomplish?

If he failed, what caused it? Circumstances? His insufficiency? Opposition of others? Could he have avoided failure? How?

What were the conditions of the period—economic, social, political, etc.?

What kind of people functioned then?

Did the conditions and the people affect his acts? How?

What was the effect of his acts on his immediate community? Were the results good? In what way? Were they bad? In what way? Why?

Did the acts and events of the story and the characters affect our lives today? Which aspects? How?

Were the acts justified—in the light of conditions then prevailing—in the light of the judgment of our historical perspective? Why?

What would I (the student) do in his place? Why?

In finding the answer to such and similar questions which arise during the process of preparing a history dramatization, the student becomes familiar with the facts of the story. He absorbs the overtones of the story which give it reality and meaning. He discovers within it the aspects of relevancy to his own life and circumstances. He recognizes therein guideposts for his own conduct in relation to similar conditions and problems, thus, in essence, truly learning from the past.

■ THE USES OF DRAMATIZATION OF HISTORY

Dramatization has its uses in every phase of the teaching process. It may be used to motivate a new lesson, to enrich the content of a lesson taught by other techniques, as the major technique for teaching new material, and for purposes of review. The teacher is careful, of course, not to use the technique of dramatization exclusively, nor to use it too often. Doing so might become monotonous and tiresome. Also, in choosing the particular type of dramatization to be utilized, the teacher considers not only the age, maturity, and how experienced the students are in the use of the technique, but also the purpose for which dramatization is about to be used. Thus, if the medium is used for the purpose of motivation, a simpler form such as "Correspondent" or "Newscaster" will be selected. If it is to help in review, a form which calls for a good deal of background knowledge on the part of the class will be selected. Particularly useful for this purpose are those forms of dramatization which permit the involvement of the entire class as participants or questioners. "Self-Defense" or "Press Conference" are useful for the purpose of review. Any of the forms are useful as enrichment material, provided the dramatization is brief and does not overshadow the balance of the lesson. Each of the different forms is also suitable for use as the major technique for teaching new material. However, if the students are ready for them, the more complex forms give the better results—particularly "Witness to History" and "Direct Dramatization." Each of these forms will be considered in detail later.

The approach varies somewhat with the purpose for which the dramatization is being used. For example, if used:

To Motivate

1. The dramatization is prepared and presented before the class by students who have volunteered or were especially selected for the task. Detailed procedure for this step is discussed at length later under "Dramatization Step by Step."

2. After the class has witnessed the dramatization, a brief discussion of the story ensues. The discussion is concluded with a series of provocative questions by the teacher, which, although they are stimulated by the dramatization just seen, require further research and study for the answers. For example:

> The class has just seen a brief dramatization showing how Don Isaac Abarbanel pleads with Ferdinand and Isabella not to expell the Jews from Spain. This has been presented as a motivation for a lesson on the Spanish Expulsion. The teacher's questions which follow will be somewhat like these:
>
> Do you think that the king and queen of Spain were moved by Don Isaac Abarbanel's pleas?
>
> Were both the king and the queen of the same opinion?
>
> What happened finally to the Jews of Spain?
>
> Why, do you think, did Don Isaac offer to give up all his wealth in exchange for permission for the Jews to remain?
>
> What happened to Don Isaac?

3. The teacher indicates reference sources in which the class will find the answers to these and other questions. The students are assigned to prepare reports.

4. Several of the reports are read at a subsequent class period.

5. Discussion of the reports by the class.

6. Teacher augments the reports and the dramatization with as much material as is necessary to bring out all the information necessary.

If the teacher prefers, steps 3 to 6 are postponed for later and the teacher proceeds, immediately after step 2 to develop the entire lesson by means of narrative by the teacher, or by a student previously selected for the task, or by other means normally used by the teacher.

To Enrich

1. A group of students prepares a dramatization of material selected, either by the teacher or by the students, for the purpose of enriching the lesson. This might be:

> A *single incident in the story*. For example: If the life of Rabbi Akiba is being studied, an incident of the struggle for existence of his wife Rachel while Akiba is away studying might be the subject of the dramatization.
>
> A *collateral story*. For example: The class is studying the Baal Shem Tov. The dramatization to enrich the lesson is of one of the wonder tales about the Baal Shem, such as "Why the *Tzadik* Laughed."

> *A story dramatizing the environment.* For example: The lesson deals with the re-settlement of Palestine by the early Jewish pioneers in the modern period, and their struggles against great odds. The dramatization might deal with an incident in a new settlement during the search for water. If the lesson deals with Jewish life in Eastern Europe, the dramatization might be of the first day in school of a Jewish ghetto child.

2. The teacher presents the lesson in the usual way.
3. At the appropriate point, the teacher stops and introduces the dramatization.
4. The dramatization is enacted.
5. A brief discussion follows, dealing with the new material brought out in the dramatization.
6. Teacher connects the dramatization with the rest of the lesson and continues with the lesson. For example:

> The lesson is about Rashi. The teacher develops the lesson in the usual way. The background, the biography, the contribution of Rashi are studied. Then the teacher tells the class of the veneration of future generations for the great scholar. So deep was their affection for him that they created wonder tales about him, for example the Tale of Godfrey de Bouillon. The dramatization of the legend about this cruel knight for whom Rashi had foretold total defeat is now enacted. After the enactment and discussion, the teacher proceeds with the balance of the lesson which, in this case, might deal with the effect of Rashi's work on the development of later Jewish life.

To Teach New Material

If the dramatization is used as the major teachnique for teaching new material, it will be but natural that the bulk of the time allotted for the lesson will be devoted to it. The steps will be somewhat as follows:

1. Teacher introduces the lesson by connecting material previously studied with the new subject to be considered.
2. The dramatization is prepared and presented. The detailed procedure to be followed for this aspect is given later when individual forms of dramatization are considered.
3. Through discussion, socio-drama, and other techniques, the dramatization is analyzed and enlarged upon. Areas not fully covered in the dramatization are explored by means of question and answer, student reports, teacher's lecture, etc.
4. The lesson is summed up and connected with the lesson to follow.
5. Other class procedures which teacher usually follows as a conclusion of a lesson, such as assignment of reports, testing, etc., are now utilized.

To Review

When dramatization is used for review, it is employed either immediately after the original presentation of the material, at the conclusion of the entire lesson, or at some later period when a good deal of time has already elapsed since the subject was first studied.

The teacher will select that form of dramatization which allows for the involvement of the greatest number of students since, in this instance, not much new research is necessary. The experience of the children in the use of dramatics will determine the degree of complexity of the form which may be undertaken.

As to the steps to be followed, it is recommended that those given hereafter individually for each form of dramatization will serve as general guides. The teacher will make the minor modifications necessary to adjust them for use for the purposes of review.

■ FROM WHY TO HOW

We have indicated at some length why dramatization is a useful—one is tempted to say—an almost indispensable technique in teaching history. We will now consider, in some detail, the forms of dramatization that might be used, and procedures suggested to be followed in using them as aids to teaching history.

Forms of History Dramatizations Step by Step

The knowing teacher will always lead his students in gradual stages from the simple to the complex and from the familiar to the new and unknown. In dramatizing history too, the teacher will begin with simple forms of dramatization, usually familiar to the children, and proceed to the more difficult and unfamiliar as the students gain experience and self-confidence.

Following are a series of forms of dramatizations. Although some of them might well be utilized, with only minor modifications, in teaching other subjects in the curriculum, these forms are especially suitable for teaching history. In all of them, the underlying principle is the re-creation in dramatic form of the historic events, providing opportunities for the students to be transported, as it were, mentally and emotionally into the historic past, allowing them to become participants vicariously in the ebb and flow of history.

In each instance the manner in which the particular form might be used is indicated in a step-by-step progression, utilizing examples of actual teacher introductions, suggested questions and answers, actual dramatizations, etc. These are given in order to serve as guides for the teacher who is not experienced in the use of creative dramatics in education and as reminders for the more experienced teacher. Let us repeat: they are quite definitely not intended as models to be slavishly followed or, still worse, to be copied verbatim. Doing so would destroy the very basic value of the entire process—its unlimited opportunities for creativity and free expression on the part of the students and the teacher as well.

It is to be noted that the very forms of dramatization here given and the occasions suggested for their use, are merely indicative of what is possible. Teachers will no doubt think of additional types of dramatization which might be enlisted in the cause of meaningful teaching of history. Similarly, they will discover other applications of these techniques—applications which are not even hinted at in these pages.

Here then are the forms of dramatization and the ways in which they might be developed and used in the classroom:

■ A. CORRESPONDENT

The technique of "The Correspondent" is most useful as a means of introducing a new lesson or for the purpose of summarizing a lesson already studied. In essence it is the oral description of an event by a student assuming the role of a reporter or correspondent. The class is the radio or television audience. The student-correspondent stands in front of the class and relates the historical event as if it were fresh news which had just happened that very day. If the teacher deems it advisable, several students might be used as correspondents, the story being divided among them.

This technique is well suited to the needs of a class without previous experience in dramatization since it does not call for the give-and-take of dialogue and the complexity of movement. Furthermore, it is possible for the correspondents to write out their parts in advance—a useful prop to self-confidence in the early stages.

"Correspondent" is particularly suitable for use with historic events which can be portrayed as having taken place in a single day and in one place as: The Sale of Joseph, The Coronation of Saul, etc.

As is the case with all forms of history dramatization, "Correspondent" has a special value in that it stimulates purposeful independent research in historical materials and other sources on the part of the students. Research is especially required of the students who assume roles in the dramatization and those who act with them in advisory or editorial capacities. In the course of the research which has been undertaken to prepare a correspondent's report, the student of necessity acquires a knowledge of the historical facts and also a deeper understanding of the backgrounds to the facts.

As for the class-audience, in listening to the dramatization they learn the facts of the lesson in a manner that is interesting to them. Furthermore, in the process of make-believe, or dramatic re-creation of history, the event under study gains a sense of immediacy and vitality which might otherwise be lacking. The discussion which follows the enactment of the dramatization provides the teacher with a strongly motivated situation for elaboration on the material presented through the dramatization and for teaching new material, directly or collaterally connected with the dramatization.

Introducing the Technique

The first time the technique of "Correspondent" is to be used it will be necessary for the teacher to introduce it to the class and to explain, at least in general terms, the manner of its operation. Little time is expended on this phase—a one time operation. It might be done somewhat as follows:

TEACHER: How many of you read a daily newspaper regularly?
(Students raise their hands)
TEACHER: Will some of you tell me why you read a newspaper?

STUDENT 1: For the jokes.
STUDENT 2: For the sports.
STUDENT 3: To get the news.
TEACHER: Do any of you know how the newspapers get the news which they print?
STUDENT 4: From reporters.
TEACHER: Yes—from reporters, from correspondents. What other ways besides reading the newspaper do we have for getting the news?
STUDENT 5: The radio.
STUDENT 6: The television.
STUDENT 7: The newsreels in the movies.
TEACHER: And how do they get their news?
STUDENT 8: The same way. From reporters.
TEACHER: That's right. The reporters and correspondents gather the news and send it on to the newspaper, the television studio, and so on. Often correspondents report to us the news directly on the television or radio broadcast. Sometimes, during a news broadcast, we are switched to a distant city and we see and hear a correspondent who tells us the story of a news event which happened in the city where he is stationed. These stories which the correspondents tell us are today's news. Tomorrow they are history. The opposite is also true. Today's history was yesterday's news grown a little older. All history was "news of the day" at its birth, when it first happened. Wouldn't it be interesting if instead of learning the stories of the Jewish past as history we could actually have heard about it as news—as it happened, the day it happened? Naturally, that is impossible. What is passed is in the past. But, by dramatization, we can make believe that our history is fresh news, something that just happened. We can all be the radio and television audience, listening to a broadcast, while some of us will act as correspondents who will tell us the story of history as if it just happened, as if it were part of a news broadcast. Naturally those who will act as correspondents will have to read up on the story and prepare it carefully. Now, our next lesson in history deals with. . . .

Having introduced the technique the teacher proceeds with the regular steps in the process of developing this type of dramatization.

The Process

The first time the technique is used, step 1, "Teacher's Introduction or Motivation" is omitted since the introduction of the technique serves as sufficient motivation. The steps usually followed are:

1. Teacher's Introduction (or Motivation)
2. Selection of Cast
3. Research Planning
4. Cast Research
5. Planning the Report
6. Preparation of Report
7. Editing the Report
8. The Enactment
9. Discussion and Generalization

The class time allocation is as follows:

Steps 1, 2, 3: The last ten minutes of a history period.

Steps 4, 5, 6, 7: are executed by the students outside of class, during the week which follows.

Steps 8, 9: A full history period, following the week of out-of-class preparation is devoted to these two steps.

The story of the *Expulsion from Spain* will be used for the following detailed illustration of the use of each step in the process.

1. Teacher's Introduction (or Motivation)

TEACHER: *(Displays a reproduction of the well known painting of Columbus discovering America)*
Who knows what this picture shows?

STUDENT 1: Columbus discovering America.

TEACHER: Excellent. Do any of you know when Columbus discovered America?

STUDENT 2: In 1492.

TEACHER: And the exact date? Don't any of you know? Well, what date is Columbus Day?

STUDENT 3: October 12.

TEACHER: Exactly! It commemorates the day he discovered America. And in 1492, October 12th was also the festival of *Hoshanah Rabbah* which we celebrate during *Sukkot*. From what country did Columbus start out on his journey?

STUDENT 4: Spain.

TEACHER: The day Columbus started out on his journey of discovery was also a special one on the Jewish calendar. It was the fast day of Tishah B'Av. This is a very sad day for Jews since it marks the anniversary when the Temple of Jerusalem was destroyed many, many years ago. On the day when Columbus started out in 1492, Tishah B'Av was an especially sad day for the Jews because on that day all the Jews of Spain were expelled from the land of their birth. The Expulsion from Spain is quite a sad event in our history. For many of the descendants of the Spanish Jews, this event is as fresh in their minds as if it had just happened. Supposing we learn about it also as if it were fresh news, as if it had just happened. We will do a "Correspondent" dramatization. All of us will be listening to our make-believe television sets. Two of us will be the correspondents who will prepare the story during the week and tell it to us at our history lesson next week.

2. Selection of Cast

TEACHER: We will need two correspondents who will divide the story between them. We would like to be the correspondents for our "broadcast?"

The first several times this technique is used, the teacher selects such students who might reasonably be expected to prepare adequate reports in an interesting manner. The teacher is sufficiently familiar with the students, and does not have to waste time on so-called tryouts. The fact is emphasized by the teacher that others will be given opportunity for future dramatizations. Having selected the correspondents, the teacher proceeds:

TEACHER: Of course, our correspondents will have to know the story they will tell us pretty thoroughly. In a few minutes I will give you some references of books in which you can read up on the story. Now we need an Editorial Committee. You may not know this, but correspondents very often receive assistance from other reporters or from an editorial committee which provides them with information and helps them in planning their reports. I am sure our correspondents will welcome such help. Supposing we have an Editorial Committee of five. Who would like to serve on this Committee?

The Editorial Comittee is selected.

3. Research Planning

As I said, our correspondents will have to read up on the story in order to prepare interesting and complete reports. The Editorial Committee will also do the research so that they will be able to help the correspondents. Please note down the references which I will now give you. You will find the information in your textbooks, pages ——— to ———. You might also read the following: *(Teacher indicates additional references)* I suggest that you do your research by next Thursday. That afternoon, immediately after class, the correspondents will meet with the Editorial Committee to plan your reports. Good luck!

4. Cast Research

Correspondents and Editorial Committee do the research indicated by the teacher. About two days should suffice for this. More time will of course be allowed for this or any other steps if the teacher deems it advisable in the light of circumstances.

5. Planning the Report

Correspondents and Editorial Committee meet, before or after class. If possible, the teacher is present. This is particularly necessary the first few times the technique is used. The correspondents tell orally the story as they plan to present it. The Editorial Committee fills in omissions. The story is now divided in two parts, one for each correspondent. In our present story Correspondent 1 would be allocated to describe the actual expulsion of the Jews from Spain. Correspondent II would fill in on the historical background, the reasons for the expulsion, the efforts of the Jews to avert it, etc. The correspondents are instructed to write out their reports at home in the exact form in which they plan to present them to the class. A final meeting of the correspondents and Editorial Committee is scheduled to take place two (or more) days later, to go over the written reports.

6. Preparation of Reports

The correspondents write their reports at home. Teacher asks to see them, if that is deemed advisable, and offers suggestions for improvement. In any event, the teacher is available to the students for consultation in this as well as during the other steps of the process.

7. Editing the Report

The Editorial Committee meets with the correspondents who read aloud their written reports exactly as they plan to present them before the class. Suggestions for further improvements in the content and text are offered. The teacher attends this meeting if possible. In some instances this meeting may be omitted, particularly if the teacher has had an opportunity to go over the reports and is satisfied that they are adequate for the purpose.

8. The Enactment

The program is presented before the class as part of a history lesson. The class is the audience. The reporters are stationed in front of the class as if that were a radio or television studio. The Editorial Committee is seated in front, directly behind the correspondents. As the "news reports" are presented the class takes notes on aspects they might wish to discuss later. The presentation about the Expulsion From Spain might run somewhat as follows:

CORRESPONDENT 1: Ladies and gentlemen: The news reports from Spain have been pouring in all day. King Ferdinand and Queen Isabella have finally made good on their threat. The order expelling all Jews from Spain went into effect today. This day of August 12th, 1492 will be long remembered in history. From every corner of Spain Jewish families have been streaming towards the seaports. They bring with them only those belongings which they can carry on their backs. All their other possessions, and in many cases their great wealth, they have been forced to leave behind to be confiscated by the Crown. The rich and the poor, the young and the old, the healthy and the sick, all are pressing towards the ships that wait in the harbors. One of our correspondents has just come from the harbor of Salamanca where he witnessed the departure of the Jews. We will hear from him now.

CORRESPONDENT 2: I watched the Jewish refugees from Spain trying to flee from the country of their birth. Most of them come from families that have lived in Spain for hundreds of years. Now they must find new homes, since the land of their birth is throwing them out. I saw them pleading with the captains of the ships that were waiting in the harbor. They were giving away all their belongings for a tiny space on deck of leaky old tubs. This was their last day to get out of Spain. I spoke to one of their leaders. He told me of their efforts to have the order of expulsion cancelled. One of their great men, Don Isaac Abarbanel almost convinced their Spanish majesties to allow the Jews to remain, but the leaders of the Inquisition headed by Torquemada insisted, and the order of expulsion was carried out.

CORRESPONDENT 1: You mentioned to me earlier about an unusual incident that you noticed in Salamanca harbor. Would you tell us about it, please?

CORRESPONDENT 2: Gladly. While watching the refugees crowding on to the ships, I saw a beautiful sight. Three pretty caravels, the Nina, the Pinta, and the Santa Maria, sailed by the refugee ships on their way to what may be a glorious adventure. The decks of the caravels were crowded with sailors. Many of them, it is said are Marranos, secret Jews. It is even rumored by some that the Commander-in-chief of the expedition himself is a secret Jew. Who can tell? Be that as it may, under the command of Christopher Columbus they have set out to find a new route to the Indies. Who can tell to what glories this adventuresome journey will lead Columbus and his gallant crew? Who can tell to what new miseries the broken down ships in Salamanca harbor will carry the Jewish refugees whom their homeland has cast out?

9. Discussion and Generalization

After words of praise for the correspondents and the Editorial Committee, the teacher leads the class in a discussion about the content of the dramatization—*not the acting of their classmates*—and helps them to generalize what they have learned. In our present example this might deal with speculation about the ultimate fate of the Spanish refugees; the new homes they found; the fortuitous discovery of America which has provided homes for so many refugees; the lot of refugees in general; refugees from World War II and their adjustment in America and in Israel; refugees whom the children might know and the way they have adjusted; the spread of Sephardic communities over many lands as a result of the Spanish expulsion; their contributions to Jewish life and cilivization in general; a visit, where possible, to an institution established by Sephardim such as the Shearith Israel synagogue in New York, etc.

B. THE NEWSCASTER

Although similar in many respects to the technique of "Correspondent," the "Newscaster" technique is somewhat more complex. Though also a simulated news broadcast of a historical event, the information is not presented to the class in the form of a unified narrative. Instead it is presented as a mosaic of individual, simulated news dispatches, much the same as radio's "News on the Hour" or television's "The Eleven O'clock News." These individual dispatches, taken together, form a unified picture of the historic event which the class is studying.

The procedure is similar in many respects to that outlined above under "Correspondent."

Introducing the Technique

The first time "Newscaster" is used, the teacher introduces it somewhat as follows:

TEACHER: We are in the habit of listening daily and often several times each day to news broadcasts over the radio or television. The reporters, or as they are known on radio and T.V., the newscasters, read for us a number of news dispatches telling of events which have occurred that day in many places. Taken together, these news dispatches present to us a picture of the state of the world, day by day.

I am sure you remember what I told you that today's history was yesterday's news. Supposing in next week's lesson about . . . . *(The dedication of the temple by the Maccabees, the death of Rabbi Akiba, the Jews return to England, etc.)* we again go back in history, as we did when we played "Correspondent" and hear the events described as if they had just happened, as if they were today's news items. However, instead of reading for us a full story as the correspondents did, your newscaster will read us a number of dispatches which will be prepared by an Editorial Committee. From these dispatches we will learn the entire exciting story of how. . . .

The Process

Following is a step by step development, utilizing "The Coronation of Solomon" by way of illustration:

1. Teacher's Introduction (or Motivation)

Here too, the first time the technique is used, the general introduction of the technique will serve as motivation for the entire lesson. During subsequent uses, the general introduction is of course no longer used. Teacher will motivate the lesson by using any of the techniques generally used to introduce a new lesson. Here, the motivation might be showing a picture of a king, followed by a discussion of kings, their coronation, their role today, the role of the king in ancient Israel, King David, etc., leading to the coronation of his heir. Teacher might begin with a discussion of a recent inaugural of a public official like the President, Governor, or Mayor, following this with questions on how the inaugural differs from the way rulers were proclaimed in ancient days, etc.

2. Selection of Cast

TEACHER: Although we will hear the dispatches read to us by a newscaster, they will actually be prepared by an Editorial Committee which we will now choose. We will not appoint the newscaster. The Editorial Committee will elect one of its own members for that role. The program will go on a week from today. That should give us enough time to get ready. Now, who would like to serve on the Editorial Committee?

The Editorial Committee is selected.

3. Research Planning

TEACHER: The Editorial Committee will have to do some research if they are to prepare interesting and authentic news dispatches. I would suggest that you read the story in our textbook, pages ______ to ______. There is an exciting account of the Coronation of Solomon in the Bible. You will find it in Kings I, Chapter I, 5-53. I will meet with the Editorial Committee for a few minutes after class for a briefing session.

4. Briefing Session

Teacher meets with the Editorial Committee for a few minutes and explains how the story is to be broken down into news dispatches:

TEACHER: Each news dispatch should tell only a single item and should be very brief. For example: after you do your research you will learn that Adonijah tried to make himself king; that the Prophet Nathan informed Prince Solomon's mother, Bath Sheba about this; and that Bath Sheba went to the king to complain. How many separate dispatches would you say we have here?

STUDENT 1: Three.

TEACHER: Excellent! What would you say is the first?

STUDENT 1: Adonijah proclaims himself king.

TEACHER: A news dispatch usually has a date line, the place and often the date where it happened. We should begin our dispatches this way. He tried to make himself king at Ein Rogel, near Jerusalem. How would your dispatch read then?

STUDENT 1: Ein Rogel, Jerusalem—Adonijah tried to make himself king today.

TEACHER: Very good. Now, since we want to tell our story in a continuous manner, describing things in the order in which they happened, what do you think would be our second dispatch?

STUDENT 2: Bath Sheba's House, Jerusalem—the Prophet Nathan has just informed Prince Solomon's mother, Bath Sheba, that Adonijah is trying to become king. Bath Sheba is very upset.

STUDENT 3: How do you know she's upset?

STUDENT 2: Sure she is. If she wasn't upset, why did she go to the king to complain?

TEACHER: I see you will be able to do this very well without further help from me. I would suggest that you read the references and then each of you prepare as many separate news items or dispatches as you think necessary to tell the story. Day after tomorrow meet here and go over all the dispatches. You will pick the best to tell the story. For instance, you might decide that Jack's dispatch tells best how Adonijah wanted to be king. You will use that then. If Billy has the best dispatch about Nathan and Bath Sheba, you will use that one. And so on.

STUDENT 1: What if we don't agree?

TEACHER: Then you'll vote on it. You'll need a chairman. Who shall it be?

STUDENT 2: Billy.

STUDENT 3: Jack.

TEACHER: How many want Billy? How many are for Jack? All right, Billy. You're it. At your meeting day after tomorrow you will also have to elect the newscaster. I would suggest that you look over a newspaper and listen to some news broadcasts to get an idea how to word your news items interestingly. Now, let's have a good show.

5. Research and Preparation

The members of the Editorial Committee are allotted two days, or more if necessary, to do their research and prepare their news dispatches.

6. Editorial Meeting

The Editorial Committee meets. They put together the final script by selecting the best of the proposed dispatches. A newscaster is elected—this is usually either the student who submitted the best dispatches, or the one who, in the opinion of the other students, has the best oral delivery.

The teacher attends this meeting if possible. However, the goal is to train the students so that eventually they will be able to work independently from beginning to end.

If found desirable, more than one newscaster might be selected. In that event the dispatches are divided between them. If the script contains many individual items, it is also possible for every member of the Editorial Committee to be a newscaster, each one being allocated the reading of several dispatches. This is a desirable procedure in the younger classes especially.

The student who was elected as chairman, acts as chairman during the enactment, introducing the program and making the final announcement.

7. The Enactment

The program is presented before the class. The physical arrangements are similar to those indicated for "Correspondents."

CHAIRMAN: Fellow students: Today we go back in history nearly three thousand years to the days when King David was very old and citizens of the Land of Israel wondered who would be their ruler after him. Come! Let us find out! Let us listen to the news!

NEWSCASTER: Ladies and gentlemen: This has been a most important day in Jerusalem. It will long be remembered in the history of this ancient city. The dispatches from that hilltop capital of the Land of Israel have been coming in rapidly and they spell out a very exciting series of events. Here they are:

EIN ROGEL, JERUSALEM—Prince Adonijah, the son of Hagith, one of King David's wives, arranged a feast today. He invited to the feast many of the outstanding men in Jerusalem. Among those present were General Joab and Evyatar the Priest. It is rumored that this is Prince Adonijah's opening move to have himself annointed king of Israel upon the death of his father, the aging King David.

QUEEN BATH SHEBA'S PALACE, JERUSALEM—The Prophet Nathan visited Queen Bath Sheba today. It is believed that the prophet reported to her about Adonijah's feast to which neither he nor Prince Solomon had been invited. When the prophet left, the queen seemed very upset.

THE ROYAL PALACE, JERUSALEM—Queen Bath Sheba appeared in special audience before King David this afternoon. The queen reminded the king about his promise to her that her own son, Prince Solomon, would some day inherit the kingdom. She urged the king to name his successor immediately, since she and Solomon would be in danger if some one else took over the throne by force. The Prophet Nathan joined her pleas. He told the king about Adonijah's feast. The king promised to consider the matter.

QUEEN BATH SHEBA'S PALACE, JERUSALEM—Queen Bath Sheba has been called to the king. It is rumored that he promised her that only her son Solomon would inherit the throne.

THE ROYAL PALACE, JERUSALEM—The king has given his answer. He summoned the Prophet Nathan, the Priest Zadok and Benaiah the Son of Yehoyadah. He ordered them to take his son Solomon down to the stream of Gihon and anoint him king of Israel.

GIHON, JERUSALEM—This little stream below the outskirts of Jerusalem was the scene today of a great historic event. Prince Solomon, the son of King David and Queen Bath Sheba was anointed king over Israel and Judah. The event is especially important since it happened while the old King David is still alive. The ram's horn was blown and the people raised a great cheer, "Long live King Solomon," when the holy oil of anointing was poured over the head of the young prince. It is rumored that Prince Adonijah was in the midst of a feast when the news of the coronation of Solomon reached him.

THE TABERNACLE, MOUNT MORIAH—Prince Adonijah has just come here in great haste. He ran to the altar and is holding on to its corner. He knows that no one will harm him while he is holding on to the altar of the Lord. It seems Prince Adonijah is afraid for his life. He has good reason to be afraid. After all, he tried to take away the kingdom from Solomon, the rightful heir.

THE GREAT MARKET, JERUSALEM—The people here are saying that the new King Solomon plans to begin his rule without bloodshed. It is reported that when the king heard that Adonijah was hiding out at the altar, he sent a messenger to call him. He swore that if Adonijah would be loyal, no harm would come to him.

THE ROYAL PALACE, JERUSALEM—The rumors are true. Prince Adonijah has just appeared and sworn to be loyal to King Solomon. The young king allowed Adonijah to return to his home in peace. Now the Kingdom of Israel and Judah has two kings—old King David who fought all his life to establish it and young King Solomon who, it is hoped, will bring to it greater glory.

8. Unifying the Story

The enactment is followed by the usual discussion and questions regarding the content of the story.

Students are then encouraged to retell the story in their own words as a unified and continuous narrative.

9. Generalizing

The discussion is led in the direction of applying ancient Jerusalem's problem with our problems today. The danger of usurpation of power by "strong men" is pointed out. Parallels are drawn with countries where such power seizure led to the destruction of individual liberty and democracy.

■ C. SELF-DEFENSE

In this technique a historic character is re-created through enactment. He appears, describes his acts and defends them before the class, which, during the dramatization, assumes the role of his neighbors, tribesmen, co-workers, etc., or in general before the court of history, sitting in judgment upon him and his deeds.

This technique makes it possible for the students, particularly those who are called upon to enact the role of the historic characters, to learn in depth the acts and motivations of history's leading figures. It provides the class with an opportunity of weighing these figures' acts and motivations, judging them in the light of both the historic period in which they played a role and their possible effect on modern events.

The student who has been selected to impersonate the historic character, prepares his material in advance. It consists of a description of his acts and a justification of them. He then appears before the class and either reads or recites his "Self-defense." The class is the "jury of history." One student is the Presiding Judge. Another student or the teacher is the Foreman of the Jury, guiding the discussion as it develops.

This technique is especially useful in connection with the study of historic characters who served as a focus of important events and about whose acts there exists some aspect of controversy. For example:

Jacob and his dealings with Esau.

One of the Twelve Spies of Moses.

The Prophet Samuel and his relationship to King Saul.

Jeroboam divides the kingdom.

Shabbetai Zvi.

The Gaon of Vilna opposes Hasidism.

Introducing the Project

The first time the technique is to be used, the teacher introduces it and explains its operation. On this occasion, the general introduction also takes the place of the usual step No. 1—the motivation.

"Self-defense" might be introduced somewhat as follows:

TEACHER: All of us are constantly called upon to make decisions: I am about to go into the street—shall I put on a sweater or wear light clothes? It is seven o'clock and an interesting program is about to be shown on television—shall I see the program and do my homework later or shall I do it now while my mind is still fresh?

Can any of you tell me about some decisions you had to make today?

The teacher permits the children to volunteer reminiscences of decisions they had to make that day. This is to be limited to a minute or two at the maximum. The teacher then continues:

TEACHER: Most of the time we have good reasons for deciding the way we do. The boy who decides to watch the television program at seven o'clock does so because he feels that he can do his homework later, while the program can only be seen at seven o'clock. If that same boy had decided to skip the program and do his homework instead, he would probably have done so for reasons which were important to him. Whatever our problems and whatever our reasons for deciding what to do, our decisions usually affect only us, or our immediate family, our friends, classmates, or a similar small group of people. When a character in history had to make a decision, the way he decided to deal with a problem usually affected the lives of many people—those who lived in his own time and, quite often, the generations that were not yet born when he was alive.

Can any of you think of some historic decision we studied?

STUDENT 1: When young David decided to fight Goliath.

TEACHER: Good. How did that affect many others?

STUDENT 1: Well, if he had not fought the giant, the Philistines might have conquered the Israelites and there might not even be a Jewish people today.

TEACHER: That's a very good anwser. Any one else?

STUDENT 2: When Joseph decided to forgive his brothers. If he had not done this, Jacob and his family would not have come to Egypt, there would have been no Egyptian slavery and all of Jewish history might have been different.

TEACHER: That's a fine example and very well explained too. Any others?

STUDENT 3: When the Jews of Palestine decided to proclaim the State of Israel on May 14th, 1948. If they had decided to wait, there might not be a State of Israel today.

TEACHER: These are all very good examples and in connection with each of them we might ask: Why did he do what he did and not otherwise? What would have happened if he had acted differently? Was he right in deciding the way he did according to the needs of his time? In the light of what we now know, did he decide correctly?

In place of the above series of questions and answers, the teacher may feel that his purpose will be better served by providing an example of his own choosing. Any previously learned lesson involving a historic decision will do. It might be offered somewhat as follows:

TEACHER: When, after the death of King Solomon, Jeroboam divided the kingdom, he started a chain of events which, in the end led to the destruction of the

Kingdom of Israel which he had established and to the complete loss of the ten tribes of Israel. Was he justified in doing what he did? What were his reasons for doing it? Were they good reasons for his time? Would he have acted differently if he could foresee the results that followed many years later?

Whether the teacher uses the questions and answers, or the teacher-provided example, the introduction thereafter continues along the following lines:

TEACHER: To really understand the acts and decisions of a historic character, we must understand the time in which he lived and the reasons that made him act the way he did and not otherwise. It would be very helpful, of course, if a historic character could appear before us, describe his acts and give us his reasons. Important public figures nowadays do this very thing. When the President of the United States negotiates a treaty with another country, vetoes an important bill, or makes other important decisions, he often appears on television and gives a report to the nation. He tells us what he did and the reasons for his acts. The nearest we can come to this with historic characters who are no longer living is by bringing these characters to life through a dramatization. We call this kind of dramatization "Self-defense" because one of us, playing the role of a person in history, appears before the class, describes his acts and defends them by giving us his reasons. Now let me ask you a question:

The Process

This concludes the general introduction to the technique. The teacher now proceeds with the usual steps in the development of a "Self-defense" dramatization.

1. Teacher's Introduction (or Motivation)

TEACHER: Did any of you ever have occasion to be offered a reward for doing something nice? Tell us about it.

The students are encouraged to tell about occasions when a reward was offered to them, and what they did about it. Then the teacher continues:

TEACHER: Next week we will study (*or, if used for review*: we have been studying) about Abraham who faced a similar problem: He was offered a reward for helping in the war of the five kings against the four. He refused to take the reward. What happened there? Why did he come to the help of the five kings? Why did he refuse the reward?

2. Selection of Cast

TEACHER: Let us find out by playing "Self-defense." One of us will be Abraham. The rest of us will be his neighbors in the Land of Canaan. We will make believe that Abraham has just come back from the war. He will appear before us, his neighbors, and tell us what happened and why he did what he did in helping the kings and refusing the reward.

STUDENT 1: Will the neighbors have anything to say?

TEACHER: Of course. As his neighbors we may interrupt him with questions if anything is not clear to us. We will make comments if we disagree with something he says. Now, we will select one of us to play the part of Abraham.

A student is selected for the part in the usual manner.

3. Research Assignment

TEACHER: Naturally, our Abraham will have to read up on the whole story, if he is to play his part intelligently. This time, the rest of us too will have to do some reading of the story so that we may ask intelligent questions as they arise.

The teacher provides the class with references for reading: the chapter in the textbook; a section in a more complete history book; literary sources; the account in the Bible (Exodus XIV, XV). The student playing the role of Abraham is asked to prepare his presentation in writing after reading the references.

4. Guiding the Protagonist

The teacher meets with the student who is to portray Abraham for several minutes each time that he comes to school. He checks on the student's reading progress and the development of his presentation. The presentation should consist of a narrative of the story up to the point where the decision is made. This is followed by a defense of his decision, giving the reasons—those of the text if indicated, otherwise the reasons as the student imagines them in the light of the conditions existing during that period in history. The teacher offers guidance for improvement until he is satisfied that the presentation is ready to be given before the class.

5. The Enactment

The class is seated as usual. The teacher, or a student who has been selected to act the role of Chairman, comes to the front and introduces the dramatization by orally setting the stage for it:

CHAIRMAN: Fellow classmates: Today we are the Canaanite neighbors of Abraham. The time is long, long ago, more than thirty-five centuries ago. We have gathered here, in this field of the Plain of Mamre, to listen to a "Self-defense." Our neighbor, Abraham the Hebrew, has just returned from war. He wants to tell us about his adventures and defend his action. Let us now listen to Abraham the Hebrew.

The protagonist rises, proceeds to the front of the room, and speaks. It is desirable that the presentation, when actually delivered, be given from memory, with occasional recourse to notes. In the early stages of the use of the technique, however, or when it is otherwise deemed necessary, the presentation might be read. If it is read, it is desirable that the student be thoroughly familiar with the material so that he reads it smoothly, interestingly, and with sufficient expressive interpretation to hold the interest of the class.

The example given here is rather lengthy since it is our purpose to indicate how a great deal of background material and collateral historical information may be woven into a "Self-defense" presentation. Under average class conditions, particularly when the presentation has been prepared by a younger pupil, it will be much briefer and contain a good deal less detail. Following then is a possible "Self-defense" by Abraham:

ABRAHAM: Thank you, my good neighbors, for having come to greet me on my return from the war. You know that I am a man of peace. I have always lived at peace with you, my Canaanite neighbors. But, when the messenger came and told me how the four kings came and invaded the territory of our neighbors and took many of them captive, among them Lot, the son of my brother, I had no choice but to go to their rescue. You remember what happened then, for some of you came to my aid, especially Aner, Eshkol, and Mamre, for which I will ever thank you. I took three hundred and eighteen of my young men and pursued the enemy. The chase took me to the North of our land past Dan, as far as Hovah near Damascus. There, in the middle of the night, my forces joined battle with the enemy. The Lord on High came to my aid. I defeated the enemy. I freed my brother's son Lot, and all the others who had been taken captive. When I returned victorious, the king of Sodom came out to greet me and Melchizedek, the king of Jerusalem, who is also a priest of the Lord on High, came out toward me with bread and wine. The priest-king gave me his blessing and the king of Sodom offered me all the wealth I had re-captured from the enemy. "Give me back the people and you take the wealth," said the king of Sodom. What would you have done, my neighbors? Do I need the possessions of the people of Sodom? The Creator has blessed me with great wealth. How much does one man need? I came to their rescue because an invader had attacked them. It was important that the enemies from outside our land learn that they cannot invade us or our neighbors without being punished. If I accepted a reward now for having done my duty, they would say that I fought this war for wealth and not to protect my neighbors. If I took the riches of the king of Sodom, they would say, "The king of Sodom made Abraham wealthy and not the One God whom Abraham serves." So I turned to the king of Sodom and said to him, "I lift up my hand to the Lord, God on High, Creator of the heavens and the earth, and swear that I shall not take even a piece of thread or a shoelace from you, so that you may never be able to say, 'I made Abraham rich.' "

6. The Class Acts

The students who have taken the role of the people before whom the historic character offers his defense, in this case Abraham's Canaanite neighbors, are encouraged to ask questions and make comments regarding the story:

CHAIRMAN: We have heard our neighbor Abraham's story. Do any of you now have anything to say to him or any questions to ask him?

CANAANITE 1: Tell us, Abraham, would you have gone to the help of the five kings, your neighbors, if your brother's son were not among the captives?

ABRAHAM: Yes, I would.

CANAANITE 1: Why? For what reason?

ABRAHAM: The five kings whom I helped are my neighbors. I had a duty to help them. What's more—if I allowed my neighbors to be attacked today, who knows if I myself might not be attacked tomorrow? Our enemies must learn that we all are together, ready at all times to defend each other.

CHAIRMAN: Any other questions?

CANAANITE 2: I have a question. Abraham, why did you refuse any reward? Didn't you have expenses in connection with the fight?

ABRAHAM: Of course I did. I had to feed my young men during the campaign. For this I did accept payment from the king of Sodom.

CANAANITE 3: What about the other clans who went with you? Did you forbid them to accept a reward?

ABRAHAM: No, I did not. The clans of Aner, Eshkol, and Mamre came with me and helped me in the fight. They accepted a reward from the king of Sodom.

CANAANITE 4: Why did you let them accept when you refused?

ABRAHAM: I had no right to tell them what to do. I have the right to refuse to accept payment for helping my neighbor. I have no right to tell others what to do.

CHAIRMAN: Are there any other questions? None? Then the Self-defense of Abraham is finished. Thank you Abraham for your fine presentation and thank you Canaanite neighbors for your intelligent questions.

7. Discussion of the Presentation

After words of praise for the participants, the teacher leads the class in a discussion of the contents of the presentation. Some questions are asked in order to determine whether the students have learned the *facts* of the story. The teacher is careful to avoid making of this an examination. After a few questions of this nature, the teacher leads the class in an analytical discussion, evaluating the acts of the characters in the story. The discussion is stimulated by means of provocative questions such as:

Was Abraham right in refusing a reward?
Why?
Should the king of Sodom have insisted?

8. Generalizing and Relating to Students' Experiences

This is probably the most significant aspect of any lesson. It is certainly so in a history lesson. Having learned the facts and analyzed the actions and motivations of the characters, the teacher guides the class in learning to give general application to the history lesson and to relate it especially to the pupils' own experiences. This may be done in a variety of ways. Following are some suggestions:

a. By teacher's summary

The teacher summarizes the lesson by pointing out general principles inherent in it and their relevancy to the students' own problems and experiences. This is done somewhat as follows:

TEACHER: Most of us, like Abraham, are called upon from time to time to make similar decisions. You are walking down the street and you see two boys teasing a younger child. Should you walk on, minding your own business, or should you help the younger child? Abraham, with a fairly small group of fighters, engaged in battle an army much larger than his in order to help his neighbors. Evidently Abraham felt that a human being has a duty to help the weak and the oppressed. What is *your* duty toward the little boy?

You are walking along the street. A car whose driver has the green light begins to cross the intersection. From a side street comes a speeding automobile, jumps the red light and crashes into the first car injuring the driver. People come running. You were the only witness. Should you give your name and risk having to waste many days later going to court or, should you walk on, minding your own business. Abraham evidently felt that we cannot mind our own business when some one else will suffer by it.

You helped the child and his mother offers you a reward; you gave your name as a witness, lost a lot of time from your work and play going to court, and the injured motorist offers you a reward; or, you did any other thing that helps your neighbor such as returning a lost piece of jewelry, you helped a neighbor clean his yard, you helped him shovel snow, and you are offered a reward. Should you accept it? Should you refuse it? What can you learn from Abraham about this? Abraham refused to take anything from the king of Sodom for doing his duty. Are you to do the same? Think about it.

b. By class discussion

The teacher leads the class in a discussion which develops the general application of ethical principles inherent in the story and their application to the students' experiences. The teacher emphasizes personal experiences of the students which parallel those of the historic character. Following are some sample questions which might activate this type of discussion:

Did any of you have an experience similar to that of Abraham? Can you recollect an occasion when you saw someone weaker than you needing help? What did you do? Tell us about it.

Were you ever offered payment for being helpful to someone?
Did it ever happen to someone you know? Tell us about it. What did he do? Did he accept or refuse the payment? Why?

In the light of the story that we just saw enacted would you, if you were he, now act differently? Why?

Should people always come to the help of others? Are there any exceptions? Should it make a difference if those in need of help are our relatives? Should it be different with strangers?

Should we refuse to accept payment for helping others? Can you think of occasions that would be exceptions?

c. *By means of socio-drama*

General principles and relevancy might be highlighted by means of socio-drama techniques. Detailed steps in the use of this technique are given in the section "Socio-Drama for Teaching Bible." Following are general suggestions:

The teacher poses a problem-situation which might arise in the normal, everyday experiences of a student paralleling that of the historical character. For example:

TEACHER: We have listened to Abraham explaining his actions and giving his reasons why he came to the aid of the five kings and why he refused a reward. Many of us often face similar situations. Let us take for example the following imaginary situation:

> William is on his way from school. He is hurrying because he wants to see his favorite television program which is about to begin. As he comes near his house he sees a man standing beside his stalled automobile. The man calls William over and explains to him that he is out of gasoline. Since he has a sprained left ankle, he finds it hard to walk. He asks William to go to the nearest gas station and bring him some gasoline. "Look," the man says, "I will give you a half a dollar for your trouble." "I don't know," William answers him. "There is a television program that goes on in a few minutes. I don't know, mister . . ."
>
> What is William to do? Should he go and miss the program? If he goes, should he accept the reward? Supposing we act this out and see what happens.

The teacher now chooses one student to play the role of William and another to play the role of the motorist.

The two act out the story beginning with the point where the man asks for help. The enactment is brief, taking no more than a minute or two. For example:

MOTORIST: What's your name, son?
WILLIAM: William.
MOTORIST: Would you do me a favor, please?
WILLIAM: I'll try. What is it?
MOTORIST: I'm out of gas.
WILLIAM: There's a gas station two blocks down.
MOTORIST: I know. But I have a sprained left ankle. It's hard for me to walk. Would you bring me a gallon of gas so I can get started?
WILLIAM: Well . . . I don't know . . . you see . . .
MOTORIST: I'll give you fifty cents for your trouble.
WILLIAM: It isn't the money, mister. There's a program I want to see. It goes on in a minute. Can you wait until it's over?
MOTORIST: I have a very important business appointment down town. I'm already late.
WILLIAM: Oh, all right. I'll go.
MOTORIST: Good. Here's some money for the gas. And here's half a dollar for you.
WILLIAM: No, thanks.
MOTORIST: Why not?
WILLIAM: You need help, mister. So I'm going. Not for your money. I'll be right back.

The enactment might not end this way. The student playing William might decide to solve the problem this way:

MOTORIST: I have an important business appointment down town. I'm already late.

WILLIAM: I'm sorry. Your appointment is important for you. My program is important for me. If you're still here when it's over, I'll go. So long, mister.

Or this way:

MOTORIST: Good. Here's some money for the gas and here's half a dollar for you.

WILLIAM: Thanks, mister. I can use it. I'll be right back.

After the enactment, the class discusses the manner in which the role players solved the problems in the dramatization. General principles are then drawn from the enactment and the discussion.

Following are several additional examples of possible "Self-defense" presentations dramatizing historical characters involved in controversial situations:

ONE OF THE TWELVE SPIES OF MOSES

The Setting

The class is a group of Israelites in the desert belonging to one particular tribe—say Shimon. It is several nights after the spies have returned from Canaan and given their reports. Now a spy belonging to their tribe, one Shafat ben Hori, appears before them to explain his actions and to defend his position.

The Enactment

CHAIRMAN: Fellow classmates: Again we go back in history, thousands of years ago. Now we are Israelites of the tribe of Shimon in the desert. A few days ago the twelve spies whom Moses our leader had sent to Canaan returned with a very disturbing report. Now it is night and we of the tribe of Shimon have gathered to listen to one of the spies, a member of our tribe. You all know him—Shafat ben Hori.

SHAFAT: Hear me my brothers! Listen to me, my tribe Shimon! Why blame me for all that happened? For years I have been the head of our tribe. I fulfilled my duties faithfully. None of you ever had reason to complain against me. Then Moses chose me to go along with the chiefs of the other eleven tribes to spy out the Land of Canaan. "Go up into the Negev and ascend to the top of the Mountain," he said. "Look over the land. Look over the people. Are they strong, or are they weak? Are they many, or are they few? Is the land good or bad? Are the cities strongly fortified or open camps? Is the land fertile or barren? Does it have trees, or is it treeless?"

Forty days we spied out the land. We brought back samples from the fruit of the land—clusters of grapes so heavy that two men had to carry them on a pole, juicy pomegranates and figs dripping honey. Honestly we reported what we had seen: "Truly the land is fruitful. Truly it is flowing with milk and honey. But the people in it are exceedingly strong." I ask you people of my tribe, what was I to say if not the truth of what I saw? Caleb of the tribe of Judah said to the Children of Israel and to Moses, "Let us go up to the land. Let us take it. We are strong and we can conquer it!" But I and the others knew differently and we told this to Moses. We said, "It is a land that destroys is inhabitants. Giants live in the land. We can not conquer it!" We reported that which we had seen. Were we to hide the truth? Caleb and Joshua were sure that God would help us conquer the Land of Canaan. But, we were not so sure and we had to tell the truth as we saw it. Are we to blame that after hearing our report the people complained against Moses? Is it our fault that God became angry and condemned us to wander in the desert for forty years? All we did was tell the truth as we saw it. Is that wrong? Is that a sin? You be my judges, O people of my tribe of Shimon!

The Class Acts

CHAIRMAN: People of Shimon, you have heard our tribesman Shafat ben Hori. Do any of you have anything to say, any questions to ask?

SHIMONI 1: Would you give us some details of some of the things you saw in Canaan?

SHAFAT: The cities are mighty. They have thick walls around them. The men are giants—tall as tall trees.

SHIMONI 2: Aren't you exaggerating?

SHAFAT: That's what they seemed like to us.

SHIMONI 3: Why did you have to report these things publicly and frighten everybody?

SHAFAT: It's the truth.

SHIMONI 3: Even if it is the truth, why couldn't you report these things to Moses in private?

SHAFAT: It was my duty to let all the people know the truth.

CHAIRMAN: Thank you, Shafat ben Hori for reporting to us. Thank you people of the tribe of Shimon for your polite attention and fine questions.

Discussion of the Presentation

The discussion then centers on the content of the story and the acts of the characters, stimulated by questions such as these:

Did the spies really tell the truth or did they exaggerate?

Should they have kept quiet so as not to frighten the people?

Even if they were sure that everything they said was the truth, should they have told it publicly or should they have reported to Moses in private?

How is it possible for the spies to say one thing and for Caleb and Joshua to say something else that is entirely different?

Generalizing and Relating to Students' Experiences

The differing procedures outlined earlier might be followed using one, several, or all of them. Some provocative questions which might be used are:

In what way were the spies wrong?

Were the Israelites really to blame for becoming discouraged on hearing the report of the spies?

Even if something is true, does a person have to blurt out everything he knows, or is it better to let some things remain unsaid?

Is it possible that the ten spies were right and that Caleb and Joshua were also right? Could there be more than one truth depending on who sees it?

Should a person accept everything he hears, even from a person whom he knows to be honest, and act on it right away as the Israelites did with the spies' report? Or, should a person think things through carefully first?

Has it ever happened to you that someone told you something and you acted on it, only to find out later that he thought he was telling the truth but he was really mistaken? Tell us about it? Would you have acted differently had you known that his information was wrong? What did that experience teach you?

JEROBOAM DIVIDES THE KINGDOM

The Setting

The class assumes the roles of Jeroboam's advisers or "Cabinet." It is immediately after Jeroboam has been proclaimed king of the new Kingdom of Israel which has just been formed by the ten tribes who seceded from the Kingdom of Judah. Jeroboam appears before the advisors to give a report of his actions.

The Enactment

CHAIRMAN: Fellow classmates: Let your imaginations wander back in history. It is the city of Samaria which is soon to be the capital of the newly formed Kingdom of Israel. The new king of Israel, Jeroboam, has appointed all of you to be his advisors or "cabinet" as it would be called nowadays. In a moment he will appear before you to report on his actions up to now. You will please give him your undivided attention. You may take notes, if you wish. When the king has finished, you are each free to make comments or ask questions. Our fellow classmate ______ will portray the role of King Jeroboam of Israel.

JEROBOAM: My advisors! You and all of Israel have proclaimed me king over the ten tribes of Israel. Now our nation has been divided. In Jerusalem, Rehoboam the son of Solomon rules over the Kingdom of Judah, over the tribes of Judah and Benjamin. The other ten tribes of the sons of Jacob now form our Kingdom of Israel. I promise to be a faithful ruler and a just one.

There will be those who will blame me for breaking up the kingdom established by King David. Do not think that I am happy that our nation has been divided. But, what choice did we have? Many years ago, as a young lieutenant serving King Solomon, I saw how he oppressed our people, how he burdened them with taxes, how he took our sons to be soldiers in his armies and our daughters to be servants in his palaces. It was then that the Prophet Ahiyah the Shilonite prophesied that the nation would one day be divided and that I would rule the Kingdom of Israel. It was not my desire to be king. But I could not remain silent while Solomon oppressed our people. Solomon was great and mighty. For speaking against him he tried to take my life. I had to run away to Egypt to save myself. For many years I remained in Egypt. I only came back when you called me back after the death of Solomon, when his son Rehoboam was about to be proclaimed our king.

Even then I would have been a faithful servant to the son of Solomon if he had only shown a little consideration for us, a little understanding. What did we ask of the son of Solomon? All we wanted was that he make our burden a little lighter, that he treat us as free human beings, that he rule over us as God had ordered, as our brother—our king, with love and understanding, not like a tyrant. Was this asking too much? Even the old ministers, King Solomon's advisors told him to speak kindly to us and we would serve him faithfully forever. But no! Rehoboam would not listen to them! Instead he listened to the advice of the young men who had grown up with him, foolish young boys without experience. And what was Rehoboam's answer to our just demands? "My father," he said, "beat you with whips. I shall beat you with scorpions." Only then did we proclaim, "What part have we in David? What portion in the son of Jesse? To your tents, O Israel!"

Only when there was no other way did I agree to the division of the nation. Only after everything else failed, did I accept your offer to become king of the Ten Tribes of Israel. You, my brothers, my advisors, you be my judges! Could I have acted otherwise?

The Class Acts

CHAIRMAN: Are there any questions you would like to ask the king?

ADVISOR 1: Was it really necessary to divide the kingdom? Couldn't we have made peace with Rehoboam and then worked quietly to change his ways?

JEROBOAM: We could not. Remember his answer! If we had given in, things would have been even worse for us.

ADVISOR 2: After all, Rehoboam is young. Isn't it possible he would have changed his ways when he got older?

JEROBOAM: I doubt it. Anyway, with his answer he left us no choice.

ADVISOR 3: Are you going to keep the nation divided, or will you work toward making peace with Rehoboam?

JEROBOAM: If Rehoboam wants peace, he shall have it.

ADVISOR 4: Does that mean that we would go back and become a part of the Kingdom of Judah once again?

JEROBOAM: It does not mean that all. We can never go back. The Kingdom of Israel is here to stay.

ADVISOR 5: The Torah requires us to make a pilgrimage to the Temple in Jerusalem three times a year. Now that the nation is divided and Jerusalem is the capital of Judah, how will we be able to do what the Torah requires of us? Have you any suggestions, O king?

JEROBOAM: We will find a way. After all the Torah requires us to visit the Lord's Temple. It does not say where. It does not mention Jerusalem.

ADVISOR 5: Would you set up a Temple to rival Jerusalem?

JEROBOAM: Perhaps. After all, there are other holy places in the Land of Israel besides Jerusalem. There's Dan. There's Beth-el. We shall see.

The Class-Advisors need not limit themselves to questions. They may comment. They may even take a position and argue one side of the problem or the other. For example:

ADVISOR 1: If you will forgive me, King Jeroboam, I would like to speak my mind, if I may.

JEROBOAM: Go ahead. Speak.

ADVISOR 1: I think we have made a serious mistake. To divide the nation means weakening it. Our enemies are just waiting for a chance to attack us. United we could stand up against them. Divided we are in danger of being destroyed.

ADVISOR 2: You are wrong. After all, we are ten tribes—strong enough to stand up against most of our enemies.

ADVISOR 3: Most, but not all. When we were united under King Solomon, all our enemies feared us. I think it would have been much better if we had been more patient with Rehoboam.

ADVISOR 4: If you like Rehoboam so much, then why don't you join him?

ADVISOR 3: I didn't say I like Rehoboam.

ADVISOR 4: You certainly did!

CHAIRMAN: Peace, now! Do not quarrel.

ADVISOR 2: There's no sense talking about being patient. We were patient with Solomon for many years and where did it get us?

JEROBOAM: There is no sense talking about what is past. Let us go on with building the Kingdom.

CHAIRMAN: Thank you, King Jeroboam for making things clear for us. Thank you Royal Advisors for your questions and your comments.

Discussion of the Presentation

The discussion analyzes the basic problems presented. It is stimulated by questions of this nature:

Do you agree with Jeroboam that there was no other way of dealing with the problem than by dividing the kingdom?

Should Jeroboam have submitted to Rehoboam for the sake of national unity?

Would you say that Jeroboam was a patriot, or was he rather a vain person, seeking power and glory?

Generalizing and Relating to Students' Experience

After the discussion of the presentation, the teacher helps the students to generalize the basic principles involved and to apply them to their own experiences and needs by utilizing one or more of the following approaches:

a. Teacher's summary

TEACHER: History has taught us how wrong Jeroboam really was. The nation was divided into two kingdoms. As one great kingdom they were strong and powerful. They were able to fight off the attacks of their enemies. As two small nations they fell victim to every ambitious conqueror. In the end, the Kingdom of Israel was destroyed by the Assyrians, its ten tribes driven into exile and finally lost to the Jewish people altogether. The Kingdom of Judah too, was finally destroyed by the Babylonians.

Wouldn't it have been better if Jeroboam and his followers had been more patient with young King Rehoboam?

Very often we find ourselves in a similar position. Some one commits an injustice against us. We know we are being treated unfairly. Should we always fight back, or is it wiser to be patient, control our anger and try to change the situation in a peaceful way?

You sit down at the table on Friday night. Your little sister across the table kicks your foot. You know she did it deliberately. What should you do? You can kick her foot in retaliation. Then she'll kick you again, then you'll kick back and, before you now it, there is a big fight, both of you expect your parents to take sides, everybody is upset and the whole Sabbath is ruined. Or, you might say to yourself, "Sure my sister is wrong. But, she's younger and doesn't know any better. It will be much better if I let this injustice go by for the sake of a quiet, peaceful Sabbath meal."

Jeroboam fought an injustice by committing a greater injustice. The result was a great catastrophe for the Jewish people.

b. Class discussion

Similar ideas to those expressed in the teacher's summary might be brought out through class discussion stimulated by questions like the following:

Did any of you ever have an experience similar to that of Jeroboam and the ten tribes of Israel? Can you remember an occasion when someone treated you unjustly and you had to decide what to do about it? Tell us about it.

What did you do then? Why?

Did you ever find yourself in a position where you gave in to someone else, even though you were right? Tell us about it. Why did you give in? Would you act the same way now? Why?

Should people always fight back when they are treated unjustly?

Are there any exceptions?

Can you think of any?

c. Socio-drama

Following is a possible use of socio-drama for generalization and relevancy:

TEACHER: You heard Jeroboam and his reasons for dividing the Jewish nation. We know now what a mistake that was. Jeroboam corrected an injustice of the moment. But his actions eventually led to the destruction of both kingdoms. Many of us often face Jeroboam's choice: When we are treated badly, should we always stand up for our rights and fight back, or should we stop to think whether fighting back would not lead to greater difficulty? Take this situation, for example:

Daniel's parents and Walter's parents each had a summer cottage on the lake. All summer long, both Daniel and Walter spent their time riding their motorboats or fishing. There were two spots on the lake where the fishing was unusually good. Daniel picked one for himself and Walter picked the other. Not that Daniel couldn't use Walter's fishing spot or Walter Daniel's. It's just that each boy preferred his own place for fishing. By mutual agreement, neither boy rode his motorboat over the other's fishing spot so as not to chase away the fish.

One day the boys had a quarrel. The next morning, when Daniel looked across at the lake, he saw that Walter was driving his motorboat back and forth, back and forth over his fishing ground. Daniel grew very angry. "Look mother," he cried out. "Walter is ruining my fishing spot. He's doing this on purpose. I'll fix him. If he can ruin my fishing spot, I can do the same to him!"

He began to run for his own motorboat. "Wait, Daniel!" His mother called to him. "Don't be foolish!" "But look, mother, look what he's doing!"

Mother tried to stop him and argued with him. She tried to convince him that . . .

Now, instead of me telling you what mother said and what Daniel said and what he finally did, let's act it out and see what happens.

Two students are selected—one to play the mother, the other to play Daniel. They begin to act out the story at the point where Daniel sees what Walter is doing.

DANIEL: Mother! Look what Walter is doing. He's driving his motorboat over my fishing spot. He'll chase away all the fish. He'll ruin it. I'll fix him. I'll get even with him right now.
MOTHER: Daniel! What are you going to do?
DANIEL: I'll get my motorboat and drive it right over Walter's fishing spot.
MOTHER: That's awfully silly, Daniel.
DANIEL: If he can ruin my spot, I can ruin his.
MOTHER: And then there won't be any good fishing spot on the lake at all.
DANIEL: I don't care.
MOTHER: O yes, you do. You love to fish.
DANIEL: But he's already ruined my spot.
MOTHER: But you can fish at his spot. It doesn't belong to him, you know.

DANIEL: I know. But why should I let him get away with it?

MOTHER: So you want to cut off your nose to spite your face?

DANIEL: But if I don't get even with him, he'll think he can walk all over me.

MOTHER: What if he does? You just keep away from him for a while. Walter is no fool. He'll realize pretty soon how wrong he was and he'll be coming to beg your pardon and make up.

DANIEL: But look, mother. . . .

MOTHER: All right. . . . Supposing you get even with him. Then he'll get mad and look for a way to hurt you, then you'll try to hurt him back and you'll be spending the whole summer looking for ways to hurt each other instead of having fun. Forget it, Daniel. Go read your book.

DANIEL: All right, mother. I guess you're right.

The enactment might end quite differently. The boy playing Daniel might say at the very end:

DANIEL: I don't want to read my book. I'm sorry, mother, but I'm just not going to let anybody walk over me. I'm going to get my boat.

From the discussion of the way the role players solved the problem general principles are drawn as guides for personal conduct.

■ D. PRESS CONFERENCE

The press conference is a technique which has long been used by public figures to present their activities and points of view before the general public. A group of reporters representing various newspapers, wire services, and more recently radio and television stations and networks, meet a public figure. The public figure makes a brief prepared statement. The reporters then proceed to ask him all kinds of questions regarding his activities, plans, etc. Thereafter the correspondents write up their reports of the press conference, describing the scene, the appearance of the public figure, and a summary of the questions and answers in such form as to present a complete and unified story.

This device is used particularly by public figures when they are to make, or have just made a crucial decision and are anxious to present the background and the reasons for their decision before the public. The President of the United States, having decided on a new course in foreign policy, calls in the correspondents for a press conference. Briefly he explains his decision. The correspondents question him about a variety of aspects dealing with his decision—the historical background, his reasons, possible effect on future foreign policy, possible reaction by other nations, etc. The articles which the correspondents then write present before the public a well-rounded report on the crucial decision. A popular movie star from Europe arrives to begin work on a new picture. She uses the press conference as a vehicle for alerting the public to the event and incidentally for continuing to keep herself in the public eye.

Teachers will find the press conference technique a useful tool in teaching history. By means of dramatization a historical character to be studied is brought to life at a decisive moment in his career. At an imaginary press conference he is faced by "a group of correspondents" who question him about his problem and his decision. During the questioning a good deal of background information about the historical character is brought out in a living and vital manner. Following are some examples of such situations:

> Moses has arrived in Egypt and is about to appear before Pharaoh to demand freedom for the Children of Israel.
>
> Samuel has passed over all the princes of Israel and has just chosen Saul, a simple farm boy, to be king of Israel.
>
> Elijah has just prophesied punishment for King Ahab for taking Naboth's vineyard.
>
> Jeremiah has just been arrested for prophesying the destruction of Jerusalem.
>
> Menasseh ben Israel is about to appear before Oliver Cromwell to request that the Jews be permitted to return to England.
>
> Asher Levy comes out of Council House in New Amsterdam following his demand of Governor Stuyvesant that Jews be permitted to stand guard in the colony.
>
> Theodor Herzl in Jerusalem is about to meet the German Kaiser.
>
> Chaim Weizmann has just been sworn in as the first president of the State of Israel.

The utilization of this technique requires a good deal of independent research and planning on the part of the students. It is implemented through a series of well-defined steps.

Introducing the Technique

The teacher about to utilize the technique of "Press Conference" for the first time introduces it and explains its operation to the class somewhat as follows:

TEACHER: Public figures such as the President of our country, mayor of our city, a senator, a movie star, or a great industrialist very often use the press conference as a means of presenting their acts and the reasons for these acts to the general public. Such public figure will meet with correspondents from the newspapers, TV and radio. He will tell them of his plans. They ask questions which he answers. Thereafter the correspondents write up a report of what they saw and heard. The following day we read it as news in our newspapers, hear it on radio, or see it on TV.

In our next lesson in history, we will learn about (Moses, or Jeremiah, or Herzl, etc.). Instead of learning about this historical character in the usual way, we will use the "Press Conference" idea to find out all we want to know about him. Through dramatization we will bring to life our historical character and the period in which he lived. One of us will portray him (Moses, or Jeremiah, or Herzl, etc.), while some other students in the class will act the roles of correspondents. A week from now (or any other period which the teacher may designate) our historical character ——— will come into this classroom and face the "correspondents" in a press conference. This press conference will be held at a very decisive moment in the career of our hero (Judah Maccabee as he is about to rededicate the Temple, Rabbi Judah Hanasi as he is about to begin codifying the Mishnah, etc.). He will tell us a little about himself and his project. Our correspondents will ask him questions. The rest of the class will be the audience watching the press conference. Members of the audience too will be permitted to ask questions from time to time.

After the press conference the correspondents will each write up individual reports of what has been said and discussed. These reports will later be (read before the class and discussed; displayed as part of our class newspaper; the best ones published in school newspaper; etc.).

Although the term "Correspondents" is used for a "Press Conference" dramatization of comparatively recent periods in history, its use in connection with more remote historical periods, before the development of newspapers, would be anachronistic and jarring. For such periods we would use types of characters who would then have been the normal disseminators of news in their community. For example:

Moses—a chief of the Levites, head of the brick makers, a delegate chosen by the Israelite women, several elders, etc.

Jeremiah—heads of the various workers' guilds of Jerusalem such as the bakers, the tanners, the cobblers, etc.; a leading *Kohen;* one of the Egyptian party in the king's court, etc.

Similarly, the very term "Press Conference" might be replaced with one that is more fitting for the period such as "*Kinus* of the elders" or "*Asefah* of the *Roshei Kahal,*" etc.

If the dramatization deals with such a period, the teacher would make this clear in the introduction as follows:

TEACHER: Since in this period of history there were no newspapers, we will use in place of correspondents characters who usually brought the news to their communities at that time, such as: the local priest, a leading merchant, etc. Also, we will call our conference with Moses a *Kinus* (or gathering) of the Elders. These people will ask the questions during the *Kinus* and will afterwards prepare the reports.

The teacher then proceeds with the normal introduction:

TEACHER: Naturally, if the correspondents (or Elders, or *Roshei Kahal,* etc.), are to ask intelligent questions, they must know quite a bit about the character they are to question—his biography, the period in which he lived, the immediate situation in which he finds himself when we are to interview him, etc. The one among us who will play the historical character who is holding the press conference (or, will be questioned at the *Kinus* of the Elders, the *Asefah* of the *Roshei Kahal*, etc.) will, of course, have to know even more about him so that he may act his part convincingly and answer questions with knowledge and intelligence. You can find this information in the reference books which you see on my desk now. I prepared a list of the exact chapters dealing with the subject. I also prepared an additional list of references which you can find in our school library. I would advise you to read those also, if you have time.

The above general introduction will be necessary only the first time that the "Press Conference" technique is used. At that time it takes the place of the first step—Teacher's Introduction (or Motivation).

Whenever the technique is used thereafter, this general introduction will of course on longer be necessary since the students will be familiar with its method of operation. The teacher will begin directly with the subject to be dramatized as hereafter indicated.

The Process

It is to be noted once again that although actual words for the various teacher presentations are here given, they are merely indicative of what might be covered by the teacher and only suggest possible ways of presentation. They are definitely not intended as models and certainly *not as "scripts" to be used directly by the teacher. As a matter of fact, they are, in nearly all instances, much too lengthy for actual use.* Since they are intended as guides, they attempt to be inclusive of many contingencies. The actual introductions, explanations, and comments of the teacher will be much, much briefer, if the risk of losing the students' interest is to be avoided.

The steps used in the "Press Conference" are as follows:

1. Teacher's Introduction (or Motivation)
2. Selection of Cast
3. Preliminary Research
4. Staff Briefing Session
5. Subject's Briefing Session
6. Summary Research
7. The Enactment
8. Class Discussion of the Dramatization
9. Reports are Prepared
10. Reports are Read and Class Discusses the Subject.

Some of the steps may need one or several days for their execution. Others are executed along with several other steps during the same session. Following is a detailed development of each of the above steps, utilizing the character of Jeremiah by way of illustration:

1. Teacher's Introduction

The teacher introduces the subject of the forthcoming press conference somewhat as follows:

TEACHER: We now come in our study of history to a very sad period of Jewish life, the downfall of the First Jewish Commonwealth and the destruction of the Temple in Jerusalem by the Babylonians.

One of the giant figures of that period was the Prophet Jeremiah. Jeremiah was important not only at that time. To this very day we feel the influence of his acts and his teachings. Naturally we want to learn all we can about him and the times in which he lived. So we will try to bring him and his period to life by means of a dramatization. We will conduct in our class an *Asefat Am* a meeting of representatives of the people of Jerusalem with the Prophet Jeremiah. Nowadays we would call it a press conference. The time will be just before Jeremiah is placed in prison by King Zedekiah.

For those of you who will take part in this dramatization, I have placed on my desk a number of reference books. You may borrow these books and read the sections which I have indicated. Each one of you may take one book. When you are finished you may exchange books with the others who are taking part. There is also a list of additional references which you will find in the library. Read those too if you have time.

2. Selecting the Cast

The teacher asks for volunteers to play the various roles. The teacher explains the function of each as he is selected. Generally the following will be necessary.

a. *The Historical Character or Subject*—this is naturally the most important role in the dramatization. It is necessary that the person playing this role know as much as possible about the historical character he is to portray—his family background; his activities leading up to the "moment of decision" for which the press conference has been called; the problems he faced and the manner in which he solved them; the social, political and economic conditions under which he lived; etc. Some teachers who have utilized this technique felt that the first few times it is tried, the teacher should personally enact the role of the historical character. After the students have learned to know what is expected, the role is allotted to a student.

In any event, the student who is selected to play the role should be of better than average intelligence, articulate, and of good scholastic achievement.

b. *Advisory Committee*—A statesman or other public figure often works very closely with an advisory committee. This committee does background research for him, acts as a sounding board for his ideas, offers suggestions and in general helps him to formulate policy. The teacher may find it advisable to select an advisory committee of students who will work closely with the one who will portray the historical character, particularly to help with the research. Students who are normally too shy to assume acting roles will be particularly interested in serving on such advisory committees. They will be making a definite contribution toward the dramatization and yet will be spared from acting in public which to them is an ordeal. The Advisory Committee will, during the enactment, sit with the subject and whenever necessary whisper suggestions to him, pass him written notes with information, and be generally helpful.

c. *The Correspondents*—Anywhere from 3 to 10 students are selected to play the role of correspondents. In our example, dealing with Jeremiah, in place of correspondents we will have representative figures such as: Chief of the Bakers' Guild, Chief of the Tanners' Guild, a leading *Kohen*, a representative of the Egyptian Party in the Court, etc. Although in this group too the brighter and more articulate students will be chosen at first, several slower students may also be included from the very beginning. The slower ones will gain confidence from the support which they will receive from the brighter students in the group.

d. *The Chairman*—A student will be selected to act as chairman of the press conference.

The chairman is in a position to affect the proceedings in a way which might spell the difference between success and failure of the project. It is important therefore that the choice of a student for this task be made very carefully. The first few times the technique is used, the teacher, if not acting the role of the hisorial character, might personally assume the role of chairman.

The task of the chairman will be to open the press conference by introducing the character to be interviewed and generally to guide the course of the proceedings so that correspondents will be called upon in proper turn, members of the audience desiring to pose questions will be given an opportunity, etc. Whenever the proceedings lag, the chairman is in a position to revive them. He is able to do so in a number of ways:

> *By pertinent comment such as:* "We know that Jeremiah was finally imprisoned. We must not forget, however, that King Zedekiah tried a number of times to keep the Prophet out of prison, pleaded with him to change his ways, and to stop prophesying the destruction of Jerusalem. Would any of you representatives care to ask Jeremiah why he refused to listen to the king's pleas? I am sure it would be interesting to know his reasons."
>
> *By prodding a forgetful correspondent:* "Chief of the Bakers, aren't you going to ask the Prophet why he refused at first to accept God's mission of prophecy?"
>
> *By jogging the memory of the student playing the Subject:* "If I remember correctly, Prophet Jeremiah, your letter to the exiles in Babylon did a lot to give courage to those Judeans who had been uprooted from their native Jerusalem. I am sure we would all want to know what was in that letter. Do you happen to remember, or shall I read it from this copy that I have here?"
>
> *By correcting errors:* "Excuse me, Prophet Jeremiah, even prophets have a right to make mistakes sometimes. Actually you were not born in Jerusalem, were you? According to the records you were born in the village of Anatot."

Obviously, if a student is to act as chairman, he would have to be quick-witted, articulate, and above all he would have to read up a good deal about his subject.

3. Preliminary Research

The students who have been selected for roles are given several days during which they will do their background reading in the references indicated by the teacher.

4. Staff Briefing Session

Correspondents are sometimes briefed by their editor before going out on an assignment to an important press conference. The editor might indicate to the correspondent the type of questions to be asked. Sometimes the briefing session might involve a number of members of the newspaper staff, who, together with the editor meet with the correspondent prior to the press conference, offering their suggestions for the line of questioning to be followed and even indicating at times specific questions to be asked. Adopting this procedure in our technique will help assure a successful lesson resulting from the simulated press conference.

After the students who are to portray the correspondents have done their preliminary research, the teacher meets with them for about a half hour before or after class. If preferred this session might be made a part of a regular history period involving the entire class which might participate by offering suggestions. They discuss together the questions to be asked. These questions are listed on the blackboard. If, in the opinion of the teacher, the questions suggested are insufficient to elicit the necessary information, the teacher suggests additional questions to be asked. Some of the questions will deal with:

The character's background such as his place of birth, family, family occupation, his current occupation, or position, etc.

The immediate problem regarding which a decision must now be made. (Jeremiah—will he give in to the king or go to prison?)

Why does he now have to make a decision?

The events leading up to this point.

What will his decision be?

What are his reasons?

What does he think the consequences will be?

After all possible questions have been listed, they are divided among the correspondents so that each will have a number of definite questions to ask. The correspondents are free to ask additional questions during the actual press conference as the need may arise.

5. Subject's Briefing Session

The teacher meets with the student who is to play the role of the historical character or subject for a briefing session to prepare him for the press conference. During this session the teacher tries to find out exactly how much the student has learned, as a result of his research, about the character he is to portray. The teacher also corrects any misconceptions, provides additional information on the subject, and helps the student to organize his knowledge so that he will have, in his own mind, a clear-cut conception of the character he is to portray. Where an Advisory Committee has been selected, the members of this committee sit in on this briefing session if possible. Each member of the committee is given an opportunity to report briefly on his research and to present the information which he has gathered. At this session a good deal of attention is paid to the possible motivation for the subject's historic decisions so that when a correspondent asks a question "Why did you . . ." a valid reason will be forthcoming. The members of the committee can be helpful in formulating these reasons. For example: The teacher asks, "Now, supposing a correspondent will ask you, Jeremiah, why did you preach in the streets of Jerusalem that the Judeans should not make a treaty with Egypt, what would your answer be?" The student portraying Jeremiah might say, "Because Babylon was strong and Judah was weak." One of the Advisory Committee might offer the suggestion "Because experience had taught us that Egypt was not to be trusted." Another member of the Advisory Committee might say, "Because Jeremiah felt that the way to safety for Jerusalem lay not in making military alliances with neighboring countries, but in obeying God's commandments." On analysis it might be decided that all of these reasons are valid and Jeremiah is to use all of them in answering the correspondent's question.

The time devoted to this briefing session will vary with the needs. Generally twenty minutes, before or after class, will prove sufficient.

6. Summary Research

At the conclusion of our briefing session, the teacher suggests additional research to Correspondents and Subject in order to augment their information in those areas in which they show themselves to be weak. The students are given a few days for this purpose.

7. The Enactment

The enactment of the Press Conference takes place during the regular history period, about a week after the project has been initiated. The teacher is, of course, free to schedule the enactment sooner or later as may be necessary.

The physical arrangement for the enactment is as follows: The Subject sits in front of the room in the center, facing the class—the audience. Behind him sit the members of his Advisory Committee who will help him during the interview when necessary. Next to the Subject sits the Chairman. The Correspondents sit on both sides of the subject facing both him and the audience.

The enactment proceeds, as follows:

a. *Chairman's introduction*—The Chairman introduces the dramatization and the Subject in general terms, somewhat as follows:

CHAIRMAN: Friends, today we are privileged to witness an important occasion. A moment in history that happened long, long ago will be enacted before our eyes. Characters that are long since dead will be brought to life again so that we may hear about them, their problems, and how they solved them.

The Prophet Jeremiah, played by our fellow student ———, appears before us as if he were alive today facing the questions which representatives of important groups in the City of Jerusalem (or, in the case of a modern personality, "correspondents from the press, radio and television") played by our fellow-students, ———, ———, etc., will put to him.

By way of introduction, Jeremiah was born of a priestly family in the village of Anatot, near Jerusalem. He has been a prophet for many years. Now he is in difficulties with King Zedekiah of Judah. He has been tried by the king and is about to be condemned to prison. The king has offered Jeremiah a way out. We are here to find out what the Prophet will do. My friends, I present to you —the Prophet Jeremiah.

b. *Subject's Introduction*—The historical Subject makes a brief introductory statement. In our hypothetical case it would run somewhat as follows:

JEREMIAH: Thank you. It is not quite true that the choice is up to me. The choice about what I am to do has never been up to me. Long, long ago when I was still a young child, the Lord God said to me "Even before I created you I appointed you, even before you were born I made you holy and dedicated you as a Prophet to the nations," and I pleaded with the Lord God saying "Please Lord God I cannot speak. I am only a child." I did not want to be a prophet then or thereafter. But the choice was not mine. The Lord ordered me to prophesy. I had to obey. I have no choice now either. I must do what God orders me to do.

c. *The Questioning*—The correspondents, or people's representatives, now raise their hands and upon being recognized by the Chairman, put their questions to the Subject. Examples:

BAKER: Jeremiah, we understood that the king did offer you a choice. Is that true?

JEREMIAH: It is true the king offered me a choice. He told me that if I stopped prophesying that Jerusalem is about to be destroyed, I would not have to go to prison. But this is a choice that I am not free to take. The Lord has ordered me to prophesy that the city will be destroyed by the Babylonians, that it will be burned to the ground. I must prophesy the way God ordered me.

KOHEN: Why does not King Zedekiah listen to you then.

JEREMIAH: He is surrounded by men who advise him to make a treaty with Egypt and to fight against Babylon. They tell him that only this way can Jerusalem be saved. But they are wrong and the king is wrong.

EGYPTIAN: Do you think that king Zedekiah should make a treaty with Babylon instead?

JEREMIAH: No! Treaties will not help Jerusalem. Going back to the ways of God will help.

TANNER: Can you tell us a little more about this?

JEREMIAH: Jerusalem has sinned. The inhabitants of Judah have worshipped idols. Its rich men have robbed the poor, the widows and the orphans. Its judges accepted bribes. Babylon has been chosen by God to punish Judah for her sins.

God says to Judah, "Submit to Babylon. Accept your punishment and change your wicked ways."

MERCHANT: Is there no hope then for Judah unless the king listens to you?

JEREMIAH: There is always hope. Even if the king does not listen to me, even if Jerusalem and the Temple are destroyed, there is hope. The Lord told me to prophesy: "I shall bring back the captives of Judah and the exiles of Israel, and I will rebuild them as in the beginning." This is what the Lord said: "There will once again be heard in this place the song of rejoicing, the song of happiness, the song of the groom and the song of the bride, the sound of happy people saying 'Bless you the Lord, for he is good, He is forever merciful.' "

ELDER 1: In your opinion what has brought us to the point where Babylon threatens to destroy us?

JEREMIAH: This began a long time ago when the kings of Judah and the people of Judah abandoned the worship of God. They thought that the Temple would protect them; that it was so holy that it could never be destroyed; and that Judah would never be destroyed because the holy Temple was in it. So they robbed and they cheated and they lied and worshipped strange gods until God, in His anger, said, "I will destroy the Temple. Perhaps then the people of Judah will change their ways."

ELDER 2: Some people say that you are a traitor because you want to see Jerusalem destroyed.

JEREMIAH: I am no traitor. But I would rather see the city destroyed than the people forget the God who brought their forefathers out of Egyptian slavery. Once we were called children of God and Jerusalem the city of God. I would rather see the city destroyed than the children abandon their Heavenly Father.

CHAIRMAN: Is there anyone in the audience that would like to ask a question?
(Students in the audience are given an opportunity to question. Example:)

STUDENT 1: Why did the king's adivsors tell him to trust Egypt?

JEREMIAH: That is hard to say. Some believe that Egypt would be able to help them against Babylon. Others were bribed by Egypt to advise the king this way.

The questions and answers proceed along this line until the time allocated for the dramatization is over, or until the chairman or teacher feels that the subject has been exhausted.

8. Class Discusses the Dramatization

When the dramatization is concluded, a few minutes are allocated for a discussion by the class. The teacher is careful to point out the praiseworthy aspects such as the fine way in which the Subject acquitted himself, the clarity of his answers, the probing questions of the Correspondents, etc. If time permits, substantive aspects of the dramatization are considered such as the validity of the Subject's answers, how convincing were the reasons which he gave, etc.

9. Reports Are Prepared

The teacher now informs the correspondents that they will each be given several days (or, until the next history lesson) during which they will prepare their written reports of the press conference. They are to read these reports to the class during the next history lesson. At that time the class will be given an opportunity to discuss the correspondents' reports as well as the actions of the Subject, the historical events in which he was involved, the behavior of the other historical characters that affected the Subject's actions, etc. An opportunity will also be given to the students to compare the answers given by the Subject during the interview with the facts as they are described in the history book.

The teacher points out to the class that in order to participate intelligently in the discussion every student will do well now to read or reread in the history book the lesson dealing with the Subject, and perhaps even some additional collateral reading.

10. Reports Are Read and Class Discusses the Subject

The reports of the correspondents are read to the class. Thereafter the class discusses the reports as well as the entire area under consideration in the light of their reading of the lesson in the history book.

The teacher then summarizes the entire lesson in the usual way.

Following are several additional examples of Press Conferences with historical figures:

DON JOSEPH NASI

1. Teacher's Introduction

TEACHER: In the dark period of rule by the Inquisition, the deeds of one family, Mendes-Nasi shined forth as a beacon. Great merchants, statesmen and bankers, they defied the Inquisition successfully. Outstanding among them is the romantic figure of Don Joseph Nasi—a Marrano who returned to his faith and made the first attempt, since the fall of Bar Kokhba in the Second Century of the Common Era, to resettle the land of Israel and re-establish there a Jewish life. Next week we will bring Don Joseph Nasi to life in our classroom by dramatizing a conference with him. He will be questioned by representatives of different groups who have a special interest in his daring scheme to resettle the land of Israel. Who do you think they should be? Any suggestions?

2. Selecting the Cast

STUDENT 1: The Venetian merchants had many difficulties with the Mendes-Nasi family. How about an agent representing them?

TEACHER: *(Writes on the blackboard) Venetian.* Who else.

STUDENT 2: The Turkish Jews living in Constantinople would be interested. How about one representing them?

TEACHER: Fine! *(Writes on blackboard) Turkish Jew.* Who else?

STUDENT 3: How about someone representing the Marrano Jews?

TEACHER: *(Writes on blackboard) Marrano.* Any other suggestions?

STUDENT 4: How about a delegate from the Arabs living in Palestine? Their interest would be affected.

TEACHER: *(Writes on blackboard) An Arab.* No others?

STUDENT 5: If Don Joseph Nasi was a Marrano from Portugal, we should have someone from the Portugese Embassy in Constantinople.

TEACHER: *(Writes on blackboard)* All right. A *Portuguese.* Now we will need someone to play Don Joseph Nasi, a few to serve as his advisors, and a chairman.

STUDENT 6: I think the chairman should be called the Major Domo. At that time all great nobles had a Major Domo.

TEACHER: *(Writes on blackboard)* Fine! a *Major Domo.*

STUDENT 7: Maybe we ought to have two Subjects to be interviewed. After all Dona Gracia was just as important as Don Joseph. *(Some students might agree. Some might object that it would complicate matters. A decision is finally made whether only one or two subjects should be interviewed. The cast is now selected.)*

Steps **3, 4, 5, 6** are followed in the manner previously indicated.

7. The Enactment

MAJOR DOMO: The noble lord, Don Joseph Nasi, Duke of Naxos, has graciously consented to appear before us and answer questions about his plan to rebuild the city of Tiberias and settle Jews there. I present to you Don Joseph Nasi, played by ______.

He will be questioned by a Venetian, played by ______, a Turkish Jew representing the Jewish Community of Constantinople, played by ______, etc.

JOSEPH NASI: *(Rises and makes his opening statement).* The Almighty has been good to me and to my family. We were born in Portugal and brought up as Marranos. I might have shared the same fate that befell so many of my brothers—to be caught by the Inquisition, tortured and killed for practicing secretly my Jewish faith. Instead my family and I managed to escape and to take with us a good part of our fortune. We have prospered as bankers and merchants. I have been raised to a position higher than that ever reached by any Jew before me, and now I have the privilege of doing something for my brothers and for the Land of Israel. In the land of my fathers which has been desolate for many centuries, I plan to establish once again a Jewish community.

TURKISH JEW: Can you tell us a little more about these plans?

JOSEPH NASI: Gladly. I plan to rebuild the city of Tiberias on the shores of Lake Kinneret in the Land of Israel. There, I will settle Jews who will earn their living as artisans and as merchants. On the outskirts of the city I will have farms and vineyards and groves of mulberry trees.

VENETIAN: Mulberry trees?

JOSEPH NASI: Of course. The mulberry trees are necessary for the silk worms which we will raise there. I plan to establish a silk weaving industry in Tiberias.

VENETIAN: I don't believe that the Venetian merchants whom I represent will be very happy about this. If you manufacture silks in your new settlement, you will be competing with us. Have you thought about that, Don Joseph?

JOSEPH NASI: Of course I did. I am a banker and merchant. I always think about possible competition. But the demand for silk is great enough to provide business for Venice and for Tiberias as well.

ARAB: What of the Arabs that are now living in and around Tiberias? How will they be affected by your plans?

NASI: Very well, I think. If we need any of their land, we will pay them for it. Our industry will bring prosperity to the area so that the Arabs too will benefit.

ARAB: Speaking for the Arabs, I am sure that most of them will welcome Jewish settlers. But I know there are many among them who are hotheads and who want to keep things just as they are. I wouldn't put it past them if they attack your settlers and . . .

NASI: Are you threatening us?

ARAB: Well, not exactly.

NASI: We have no fear of your hotheads. We will fortify Tiberias and defend it. We will build a wall around it strong enough to withstand any of your attacks.

ARAB: That would be just about the worst thing that you could do. If you fortify Tiberias . . .

NASI: Look my friend. I told you that resettling the Jews in the Land of Israel will benefit not only the Jews, but the Arabs as well. We will try to be friendly. But, if your Arabs attack us, we will know how to defend ourselves.

PORTUGESE: Where will you get the settlers?

NASI: From every land where Jews are denied the right to live as Jews. They will come from Venice and Florence, from Spain and Portugal . . .

PORTUGESE: Portugal? We have no Jews in Portugal.

NASI: You have many thousands of Jews in Portugal. They have to hide the fact that they are Jews. They are Marranos—non-Jews in public, Jews in secret. We will rescue them from your hands and bring them to live in peace in the land of their fathers.

TURKISH JEW: There are so many Jews who need to be rescued from persecution and Tiberias can only take in a few thousand at best. Have you greater plans perhaps, Don Joseph?

NASI: Tiberias is only the beginning. If we succeed there, we will open other areas in the Land of Israel to Jewish settlement until the whole land is once more a Jewish homeland.

MAJOR DOMO: Are there any other questions? Does anyone in this audience chamber have any further questions?

(Students are given an opportunity to ask questions. When they are at an end, the Major Domo concludes the conference.)

MAJOR DOMO: There being no further questions, the Conference is at an end. Thank you for your interesting questions and for your attention.

Steps **8, 9, 10** follow as previously indicated.

RABBI ISRAEL BAAL SHEM TOV

1. Teacher's Introduction

TEACHER: In the year 1700, a child was born in the village of Okup near the southern border of Poland. When this child grew up, he changed the lives of thousands of Jews, giving them new hope, a new spirit and a new understanding of how God is to be worshipped. His name was Israel. His followers called him the Baal Shem Tov—The Master of the Good Name. We have had many important historical personalities whom we interviewed in this classroom during our mock press conferences. Next week we shall interview Rabbi Israel Baal Shem Tov. We will make believe that this room is the synagogue in the village of Medzibuz in Poland. Rabbi Israel Baal Shem Tov has just come to our town where he plans to settle permanently. All the inhabitants want to know more about him so we will gather here in the synagogue for a make-believe *Asefah* of the *Roshei Kahal,* a meeting of representatives of the community during which several important men of the town will question him. Who do you suggest should be among the questioners?

STUDENT 1: The Rabbi of the town.

TEACHER: Good! *(Writes on the blackboard) Rabbi (She continues to write on the blackboard the names of the other characters suggested by the students.)* Any others?

STUDENT 2: The president of the *Kehillah.*

STUDENT 3: A member of the Burial Society.

STUDENT 4: I think the merchants of the town should be represented.

TEACHER: That's a good idea. I am sure the merchants should be very interested in this man who planned to settle in their town.

STUDENT 5: I think the working people would also be interested. How about someone representing them like a tailor, or a shoemaker.

TEACHER: Fine! We will also need Rabbi Israel Baal Shem Tov himself, a few of his followers to act as his advisors and, of course a chairman. What do you think we should call our chairman in this dramatization? You remember when we dramatized Don Joseph Nasi, one of you suggested that the chairman be called the Major Domo. Well, you will learn later that rabbis such as the Baal Shem Tov usually had a person who acted as their assistant, agent, manager, and general representative. He was called a *Gabbai.* So, for this dramatized press conference we will have a *Gabbai* as chairman.

The cast is selected. Steps **3, 4, 5, 6** follow in the usual pattern.

7. The Enactment

GABBAI: Friends: Today we are going back in history, almost two hundred and fifty years ago to relive an important moment. This room now becomes the Synagogue of Medzibuz, a small town in Poland. All of you imagine yourselves as Jewish inhabitants of this town. I am the Gabbai, the helper to the great Hassidic Rabbi and teacher, Rabbi Israel Baal Shem Tov, who is seated up here, ready to answer the questions which will be put to him by your representatives.

(The following may be added, if desired)

The part of the Baal Shem Tov is played by ______. His advisors are: ______. ______. He will be questioned by the Rabbi of the town of Medzibuz, played by ______, the President of the *Kehillah*, played by ______, etc.

(The Gabbai then continues)

After your representatives have asked their questions, you, the citizens of Medzibuz, will also be given an opportunity to ask questions should you have any. We will now hear an opening statement from Rabbi Israel Baal Shem Tov whom many call simply the Besht.

BESHT: *(Rises, stands before the class and makes his opening statement)* Honored Rabbi, Jews of Medzibuz: From my earliest childhood I learned many things which I hoped to teach to my brother Jews some day. But I felt that before I could become a teacher to others, I must learn a great deal more myself—and so I waited. I have now reached my thirty-sixth birthday. The time has now come to proclaim to the world that which I learned about the world and about the Almighty who created it. I have therefore decided to settle in your town, with your permission and with the permission of your Rabbi, and to teach these things to all who will care to listen and learn.

RABBI: All that one needs to learn is written in the Holy Books. Tell me, what can you teach that is not already to be found in the sacred writings?

BESHT: I will teach our people that the Almighty is not only the Creator and the Judge of the world, but also the Father of all Creation.

PRES. OF KEHILLAH: Every learned Jew knows that.

BESHT: But there are many Jews who are not learned. There are tailors and cobblers and small merchants who work all day and far into the night to earn a livelihood. They never had a chance to acquire learning.

TAILOR: You mean that even the ignorant can worship God?

BESHT: What a question! Of course! Everyone can worship God if he loves God with all his heart and with all his soul.

COBBLER: How are we to do this? If I, a cobbler or my friend here, a tailor are too ignorant to worship God by study, how are we to serve Him? Are we then to fast and torment our bodies?

BESHT: No. God does not want our suffering. God is best served with our love—with our joy. When we sing a song of praise to Him, we are worshipping our Heavenly Father. When we dance with joy because of our great love for Him, we serve Him and give honor to His glory.

MERCHANT: I am a plain merchant. I find this hard to understand. You mean that by singing and dancing we give honor to Heaven?

BESHT: To our Heavenly Father. Not to Heaven.

COBBLER: But that's where God is—in heaven. Our Rabbi told us . . .

BESHT: No, my son. God is to be found everywhere. Wherever you turn, you will find His glory. The "Sparks of God" are to be found in every tree, in every stone, in every blade of grass. That is the meaning of the saying in the Bible: "*M'lo khol ho-oretz k'vodo*—the whole earth is full of His glory."

CHAIRMAN OF BURIAL SOCIETY: Why did you decide to settle in our town, Rabbi Israel?

BESHT: Because in this town and in the towns all around yours, there are thousands of Jews who are in need of my help to bring them nearer to God.

PRESIDENT OF KEHILLAH: You were not born near our town, were you?

BESHT: No. I was born in Okup in the Carpathian Mountains.

PRESIDENT OF KEHILLAH: If you are to live among us, we should know more about you. Won't you please tell us a little about yourself?

BESHT: There is not much to tell. As a young child I lost both my parents. I earned my livelihood as a lime-digger, as an inn-keeper, and, when I was very young, as a teacher's helper. I remember I used to take my pupils for walks in the woods and in the mountains. There, my little pupils and I learned together to love our Father the Creator. The birds sang to us of the glory of the Creator. The brook whispered to us of His loving kindness.

CHAIRMAN OF BURIAL SOCIETY: You mean to tell us that you wasted your pupils' time walking through the woods? What about learning, study? Have they no importance at all? Is that what you mean to tell us?

BESHT: I mean no such thing. A Jew, if he is able, should study the Bible, the Talmud, our holy tongue, the lessons of our sages. But, even if he is unable to study, he still has a share in Jewish life. It is this that I will teach in Medzibuz to all who will listen.

GABBAI: Does any one else have any questions? *(He turns to the class.)* Townsmen of Medzibuz?

STUDENT 1: If Medzibuz already has a town Rabbi and you settle here, what will happen to him?

BESHT: He will stay on and fulfill his duties as before—as leader and judge of the community. I am here only to teach my fellow Jews the road to God as I see it.

STUDENT 2: Do you think all the Jews will follow your teachings?

BESHT: Probably not. As a matter of fact, I am sure that many will be against me and my followers. They may even persecute us.

STUDENT 2: Why should they do that?

BESHT: Because my teachings will be something new. Many are afraid of everything that is new. They don't trust it.

STUDENT 3: Will you write down in books the things you want to teach the Jews?

BESHT: I am afraid I will write down very little. There simply will not be enough time both to teach and to write—and after all, I must have time also to worship my Father in Heaven and Earth.

STUDENT 4: Then how will future generations learn your teachings?

BESHT: By word of mouth. One will tell the other.

STUDENT 4: From stories?

BESHT: From stories too. One can learn a great deal from stories. And there will probably be those who will write down the things they hear from me and later print them in books for all to read.

GABBAI: Are there any further questions? There being no more questions (or, our time is now up and therefore) the conference with the Rabbi Israel Baal Shem Tov is now at an end.

Steps ***8, 9, 10*** follow as outlined above. In the discussion the teacher connects the dramatization and the historic period it treats with the students' present-day knowledge and experiences, viz. "Who comes from a Hassidic family? Have they seen Hassidim? Is Hassidism as widespread today? Why? What can the Hassidic teachings mean in our lives in modern times?" There is of course room in this lesson for the inclusion of Hassidic songs, dances, stories and, of course, graphic art. While the Representatives are preparing their reports of the press conference, other students might be asked to do some research and bring in Hassidic tales which they may relate to the class, Hassidic songs which they might teach to the others, etc. In a program such as this there are also many opportunities for correlation with classical music on records such as: Ernest Bloch's *Baal Shem Suite.*

MAJOR MORDECAI MANUEL NOAH

1. Teacher's Introduction

The lesson might be motivated by a display of stamps from the State of Israel. This would lead to a discussion about the State, reports of some students who visited Israel, or whose parents, relatives or friends recently returned from a visit to Israel. A few questions about the State and the story of its establishment in 1948 serve as a jumping off point for the teacher's introduction to the lesson at hand somewhat as follows:

TEACHER: In our study of history we have had occasion, from time to time, to learn about various men who tried to re-establish a Jewish state in the Land of Israel. We studied about Don Joseph Nasi, the Jewish Duke of Naxos, who tried to establish a Jewish state, with a rebuilt city of Tiberias as a beginning. We learned about Shabbetai Zevi, who claimed to be the Messiah, the Lord's anointed, sent by God to bring the exiled Jewish people back to the Land of Israel.

There was one man who, only a little more than a hundred years ago, tried to establish a Jewish State right here in America. His name was Mordecai Manuel Noah. He was a major in the United States Army, a man of romance and adventure and . . . we will meet him right here, in our own classroom, in a dramatization of a press conference next week. We will make believe that we are in Buffalo, New York on the morning of the dedication of the place he chose for his Jewish state. Just before the dedication Major Noah will face the newspaper correspondents from a number of important newspapers in New York, Philadelphia, Buffalo, Boston, and so on, who will gather here for a press conference with him.

The teacher indicates a number of references for the students to examine in preparation for the dramatization.

2. Selecting the Cast

Class discussion determines the needed cast. Then students are selected to play Major Noah, the correspondents representing the various newspapers of the period, and a chairman. If time permits, a committee might be appointed to find out what newspapers were actually published in 1825 in New York, Buffalo, Philadelphia, Boston, etc., so that their names might be used in connection with the correspondents "representing" them.

Steps ***3, 4, 5, 6*** follow as outlined previously.

7. The Enactment

In front of the room are seated Major Noah and the Chairman. Behind them is the Advisory Committee. At either side, and facing them, are the Correspondents. The class represents the citizens of Buffalo, local politicians, Jews who came from other cities to observe this event, etc. The Chairman steps forward and opens the proceedings:

CHAIRMAN: Ladies and gentlemen: I have the honor to present to you Major Mordecai Manuel Noah, formerly of the United States Army, formerly American Consul in Tunis, and now, like Gideon and Jephtah of old, a Judge in Israel. Major Noah . . .

NOAH: Friends: It was good of you to come. This is a great day in my life, a great day for the exiled people of Israel and a great day for the United States of America. We in America, who only less than fifty years ago had to fight a Revolutionary War against Great Britian for our freedom, know what it means to be enslaved. We are today stretching out a welcoming hand to the enslaved children of Israel, offering them a life of freedom on our shores.

CORRESPONDENT 1: Are we to understand, sir, that your new colony will be part of the United States?

NOAH: Yes and no. The colony will be under the flag of the United States but we will establish there a Jewish state in which the oppressed Jews will find refuge.

CORRESPONDENT 2: Will the place which you have chosen be large enough for all the Jews?

NOAH: Of course not. I have chosen Grand Island in the Niagara River, near this city of Buffalo, because it has enough place for a large colony. But it cannot possibly take in all the Jews who need a place of refuge.

CORRESPONDENT 3: If that is so, then is the whole effort worth it?

NOAH: Of course it is. Our sages have taught us: "He who preserves a single life, it is as if he had preserved the entire world."

CORRESPONDENT 4: The Jews, I understand, have always prayed for a return to Zion. Does the establishment of this Jewish state on your Grand Island here mean that you are giving up the hope for a return to Palestine?

NOAH: Definitely not! Whenever, in God's good time, it will become possible, Palestine will be restored as an independent Jewish state. In the meantime, Grand Island will serve this purpose.

CORRESPONDENT 5: Major Noah, what do you plan to call this state?

NOAH: When the biblical Noah, after whom I am named, braved the raging flood in his frail ark, he did so because he believed in God's promise that one day the storm would end and his ark would come to rest safely on dry land. The Lord kept his promise. Noah's ark withstood the flood and finally came to rest at Ararat. Here, in this new colony, my persecuted brothers will find rest. I shall therefore name this resting place "Ararat."

CORRESPONDENT 1: Will the Jews come here to your Ararat?

NOAH: I hope so. I have sent out proclamations to all the Jewish communities in Europe inviting Jews to come here.

CORRESPONDENT 2: I do not mean to be impertinent, sir, but, you were introduced as a Judge in Israel. What experience in government do you claim?

NOAH: I have been a playwright and a soldier, a newspaper editor and a United States Consul as well as a major in the United States Army. In my service to my country in North Africa I had to deal with the Berber pirates and I believe I represented my country with dignity and with honor. With the help of the Almighty, I shall do the same as a Judge in Israel of the Jewish State of Ararat which we shall dedicate today.

CHAIRMAN: Are there any questions from the audience?

STUDENT 1: Who is helping you pay for Grand Island?

NOAH: No one. The funds come from my private fortune.

STUDENT 2: How many houses are already built on Ararat?

NOAH: None yet. Every colonist will build his own, with help from his brother Jews if needed.

CHAIRMAN: Are there any other questions?

There being no further questions, this press conference is at an end. We will all gather at two o'clock for the Grand Parade and the ceremonies of dedicating the cornerstone of the new Jewish state. For the benefit of the correspondents who must send off their dispatches promptly I will now read the inscription that appears on that stone: "*Sh'ma Yisrael, Hashem Elokenu, Hashem Ehad.*" This means: "Hear, O Israel, the Lord our God, the Lord is one." I continue to read the inscription: "Ararat, a city of refuge for the Jews, founded by Mordecai Manuel Noah in the Month Tizri, 5586, September 1825 and in the 50th year of American Independence." Thank you all for your attention.

Steps ***8, 9, 10*** follow as outlined previously. In the discussion the teacher will draw comparisons between the Grand Island effort which failed and the efforts on behalf of a Jewish state in the Land of Israel which ultimately succeeded. The reasons for both will be explored to the extent possible, considering the maturity of the students.

■ E. WITNESS TO HISTORY

Through this technique a historical event is recreated by means of dramatization as if it were taking place in our very presence. This form of history dramatization has been used with telling effect in such radio and television programs as "You Are There," "See It Now," and in publications like "*Chronicles.*" It is particularly useful for teaching history in that it provides historic events with a sense of immediacy; gives to both participants and class-audience a feeling of actual participation in the flow of historical incident; allows for the creation of background incidents making for a more rounded presentation of history; serves as a stimulant for independent research by the students.

The "Witness to History" technique is especially suited for presentation of climactic moments in history such as:

Abraham arrives in Canaan.

Joseph makes himself known to his brothers.

The exodus from Egypt.

The fall of Jericho.

Ezra and Nehemiah rebuild the walls of Jerusalem.

Mattathias proclaims the revolt against the Syrians at Modin.

Titus breaches the walls of Jerusalem and sets fire to the Temple.

Rabbi Judah Hanasi codifies the Mishnah.

Sabbatai Zevi renounces Judaism.

The birth of the State of Israel is proclaimed.

"Witness to History" utilizes a combination of several techniques, some of which have been dealt with above. Straight reporting from the scene, interview, and simple dramatization are its basic elements. The way these elements will be used and the manner in which they will be combined and emphasized is entirely discretionary with the individual teacher and class. Some classes may choose to convey the story through a dramatization consisting solely of a series of "news reports." Others may create a dramatization that is a mosaic of interviews only. Generally however, the combination of many forms makes for variety and interest.

In its most familiar form, the "Witness to History" dramatization opens with a Narrator. Briefly, he informs the audience that they will now, by means of the dramatization, be transported in time and place so that they may witness the historical event as it occurs:

NARRATOR: Friends, today we will, by means of dramatization, recreate the stirring events of the fall of Jericho. We take you back now more than thirty-one hundred years ago, to the outskirts of the city of Jericho in the Land of Canaan. Each of you now is a Witness to History! The first person you will hear will be our reporter David who is stationed near Joshua's tent.

A number of reporters who are "stationed" at different vantage points now describe the various aspects of the event as they "see" them:

REPORTER DAVID: I am speaking to you from my position near the Headquarters tent of Joshua ben Nun, Commander-in-Chief of the Israelites. The tent is located on a small hill in the center of the Israelite encampment. As far as the eye can see, stretching in every direction, are the tents of the Israelite hosts. The camp is unusually quiet. For the past six days silence has reigned in the Israelite camp. . . .

Occasionally, a reporter will interview someone in order to clarify something, to provide background information, or to advance the thread of the story in an interesting way. Subjects of such interviews may be the leading character in the story (Joshua), an important participant (a priest, one of the spies, etc.), or simply one of the people (a soldier). By way of illustration we will return to our Reporter David:

REPORTER DAVID: For the past six days, silence has reigned in the Israelite camp. Joshua's orders were very strict and the Israelite army has been trained to obey orders. An Israelite soldier has just come out of Joshua's tent. Let us ask him about this. Soldier! A moment please . . .

SOLDIER: Yes sir!

REPORTER D: I would like to ask you a few questions, if I may.

SOLDIER: Go right ahead. If it's not about military secrets. . . .

REPORTER D: Naturally not. What is your name?

SOLDIER: Shimon ben Er.

REPORTER D: Your rank?

SOLDIER: Messenger, attached to Headquarters.

REPORTER D: Can you tell me why Joshua has ordered the Israelites to be silent during the past six days?

SOLDIER: I really don't know. The Commander-in-Chief does not give me his reasons for the orders he issues.

REPORTER D: Naturally. But you must have some idea.

SOLDIER: Well, the people think that it is to make the march of the Priests even more frightening to the inhabitants of Jericho.

REPORTER D: Could you explain this, please?

SOLDIER: Sure. You see, when our soldiers arrived before the walls of Jericho, we found all the gates locked. The Canaanites inside the city have enough food, the walls are thick enough to withstand any siege.

REPORTER D: But Joshua means to conquer the city, no matter how strong its defenses are?

SOLDIER: Naturally. Jericho is the first city in Canaan which we approached. If we capture it the defenders of other Canaanite cities will see that the Lord is with us and be afraid. Their fear will make them weak, easier to be conquered. If we do not take Jericho, they will all gather courage and resist us mightily.

REPORTER D: That's why the silence in the camp and the priests marching round about the city?

SOLDIER: So we think. Joshua ordered the priests to march, blow their trumpets, while the rest of the camp is absolutely silent. How would you feel if you were a Canaanite inside Jericho waiting for the Israelites to attack? Instead, all they see is priests marching and a silent army surrounding them. How would you feel?

REPORTER D: Frightened.

SOLDIER: Exactly! I must go now. I have a message from Joshua to the princes of the tribes. They and their soldiers are to gather now to hear the words of Joshua.

REPORTER D: Thank you very much.

In this way the dramatization shifts from reporting to interviewing, from one position to another. For example:

REPORTER D: That was an Israelite soldier attached to Headquarters. While we have been talking to him, a group of Israelite soldiers and priests has been continuing their march around the walls. Our reporter Jacob is stationed near the main gate. I will switch you to him now.

REPORTER JACOB: I am standing near the main gate of the huge walls surrounding Jericho. The walls defending the city are of a type known as "casemate walls." They are so thick that there are actually dwellings built into them, with people living right inside the walls. The woman Rahab who rescued Joshua's spies lives in such a dwelling. From my right, a strange procession is approaching. First there is a small group of Israelite soldiers. They are followed by seven priests carrying seven trumpets. They are followed by a group carrying the Ark of the Covenant after which comes another group of soldiers. They have stopped marching now, probably to rest. I will see if I can't talk to one of the priests in the procession. Excuse me. Will you please tell me why you have stopped marching?

PRIEST: We are getting ready for the seventh march.

REPORTER J: Could you explain this?

PRIEST: Gladly. For the past six days, our small procession has marched around the walls of Jericho, once each day.

REPORTER J: And each time, as you ended your march, you blew your trumpets.

PRIEST: Exactly.

REPORTER J: While all the Israelites remained absolutely silent.

PRIEST: Yes. Today, the seventh day, we marched around the city six times. Now, we will march around a seventh time. Then, when we blow our trumpets, we will raise a great shout. All the Israelites will join in the shout, the walls of Jericho will crumble and fall, and the Lord will give the city of Jericho into our hands.

REPORTER J: How do you know this?

PRIEST: Joshua ben Nun has told us so, in the name of the Lord Most High.

REPORTER J: How soon will you begin your final march?

PRIEST: We are waiting for Joshua to speak to the people. There he is now, coming out of his tent . . .

Occasionally straight dramatization is used, the reporter retiring into the background while the incident is dramatized in the familiar manner. To illustrate, we will continue where we left off with Reporter Jacob and the priest:

REPORTER J: Then you must go back to your group of priests?

PRIEST: Yes. We will soon begin our seventh march.

REPORTER J: Thank you very much. And now, friends, the great moment has arrived at last. The walls of Jericho are about to fall. Let me switch you back to Reporter David near the Headquarters tent so that you may hear Joshua who has begun to speak to the people.

REPORTER DAVID: The great moment is at hand now, the moment for which all the Israelites have been eagerly waiting. After the great Exodus from Egyptian slavery, after forty years of suffering and wandering in the desert under their great leader Moses, they are now about to begin the conquest of the land which the Lord has promised to their fathers, Abraham, Isaac, and Jacob. For the past few moments Joshua the son of Nun, whom Moses had appointed to lead them into the Promised Land, has been speaking to the Israelite hosts. Let us listen . . .

JOSHUA: People of Israel, shout, for the Lord hath given you the city. And the city shall be devoted, even it and all that is therein, to the Lord!

SPY: Joshua! Our master!

JOSHUA: What is it?

SPY: I am one of the two spies you sent into the city of Jericho.

JOSHUA: I remember you well.

SPY: When the inhabitants of Jericho found out about us they sought to kill us. Our lives were saved by Rahab who lives in the city wall. She hid us in the flax bundles until the danger was past. We promised her that when the Lord will give the city of Jericho unto our hands she and her family would be spared. She is to hang a red string out of her window so that all may know her house and keep it safe.

JOSHUA: I have not forgotten. Rahab shall live, she and all that are with her in the house, because she hid the messengers that we sent.

But you are to take nothing from the city for yourselves. All the gold and silver and vessels of brass and iron are holy unto the Lord; they shall come into the treasury of the Lord. Now, blow your horns, O you priests! Shout aloud, O you children of Israel!

NARRATOR: Round about the city they marched, blowing their trumpets, raising a great shout and the mighty walls of Jericho fell. The children of Israel conquered their first city in the land which the Lord had promised unto their fathers.

Introducing the Technique

The first time the technique "Witness to History" is to be used it would be well to introduce it to the class and to explain it briefly. This might be done somewhat as follows:

TEACHER: Most of us, while reading an interesting story of adventure, of exciting happenings from the past, or of occurrences in distant places have often wished that we had been able to be part of that story or at least to witness it as it happened. This is particularly true when we read of a great event in history. How exciting if we all could have witnessed the Battle of Gettysburg, the inauguration of George Washington as the first President of the United States, or the Exodus of the Israelites from Egypt! Naturally that is not possible. What has happened in the past is over and done with. And yet, we need not be satisfied with merely reading about the great events of history. With a little bit of imagination, we can bring them to life. We can make believe that they are happening before our very eyes; that we are truly, each one of us, a "witness to history." Isn't this a more interesting way for us to learn our history than just read about it? Our next lesson is to deal with the beginning of the revolt of the Judaeans against the Syrians. Shall we bring it to life? Would you like to be witnesses to it?

VOICES: Yes. That ought to be interesting.

STUDENT: How do we do it?

TEACHER: We will make believe that the revolt is beginning while a number of reporters are watching and describing for us everything they see. They will describe to us the situation in Modin, the arrival of the Syrians with their idol, the call to sacrifice, Mattathias' call to revolt, etc. Some of the reporters will interview some of the people taking part in the happenings—perhaps a citizen of Modin, the Syrian Captain, Mattathias, and others. Some parts of the story might even be acted out before our very eyes, as if they were happening just now instead of more than two thousand years ago. Supposing we try a dramatization of "Witness to History" with this lesson. If we find it interesting, we may do it quite often with other lessons. We will plan this thing together of course, deciding what parts to dramatize, what characters are needed, and so on.

STUDENT: How can we do this if we don't know the story?

TEACHER: That's a good question. Naturally we must know at least a little about the story—the most important incidents, the leading characters and so on. We will postpone our planning and the selection of a cast to our next history lesson. In the meantime, we will all read pages —— in our history book so as to get some idea about the Maccabean Revolt.

As in other forms of history dramatization, here too the general introduction of the technique "Witness to History" will be used only the first time. Thereafter, when the technique is used the teacher begins directly by mentioning the subject to be dramatized and indicating the section in the text to be read for preliminary preparation.

The Process

The process of dramatization proceeds according to the following steps:

1. Teacher's Introduction (or Motivation).
2. Assignment of Preliminary Reading.
3. Planning the Dramatization.
4. Determining the Cast.
5. Selecting the Cast.
6. Developing the Dramatization.
7. Research by Cast.
8. Home Preparation by "Reporters" of Their Reports.
9. Rehearsal of Dramatization.
10. The Enactment.

11. Class Evaluation of the Enactment.
12. Generalizing and Applying the Lesson.

This plan assumes that three sessions will elapse from the first introduction of the subject until the final discussion following the enactment. At least one third of a history period will be devoted to the introduction by the teacher, preliminary planning, and giving the reading assignment. The entire succeeding lesson is devoted to planning the dramatization, determining the cast, selecting the cast and developing the dramatization. In some instances an additional period may have to be devoted to this aspect. The third (sometimes fourth) period is devoted completely to the enactment, evaluation, and generalizing. The teacher is of course constantly on guard not to devote too much time to one aspect of the process to the detriment of the others. Unless guarded against, a discussion may consume so much time that there is none left for planning the dramatization, selecting the cast, etc. A preliminary allocation of time to each step, noted in the teacher's plan book, will be of great help. A watch is an invaluable asset.

In addition, the teacher might meet with the cast once for a rehearsal of the dramatization, outside of class time. When the students have gained experience, they may be permitted to have their rehearsal without the presence of the teacher.

Following is a detailed development of the steps outlined above. The "Beginning of the Maccabean Revolt" will be used by way of illustration.

1. Teacher's Introduction

TEACHER: What is, in your opinion, the most important American national holiday?
STUDENT 1: Washington's Birthday.
TEACHER: Why?
STUDENT 1: Because Washington was the "father of our country."
TEACHER: Does anybody have another opinion?
STUDENT 2: July 4th.
TEACHER: Why?
STUDENT 2: Because it's our Independence Day.
TEACHER: Does that make it more important than Washington's Birthday, or Thanksgiving, or Memorial Day?
STUDENT 2: Sure.
TEACHER: Could you explain to us why?
STUDENT 2: If not for the Declaration of Independence on July 4, 1776, we would have no United States and no national holidays to celebrate.
TEACHER: That sounds like a very good reason. As a result of the Declaration of Independence we have a free America.

The teacher has begun the introduction of the project by discussing with the students a subject with which they are thoroughly familiar from their general studies and the culture about them. Now the teacher proceeds to develop the connecting link between the familiar and the new in the lesson.

TEACHER: The Declaration of Independence was certainly important in American national life. But, tell me, was that all the original thirteen American colonies had to do to gain their independence? Did they just have to draw up a declaration and sign it and be free forever after?

STUDENT 3: No. They had to fight the Revolutionary War.

TEACHER: Yes. Against England. Why did they fight England?

STUDENT 4: Because the British were oppressing them and the colonists wanted to be free.

TEACHER: That's exactly it. Now, who would you say was stronger when the Revolution broke out? Who had the bigger army, more arms and ammunition?

STUDENT 5: The British, of course.

TEACHER: And yet, the American colonists signed the Declaration of Independence and went to war against a country so much stronger than they were. Weren't they afraid for their lives?

STUDENT 4: I guess they were.

TEACHER: Still they fought. Why?

STUDENT 5: I suppose because they wanted to live in freedom. I guess their freedom meant more to them than their lives, so they just took the chance.

TEACHER: And in the end they won their independence. The few fought against the many, the weak against the strong and they gained their victory. History can show us a number of examples of a weak people fighting against a strong people and winning their fight, because they were fighting for the right to live free and independent. Can any of you think of a similar case in modern Jewish history?

STUDENT 6: Sure. The State of Israel.

TEACHER: In what way is Israel's independence similar to American independence?

STUDENT 6: Well, Israel also issued a Declaration of Independence.

TEACHER: What else?

STUDENT 6: Israel had to fight many Arab nations that had bigger armies and more arms, in order to establish her independence.

STUDENT 7: And, like America, Israel fought for her freedom and independence.

TEACHER: Very good. Both countries fought, the few against the many, for the right to live as a free people in their own homeland. But Israel and America were not the first in history to declare their independence and fight for it against great odds. There was another such case many, many hundreds of years ago that probably served as an example to the American colonists, and most certainly inspired the Jews in Israel in 1948 since it had happened in Jewish history. Does any one of you know what that was?

STUDENT 8: The Exodus from Egypt?

TEACHER: Not quite. The Exodus is certainly important in our history. It marked the beginning of our existence as a free nation and we have our beautiful holiday, Pesah, to celebrate the event. But we didn't fight a war then. What other holiday do we have to celebrate the winning of our Freedom?

STUDENT 9: Purim?

TEACHER: No. Purim celebrates an event that happened when we were in exile. I am referring to an event that happened during our life as a nation in the Land of Israel. We have a beautiful holiday to celebrate it. The Feast of Lights.

STUDENT 7: Hanukah?

TEACHER: Of course! Hanukah! It marks the victory of the few against the many, the weak against the strong. It commemorates the victorious Maccabean Revolt which began in a small village in Judea, more than two thousand years ago. You have enjoyed doing "Witness to History" dramatizations in the past. Supposing we become witnesses to history at the beginning of the Maccabean Revolt. Shall we?

STUDENT 1: Will we have to do a lot of research?

TEACHER: Some—although not as much as the last time.

STUDENT 1: When we did "Witness to History" with Ezra and Nehemiah I had to read so much that I couldn't do my other homework.

TEACHER: That was not good. You should have told me about it and I would have given you more time to prepare. But this time you already know about the life of the Judeans during the days of the Second Temple from our earlier lessons. That will save us a lot of work. A little, you will have to do, even now.

STUDENT 1: A little research I don't mind.

TEACHER: Good. *(Teacher proceeds to step 2)*

2. Assignment of Preliminary Reading

TEACHER: *(Continuing)* Next time, when we have our history lesson, we will decide which scenes we will "witness" in our dramatization, what characters we will need in our cast, and choose the cast. We will also plan the whole dramatization. To do this, we will of course have to have at least a general idea about the story. I would suggest therefore that you all read at home from page 74 to the bottom of page 81 in our history book *The Jewish People, Book II (Or indicate the proper pages in whatever other text is being used by the class, that tells the story of the Syrian oppression and the beginning of the Maccabean Revolt.)*

STUDENT 1: That's eight pages!

TEACHER: Well, if you find that too much, reading from page 78 to the bottom of page 81 might be enough. This tells the story of the actual beginning of the revolt. However, if we are to do an intelligent dramatization, we should know a little about what led up to the revolt. So, if it is at all possible, try to read from page 74. It's only another three pages in our book.

3. Planning the Dramatization and 4. Determining the Cast

TEACHER: During the last history lesson we decided to do a "Witness to History" dramatization of the beginning of the Maccabean Revolt. Now, let us decide what parts we will dramatize and how we will dramatize each part. What do you think should be the first thing we will witness?

STUDENT 1: How the Syrians bring the idol to Modin.

TEACHER: That's good. The bringing of the idol to Modin was the spark that lighted the fire of revolt. But how about the events that led up to this—the Syrian oppression and so on—shouldn't we show this somehow?

STUDENT 2: That's very important.

TEACHER: How shall we show that?

STUDENT 3: We could dramatize some of the scenes of persecution of the Judaeans.

STUDENT 4: That would take us away from Modin and complicate things.

STUDENT 5: Couldn't we have a Narrator, who would start the dramatization by telling us about this?

TEACHER: That's a very good idea. We will have a Narrator open the scene by describing briefly what had happened in Judaea under the Syrian oppression.

STUDENT 6: I have another idea. Couldn't we show some Jews in Modin talking about these things, complaining about what the Syrians are doing?

TEACHER: We certainly could. As a matter of fact, we could begin the dramatization with a Narrator who would give the general background. We would then switch to Reporter 1, who is stationed in the market place of Modin who would let us listen in on the conversation of two Judaeans.

(Teacher now divides the blackboard in two columns. Over column one teacher writes the heading "Action," over column two the heading "Cast." Now, teacher writes in the "Action" column a brief outline of the first two scenes just decided, somewhat as follows:)

1. *Narrator:* Title of dramatization; describes persecutions; describes Modin market place; switch to Reporter 1.

2. *Reporter 1:* Describes place where he is; mentions Judaeans talking; switch to Judaeans.

(Teacher now resumes discussion with class)

I have written on the blackboard an outline of what we decided. When we choose people for the parts, I would suggest that each one write down that section of the outline which deals with his part. It would help you remember what we have decided about each part. Now let's see—what cast do we need for these first two sections of our dramatization?

STUDENT 6: We will need a Narrator.

TEACHER: A Narrator.

(Teacher writes on the blackboard, in the column labeled "Cast" the word "Narrator.")

Who else?

STUDENT 7: Reporter 1.

TEACHER: *(Writes in the "Cast" column: Reporter 1)*

Who else?

STUDENT 8: Two Judaeans.

TEACHER: Shall we have men Judaeans or women?

STUDENT 9: I think we should have women. Most of the people in the story are men. Let's give the girls a chance while we can.

TEACHER: You're absolutely right. Women it shall be.

(Teacher writes under "Cast" Woman 1, Woman 2)

TEACHER: Let's put down in our outline what we decided about the part of the Judaean women so that we don't forget it.

(In the column labeled "Action" teacher writes:)

3. *Judaean Women:* Conversation—things are bad; Syrians oppress Jews; forbid Jewish religion, etc.

(Teacher resumes the discussion)

Now that we have our background to the story, we can go back to your earlier suggestion that we show how the Syrians bring their idol to Modin. How, do you think, we ought to do this?

STUDENT 1: We could have a reporter describe it.

TEACHER: Fine. Shall we have Reporter 1 do it?

STUDENT 1: I think so. He's already in the market place so he can see what's going on when the Syrians arrive.

TEACHER: Does anyone think differently?

STUDENT 9: I think we should have a second reporter describe the arrival of the Syrians.

TEACHER: Why?

STUDENT 9: Well, first of all, it might become monotonous to listen to Reporter 1 all the time. In the second place, the more parts we have, the more people will get a chance to act in the dramatization.

TEACHER: These are two excellent reasons. How shall we switch from Reporter 1 and the two Judaean Women to Reporter 2?

STUDENT 9: The Narrator could say, "I take you now to Reporter 2."

TEACHER: That's one way. Any other suggestions?

STUDENT 2: Couldn't Reporter 1 say that he hears a commotion at the other end of the market place? Then he could say, "Our Reporter 2 is stationed there. I will switch you now to him so we can find out what's going on."

TEACHER: That's a very good idea. Which shall we choose? Those who prefer that we have the Narrator switch us to Reporter 2 raise your hands. *(Students raise their hands)* How many prefer that we have Reporter 1 switch the action to Reporter 2? *(Students raise their hands)* It seems that most of you want Reporter 1 to do it instead of the Narrator. Why?

STUDENT 3: It's livelier.

STUDENT 4: It keeps the action continuous instead of being interrupted by the Narrator.

TEACHER: These are very good reasons. I would say that generally it's better to avoid using the Narrator too much since, every time he speaks, there is a break in the action of our play. At any rate, now we have another character: Reporter 2.

(In the column "Cast" teacher writes "Reporter 2" in the column "Action" teacher writes:)

4. *Reporter 2:* Describes commotion; tells of procession of Syrians with Captain bringing in idol and altar.

It is to be noted once more that this Teacher-Students dialogue is given here merely as an indication of the classroom process to be followed. Obviously, the actual Teacher-Student dialogue will differ, often quite radically, with each class. The alert teacher will guide the discussion so that it does not go off in tangential directions but hews to the line of planning the progress of the dramatization and determining the cast needed. Naturally, the teacher will be continuously on the alert for opportunities to bring out various aspects of the history lesson under consideration. Whenever possible, the teacher enriches the discussion with background information, Midrashic material, etc. bearing in mind that basically the dramatization is not the real goal. It is rather a tool, a means for more effective teaching of the history lesson.

The teacher is aware that not in every instance will students come forth with positive suggestions. At times, things will bog down and the teacher will find it necessary to keep the process moving by "priming the pump" with leading questions or even direct suggestions. For example:

TEACHER: Now that the Syrians have arrived with their idol, what do we show next? *(Silence)* Does anybody have any suggestions? *(No answer)* What's the matter? Did your inspiration dry up? Well, let's see . . . What happens next in the story? The Syrian Captain asks Mattathias to sacrifice to the idol. Shall we show that next in our dramatization? How?

STUDENT 4: Reporter 2 could describe it.

TEACHER: That's one way. But we just heard from Reporter 2. It might become monotonous listening to him all the time.

STUDENT 5: Let's use Reporter 1 then.

Obviously the class has arrived at a plateau. The time has come for the teacher to point out possibilities in order to start the creative process operating once again. Teacher therefore takes the lead at this point.

TEACHER: *(Continuing the discussion)* That's a possibility. But, maybe it might prove more interesting if we begin by having Reporter 1 describe for us what he sees as the Syrian Captain turns to the Jews and begins to speak. Then Reporter 1 says, "Let's listen" and we now dramatize the actual dialogue between the Captain who asks Mattathias to offer the sacrifice and the old priest's answers. What do you think of this idea?

STUDENT 5: I like it.

TEACHER: Do you think this will make it more interesting than just having the scene described by one of the Reporters?

STUDENT 7: It will be lot's more interesting—like a real play.

TEACHER: Then shall we do it this way?

STUDENTS: Yes.

TEACHER: That gives us two more characters and another dialogue scene. *(Teacher writes under "Cast" "Captain" and "Mattathias." Under "Action" teacher writes:)*

5. *Captain and Mattathias:* Captain asks Mattathias to offer sacrifice; Mattathias refuses; Captain asks for volunteer from crowd.

(As each segment of the dramatization is developed the teacher notes it down in outline form under "Action." As new characters are added, they are noted down on the blackboard under "Cast.")

STUDENT 7: What about the traitor who offers the sacrifice?

TEACHER: Right. What shall we call him?

STUDENT 6: He should have a Greek name since he was a Hellenist.

TEACHER: That's an excellent idea. *(If no student offers this suggestion the teacher might volunteer it since it provides an opportunity for defining the term.)* Many of the Judaeans of that period took Greek names, wore Greek clothes, took part in Greek games, ate forbidden food and in general followed the ways of the Syrian Greeks. They were called Hellenists—Hellene being another name for Greek. Now, does any one know by what Greek name this traitor called himself?

STUDENT 6: It's not in our book.

TEACHER: You will find it in the Book of Maccabees. The Books of the Maccabees are ancient chronicles that tell the entire story we are studying in great detail. Whoever gets the part of the traitor can look it up and find out his name. It's on page ______ in the edition we have here. Whoever looks it up will also be able to report to us more about him. For now, we'll just call him Traitor. *(The name is noted under "Cast.")* Now, let's see. How far did we get with our story?

STUDENT 8: Where the traitor offers the sacrifice.

TEACHER: What happens next?

STUDENT 9: Mattathias kills him and calls out, "Who is for the Lord? Follow me!"

TEACHER: This was the call to revolt—sort of the Declaration of Independence of the Maccabeans. I guess this ends our dramatization, unless you feel we need a closing statement by our Narrator, summarizing what happened afterwards and how the Judaeans were finally victorious. What do you think of this suggestion?

STUDENT 1: Since we opened with the Narrator, I think it would be good to close with him. It would make our play complete.

TEACHER: Very well. That's what we'll do then. And that just about does it for our "Witness to History."

As indicated earlier, throughout the entire discussion reference is constantly made to the story. The teacher from time to time elaborates on details and background. In that way the students who have read the story fix it better in their minds. Those who have not read it have their curiosity aroused to the point where they might now be eager to read it at home.

Having planned the dramatization and determined on the characters, the teacher proceeds to step 5.

5. Selecting the Cast

The teacher asks for volunteers for each part. The first few times "Witness to History" is utilized, acting roles, such as the Judaean Women, Syrian Captain, and Mattathias in this dramatization, will be assigned to the more able students, because much of their dialogue will have to be improvised during the actual presentation. More retiring children might be chosen for the Narrator and Reporters, since the greater part of their reports can be prepared in advance and memorized if they so wish it. The first few times "Witness to History" is used, such students, having written out their parts in advance, might even be permitted to read from script during the presentation. Teachers may have to resort to this in order to bolster their students' confidence.

Parts of villains should rarely be assigned but given to volunteers. Certainly extreme care is exercised if there are no volunteers and the part must be assigned. No amount of explanation by the teacher that it is "only make-believe" will spare the student who gets such a part the annoying teasing of his fellows. Consequently, when villainous parts are assigned, they are given to students who are normally the class leaders and who can well withstand such teasing or discourage it if they have a mind to.

Small parts, requiring a minimum of speech and action, are allocated to the very shy and retiring, thus helping to bring them out slowly and gradually. It is a mistake to assume, as some teachers do, that giving a shy student a major part in a play will help him to overcome his shyness. On the contrary, it will usually only add to his difficulties. The enormity of his responsibility will overwhelm him. Instead of building up his ego, being forced into such a situation only has the opposite effect. Certainly students can often be helped to build up their self-confidence and it is definitely the task of the teacher to do so. But this must be done in easy stages, in small, almost imperceptible doses. The teacher, in assigning a part to such a child, should be practically certain in advance that the student will handle it successfully. Failure would be a serious blow to the student's ego development.

If several students volunteer for a part, the teacher is very careful in making a selection, justifying the choice, so that those who are not selected will accept it in good grace. Students might be chosen because they more closely resemble the character they are to portray in physical characteristics; each volunteer might be asked to improvise extemporaneously a brief scene from the story involving the character, the class deciding by vote who is to get the part; students might be selected by "choosing up," drawing lots, "counting out," or similar method of chance generally acceptable to children.

In any event, the teacher is careful not to spend too much time in allocating parts. He is usually sufficiently familiar with the children to be able to cast intelligently without time-consuming methods such as "tryouts." After all, when using this technique, the lesson is the thing not the play.

The teacher will in all instances soften the disappointment of those who failed to get a part they wanted by pointing out that there will be other opportunities when the class does dramatizations again.

The teacher will be on guard to provide other opportunities to students who had volunteered for a part and were not chosen. Such students will be given preference for parts in future dramatizations. Often, a student who has been disappointed, may not volunteer again, fearing another rebuff. The teacher bears this in mind. When selecting a cast in the future, the teacher might say to such a student, "When we did 'Witness to History' about Ezra and Nehemiah you missed out on getting the part of Ezra. This time it's your turn. Supposing you do the part of the Syrian Captain (or Mattathias, Reporter I, or other)."

There may be occasions when the reverse happens—there is a complete lack of volunteers. In that event, the teacher will assign parts. Frequent resort to this expedient is rarely necessary. One successful dramatization usually motivates a desire for more such experiences and an eagerness on the part of many students to take part.

Having selected the cast, the teacher proceeds directly to the next task—developing the dramatization.

6. Developing the Dramatization

The object of this step in the process is fourfold:

a. To plan the dramatization in full detail, involving the participation of the whole class.
b. To determine the individual task of each member of the cast.
c. To stimulate a desire for additional text reading and research.
d. To provide an additional learning opportunity during which the history lesson is developed in greater detail.

If the time allocated for the history period is long enough, the class will proceed to develop the dramatization during the same session, immediately after the cast is selected. If not enough time is available, the succeeding history session is devoted to this step.

The following example of procedure in this step of the process is offered as a guide:

TEACHER: Now that we have a general idea about what our "Witness to History" dramatization of the Beginning of the Maccabean Revolt will be like, and we have our cast, we can proceed to develop our dramatization in full detail. Let's see now—we decided to begin with the Narrator. Jack, since you will be playing the part of the Narrator, supposing you tell us what you might say.

JACK: I think I'll sort of introduce things by inviting everybody to witness what's going to happen.

TEACHER: That's the general idea. Why not tell us how you might say it—using more or less the actual words you plan to use in the dramatization. Go ahead. Try it.

JACK: I think I'll say, "Come with me to Modin where you will see the beginning of the Maccabean Revolt."

TEACHER: That's a very good opening, Jack. When we hear it, we know immediately what to expect to see—the beginning of the Maccabean Revolt, and where the action will take place—in Modin. Do you think we ought to be even more specific in identifying the place—like, "Come with me to Modin, a little village in the Hills of Judaea?"

STUDENT 1: That's a good idea but I think we ought to add also, "in the Land of Israel."

TEACHER: That's an excellent suggestion. This way the audience knows immediately where the Revolt began, what kind of a place Modin was, in what country and in what section of the country the village was located. Will you try it again now, Jack?

JACK: "Come with me to Modin, a little village in the Hills of Judaea in the Land of Israel, where you will see the beginning of the Maccabean Revolt."

STUDENT 2: I think instead of using the word "see" the Narrator should say "where you will witness."

TEACHER: Why?

STUDENT 2: Because the kind of dramatization we are doing is called "Witness to History."

STUDENT 3: Then why not use the whole title? Why not say "where each of you will be a witness to history, where you will see the beginning of the Maccabean Revolt"?

TEACHER: How about this, class? How many think the Narrator should begin this way? Please raise your hands if you agree to this. *(Students raise their hands)* Very well this is the way it will be.

STUDENT 4: I think it's important that the Narrator tell when this took place. After all, it's only make believe that we are witnessing the beginning of the Revolt today. We shouldn't fool the people into thinking that it just happened when really it happened hundreds of years ago.

TEACHER: I don't believe that we would be fooling anyone. Everyone would know that we are doing a dramatization. But fixing the date is a very good idea. How would you say it?

STUDENT 4: "This took place more than two thousand years ago."

BILLY: I don't like this at all. We're making believe that we're *witnessing* everything. We can't suddenly say that we're *not* witnessing it but it's only a story.

TEACHER: I think I know what you are trying to say, Billy. How would you suggest that we fix the time?

BILLY: Well, just as the Narrator says to the audience to come with him to the place where the thing happened, he could tell them to come with him to the time when the thing happened.

JANE: Sort of like in science-fiction, "Come with me back in time to the year. . . ." What year did the Revolt begin?

TEACHER: Does any one know when the Maccabean Revolt began? No one?

BILLY: Well I know that the Maccabean Revolt happened after the Jews returned from the Babylonian exile.

TEACHER: How do you know that?

BILLY: Because in our text book the Maccabean Revolt comes after the Return from Babylon.

TEACHER: That's logical. Correct, too. And what year was the Return?

BILLY: Well, Ezra and Nehemiah came to Jerusalem in the year 458 B.C.E. I also know that the Maccabean Revolt happened before the destruction of the Temple in the year 70 C.E. They told us that in Camp on Tisha B'Av. So, since the Temple was still standing in the days of the Maccabees, all this must have happened some time after Ezra and before the Destruction.

TEACHER: Excellent reasoning, Billy. Very logical. But that still does not give us the exact date. Why don't we just use the letter X for the year for now? Before our next session you can all look it up. I will write on the blackboard several sources where you can find it. Note them down, please. *(Teacher writes the references on the blackboard)* You'll find the information in the *Jewish Encyclopedia* under "Maccabees"; Gratz, *History of the Jews,* Volume — Pages — to — deal with this period. Also in *Birdseye View of Jewish History* by Cecil Roth there is an excellent chapter on "The Maccabean Struggle." As a matter of fact, you will do well to read the entire chapter. It will give you much more information than there is in our textbook. Now, Jack, let us hear your opening section.

JACK: "Come with me back in time to the year X. Come with me to the small village of Modin, in the hills of Judaea, in the Land of Israel, where you will be witness to history, where you will see the beginning of the Maccabean Revolt."

TEACHER: Very good, Jack.

It would seem that much more time than is warranted has been devoted to the development of the very opening section of the first narration. It is to be borne in mind, however, that this holds true only the first time that the technique is being used, when the pupils are completely unfamiliar with it. After doing "Witness to History" once, many of the things discussed in the example given here will be done by the students as a matter of course. The very next time such a dramatization is attempted, the Narrator will quite naturally open by setting the time and the place in his narration without need of discussion. Should he forget and fail to do so, some student can be counted on to call him to task at once with, "You forgot to say, 'Come with me back in time to the year . . .' " So that much of the discussion indicated here will be completely unnecessary after the first few times the technique is used, and the process will consequently consume a great deal less time, a commodity that is in very short supply and extremely precious in our schools.

The discussion about how the Narrator is to open, has also provided the teacher with an opportunity to stimulate independent research. In trying to find the exact date of the Maccabean Revolt which they need for the dramatization, the students become involved in research that is to them purposeful. They go outside of the confines of their textbook, thus widening and deepening their knowledge of the historical period under study. The teacher is of course ready to offer suggestions of research sources. In the example given here, the teacher was prepared to refer the students to the *Jewish Encyclopedia,* the exact volume and pages in Gratz, and the correct chapter in Roth's history. This requires careful advance preparation and research on the part of the teacher—a task which will be of great benefit to teacher, students, and the learning process.

Having developed the first section of the opening narration, the teacher continues the discussion:

TEACHER: Now that our Narrator has set the time, the place and the event we are to witness, what else should he tell us?

JOAN: I think he ought to give us some information about what happened up to this point.

TEACHER: You mean the background of our story—the events which led up to the revolt?

JOAN: That's right.

TEACHER: How do you suggest he say it, Joan?

JOAN: Well, the Narrator might say, "The Syrian Greeks had conquered Judaea. They passed cruel laws forbidding the Jews to practice their religion. They ordered everyone to worship Greek idols. Many Jews obeyed their orders. They were called Hellenists. But many refused to worship idols. The Syrians tortured and killed thousands for following the Jewish religion."

TEACHER: That's very good, Joan. Did you note this down, Jack?

JACK: I'll remember it.

TEACHER: Good. You'll be able to write out your narration when you get home. Now our Narrator must do only one more thing for us. Can any one tell us what that is? How about you, Jack?

JACK: I can't think of anything.

TEACHER: Joan?

JOAN: I don't know.

TEACHER: Billy?
BILLY: I have no idea.
TEACHER: Anybody?

Once again the wellsprings of creativity have momentarily dried up. The teacher will have to get things moving again by making suggestions, using leading questions, etc.

TEACHER: Let's see now—what is the main task of the Narrator?
JOAN: To introduce the play?
TEACHER: That's right! He introduces the play by setting the period, by fixing the place of action, by giving the background and then he brings the audience in their imagination right into the midst of the action that is taking place—right into the market place of Modin where Mattathias and his five sons lived. Now then, Jack, after you tell them that many Jews were killed, how would you move on to Modin?
JACK: I would say, "There was a small village in the mountains of Judaea to which the Syrians did not come immediately. There lived the old Mattathias with his five sons . . ."
STUDENT 5: I read that their family name was Hasmonean. I think the Narrator should mention that.
TEACHER: How?
STUDENT 5: He could say, "There lived Mattathias Hasmonean and his five sons."
JACK: "There lived the old Mattathias Hasmonean with his five sons. But finally the Syrians came even here. Come with me to the market place of Modin where we will witness what happened."
TEACHER: Very, very good. Only one thing more now, you have to introduce our Reporter 1—that's Morris. You might finish by saying, "Our Reporter, Morris, is stationed near a group of citizens of Modin. Let us hear from him now." Now Jack, I would suggest that you write out at home your opening narration so that you don't leave out anything important.
BILLY: He shouldn't make it too long.
TEACHER: Billy is right, Jack. Be careful not to make a long speech. But don't leave out anything important. I would suggest, Jack, that you read all of Chapters Two and Three in our book. If you have time, you might look up some other history books that we have in our school library and read the chapters dealing with the Maccabean Revolt. The rest of you might do the same. Now Morris, you are our Reporter 1. It's your turn.
MORRIS: I would tell them, "I'm standing in the market place of Modin next to some Judaean women. Like everybody in Modin, they are complaining about the Syrians. Let's listen to them."
TEACHER: Good. Jane and Mildred—you are the Judaean women. What will you be saying? Jane?
JANE: "Isn't it awful what the Syrians are doing to our people?"
TEACHER: Mildred?
MILDRED: "It's terrible."
TEACHER: You are complaining about the Syrians. Tell us about some of the things they have done.

JANE: "Did you hear what happened to Hannah?"

MILDRED: "Yes. They killed her seven sons because they would not worship idols."

TEACHER: Maybe you could bring out more facts, Morris, by interviewing them. After all, you are a reporter in this dramatization.

MORRIS: I don't know what to ask them.

TEACHER: You might ask them about conditions in Modin.

MORRIS: "Excuse me, women of Modin, I heard you talking. Are things bad in Modin too?"

JANE: "Not yet. The Syrians haven't come here yet."

MORRIS: "Do you think they'll come?"

MILDRED: "I'm sure they will and they'll bring their idols with them."

MORRIS: "What will you do then?"

MILDRED: "I don't know."

TEACHER: What about you, Jane? If you were really a woman of Modin, how would you answer this question? Would you worship the idols? Why not ask her, Morris?

MORRIS: "How about you? Would you worship their idols?"

JANE: "Never!"

MORRIS: "Would anybody in Modin?"

JANE: "Nobody would!"

TEACHER: This might be a good place to introduce us to the traitor. You might say, "Except maybe that Hellenist that's living in Modin. He might." Do you think we might move away from the women and bring on our Syrians?

NAT: I was wondering when I would get my chance.

TEACHER: Now, Nat. We had decided that our Reporter 1 would introduce Reporter 2. How would you do this, Morris?

MORRIS: I could say, "We will now hear from our Reporter Nat."

TEACHER: Perhaps we could do it in a more interesting way. Think! What, for example, would make you turn things over to another Reporter?

BILLY: Maybe Morris hears a commotion at the other end of the market place.

TEACHER: Excellent! Do you like this, Morris? All right, go ahead then. How will you say it?

MORRIS: When Jane answers me that nobody in Modin would bow to the idol except maybe the Hellenist, I will suddenly look up and say, "There is a commotion at the other end of the market place. A large group of people is coming out of a side street. Our Reporter Nat is stationed there. I will switch you to him so we can find out what's happening."

TEACHER: Good. Now you, Nat.

NAT: "There is a lot of excitement here. A troop of Syrian soldiers, led by a Captain has just come from the Jerusalem Highway. They are carrying a large statue of the Greek idol Zeus and a portable altar. Now they have entered the market place. They are setting up the idol and the altar in front of it. From all sides the people of Modin are gathering. The market place is now filled with a large crowd."

TEACHER: That's an excellent description, Nat. Do you think you will remember it? Maybe you had better write it out when you get home, just to be sure. Now, what should come next?

SAM: I think it's about time we got down to business. We ought to begin the action of the play.

TEACHER: You're right, Sam. How do you suggest we do this?

SAM: Well, let Reporter 2—that's Nat—introduce the Captain. I'll take it from there.

TEACHER: All right. Go ahead, Nat.

NAT: "The Syrian Captain raises his hand. The crowd grows silent. Now the Captain speaks."

TEACHER: All right, Sam.

SAM: "People of Modin. I have come here by order of our great king Antiochus to inform you that by law it is forbidden for you to practice the Jewish religion. From now on you must all worship the Greek gods. Now, who will be the first to offer the sacrifice to Zeus at this altar?"

BILLY: Is it my turn now?

SAM: I think Mattathias should wait until I ask him. He wouldn't go out of his way to look for trouble.

TEACHER: That sounds reasonable. Continue, Sam.

SAM: After I ask "who'll be the first," I turn to Billy and say, "You there, old man, what's your name?"

BILLY: "Mattathias."

SAM: "I see that you are dressed like a priest. Are you?"

TEACHER: That's a very good way to let us know that Mattathias is a priest, Sam. Very good. Go on, Billy. You have to answer him.

BILLY: "Yes. I am a priest of the One God."

SAM: "Then you must be the leader of the Jews here. You offer the sacrifice. If you do it, the others will follow you and worship Zeus."

BILLY: "I will not."

SAM: "Come, don't be a fool. If you make the sacrifice, the king will give you much gold and silver."

BILLY: "Even if King Antiochus gave me all the gold and silver in the world, I would not give up my religion, I would not worship your idol."

SAM: "You are a foolish old man. The king will punish you for this. I am sure somebody else will be glad to offer the sacrifice and earn the king's gold and silver. Who will offer the sacrifice?"

JANE: I think that before Sam, I mean the Captain, asks for another volunteer, Mattathias should tell him that he's sure no Jew will offer the sacrifice.

TEACHER: Why do you think this is necessary?

JANE: Because that will show how much faith Mattathias had in his people and. . . .

TEACHER: Yes?

JANE: And it will explain why he got so excited when the traitor did offer it.

TEACHER: Because he was so terribly disappointed?

JANE: That's part of it. The other is that he was afraid if one Jew could be a traitor, others might also give up their faith unless they are shown how to fight for their rights.

TEACHER: That's very important. We must bring this out in our dramatization. Do you think though, that a statement by Mattathias that no Jew will obey the king would tell us all this?

JANE: Well . . . partly. . . .

NAT: Why can't one of the Reporters, Morris or I, interview Mattathias later and get his reasons from him?

TEACHER: That's a good suggestion. But the speech which Jane suggests is also important. Let's use it. Let's go back to the Captain's last part. Go on, Sam.

SAM: "Mattathias, if you won't offer the sacrifice, somebody else will. Anybody will be glad to take the king's gold and silver."

BILLY: "You are wrong, Captain. No Jew in Modin will be a traitor to his people and to his religion."

SAM: "We'll see about that. Jews of Modin! Who will offer the sacrifice? Come! You'll be rich if you obey the king's command. Who will offer the sacrifice?"

LOUIS: "I will."

TEACHER: Very good, Louis. You came in exactly on cue. You keep this up and you'll be playing lead parts before long. Now how will the audience know that the part Louis is playing is of a Hellenist?

MILDRED: The people could be shocked and whisper it to each other.

NAT: I think one of the reporters should say it.

MILDRED: You just want to take all the parts for yourself.

TEACHER: Now, Mildred, I'm sure that's not why Nat made his suggestion. Why do you think a reporter should say it?

NAT: Well, for one thing we don't have enough people in the cast to make up a crowd. Also, the audience couldn't hear a whisper.

BILLY: I think they are both right. As soon as Louis says that he'll offer the sacrifice, everybody in the crowd begins to whisper about him, then a Reporter explains in more detail.

SAM: But we don't have a crowd in the cast.

BILLY: Sure we have. The whole class could be the crowd. Aren't we doing, "Witness to History"? Everybody is seeing what's happening. Everybody can take part.

This suggestion of Billy is a very fortuitous one. It provides all the students with an opportunity to participate actively in the dramatization. Not always, however, will one of the students arrive at this idea. If such a suggestion is not offered by a student, the teacher makes it. This is especially important the first several times "Witness to History" is used. Once the pattern of involving the class in crowd scenes is established, the students will look for an opportunity to create class-crowd scenes.

TEACHER: Billy, that's a real fine suggestion. Now, what would the people in the crowd be saying? *(Teacher turns to class)* Any suggestions?

STUDENT 1: I would say, "That's the Hellenist!"

TEACHER: Good. You say this when we do the dramatization. All of you decide what you want to say as part of the crowd. Marty?

MARTY: I'll say sort of shocked like, "He's going to offer the sacrifice!"

LEAH: I'll say, "I don't believe it."

SARAH: I'll say, "He's a traitor."

TEACHER: Between now and the time we do the dramatization you will all have a chance to think up something to say. You are shocked. You are angry. You don't believe that any Jew would do such a thing. Now, which of our Reporters should describe what happens next?

STUDENT 1: Since Nat has been describing things, he should be the one to continue.

TEACHER: Go ahead, Nat. You will now describe what's happening.

NAT: "A fat man pushes his way out from the crowd toward the altar."

STUDENT 2: How do you know the Traitor was fat?

NAT: How do you know he wasn't?

TEACHER: I suppose Nat feels that a Hellenist should be fat for some reason. Is that it, Nat?

NAT: Sure. It sort of fits.

TEACHER: Continue, Nat.

NAT: "The crowd is shocked. They can't believe that any citizen of Modin would sacrifice to the idol. They recognize him. He is X the Hellenist."

TEACHER: X?

NAT: Well, Louis is supposed to find a Greek name for himself as the traitor. Since we don't know the name yet, I shall call him X.

TEACHER: I forgot. Go on, Nat.

NAT: "The Hellenist goes over to the altar. He kneels. He begins to offer the sacrifice. The Priest Mattathias the Hasmonean seeing this great sin, draws a knife . . ."

STUDENT 3: *(Interrupts)* I don't think the Reporter should describe this. I think we ought to show by acting it out.

TEACHER: *(To class)* What do you think of this idea?

STUDENT 4: I don't like it. We can't really show this scene of killing and make it real. I think it's better if we describe it and leave it to the imagination of the audience.

TEACHER: We'll vote on it. Those who think we should act it out, raise your hands. *(Teacher counts votes)* Those who feel that the Reporter should describe it, raise your hands. *(Teacher counts the votes)*. It seems most of you feel that we leave it to Nat. Go ahead.

NAT: "Mattathias rushes at the Traitor and stabs him. The Traitor falls dead across the altar. The crowd attacks the Syrians who run away. Mattathias jumps up on a large stone and calls out . . ."

BILLY: "Who is for the Lord? Follow me!"

TEACHER: Bravo, Billy. You came in perfectly. What do we do now?

STUDENT 5: We had decided that a Reporter was going to interview Mattathias.

TEACHER: How do we shift to him?

STUDENT 6: Why not have the Narrator tell what happened next in Modin and then say, "That night our Reporter interviewed Mattathias" and we hear the interview?

TEACHER: Very well. We'll try it. Jack, you're our Narrator. Take it over.

JACK: "The call of Mattathias was the Declaration of Independence of the Judaeans. All the Jews of Modin followed Mattathias into the hills. Others heard about the happenings in Modin and came to Mattathias to fight with him for freedom. Come with me now into the hills to the Camp of Mattathias where he is being interviewed by our Reporter . . ." Which one?

TEACHER: Nat has just had a long part. Let's give Morris a chance.

JACK: "Where he is being interviewed by our Reporter Morris."

TEACHER: You remember, Morris, we decided you were to find out from Mattathias why he killed the Traitor. Go ahead now.

MORRIS: "Mattathias, will you please tell me why you killed the Hellenist?"

BILLY: "Because he offered the sacrifice to the idol."

MORRIS: "Other Jews before him listened to the Syrians and worshipped the idols."

BILLY: "Not in Modin. In my city I was sure nobody would be a traitor to our religion."

MORRIS: "Is it so important if one Jew is a traitor? All the other Jews refused to give up their religion."

BILLY: "Today it is one. Tomorrow others will see the traitor with the gold and silver of the Syrians and they'll do the same. I had to stop this right away."

MORRIS: "Why did you call for all those who are with the Lord to follow you?"

BILLY: "I saw our religion in danger. The time has come to fight for our God and for the right to worship Him."

MORRIS: "You intend to make war on the Syrians with so few men and almost no ammunition?"

BILLY: "We will fight for our freedom. The Lord will help us. With His help, we're sure to win."

TEACHER: That is very, very good, boys. This is the perfect place to finish our drama. All right, Jack.

JACK: "And with the help of God, the Jews won their fight for freedom and to this day we celebrate their fight and victory with the festival of Hanukah. You have seen the Beginning of the Maccabean Revolt. Today you have been Witness to History!"

TEACHER: Now, that's very nice. I should think you are ready to do the dramatization right now. All of you in the cast, don't forget to look up the references I gave you. It will help you to give a much richer performance when you know more of the facts. The Reporters and the Narrator should write out their parts at home and then go over them several times until you know them very well. It might be a good idea if you all got together once for a rehearsal. How about next Monday a half hour before class? You can have the rehearsal without my help since we worked it all out today. If possible, I may join you. At out next history lesson we will have the enactment of our dramatization.

7. Research by the Cast

The teacher arranges with the school librarian to make available to the cast the reference books which have been suggested as well as other sources which might prove helpful in enriching the background and knowledge of the students. If there is no library in the school, the teacher places the reference books in the classroom and arranges for the students to use them on a rotating basis so that all will have an opportunity to read them. The teacher is of course available freely for consultation with any of the students who seek guidance in their research.

8. Home Preparation of Reports by "Reporters" and Others

Those members of the cast who have long narrative sections, such as the Narrator, Reporter 1, and Reporter 2 are urged to write out at home what they will say in the dramatization. If time permits, the teacher looks over these written reports and offers suggestions for improvement. The students then go over what they have written until they become thoroughly familiar with their parts.

9. Rehearsal of Dramatization

The teacher determines whether or not a rehearsal is necessary. If the dramatization has been carefully developed in class, it is quite possible to do without any further rehearsal. If the teacher feels that a rehearsal would be beneficial, it is scheduled for a mutually convenient time outside of class hours. The teacher attends the rehearsal if possible. This might be essential with younger children. Older students, particularly those who have had previous experience with this type of dramatization, might be permitted to hold their rehearsals without the presence of the teacher. In this event it is advisable to elect or appoint one of the students as Director or Chairman, to keep the rehearsal going in an orderly fashion.

10. The Enactment

The dramatization is presented before the class during the succeeding history period. No attempt is made at costuming the cast, and scenery certainly has no place in this type of classroom dramatization. It is of course discretionary with the teacher to permit a minimum of costuming and props if the students ask for it. The teacher is careful, however, not to permit such physical aspects to overshadow the dramatization itself and to assume primary importance.

On occasion it might be advisable to invite another class to witness the enactment. In some instances the dramatization may be of sufficiently high quality and general interest to warrant its presentation before a general school assembly. The teacher bears in mind, however, that the aim in utilizing the "Witness to History" technique is not the creation of a dramatic performance for showing to others but rather as a means for vitalizing a lesson in history. It is first and foremost a device for teaching. Consequently, the process of creating the dramatization is of primary importance. The quality of the enactment is of relatively minor significance.

During a session of an in-service course for teachers which dealt with the use of this technique, a certain teacher reported on her experiences with it. They had dramatized "The Arrest of Jeremiah." The members of the cast were asked to write up their parts where possible. The teacher reported that "The whole year I didn't get such papers as I did on Jeremiah. One boy who usually writes only several lines gave a two page paper discussing religious conditions." When asked to characterize her experience, the teacher said that she was disappointed in the result. "The children often hesitated. They often groped for words. The dialogue wasn't smooth. I wanted to invite the principal to the presentation. I was glad he could not come. It wasn't a smooth show." After this "discouraging" report this teacher was asked, "Is there anything favorable you can say about your experience?" She shook her head rather doubtfully. With a good deal of hesitation she said, "Well . . . I don't know . . . The show was disappointing . . ." Then, almost as an afterthought she added, "One thing I will say. The children learned more about Jeremiah than about any other character they studied in history this year. I don't think they'll ever forget what they learned about Jeremiah." "Why," she was asked. "Well . . .

They were excited about him. They did research. They talked about him in class and after class. They really learned about Jeremiah and the destruction of the First Temple."

Here is a classic example of a teacher who finds gold and spurns it because she does not recognize its value. The teacher who keeps in mind the true purpose of utilizing this and other dramatic techniques will not mind an unsmooth enactment—particularly with a younger class or the first few times the technique is used even with an older class. The true measuring rod of success or failure will be how much better, how much more willingly, how much more intensively did the children learn with this technique than they usually learn without it.

Naturally, the teacher always aims for improvement in every aspect of the process, including the final presentation. The discussion period which follows the enactment is quite useful in this regard.

11. Class Evaluation of the Enactment

The students are encouraged to comment on the quality of the dramatization. The teacher is careful to guide the discussion so that positive aspects receive due recognition and praise. He uses guiding questions such as, "Wasn't it nice, the way our Reporter Nat lowered his voice almost to a whisper when he described the Traitor's appearance? Wasn't it dramatic?" "What did you like best about Billy's portrayal of Mattathias?"

Comments of this type are followed with requests for suggestions for improvement of the portrayals. This has value since it will tend to raise the level of quality of future dramatizations. The teacher is extremely careful, however, in guiding this aspect of the discussion. It can readily offer opportunities for the students to vent their animosities against each other under the guise of criticism. Furthermore, if criticism is allowed to get out of hand it will have the exact opposite effect from what it is intended to produce. Instead of helping to improve future dramatizations, it might frighten off many from participating for fear of exposing themselves to sharp criticism. Consequently the teacher frames the questions in such a way as to elicit suggestions for improvement rather than criticisms. For example:

> "When Mattathias spoke to the reporter would he have been more effective if he had spoken quietly rather than sounding angry?"
>
> "In describing the killing of Hannah's sons, what could the Judaean woman have done to make us feel that she was really sad about it?"
>
> "What would have helped us to understand the narration of Reporter I better? Should he have spoken slower? Would raising his voice have been an improvement? What else could you suggest?"

During this phase of the discussion the teacher is careful to avoid using the names of the students who took the part. Reference is always made to the name of the character portrayed. It is not, "What should *Billy* have done to make his call 'Who is for the Lord' more effective?" It is, "What should *Mattathias* have done to make his call 'Who is for the Lord' more effective?"

Suggestions are also encouraged for improvement of the dramatization. By developing their critical faculties toward their own work the students learn to improve it from one dramatization to the next. Thus there is room in this phase of the discussion for such questions as:

"What part of the story could have been left out of the dramatization? Why?"

"What part was omitted and should have been included? Why?"

Finally, in some situations, the teacher might find it valuable to encourage self-criticism on the part of the participants. Thus:

"Billy, if you were to do the play over again, what would you do differently to improve your part?"

"Jane, what part of your portrayal do you think was most effective? What part didn't satisfy you?"

From evaluating the enactment, the discussion is guided in the direction of evaluating the story. The actions of the characters are analyzed, discussed, and evaluated in the light of their motivations, the conditions under which they lived, the effect of their acts on later history, etc. The type of questions raised for discussion will depend on the age and maturity of the students. Following are some examples:

"Why did Antiochus want everyone to worship the Greek idols?"

"In your opinion, what caused many Jews to become Hellenists?"

"Why did Mattathias and his followers oppose them?"

"Why did every one in Modin look to Mattathias for leadership?"

"In your opinion, why didn't the Jews of the big cities revolt against the Syrians?"

"What, do you think, made it possible for the small and poorly equipped army of the Judaeans to win against the might of the Syrians?"

12. Generalizing and Applying the Lesson

The lesson assumes its true significance when the students are helped to recognize its general implications and its relevance to their own lives and value-scheme. The discussion therefore proceeds in this direction—the final step in the process. For example:

TEACHER: One of the strange things about history is that on occasion similar things happen in far separated countries and in different times. Take for example, the Traitor whose acts were a turning point in the Maccabean Revolt. Can you think of a similar incident in American History?

STUDENT: Benedict Arnold.

TEACHER: Why is the Maccabean struggle such an important landmark in Jewish history?

STUDENTS: It was the first fight for religious freedom in Jewish history.
It saved the Jewish way of life.

TEACHER: There have been many examples in history of similar struggles by an oppressed people fighting for freedom. Can you think of any?

STUDENTS: The American Revolution.
Bolivar, San Martin, and O'Higgins in South America.
Israel's War of Independence.
Garibaldi in Italy.
The Greek Revolution against Turkey.
The Ghetto Fighters' struggle against the Nazis.

TEACHER: What did all these have in common?

STUDENTS: They fought against oppression.
They fought for their rights.
They fought to be free.

TEACHER: What do we mean by freedom?

STUDENTS: The right to worship God.
The right to speak our mind.
The right to earn a living.
The right to run our own country.
etc.

TEACHER: Should a person always put up a fight when his rights are denied him?

STUDENTS: *(Free discussion).*

TEACHER: Are there occasions when one should give up his rights for the sake of peace? Can you think of some examples in your own experience?

STUDENTS: *(Free discussion).*

TEACHER: Should a person put up a fight to defend some one else's rights? Can you think of some actual situations?

STUDENTS: *(Free discussion).*

TEACHER: Every year, for eight days, we observe the festival of Hanukah to celebrate the Maccabean victory. Can you tell me, what is the literal meaning of the word "Hanukah"?

STUDENT: Dedication.

TEACHER: What does it describe?

STUDENT: The fact that the Maccabees re-dedicated the Temple in Jerusalem to the service of God.

TEACHER: The Maccabees not only re-dedicated the Temple. They also dedicated themselves, their own lives. Can any of you tell me to what the Maccabees dedicated themselves?

STUDENTS: To fight on for freedom.
To be true to the Jewish religion.
To protect the Land of Israel from enemies.
etc.

TEACHER: The main reason we observe a festival is to remember the events it commemorates and to feel them once again as if we had been there in person. Thus on Pesah the *Hagadah* tells us, "*B'khol dor va-dor ha-yav a-dam lir-ot et atz-mo k'ee-lu hu ya-tza mi-mitz-ra-yim.* In every generation each person must feel as if he personally had been delivered from Egypt." On Shavuot we celebrate the receiving of the Torah and we renew our pledge to be faithful to its teachings. If Hanukah means dedication, to what do you dedicate yourselves each year on Hanukah?

STUDENTS: To be true to our religion.
To live a good Jewish life.
To love freedom.
etc.

TEACHER: I'll tell you what—we are running out of time and this is very important. I want to be sure you will each get your turn. Supposing, when you get home, each of you sits down and writes a short composition on "What Hanukah means to me and to what do I dedicate myself on Hanukah."

(Teacher writes topic on blackboard)

I will of course read every composition. Then I will pick out three at random and the ones who wrote them will read them aloud to the class.

The teacher may suggest other uses for the compositions. For example:

The best one to be published in the school newspaper.
The best three to be posted on the class bulletin board.
The best one to be read at a school assembly.
All the compositions are to be issued as a class newspaper which will also contain a report of the dramatization.

Having given the class this assignment, the time has come for the teacher to proceed with the next lesson in history. Whatever technique the teacher might now choose to utilize in teaching the new lesson, it would be advisable to indicate to the students in some manner both the fact that their work on the dramatization is at an end and that there is a continuity in the historical process. The teacher's closing statement might then run somewhat as follows:

TEACHER: Now that we have witnessed the beginning of the Maccabean Revolt, it will be interesting to find out what happened to Jewish life in the Land of Israel after the struggle was won. Were all the Jews united now? Did they all follow the religion of their fathers, believing in the same things, worshipping in the same manner? Or, did the influence of the Hellenists remain in Judaea? Did religious differences develop? You will find the answers to these questions in your book in Chapter Four which begins on page 90. I suggest that you all read it at home. We will talk about it at our next history lesson.

Additional Examples

Following are several additional examples of "Witness to History" dramatizations:

DEBORAH THE PROPHETESS

1. Teacher's Introduction

TEACHER: Who can mention some names of great generals of history?
STUDENT 1: General Eisenhower.
STUDENT 2: General Grant.
STUDENT 3: General Pershing.
TEACHER: What about some generals who were not Americans?
STUDENT 4: General Montgomery.
STUDENT 5: Napoleon.
STUDENT 6: Caesar.
TEACHER: All men? Don't you know even a single woman military leader? There's one that's very famous in French history.
STUDENT 1: Joan of Arc?
TEACHER: Of course! She not only inspired the French generals of her day to fight for France but actually led the French armies in battle. Jewish history also has such a woman. Does any one know her name?
STUDENT 2: Hannah Senesh?
TEACHER: No. Hannah Senesh was a great heroine. She gave her life for the cause of freedom in World War II. Some day soon we will study about her. But she was not a leader of armies. The woman I mean is mentioned in the Bible.
STUDENT 3: Deborah?
TEACHER: Of course! Deborah the Prophetess. She is one of the very few women in history who was a great military leader. Don't you think it would be fun to do a "Witness to History" dramatization about a woman for a change?

(Usually the boys would say "no" and the girls "yes")

Well, I think the girls deserve a chance for once. The men have been having it their way in history for a long time.

2. Assignment of Preliminary Reading

TEACHER: *(Continuing)* During our next history lesson we will decide which scenes we will "witness" in our dramatization, the characters, and we will plan the details. Naturally you will have to read up on the story before then. You will find the information in your textbooks on page ______ and of course in the Bible in the Book of Judges, Chapters 4 and 5.

Steps **3** to **9** are followed as outlined above. During these steps the play is outlined, the cast selected, more research undertaken and the final dramatization developed, ready for the enactment.

10. The Enactment

NARRATOR: Come with me back in history, about three thousand years ago. Come with me to the Land of Israel to a great open space in the Hills of Naphtali where the armies of the Children of Israel are gathered, where you will be witness to history at the great celebration of Israel's victory over Jabin the king of Canaan. Our reporter Philip is stationed right in the middle of the plain. We will hear from him now.

PHILIP: I am right in the middle of a great plain in the hills of Naphtali. It is night but the plain is as bright as in the middle of the day. As far as the eye can see there are burning torches, held by thousands of Israelite warriors. The great celebration is about to begin. Here, let me speak to this warrior. Your name please?

ANATH: Anath ben Bildad.

PHILIP: From what tribe are you?

ANATH: Zebulun.

PHILIP: Were there many from your tribe in the fighting?

ANATH: Every one who could carry arms.

PHILIP: You seem proud of what you accomplished.

ANATH: Of course I am proud. For twenty years Jabin king of Canaan oppressed the Children of Israel. He had nine hundred iron chariots. He sent his soldiers from his capital city Hazor . . .

PHILIP: Excuse me for interrupting, but where is Hazor?

ANATH: Far, far to the north of our land. It is a great and mighty city. Jabin sent his iron chariots commanded by his general Sisera and they oppressed us greatly.

PHILIP: And what finally happened that you revolted against Jabin and his general Sisera?

ANATH: Every Israelite knows this. Deborah!

PHILIP: The Prophetess?

ANATH: The Prophetess, the Judge in Israel. She inspired us.

PHILIP: And Barak the son of Abinoam?

ANATH: Barak from the tribe of Naphtali led us in the fight. But without Deborah he would have been nothing.

PHILIP: Really?

ANATH: That's what all the soldiers are saying.

PHILIP: But you don't know this for a fact, do you?

ANATH: Why not ask the Ephraimite Yizhar ben Paltiel? He lives right near the home of the Prophetess. Hey! Yizhar! Come here a moment!

YIZHAR: What do you want, Anath?

ANATH: This man wants to ask you some questions.

YIZHAR: Go ahead! Ask!

PHILIP: You are from the tribe of Ephraim?

YIZHAR: Yes.

PHILIP: Where is your home?

YIZHAR: Not far from the home of Deborah the wife of Lapidoth.

PHILIP: The Prophetess?

YIZHAR: Yes.

PHILIP: So you knew her before the war?

YIZHAR: I knew her then.

PHILIP: Tell me about her.

YIZHAR: There isn't much to tell. She was always a wise woman. The people said she was a prophetess, that the spirit of God rested on her. So we made her a judge in Ephraim.

PHILIP: And the men of Ephraim obeyed the judgments of Deborah the wife of Lapidoth?

YIZHAR: Not only the Ephraimites. They came to her for judgment from the tribes of Naphtali and Zebulun and Issachar and many far places. She would sit in the shade of what we now call the "Tree of Deborah" that is between Ramah and Beth-El in Mount Ephraim and judge the people.

PHILIP: Now about this war?

YIZHAR: Well, it was this way: The children of Israel came to Deborah and cried out about their oppression by Jabin. So she sent for Barak the son of Abinoam . . .

PHILIP: The Naphtalite?

YIZHAR: Yes. She told him to go with ten thousand men of Naphtali and Zebulun and others to Mount Tabor. There, she said, General Sisera would come with Jabin's nine hundred iron chariots and the Lord would deliver them into Barak's hands.

PHILIP: But Barak refused to go.

YIZHAR: Not exactly. He said he would go, on condition that Deborah went along with him to help lead the warriors.

PHILIP: And Deborah went?

YIZHAR: She went and the Lord gave the victory into the hands of Deborah and Barak.

PHILIP: And Sisera?

YIZHAR: We fought him near the brook of Kishon. When he realized that he had been defeated he escaped and hid himself in the tent of Heber the Kenite. That was the mistake he made.

PHILIP: Why? I thought that Heber sided with the Canaanites.

YIZHAR: Heber did. But his wife Yael did not, and she was alone in the tent when Sisera came. When he fell asleep, she killed him and the Children of Israel were then really saved.

PHILIP: Again by a woman.

YIZHAR: And what is wrong with women?

PHILIP: Nothing. Nothing at all—especially if they are like Deborah the Prophetess and Yael the wife of Heber. Thank you very much Yizhar. Friends, I see a commotion near Deborah's tent. I will switch you now to our reporter Shimon who is stationed there.

SHIMON: I am speaking to you from the entrance to Deborah's tent. General Barak has just come in to speak to the Prophetess. She seems very upset about something. Let us listen.

DEBORAH: I tell you Barak, I will not have them join with us now.

BARAK: But why, Deborah? We can use every single warrior.

DEBORAH: Warrior? You call the men of Reuben and Gilead and Dan and Asher warriors? Where were they when we went to fight the armies of Sisera?

BARAK: Still, we could use them even now.

DEBORAH: No! When Israel cried out, Ephraim and Benjamin, Machir, Zebulun, Issachar and Naphtali endangered their lives. Where were they then? Among their sheepfolds, the divisions of Reuben searched their hearts and stayed home. Gilead remained beyond the Jordan. Dan remained in his ships. Asher stayed on at their seashore. They closed their ears to the cries of their brothers . . . Enough of this. Come Barak. The people are waiting to begin the celebration.

SHIMON: Deborah and Barak are leaving the tent. They are walking toward a small rise right in the middle of the plain. As far as the eye can see there are the thousands of victorious Israelite warriors with their torches in their hands. Now the sound of the *shofar*, the blowing of the ram's horn can be heard. Only a few days ago its sounds called the warriors of Israel to battle. Now it blows for victory. Deborah and Barak ascend the little hill. A great shout goes up. Wait! I will switch you to our reporter Sarah. She is stationed near the hill. Come in, Sarah.

SARAH: I am speaking to you from a hill right in the middle of the plain. Deborah and Barak are standing right close by, so near that I can almost touch them. The warriors are waving their torches and cheering in honor of their leaders. Now Deborah raises her hands for silence. She is going to speak. No, she isn't either! In the background musicians have begun to beat the drums and strike the cymbals. The Prophetess will recite a song of victory. Listen!

DEBORAH:

> When men let grow their hair in Israel,
> When the people offer themselves willingly,
> Bless ye the Lord!

SARAH: A great shout goes up from thousands of throats: "Bless the Lord! Bless the Lord!" they are shouting. Now the Prophetess speaks again her Song of Victory. Listen!

DEBORAH:

> Hear, O ye kings; give ear, O ye princes;
> I, unto the Lord will sing;
> I will sing praise to the Lord, the God of Israel.

SARAH: The Prophetess has stopped. She has finished the introduction to her song. Now she seems to be gathering her thoughts, searching for the right words. In the background the drums are beating louder. She speak now:

DEBORAH:

> Lord, when Thou didst go forth out of Seir,
> When Thou didst march out of the field of Edom,
> The earth trembled, the heavens also dropped,
> Yea, the clouds dropped water.
> The mountains quaked at the presence of the Lord.

SARAH: The Prophetess goes on with her song. She is telling about the war. Israel was silent, in mourning under the oppression of Jabin and Sisera. Now she describes the war and the victory. The warriors keep up a continuous roar of cheering now. Now comes the end of the Song of Deborah. Listen!

DEBORAH:

So perish all Thine enemies, O Lord;
But they that love Him be as the sun
when he goeth forth in his might.

NARRATOR: You have been witnesses to history at the victory celebration of the Israelite armies who won their freedom from the oppression of Jabin the king of Canaan and his general Sisera. You have also heard portions of Deborah's song of victory—a song that will go down in history as one of the great literary masterpieces of all time.

THE DEGRADATION OF DREYFUS

NARRATOR: It is January 5th, 1895. This place is now the Field of Mars in Paris. We will all be witness to history, to the degradation of Captain Alfred Dreyfus. For the background to this moving moment we take you to our Reporter Leon.

LEON: The crowds have been gathering all morning. They have come here to witness the final act of a great human drama. Alfred Dreyfus, Captain in the Army of France is about to be publicly degraded, stripped of his rank, and transported to Devil's Island. He has been condemned as a traitor to France. Interestingly enough, even though a military court found him guilty, there are those who believe him innocent. There is Monsieur Duval. I spoke with him earlier. Monsieur Duval, would you please repeat what you told me before.

DUVAL: Gladly. I will keep repeating it until all will believe what I have to say.

LEON: And that is?

DUVAL: That is, that Captain Dreyfus is innocent.

LEON: That is what the Captain has been saying from the moment he was arrested.

DUVAL: And it's true! Captain Dreyfus is loyal to France. He never turned over military secrets to the Germans.

LEON: But they say that the documents proving his guilt are in his own handwriting.

DUVAL: Forgeries!

LEON: But handwriting experts have sworn in court that . . .

DUVAL: What experts? What court? The experts are from the Army, the officers of the Court Martial that tried him are from the Army. The army generals and the experts and all the others got together and arranged to condemn an innocent man.

LEON: But why?

DUVAL: Because he is a Jew, that's why!

LEON: What has this to do with it?

DUVAL: Everything. The army officers hate the Republic. They would like to have the monarchy back again. So they say that the Republic is controlled by Jews and that the Jews are traitors to France. To prove it, they now have this Captain Dreyfus. I tell you, sir, he was framed—as simple as that!

LEON: What about you, Monsieur Duval? Tell us who you are?

DUVAL: I? I am a Frenchman who fought for France and to establish the Republic. I will continue to fight for the Republic and against these army officers who are the real traitors.

LEON: Are there many Frenchmen who think about this Dreyfus affair as you do?

DUVAL: Unfortunately no. Most have been hoodwinked by the liars and the forgers from the Army General Staff. But, mark my words, Monsieur! There will be many more who think as I do as time goes on. Mark my words, Monsieur!

LEON: One more question, Monsieur Duval? Are you Jewish?

DUVAL: No sir. I am a Roman Catholic.

LEON: Thank you, Monsieur Duval. While I have been talking with Monsieur Duval, they have brought out Captain Dreyfus. Nearly a full regiment of French soldiers is drawn up. Now an officer steps up to Dreyfus. Listen!

OFFICER: Captain Alfred Dreyfus, you have been found guilty of treason. You are an enemy of France!

DREYFUS: I am no traitor! I love France! I swear it!

OFFICER: Alfred Dreyfus, give me your sword. Here now, I break your sword which you have dishonored!

LEON: They are publicly degrading Alfred Dreyfus. Now the army officer rips the braid from Dreyfus' uniform—now the epaulettes go—now the gold buttons are cut away and Alfred Dreyfus is no longer an officer of France. The crowd roars, "Down with the traitor!" Dreyfus too is shouting. What is he saying? Let us listen.

DREYFUS: I am innocent! Long live the Army! Long live France!

LEON: Now the mob is shouting "Death to the Jew! Death to the traitor!" They are leading Dreyfus away to his prison cell. Here, sir! A word with you, please . . .

JACQUES: What do you want?

LEON: What is your name, Monsieur?

JACQUES: My name is Jacques.

LEON: What did you think of this, Jacques?

JACQUES: What's there to think? The man is getting what he deserves. He betrayed our military secrets to the Germans.

LEON: How can you be sure?

JACQUES: He was found guilty, wasn't he? If the Army says he is guilty, then he is guilty and that's all there is to it.

LEON: Isn't it possible that there may be a mistake?

JACQUES: There is no mistake. The man is a traitor to France. No question about it.

LEON: No question at all?

JACQUES: None. The man is a Jew, isn't he? I must be going, Monsieur. Au revoir.

LEON: Au revoir. Ladies and gentlemen, there has been a man with a black beard standing next to me all this time. I will have a word with him. You have seen everything, Monsieur?

MAN: Everything.

LEON: What did you think?

MAN: It was horrible.

LEON: Horrible?

MAN: To condemn a man for treason, to degrade him publicly—and only because he is a Jew.

LEON: You believe that?

MAN: What else am I to believe? You heard the mob. You heard them shout, "Death to the Jew!" Every single one of them hates the Jew—without even knowing why.

LEON: And you, Monsieur know why?

MAN: Yes. Because the Jew is a wanderer on the face of the earth. Because he has no land on earth he can call his own. Because he is homeless. Because he has no government of his own that will speak out for him, that will protect him.

LEON: And if the Jews had a homeland?

MAN: It is not a question of "if" Monsieur but rather of "when." The day *must* come when the Jew will have a national home, internationally guaranteed, legally secured.

LEON: Interesting.

MAN: True. The conscience of the world demands it.

LEON: I see. And where will this home be?

MAN: In their old homeland naturally—in Palestine.

LEON: I see. And that would help Dreyfus?

MAN: That would avoid affairs like that of Dreyfus.

LEON: You are Jewish, aren't you Monsieur?

MAN: Yes, I am.

LEON: And with whom have I the honor?

MAN: Theodor Herzl, journalist, for the *Neue Freie Presse* of Vienna.

NARRATOR: With this we end our dramatization. You have seen the degradation of Dreyfus. The story did not end there. In the end, the conscience of France won out over the evil men of the Army General Staff. Alfred Dreyfus was declared innocent and given back his post with honor. The man in the black beard gave birth that day to the Zionist idea which, in 1948, brought about the establishment of the State of Israel.

F. DIRECT DRAMATIZATION

This is a dramatic technique which permits the students to relive a historical situation directly, as if they were actually participating in it. It is creative acting out of a story with complete self-involvement. As its name implies, it is direct, straight playmaking. There are no psychological props of the kind used in the techniques discussed previously such as: Written scripts for the participants to read, notes to be glanced at to jog a failing memory, commentators to keep the action moving, chairmen to guide the dramatization along its pre-determined path, etc. All of these devices are useful in that they bolster the self-confidence of the group or the individual students who have not had sufficient previous experience with dramatization. However, they often get in the way of the historic re-creation and are inimical to the complete involvement of the students since they act as a physical tie to the here-and-now. "Direct Dramatization," on the other hand, requires of a participant a suspension of reality, a vicarious immersion in the events of the past, and an emotional identification with the characters whom they are called upon to portray, characters who were part of these events and helped to shape them. This undoubtedly makes "Direct Dramatization" the most difficult of the dramatic techniques suggested here and, by the same token, it probably offers the greatest opportunities for effective teaching and learning of history.

Almost any event in history may be the subject of a "Direct Dramatization." It is most effective, however, when used in connection with a story revolving about a well-defined conflict—a conflict of personalities, of desires, of ideas, or of spiritual movements:

Jacob meets his brother Esau.

Moses in the bullrushes.

David and Saul.

The Samaritans and the Judaeans.

Pharisees against Saducees.

Marranos.

Yehudah Halevi's longing for Zion.

Hassidim versus Mitnagdim.

Zionism versus assimilation.

"Direct Dramatization" tells the story of its dramatic conflict within a distinct framework—a beginning which gives the background, introduces the protagonists, and states the central conflict or problem; the rising action which develops the problem and brings it to a climax; and the resolution which states the solution to the problem and brings the story to a conclusion. Within this framework the story may be told briefly, in one scene, or a number of acts and several scenes may be necessary.

A "Direct Dramatization" gains in interest and strength if it deals with human beings, with personalities with whom players and audience can sympathize in their struggle. Even when the subject is the conflict of ideas, it is best portrayed through the medium of a dramatization of the problem of human beings who are caught up in this struggle, and through whose personal story the conflict of ideas is brought to light.

Often the history text itself states a conflict of ideas in personal terms, emphasizing the role of specific individuals as the protagonists of those ideas. In such instances the class is able to dramatize the text itself, enriching it by filling in the background and rounding out the characterization of the historical figures with material discovered by the students as a result of independent research. In this category belong stories like:

Ezra and Nehemiah defy the Samaritans and rebuild Jewish life.

The Maccabean revolt against the Syrians.

Judah ben Baba ordains scholars in defiance of Hadrian's edicts.

Judah Hanasi overcomes the oral tradition and codifies the Mishnah.

Saadia Gaon's struggle against the Karaites.

Asher Levy's fight for equality for the Jews of New Amsterdam.

Theodor Herzl.

Joseph Trumpledor.

Chaim Weizmann.

The study of the history of certain ideas and movements might also be considerably enriched by direct dramatization of selections from the Midrash, literature, folk tales and similar materials which project through the personality of certain individuals the broader meaning of those movements or ideas. Take for example the following:

The ideal of learning—This is one of the central ideals in Jewish life. It has been restated time and again in many periods of Jewish history. Studied as an abstraction it may be difficult for an elementary school student to identify with it and make it part of his personal concept-structure. Fortunately this ideal is brought to the fore time and time again through the struggles and sacrifices in its behalf by personalities who evoke our sympathy and emotional involvement—personalities who are the central characters of history, literature or legend. Innumerable examples are at hand. Only a few will be mentioned by way of illustration:

The sacrifices of Rachel, daughter of Kalba Savua, to help the ignorant shepherd Akiba to become a great scholar.

Rabbi Johanan ben Zakkai risks his life during the Roman siege of Jerusalem to gain permission for the establishment of an academy at Yavneh, so that Jewish learning would continue.

Rabbi Moses ben Enoch establishes the academy at Cordova.

The legend of the *Seven Good Years*. The mother uses Elijah's fortune only to do good deeds and provide learning for her children.

The many folk tales about Elijah, Goan of Vilna, detailing his denial of self for the sake of learning.

Yearning for Zion—The love of a people for a land from which it has been exiled for many hundreds of years is an abstract idea. Stated through the stories of individuals whose lives were climactically affected by this ideal, we may find ourselves carried along with it, absorbing it, making it our own. Consider the stories of:

Judah Halevi honored as a philosopher, poet, and physician, leaves his loved ones to return to Zion.

Solomon Molkho dies at the stake refusing to renounce his self-imposed mission of leading a messianic return to Zion.

Any of the stories of Russian-Jewish students who abandoned their careers to join the Bilu in rebuilding Zion.

The romantic tale of any of the early *Shomrim* in Palestine.

Throughout Jewish literature are scattered dramatic tales which highlight the different ways of life of Jewish communities in many parts of the world and in many periods. These stories or excerpts from them offer rich material for direct dramatizations for history study. For example:

> The story of Bustanai dramatized in class, will help the students to an understanding of Jewish life in the Gaonic period and under the early Caliphate.
>
> The scene in Sholem Ash's *Kiddush Hashem* which describes how Shloimele leaves his child-bride Dvorah to go to the big city where he will remain for many years, a student in the *Yeshivah,* not only conveys a picture of Jewish life in Poland early in the 17th Century, but also highlights the central role of learning in Jewish life.
>
> Many of the folk-tales and other stories of I. L. Peretz might be dramatized to convey a clearer understanding of Jewish life in Eastern Europe up to World War II.
>
> Sholem Aleichem's Mottel stories offer many opportunities for direct dramatization to enrich the study of the East European immigration to America.

Finally, there is the original story, created by the students themselves as the plot for their direct dramatization, bringing to the fore, through the actions of the story's characters the ideas and movements under study. The original story will be used sparingly due to the fact that its development requires more time than can usually be allocated to this in the supplementary Jewish school. Where time is available, the creation of original story material for direct dramatization is to be encouraged. The following examples will illustrate the kind of plots it is possible to develop to highlight ideas or movements.

> *The Inquisition*—A Spanish boy learns of his Jewish origins when his parents are arrested by the Inquisition. He is rescued by a monk—in reality a Marrano—who is related to him. He is smuggled out of the country to Holland where he can live openly as a Jew.
>
> *Learning*—The tribulations of a twelve year old boy who has had to leave his home to come as a stranger to a strange city in order to pursue his studies in the *Yeshivah.*
>
> *Democracy*—A young man escapes from Russia to America so as to avoid serving in the army of the Czar who oppresses the Jews. Here he finds he is treated as an equal in getting a job, finding a home, speaking his mind. When America enters World War I, he volunteers to serve in the fight for democracy.

Introducing the Technique

Since it is assumed that "Direct Dramatization" will be used only after the students have had previous experience with other forms of dramatization, elaborate introduction of this technique will generally not be necessary. If their previous dramatizations provided the students with pleasant and satisfying experiences, it is safe to assume that they will themselves ask to dramatize the lesson. In that event the teacher will only have to indicate that a departure will be tried, and will point out the differences between "Direct Dramatization" and the other forms with which they are familiar. If the students do not come forth with the proposal that the lesson be dramatized, the teacher might simply say, "Let's play the next lesson," or "Let's show it instead of telling it." Thereafter the teacher goes on to indicate that a new form of dramatization will be used, somewhat as follows:

TEACHER: This time we will play the story a little differently than usual. We will do a "Direct Dramatization." We will act out the incidents of the story, making up our own dialogue for each of the characters. We will not use a written script. We will not refer to notes. There will be no outside characters such as a commentator, a chairman or even a narrator. It will be a straight play which we ourselves will create out of the incidents in our story.

Generally, even this simple introduction may not be necessary. The teacher might feel that it is best to proceed directly with the dramatization without any explanation about its form. An awareness of the difference between this dramatization and the ones previously done will come to the students as they see the play develop.

The Process

A "Direct Dramatization" is developed according to the following steps:

1. Motivation

The teacher motivates the new lesson using one or more approaches, depending on the subject. Following are possibilities:

a. *Pupil experience*—One or more students are encouraged to relate personal experiences which either parallel the subject of the lesson or are somewhat related to it:

TEACHER: Who remembers his first day in school? Tell us about it.

Several students are given an opportunity to describe their first day in school. The teacher then goes on to tell about a Jewish child's first day in a *Heder* and to develop the lesson about Jewish education in Eastern Europe.

b. *An object or picture*—Teacher exhibits an object or picture, allows the students to examine it and handle it, then proceeds to connect it with the lesson:

Exhibiting a *Doar Ivri* stamp motivates a lesson about the establishment of the State of Israel in 1948. The teacher relates how the stamps were printed without the name of the state since that was not decided upon until practically the last minute.

The teacher shows a clay lamp of ancient Palestine. "If this lamp could talk, what stories it would tell about the people who used it! It might tell us about the dark cave in which the Jewish sages hid out during the Roman oppression under the Emperor Hadrian, etc., etc."

c. A *poem*—Teacher reads a poem or excerpt that is related to the subject of the lesson. Having captured the students' interest the teacher proceeds to connect the poem with the lesson on hand.

A number of examples of the use of poetry follow. All of the poems suggested are in English, having either been written in that language originally, or translated from Hebrew, Yiddish or other languages. The references are as follows:

A: *The Golden Peacock*, edited by Joseph Leftwich, Robert Anscombe & Co., London, 1939.

B: A *Golden Treasury of Jewish Literature*, edited by Leo W. Schwarz, Farrar & Rinehart, Inc., New York, 1937.

C: *Modern Jewish Life in Literature*, Revised edition, Azriel Eisenberg, United Synagogue Commission on Jewish Education, New York, 1952.

The death of Saul might be introduced by the reading of an excerpt from "David's Lament," Samuel II, 1:19-27.

The Prophets may be motivated by reading a short excerpt from one of the better known prophecies, such as "The Vision of Peace," Isaiah, 2:2-4.

The Golden Age of Spain—Yehudah Halevi's "Longing for Jerusalem," B. page 579.

The Middle Ages, lessons dealing with persecutions, book burnings, forced disputations—"The Burning of the Law" by Meier of Rothenburg, B. page 586.

The Messianic Ideal, or lessons about false Messiahs—"The Messiah" by David Frishman, A. page 802.

Hassidism—Any of the following: "The Holy Baal Shem" by Zisha Landau, A. page 325; "Kaddish" by Rabbi Levi Yitzhok of Berditchev, A. page 864; "Rabbi Nachman of Bratzlav" by Aleph Katz, A. page 431.

Ghetto Life—"The Ghetto" by Leib Malach, A. page 472.

Learning in Eastern Europe or the converse, the Haskalah revolt against *Yeshivah* learning—"Mah Komashmo Lon" by Abraham Reisen, A. page 11; "The Mathmid" by Hayim Nahman Bialik, C. page 36.

Immigration to America—"Greenhorns" by Abraham Reisen, A. page 17; "My Son" by Morris Rosenfeld, C. page 77.

ICA, the Jewish colonization movement in Argentina—"The Colonist Senor Moses Katzenelbogen" by Leib Malach, A. page 475.

Pioneering in Palestine—"The Watchman De Haan" by Abraham Lev, A. page 618.

"Illegal" Jewish Immigration to Palestine (Aliyah Bet)—"To the Captain of the Hannah Senesh" by Nathan Alterman, C. page 193.

The Warsaw Ghetto—"Natasha" by a child in the Warsaw Ghetto, C. page 125.

d. A *community event*—The celebration of a special event in the community is used as a motivation for a lesson in Jewish history. For example:

The opening of the local Federation, United Charities, or Community Chest campaign is tied in with lessons dealing with the *Vaad Arba Aratzot;* the *Kahal;* Jewish community organization in differing lands such as Babylonia in the Gaonic period, in the ghettos of the Middle Ages, in Eastern Europe, in modern Israel, etc.

The dedication of a new synagogue may motivate lessons dealing with the building and dedication of any of the ancient sanctuaries as the Tabernacle, the Temple of Solomon, the Second Temple, Herod's Temple. It may also motivate lessons dealing with the history of the local Jewish settlement.

e. A *festival*—The traditional Jewish festivals offer of course obvious opportunities for motivation of lessons dealing with the stories of the festival. Some of the modern occasions, such as, Balfour Day, Herzl Day, or Israel Independence Day may be used to motivate the study of many aspects of recent Jewish history, particularly that which deals with the many aspects of the modern revival of Israel.

2. *Stimulation*

Although quite often the students who are ready for "Direct Dramatization" will themselves ask for permission to dramatize the lesson, the teacher may find it necessary to stimulate the activity. A good way to do this is for the teacher to begin telling the story in its general outlines. This arouses the students' interest in the material. The teacher then turns the task over to the students, to continue the story by telling it and showing it:

TEACHER: The dedication of the Jewish people to their Torah is unusual in the history of the world. Many, many Jews, in many generations risked their lives and often gave up their lives so that Jewish learning might continue. Take for example the case of Rabbi Johanan ben Zakkai. In the midst of the Roman siege of Jerusalem the Rabbi plays dead and risks death at the hands of both the Jewish defenders of the city and the Roman attackers, for the sake of Torah study. Just picture the drama of it! With death all around, the Rabbi has himself placed in a coffin. . . . You know something? The story would gain so much more if we not only told it but actually showed it, played it out in a dramatization. Here's what we'll do: we will all read the story at home. Then, the next time we have a history lesson, not I but you will tell the story—each one telling a little of it. Then we will act it out so that we can actually show this great drama of Jewish history and become a part of it. You will find the story on page ——— of your textbook . . .

3. *Research*

The students read the text at home. In addition, the teacher appoints several committees of student volunteers to do special research to augment the text and report their findings to the class. Separate committees are appointed to find out about social customs, the internal political situation, the international situation as it affects the story, economic conditions, supplementary legends, etc.

4. Story Told by Students

During the succeeding lesson, students tell the story, piece by piece until the entire story is related. As many students as possible are given an opportunity to do so. The procedure might be somewhat as follows:

TEACHER: We undertook to read at home the story of the Rabbi in the Coffin so that we might dramatize it in class. I told you a little about the story. But, let us now go back to the beginning of the story and tell it as it happened, each one of us telling a little at a time. Perhaps I should be the first:

"The Roman armies were encamped outside the walls of Jerusalem. Day in and day out, their battering rams hammered at the walls, trying to break them down. Their war machines hurled death and destruction over the walls and into the city. Still, after more than two years of siege, the city of Jerusalem remained unconquered. Inside the city were crowded hundreds of thousands of Jews. Food gave out. Still they did not give up. They fought on bitterly, stubbornly. However, they all knew that it was only a matter of time. The city must fall in the end before the might of Rome. 'What then?' The great Rabbi Johanan ben Zakkai, along with every one else, suffered in the besieged city and asked the same question: 'What then?' He called his students and disciples to him and said to them: 'The Lord's anger has poured out on Judea. Jerusalem will fall. What will we do then about . . .' "

Now, who will continue? Good. You keep going with the story from where I left off until I signal to someone else to take up the story. Go on:

STUDENT 1: "Rabbi Johanan ben Zakkai called his disciples and told them: 'We can not win against Rome. Jerusalem is sure to fall. What will happen to the Jewish people then?' One of his disciples answered him":

TEACHER: Student 2, continue please:

STUDENT 2: I don't know what the disciple answered. The textbook doesn't say it.

TEACHER: You are right. The book does not say it. But student 1 was imagining the conversation that must have taken place. Let us continue to use our imaginations. What do you think the disciple might have said?

STUDENT 2: "So one of his disciples answered the Rabbi: 'If the Jewish people continue to study the Torah, they will not be lost, even though Rome conquers Jerusalem.' The Rabbi agreed. Another disciple asked: 'How can Jewish learning continue if Jerusalem is destroyed?' To this the Rabbi had his answer. He said":

STUDENT 3: " 'If I could only set up an academy in some small place. It would have to be so small and unimportant that the Romans would not care to take it over.' The Rabbi thought for a moment and then he said: 'I know just the place . . .' "

STUDENT 4: "The Rabbi said: 'I know just the place. We will have our academy in Yavne. It's so small that the Romans won't even look at it.' A disciple then said: 'We must have the permission of the Romans because except for the city of Jerusalem all the rest of Judea is under their control.' "

TEACHER: Who is on the research committee for the internal political situation? All right Jackie—is this last statement correct?

JACKIE: No. The fortress of Massadah was still in Jewish hands even after Jerusalem fell.

TEACHER: Very good, Jackie. I won't stop the story telling again. I only did it this time to point out to you members of the research committees what to look out for. If you hear any other errors which you are able to correct because of your research, just make notes and we will point these things out when we work on the dramatization. All right, Student 4, please forgive the interruption. You couldn't have known this from the text lesson alone. Continue please.

STUDENT 4: "So the disciple said: 'We must have permission from the Romans because except for Jerusalem and the fortress of Massadah, all the rest of Judea is in their hands.' So the Rabbi's disciples tried to get permission from the defenders of . . ."

STUDENT 5: ". . . from the defenders of the city for the Rabbi to leave and speak to the Roman commander Vespasian."

STUDENT 6: "But the defenders refused to let any one leave the city. They were afraid that if any one left Jerusalem he would . . ."

STUDENT 7: ". . . he would give away military secrets to the Romans. Then the Rabbi thought of a plan. He told his disciples to pass around a rumor that . . ."

STUDENT 8: ". . . that the Rabbi had died. Now, nobody was allowed to be buried in Jerusalem because the city was holy. So his students placed the Rabbi in a coffin to carry him out of the city. The Rabbi of course made believe that he was dead. When they got to the gates . . ."

STUDENT 9: ". . . the defenders of the city stopped them. They didn't trust any one. But, when they heard that the dead man was the great sage Rabbi Johanan ben Zakkai . . ."

STUDENT 10: ". . . they allowed the coffin to be carried out of the city. Outside the city, the Rabbi got out of the coffin and went straight to the Roman commander Vespasian."

STUDENT 11: "Rabbi Johanan ben Zakkai greeted the general by saying: 'Hail Emperor Vespasian!' This pleased the general very much since he hoped to be emperor some day. So he asked the Rabbi what favor he would like. The Rabbi answered":

STUDENT 12: " 'Give me the small town of Yavne so that I could open a school there.' The general wondered . . ."

STUDENT 13: " 'When all of the Jewish land was being destroyed, why should this Rabbi want such a small favor as permission to build a school?' Still, he granted the request. Rabbi Johanan ben Zakkai thanked him and went away satisfied. He knew that if Jewish learning would be safe, Jewish life would continue even though Jerusalem, the Temple and all of Judea were destroyed."

TEACHER: That was beautifully told! I am glad that you included so much dialogue in the story. It will make it a lot easier to dramatize. Now, let's begin with our dramatization.

5. Break Down Story into Scenes

The teacher guides the students in breaking down the story into scenes or blocks of action. Simultaneously the story is enlarged by the inclusion of additional action, background, and plot and character development created by the pupils in the course of the discussion. To continue with our example of Rabbi Johanan ben Zakkai, the division into scenes might proceed somewhat as follows:

TEACHER: Now that we have told our story we are ready to prepare it for showing in dramatic form. Now, a number of things happen in the story. What would you say should be the first thing we would show or, to use dramatic language, what should be our first scene?

STUDENT 1: The first scene should be the Roman siege of Jerusalem.

STUDENT 3: I know the story begins with the siege of Jerusalem and that's very important to the story, but how can we show this in class? For a siege you need a lot of soldiers and things like that.

TEACHER: Well, does any one have any suggestion about this? No one? Well, let's see now—do we really have to show an actual siege to bring out this point? Can't we tell about it?

STUDENT 4: A narrator could begin the play by saying: "Jerusalem has been besieged by the Romans for two and a half years."

TEACHER: That's a very good idea. But maybe we can accomplish the same thing without having to use a narrator.

STUDENT 5: The Rabbi could say it to his students.

TEACHER: This sounds like a very good suggestion. What would be our first scene then?

STUDENT 5: The Rabbi meets with his students.

TEACHER: And what happens during this meeting?

STUDENT 6: They decide to try to set up a school at Yavne.

TEACHER: Billy, will you please be our Scene Secretary. Write on the blackboard what we decide about each scene, so that we don't forget.

BILLY: Should I put down everything?

TEACHER: No. Just put down the main things, like: "Scene 1—Rabbi J. meets disciples. Decide to establish academy." What should be the second scene?

STUDENT 7: The students try to get permission from the defenders to let the Rabbi out of the city.

STUDENT 2: That's not in the story. Furthermore, they'd have to be pretty dumb to do a thing like that.

TEACHER: Why do you say that?

STUDENT 2: Well, once the defenders find out that the Rabbi wants to leave the city, they'd watch for him and never let him out, coffin or no coffin.

STUDENT 7: All right. What do you suggest?

STUDENT 2: Don't ask the defenders.

STUDENT 7: Then how will we show that nobody can get out of the city?

STUDENT 2: Easy. Let it all come out in the first scene. They decide to get permission from the Romans. Somebody says, "How will the Rabbi get out? Nobody is allowed out." Then somebody comes up with the idea of the coffin and that's it.

TEACHER: Does any one have any other suggestion? No? How many think all this belongs in the first scene? It seems to be unanimous. It's really a very good suggestion, Student 2. All right Billy. Please add to your notes on scene 1: "Discussion how to get out. Suggestion about coffin. Now, scene 2—

STUDENT 8: That should take place near the gate when the students take out the Rabbi.

STUDENT 9: What will we use for a coffin?

STUDENT 10: Nothing. We're not having any scenery so we'll just make believe we're carrying one, that's all.

TEACHER: Anybody think differently? All right, Billy, note down scene 2 please. What will be our third scene?

STUDENT 2: I think we ought to have a scene between the Rabbi and the Roman guards, where he asks them to bring him to the General.

STUDENT 11: I don't see why that's necessary. Why can't we just begin the third scene when the Rabbi comes before the General?

STUDENT 2: Well, a scene with the guards would be exciting, like, "Halt! who goes there?" and that kind of stuff.

STUDENT 11: Sure. But what does that add to the story?

TEACHER: Both suggestions are good, so we will just have to make a choice. Those in favor of having a scene with the Roman Guards, please raise your hands. Those in favor of having scene 3 take place between the Rabbi and the General, please raise your hands. Very well. Please note it down, Billy. "Scene 3—the Rabbi before General Vespasian." Now, we are just about at the end of our story. Shall we stop at the end of scene 3 when Vespasian grants the Rabbi's request?

STUDENT 1: I think we ought to have a last scene in which the Rabbi explains to his disciples why Yavne is so important.

STUDENT 2: I think student 1 is right. And we could finish off maybe with a prayer of thanks by the Rabbi, because God helped him to save Jewish life.

TEACHER: Are you all agreed that we add such a 4th scene? Very well. Note it please, Billy. "Scene 4—Rabbi tells disciples. Prayer of thanks."

6. Determine Characters

From this point on, through step 9, the play is developed scene by scene. The class discusses the characters who are needed for the scene, and determines their functions and characteristics. The teacher points out the need for making each person in the dramatization an individual with individual characteristics and not merely a type. From this comes much of the educational value of dramatization—the figures of history cease being shadows and become human beings, identifiable personalities.

TEACHER: Now that we know what scenes our dramatization will have, we are ready to begin making our play. Let us go back to scene 1. Joseph, you've been rather quiet today. I think I have a special job for you. You'll be our Stage Manager. You will watch out that we don't make mistakes or leave out anything important. Billy will help you with it. Now, supposing you read for us what Billy has on the blackboard for scene 1.

JOSEPH: *(Reads)* "Scene 1—Rabbi J. Meets disciples. Decide to establish academy. Discussion how to get out. Suggestion about coffin."

TEACHER: Thank you, Joseph. Let us decide now what characters we will need for the first scene. Jane, you be our Characters' Secretary. You will write down on the blackboard the names of the characters just as Billy has done with the scenes. Now, let us see. Whom will we need for the first scene?

STUDENT 1: The Rabbi.

TEACHER: Good. Write it down Jane. "Rabbi Johanan ben Zakkai." Who else?

STUDENT 2: The disciples.

TEACHER: How many disciples shall we have?

STUDENT 2: I think two.

STUDENT 3: We ought to have more—at least five.

TEACHER: Why?

STUDENT 3: For one thing it will make it more interesting, and if we have more disciples each one will have to learn less lines.

TEACHER: Nobody will have to learn any lines by heart. We will each make them up as we go along.

STUDENT 3: Even so, it'll be a lot easier for everybody and it will give more people a chance to play.

TEACHER: These are all good reasons. We will leave it at five unless anybody has objections. Nobody objects? Very well, five disciples. Now what kind of a person do you think Rabbi Johanan ben Zakkai was?

STUDENT 4: He was very wise.

STUDENT 5: He was learned in the Torah.

TEACHER: Was he old or young?

STUDENT 6: He was very old—at least forty, maybe more.

TEACHER: Some people might not think that forty is very old—at least not old enough to be the chief sage of his generation. Let us say he was sixty, all right?

STUDENT 6: O.K.

TEACHER: What else can we say about him? Would you say he was a kindly person, patient, speaking softly, or would you make him a person who gets angry very easily, shouts all the time?

STUDENT 7: He must have been wise, kindly, speaking calmly. But sometimes he would get excited about things, if he thought they were important enough.

TEACHER: Like what things?

STUDENT 7: Like this academy that he wanted to set up.

TEACHER: Very good. Now, what about our five disciples? What are they like?

STUDENT 7: They're a lot younger. About twenty maybe.

TEACHER: All of them?

STUDENT 8: Well, no. Some are twenty, some are eighteen, some different ages.

TEACHER: Which shall we make twenty?

STUDENT 9: The first one.

TEACHER: Maybe we had better give them names. That will make it a lot easier for us to know whom we are talking about. Let's do that. Any suggestions?

STUDENT 10: Let's call one Jacob.

TEACHER: Jacob is a very good Jewish name. Jane, please write on top the word "Disciples" then put down the names of the disciples as we pick them. "Jacob" is the first one. Another name, please?

STUDENT 11: Judah.

TEACHER: Good. Others?

STUDENT 12: Mordecai.

STUDENT 1: John.

STUDENT 2: That's not a Jewish name.

TEACHER: John is the English equivalent for Johanan which is a very fine Jewish name. But since we already have a Johanan in Rabbi Johanan ben Zakkai, perhaps we'd better leave John out. Any other suggestions?

STUDENT 3: Moshe.

STUDENT 4: Isaac.

JANE: That's five.

TEACHER: Thank you, Jane. Now, let us take one disciple at a time. We will begin with Jacob. What is he like? How old is he? Is he tall or short? How does he act? How does he speak?

STUDENT 5: I think he's eighteen years old. He's a little guy, gets excited, talks very fast.

TEACHER: Good enough for now. Judah?

STUDENT 6: He's about the same age as Jacob but tall and talks very slow. Smiles all the time.

TEACHER: What about Mordecai? What is he like? For instance what does he do for a living?

STUDENT 7: He's a disciple of Rabbi Johanan. He studies.

TEACHER: Of course. But how does he earn his livelihood? Most of our great sages and scholars made their living from working at a trade, a business, or profession. Let us just turn for a moment to our *Siddurim* and look at *Pirke Avot*, that's Ethics of the Fathers, Chapter 2, sentence 2. Paula, will you read the Hebrew, please?

PAULA: "*Raban Gamliel b'no shel Rabbi Yehudah ha-Nasi omer: yafeh talmud torah im derekh eretz, sh'yegi-at sh'neyhen mashkahat a-von. Vekhol torah sh'eyn imah m'lakhah, sofah b'tey-lah vego-reret a-von.*"

TEACHER: Thank you, Paula. I'll tell you what that means: "Rabban Gamaliel, the son of Rabbi Judah the Prince, said, 'An excellent thing is the study of the Torah combined with some worldly occupation, for the labor demanded by them both makes sin to be forgotten. All study of the Torah, without work, must in the end be futile (that means useless) and become the cause of sin.'" That's how important the sages felt that work was. That's why we had very great scholars who were shoemakers, blacksmiths and so on. What should Mordecai then be doing for a living?

STUDENT 8: Let's make him a blacksmith. Then we can make him strong, "a mighty man" like in "The Village Blacksmith." He would talk in a loud voice . . .

TEACHER: Would he be the kind to make up his mind quickly and change it just as quickly?

STUDENT 8: I don't think so. I think he would take a long time to make up his mind but, once he made it up, he would stick to his decision.

TEACHER: Now, what is Moshe like?

STUDENT 9: Let's just make him the opposite of Mordecai—skinny, one minute he thinks this way, the next minute the other way, always agrees with everybody, never has his own ideas.

TEACHER: Very good. Each one of these is really different. They have one thing in common, I suppose, in that they have courage and are not afraid to take chances for the sake of their ideal of Torah study—or should we make one not so brave? How about the last one, the one we named Isaac?

STUDENT 10: I think they all should be brave but we could make Isaac cautious, maybe even afraid, but taking the same chances as the others in the end.

TEACHER: That gives us five disciples—five distinct personalities, five individual human beings—as in real life—each one different from the other but they all work together for their cause, for their ideal.

SARAH: I think it's unfair!

TEACHER: What is unfair?

SARAH: The boys get all the parts. There's nothing for the girls. Why does history always have to be about men?

TEACHER: That's not quite true, Sarah. There were quite a few great women who are mentioned in history. There is your own namesake Sarah the wife of Abraham. Who can think of other important women in Jewish history?

STUDENT 1: Miriam, the sister of Moses.

STUDENT 2: There was Rebekka the wife of Isaac, and Rachel and Leah the wives of Jacob.

STUDENT 3: Deborah the Prophetess.

STUDENT 4: Zipporah the wife of Moses.

STUDENT 5: Hannah the mother of Samuel.

STUDENT 6: And Hannah from the Hanukah story.

STUDENT 7: And Queen Esther.

TEACHER: I think this ought to do us for a while. There were a great many more. Women always were highly respected in Jewish life and many of them were very important. Why, less than 140 years before the time of our story, all of Judea was ruled by a woman. Who remembers her name?

JANE: Queen Salome Alexandra.

TEACHER: Very good, Jane.

SARAH: Then why can't we have women's parts in our play?

TEACHER: Who for instance?

SARAH: I don't know. They are not mentioned in the story.

TEACHER: But we can assume that there were women in the Rabbi's house—relatives, for instance.

SARAH: Daughters?

TEACHER: Well, it may not be such a good idea to say that Rabbi Johanan ben Zakkai had daughters when we really don't know. But we might assume he had other relatives, like nieces, without changing history in any way. Shall we have three nieces then? Good. What will be their names and what will they be like?

STUDENT 4: Let's call one Rebekka. She'll be very gentle, very worried about the Rabbi's health.

TEACHER: Fine. The second one?

SARAH: We could call her Miriam. She would be bossy, always worried that the house isn't clean enough, that the food isn't just right.

TEACHER: That's a good character. Now the third niece?

STUDENT 7: Let's call her Salome, like the queen. She can be flighty, worried about her looks all the time, giggling about everything.

TEACHER: Very, very good. That just about does it for the characters for scene 1. We really have made up a very interesting group of people for our play.

7. Select the Cast

TEACHER: Let us pick our cast now for the first time that we will play scene 1. Others will be given a chance to play the same parts when we do scene 1 again later on. Let us begin with the nieces. We'll start with Salome. Who would like to giggle?

In this manner the entire cast for scene 1 is selected. In this step the very same process is followed as in the selection of the cast for other types of dramatizations which we have considered previously.

8. Discuss the Scene

The scene is now discussed again in greater detail, prior to its enactment. This, of course, not only clarifies for the students the progression of the action and their separate tasks but also serves as a further opportunity for fixing the history lesson in their minds.

TEACHER: Let's go over in detail now what will happen in the first scene. How shall we begin?
STUDENT 1: Let's begin with the Rabbi telling the problem to the disciples.
STUDENT 2: I think we should begin before they come. That would give the girls a chance. They could talk to each other about the situation in Jerusalem.
TEACHER: That's an excellent suggestion. It will give us an opportunity to bring out the facts about the siege.
STUDENT 3: They could talk about the famine.
STUDENT 4: They could also start off the story by talking about the Rabbi, how he was worried and has called for his disciples.
STUDENT 4: Then one of them would say, "Here they come," and greet them and go call the Rabbi.
TEACHER: Now the Rabbi comes in and is greeted by his disciples. What do we show next?
STUDENT 5: The Rabbi tells them about his problem. Then the disciples make all kinds of suggestions how to get out. Then someone, maybe Mordecai the blacksmith, suggests that the Rabbi play dead and get out of the city that way.
TEACHER: Very, very good. Let's play the scene. The front of the room is our stage. When the scene opens, the nieces are on stage. The Rabbi is waiting to enter on the right. The disciples are waiting on the left side. Ready? Places everybody. When I say "curtain," you begin. The rest of you watch carefully and listen, so that we can discuss the scene when it is over. All right—curtain!

9. Enact the Scene

The cast which was chosen to play the scene the first time it is tried, now enacts the scene, the participants making up their own dialogue as they go along. This step is more fully discussed in the section "Story Dramatization." The first enactment of the scene might proceed somewhat as follows:

SCENE *(On stage are the three nieces)*

MIRIAM: I don't know what we will do for food. There was nothing in the market.
SALOME: Couldn't you buy a bread at least?
MIRIAM: No. There's a famine in the city. Everybody is starving.
SALOME: I don't mind not having bread, as long as I can get pretty dresses.
REBEKKA: You're silly, Salome.
SALOME: Why don't the bakers bake bread, Miriam?
MIRIAM: Don't you know there's a war on? The Roman armies are surrounding the city. Nothing can go in.
REBEKKA: I am worried about our uncle, Rabbi Johanan. I have nothing to give him for supper.
SALOME: What are we going to do, Rebekka?
REBEKKA: I don't know. Rabbi Johanan is worried also.
MIRIAM: He sent for his disciples. I wonder why.
SALOME: Here they come now.

(Disciples enter)

JACOB: We came as quick as we could. What does Rabbi Johanan ben Zakkai want?
MIRIAM: How would I know? The Rabbi does not tell me everything.
MORDECAI: Please tell the Rabbi that we are here.
MIRIAM: Salome! Go call uncle.
SALOME: Why me?
REBEKKA: Never mind. I'll go. *(She leaves and returns immediately, followed by Rabbi Johanan ben Zakkai.)*
RABBI: Welcome, my disciples.
MOSHE: Why did you send for us, Rabbi?
RABBI: The Romans have been besieging the city.
JUDAH: Yes, Rabbi.
RABBI: I know the city will fall some day. What will happen? We must find a way for the study of the Torah to go on even if Jerusalem falls.
MORDECAI: What do you suggest, Rabbi?
RABBI: We must set up a school where learning will go on.
MOSHE: That's a good idea. Where will the school be?
RABBI: In Yavne.
JACOB: Yavne is in the hands of the Romans. We will have to get their permission.
RABBI: I'll see the Roman general, Vespasian. I'll ask his permission.
ISAAC: How will you get out of the city? The defenders won't let you.
MOSHE: That's right. They won't let you go out.
RABBI: We must find a way.
MORDECAI: I have an idea. We'll tell everybody that you died.
REBEKKA: Oh, no!
MORDECAI: It's only make-believe. Then we'll put you in a coffin and carry you out of the city. Then you'll go out of the coffin and go to the Roman general.
ISAAC: Supposing they don't let us take out the coffin?
MORDECAI: Sure they will. Nobody is allowed to be buried in Jerusalem because the city is holy. They always let people carry out the dead.

ISAAC: Supposing they look inside the coffin and find out we fooled them?
RABBI: We have to take a chance. It's the only way.

10. Critically Analyze the Scene

The pertinent information has been brought out. The scene is completed and its analysis begins. It might be mentioned again that except for some remarks of praise, the discussion centers mainly about the content of the scene, not about the way it was acted. In our current example the discussion might go along the following lines:

TEACHER: Thank you very much. That was a very fine scene, very well done. You may go back to your seats and we will discuss the scene a little. I wonder, class, if any one can tell me what made the scene so fine?
STUDENT 1: I liked the way nobody looked at the audience.
TEACHER: That is true. Every one in the cast was paying attention to the scene. Now aside from the acting, what was especially good about the scene itself?
STUDENT 2: They brought out all the information.
STUDENT 3: They brought out about the siege and the famine and the rest of the story.
TEACHER: What made the scene so very interesting?
STUDENT 4: Everybody was a real person.
STUDENT 5: The things Salome said reminded me of my kid sister.
STUDENT 6: I liked the fact that Isaac kept worrying every minute about something else.
STUDENT 7: I liked how Mordecai explained the whole plan.
TEACHER: What should have been included in the scene?
STUDENT 8: Nobody mentioned that the war was going on for a long time.
STUDENT 9: That's right. It wasn't brought out how the Jews fought heroically against the Romans.
STUDENT 10: When the disciples came in they didn't say hello to anybody.
TEACHER: Hello?
STUDENT 10: I mean *Shalom*. And when the Rabbi came in and said welcome, they should have said *Shalom* also.
STUDENT 11: I think somebody should have brought out the reasons why the Jews and the Romans were fighting.
STUDENT 12: What's that got to do with the story?
TEACHER: Student 12 is right. We can't put everything into a dramatization. If a thing doesn't help in telling our story, we might as well leave it out. As a matter of fact, can you think of anything that should have been left out in the scene?
STUDENT 1: Why did we need the bit about Salome's pretty dresses? We could have left that out.
STUDENT 2: I think that was very good.
TEACHER: Why do you think Salome said that?
STUDENT 2: By talking about dresses when people were starving she showed that she was a dizzy dame. That made her a real person.

TEACHER: We've taken our play apart pretty thoroughly. Now let's give our players a chance. If you could play the scene over, what would you fix?

REBEKKA: I don't think that we, the nieces, should call him Rabbi Johanan. We should just call him uncle.

SALOME: The audience has to know whom we are talking about.

MIRIAM: I think Rebekka is right. The audience finds out his full name when the disciples come in.

RABBI: I think I made a mistake when I began to talk about a school without saying how badly I felt about Jerusalem. Even though I thought that a school was very important, I am sure that I must have felt awful about the destruction of Jerusalem.

TEACHER: I must say that not only was the scene very well played, but your analysis and criticisms are very much to the point. I am sure that when we play this scene over, later on, it will be a good deal better. Now let's take the next scene.

11. Repeat With Following Scenes

Steps ***6, 7, 8, 9*** are repeated with each of the following scenes. If the class is large enough, new players assume the roles in the succeeding scenes, so that as many students as possible have an opportunity to participate in acting roles.

12. Enact the Story

After each scene has been enacted and discussed, the entire story is played through, from beginning to end by a single cast without interruption. The final enactment might be as follows:

THE RABBI IN THE COFFIN

SCENE 1

SCENE *(In the house of Rabbi Johanan ben Zakkai in Jerusalem. Rebekka and Salome, the Rabbi's nieces are on stage.)*

MIRIAM: *(Another of the Rabbi's nieces, enters)* It was a waste of time.

REBEKKA: Couldn't you get any food, Miriam?

MIRIAM: There wasn't a scrap of anything in the market.

SALOME: Not even bread, Miriam?

MIRIAM: I said there wasn't a scrap of anything, Salome.

SALOME: I should have gone.

MIRIAM: Oh sure. You would find food on the empty stalls. Thousands of people were crowding around, begging for a bite to eat, for a piece of bread, a scrap of vegetable.

REBEKKA: What will be the end of this?

MIRIAM: We'll all starve or be killed by the Romans.

SALOME: Things can't really be as bad as you say, Miriam. My friend Dvorah bought a very pretty dress in the market yesterday.

MIRIAM: Sure. Pretty dresses you can get all you want and gold and silver jewelry, too.

SALOME: You see! Oh, I love pretty dresses and beautiful jewels!

REBEKKA: You can't eat them though. When you're starving the dresses and the jewels won't fill your stomach.

MIRIAM: I saw mothers give away diamonds worth a fortune for a scrap of bread to feed their children.

REBEKKA: It's grown quiet. The Roman battering-rams have stopped.

MIRIAM: Sure. That's to give us a chance to bring out of the city all those who were killed by their arrows and war machines.

SALOME: We haven't a chance. Why don't we surrender?

REBEKKA: The Jewish defenders of Jerusalem will never surrender to the Romans. For two and a half years the Romans have tried to break down the walls of Jerusalem. When they break down one wall, we build a new one right behind it.

MIRIAM: If our defenders would only stop fighting each other. . . .

REBEKKA: We have many groups and each one thinks their way is the only way to win against the Romans. In one way they're together—they all fight for Jerusalem.

SALOME: We haven't a chance. The Romans will take the city in the end.

MIRIAM: They will have to capture it street by street and house by house. How is uncle?

REBEKKA: The same. He's very upset. He sent for his disciples.

SALOME: Here they come.

(Disciples enter. They all incline their heads to the girls.)

MORDECAI: *Shalom,* nieces of our master and teacher, Rabbi Johanan ben Zakkai.

(Nieces reply "Shalom")

JACOB: We came as quickly as we could. What does Rabbi Johanan ben Zakkai want of us?

MIRIAM: How would I know, Jacob? The Rabbi does not tell us everything.

MORDECAI: Please tell the Rabbi that we are here.

MIRIAM: Salome, go call uncle.

SALOME: Why me? Why does it always have to be me?

REBEKKA: Never mind. I'll go.

(She leaves)

MOSHE: I wonder what our master and teacher wants of us.

ISAAC: We will soon know. I am afraid it means trouble.

JUDAH: Everything nowadays is full of trouble, Isaac.

(Rabbi Johanan ben Zakkai enters with Rebekka close behind him.)

RABBI: Welcome to you my disciples.

DISCIPLES: *Shalom,* our master and teacher.

RABBI: I sent for you because of something that is very important.

MORDECAI: We know, Rabbi. You would not have asked us to leave our posts with the defenders of the walls of Jerusalem, unless it is really important.

RABBI: The Roman siege of Jerusalem has lasted more than two and a half years.

MOSHE: A long time to fight and starve, Rabbi.

RABBI: Our defenders have fought like lions against the Romans. Every one of them, and you too my disciples, Mordecai, Jacob, Judah, Moshe and Isaac, have endangered your lives a hundred times a day fighting the Romans.

JUDAH: We have tried everything, Rabbi. Small groups of Jewish fighters go out all the time to attack whole legions of Romans.

RABBI: I know Judah. Nothing has helped. Nothing will help.

MORDECAI: Rabbi!

RABBI: You are surprised to hear me say this, Mordecai? Believe me, my heart pains for Jerusalem. Every night I weep for the holy city. But I know that the city will fall in the end. But Jewish life must not fall with it!

JACOB: Is that why you called us, Rabbi?

RABBI: Yes. Only if we continue to study the Torah will Jewish life be saved. The Torah will keep our people alive, even if Jerusalem falls.

JUDAH: That is true, Rabbi. Do we not say in the *Ma'ariv* prayer every evening, "*Ki hem hayenu, v'orekh ya-menu*—for the Torah and the commandments are our life and the length of our days"?

RABBI: Well said, Judah my son.

MORDECAI: What do you suggest, Rabbi?

RABBI: You are always the one to ask the right question, Mordecai my son. We must set up a school where the study of the Torah will go on, even if Jerusalem falls.

MOSHE: Where will the school be?

RABBI: In Yavne.

MORDECAI: Yavne is in Roman hands. They would have to give permission for us to establish an academy there.

RABBI: I know I can get the Roman general Vespasian to give us permission.

ISAAC: But how will you get to Vespasian. The defenders of Jerusalem will not let anyone get out of the city.

MOSHE: That's right, Rabbi.

RABBI: We must find a way.

MORDECAI: I have an idea. Since no one may be buried in Jerusalem because the city is holy, the defenders permit taking out the dead for burial.

RABBI: I think I understand, Mordecai.

MORDECAI: Exactly, my master and teacher! We will tell every one that the sage Rabbi Johanan ben Zakkai died.

REBEKKA: *(Frightened)* Oh no!

MORDECAI: It is only make-believe, Rebekka. Then Rabbi, we will place you in a coffin and carry you out of the city.

MOSHE: I see! Once outside the city, our Rabbi will leave the coffin and go directly to General Vespasian.

ISAAC: Supposing they look inside the coffin and see that we fooled them?

MORDECAI: Then all our lives will be in danger. The defenders will probably kill us all.

ISAAC: It's a great risk.

JACOB: Isaac! You mean you would refuse to go with us?

ISAAC: I didn't say that, Jacob. Of course I'll go along. But it is a great risk.

RABBI: We will have to take that risk, for the sake of the Torah, for the sake of the future of Jewish life. Come, my sons, let us get ready.

(They all walk off the stage area)

SCENE 2

SCENE *(Near the gate of Jerusalem. Two guards, Reuben and Shimon, walk on, one from each side.)*

REUBEN: You look tired, Shimon.
SHIMON: I am tired, Reuben. I've been on guard at this gate all day.
REUBEN: So have I, but I'm not complaining.
SHIMON: Good for you. You're a hero.
REUBEN: I am no hero. But I want no Romans in Jerusalem.
SHIMON: Who does?
REUBEN: Then why do you complain?
SHIMON: Because my feet hurt. All day long, that's all I've been doing, walking up and down in front of this gate. No Roman will try to get in anyhow.
REUBEN: Maybe not. But some traitors might try to get out of the city.
SHIMON: Why call them traitors, Reuben? They are starving. All they want is to get out to get some food.
REUBEN: I am starving also, and so are you, Shimon. But we stay here and guard Jerusalem and fight the Romans.
SHIMON: I hear Rabbi Johanan ben Zakkai died.
REUBEN: So they say.
SHIMON: Now, what does that mean?
REUBEN: I don't know. I don't trust him. I heard he is with the peace party that wants us to surrender to the Romans.
SHIMON: Reuben! That is no way to talk about Rabbi Johanan ben Zakkai. He was the greatest sage of our generation.
REUBEN: But he was with the peace party they say.
SHIMON: I am not so sure that the peace party is wrong.
REUBEN: Shimon! Would you surrender to Rome?
SHIMON: At least Jerusalem and the Temple would be saved. If your Zealots would . . .
REUBEN: You better be careful what you say Shimon. If my Zealots hear you talk this way . . . why they would . . .
SHIMON: Look, Reuben. A funeral procession.
REUBEN: It is coming our way.
SHIMON: I wonder who they are.

(A procession consisting of all the disciples approaches. They pantomime as if they are carrying a coffin.)

REUBEN: Halt!
MORDECAI: We request permission to go through the gate to bury our dead outside the city.
REUBEN: The name of your dead?
MORDECAI: Rabbi Johanan ben Zakkai.

REUBEN: Oho!
SHIMON: What do you mean, Oho?
REUBEN: Open the coffin!
MORDECAI: I told you, we are carrying Rabbi Johanan ben Zakkai.
SHIMON: Reuben! This is our great sage!
MORDECAI: I will not dishonor the great sage Rabbi Johanan ben Zakkai by opening his coffin.
REUBEN: I wonder, I just wonder . . .
SHIMON: What do you wonder, Reuben?
REUBEN: I just wonder if the Rabbi is really dead or he is trying to get out of the city to go to the Romans to surrender Jerusalem to them.
SHIMON: Reuben, you're a fool. How can one man, even a great man like Rabbi Johanan ben Zakkai, give Jerusalem away?
REUBEN: Maybe not. But I'm suspicious by nature. If you will not open the coffin, I will run my spear through it to make sure he is dead.
JUDAH: You will have to run your spear through us first before we permit you to do this.
SHIMON: You will have to kill me first also, Reuben. You cannot dishonor the great sage this way.
REUBEN: Shimon, what if it turns out later that . . . ?
SHIMON: That I was wrong? I am ready to go before your Zealots and pay with my life for the honor of Rabbi Johanan ben Zakkai.
REUBEN: All right. Let them get out.
SHIMON: Pass on with Rabbi Johanan ben Zakkai.

(The disciples leave. The two guards walk off, one to each side.)

SCENE 3

SCENE *(Inside Vespasian's tent. Vespasian enters from right, walks up and down several times. Roman guard enters from left.)*

GUARD: General Vespasian . . .
VESPASIAN: What is it?
GUARD: An old Judaean who got out of Jerusalem wants to see you.
VESPASIAN: Who is he?
GUARD: He says his name is Johanan ben Zakkai.
VESPASIAN: Rabbi Johanan ben Zakkai! The great scholar! Send him in at once.

(Guard leaves and Rabbi enters immediately.)

VESPASIAN: Welcome to my tent on the battlefield, Rabbi Johanan ben Zakkai.
RABBI: Peace to you, Emperor Vespasian.
VESPASIAN: Emperor?
RABBI: God's special glory rests on those whom He appoints as rulers. I see that glory on you, Emperor Vespasian.
GUARD: *(Enters)* Forgive me, my Emperor for coming in like this.
VESPASIAN: You too?
GUARD: A messenger has just arrived from Rome. He brought news. You have been proclaimed Emperor of Rome. Hail!

(Guard bows himself out)

VESPASIAN: So, my honored guest. You were the first to bring me this wonderful news. How can I pay you back? Ask anything you want of me.

RABBI: Anything, Emperor?

VESPASIAN: Anything.

RABBI: Give me the little town of Yavne, O Emperor.

VESPASIAN: Yavne? I said anything! Why didn't you ask me for Jerusalem?

RABBI: Because the Lord our God will destroy Jerusalem as punishment for the sins of her inhabitants. Also, there are limits even to an Emperor's generosity.

VESPASIAN: Yes, there are limits. What will you do with Yavne?

RABBI: I want to establish an academy there, a school where sages will come to study the Torah.

VESPASIAN: A school? I see no harm in a school. If you were to train soldiers, it might be another matter, but scholars to study the Torah—Rome has nothing to be afraid of that. Go ahead. Take your Yavne. Establish your school.

RABBI: *(Bows)* Thank you. Peace, O Emperor.

VESPASIAN: Go in peace, Rabbi Johanan ben Zakkai.

(They each walk off at either side.)

SCENE 4

SCENE *(A field outside Jerusalem. The disciples come on in a group.)*

ISAAC: The Rabbi is coming.

RABBI: *(Enters, greets them)* Peace, my children.

ALL: Peace, Rabbi.

MORDECAI: Did he agree?

RABBI: He agreed.

JACOB: Then we have our academy?

RABBI: We have our academy.

MOSHE: You are sad, Rabbi?

RABBI: Shall I not be sad when Jerusalem is to be destroyed, the holy Temple is to be burned?

ISAAC: It is the will of God.

RABBI: True, my son. As in the days of Zedekiah, Jerusalem will be punished for her sins.

JACOB: But we have Yavne.

RABBI: We have Yavne. Now the study of Torah will go on. Now Jewish life will go on from generation to generation.

JUDAH: What of Jerusalem? Will it ever be rebuilt? Will it be the crown of a Jewish land?

RABBI: Jerusalem will be rebuilt. Jerusalem will be ours once again.

ISAAC: When, Rabbi?

RABBI: When God wills it. *Shalom* my children.

MORDECAI: You are leaving us?

RABBI: Yes. I go to Yavne to begin the establisment of the academy.

MORDECAI: *Shalom,* our master and teacher. We too are going.

RABBI: Where to, my children?

MORDECAI: Back. To Jerusalem. To fight in her defense against the Romans.

RABBI: And when the city falls?
MORDECAI: We will fall with her. *Shalom.*
RABBI: God be with you, my sons.

(The disciples leave)

Blessed art Thou, O Lord our God, King of the universe who has given courage to men to die for Thy sacred name.

Blessed art Thou, O Lord, who teachest the Torah to Thy people Israel.

(He walks off)

13. Evaluate the Dramatization and Generalize

Once again, the teacher begins with words of praise and then leads into an evaluation discussion. The emphasis now is almost entirely on the material itself—the deed that was performed, the reasons for it, its effect on history, etc. Students are encouraged to express their opinions about the deed itself—whether it was justified, necessary, properly done, etc. They are given opportunities to speculate "if"—what *if* the deed had not been performed or had been done differently—what would conditions be like now? How would Jewish life be affected? How would the rest of the world be affected? The discussion might go as follows:

TEACHER: Wasn't it a moving play? I honestly think we are getting better and better each time we do a dramatization. I am sure you all agree this is an interesting and pleasant way to learn our history. Now, let's think a little bit about what we saw. Why did the disciples go back to Jerusalem?
STUDENT 1: To defend the city.
TEACHER: But they knew that the city was going to fall. Why didn't they stay out?
STUDENT 2: I guess they were patriots, you might say. They loved their city so much that they didn't want to live if it was destroyed.
TEACHER: What about Rabbi Johanan ben Zakkai? Why didn't he go back?
STUDENT 3: I guess he was too old to fight.
STUDENT 4: I don't think that's it at all. The Rabbi had a more important thing to do. He had to set up the school.
TEACHER: And you think that was even more important than fighting for Jerusalem—why?
STUDENT 4: Because that way he felt the Jewish people would continue to exist.
TEACHER: That's the point of the whole thing. If the Jewish people continued, there was hope that some day they might rebulid Jerusalem and make it a Jewish city again.
STUDENT 5: That's exactly what the Rabbi said: Someday Jerusalem would be rebuilt.
TEACHER: What, would you say, was the effect of Rabbi Johanan's establishment of the school at Yavne on later Jewish history?
STUDENT 6: The Jewish people continued to exist.
TEACHER: Just what do you mean by that?
STUDENT 6: There continued to be Jews.
TEACHER: But how did the school at Yavne help with this?

STUDENT 6: Well, the school taught the Jews how to live according to the laws of the Torah. I guess it helped them to continue being Jews instead of just anybody.

TEACHER: That's clear enough. Could Rabbi Johanan ben Zakkai have accomplished the same thing without asking Vespasian?

STUDENT 7: Not the way things were then. The Romans controlled everything. He didn't have much of a choice.

STUDENT 8: He could have gone to another country.

STUDENT 9: Rome controlled the whole world at that time.

TEACHER: At least a great part of it. What do you think might have happened if Rabbi Johanan ben Zakkai had not established the academy at Yavne?

STUDENT 11: The Jewish laws would have been forgotten.

STUDENT 12: We wouldn't have the Bible now.

STUDENT 1: That's not so. The Christians have the Bible and the Mohammedans also.

TEACHER: That's true, of course. But would you say that the Torah, Jewish knowledge means the Bible alone?

STUDENT 2: No. There are other things.

TEACHER: For instance.

STUDENT 2: I don't know for sure, but there's the prayer book and the Talmud and other things . . .

TEACHER: Yes, a great many other things which the Jews created in Yavne and in the schools and academies that followed Yavne—a great treasure house of knowledge which, taken together, are our Torah, which studied teach us the Jewish way of life.

14. Relate to Students' Experiences

Most lessons offer opportunities for relation to the students' personal experiences and to their own problems—some lessons more, some less. To the extent that this is possible, the teacher does so without, however, forcing the matter. The process is the same as that which has been fully described in connection with other forms of dramatization given previously.

Additional Examples

Following are several other Direct Dramatizations for teaching history:

MOSES IN THE BULLRUSHES

SCENE *(On the bank of the river Nile. Princess enters with three girls.)*

GIRL 1: This looks like a good place to bathe.

PRINCESS: I think you are right. It does look nice.

GIRL 2: Be careful, Princess. The river here is deep.

GIRL 3: She is right, Princess. The Pharaoh, your father, will be angry with us if you hurt yourself.
GIRL 2: Maybe we had better go some place else. This is near where the Hebrews live.
PRINCESS: What has this to do with it?
GIRL 2: They say the Hebrews are bad.
PRINCESS: Who says that?
GIRL 3: Everybody. That's why the Pharaoh ordered that all Hebrew children should be drowned in the Nile.
PRINCESS: That's a wicked law.
GIRL 1: Princess!
GIRL 2: It is your father's law.
GIRL 3: Pharaoh is holy and his laws are holy.
PRINCESS: No law is holy if it says that babies should be drowned, even if my father did make the law.
GIRL 1: Let's go swimming, Princess.
PRINCESS: You're right. Let us bathe. Wait now! I hear a baby crying. It seems to come from the river, right there!
GIRL 1: I'll take a look.
GIRL 2: Be careful!
GIRL 1: Look what I found, Princess.
PRINCESS: It's a baby!
GIRL 3: In a basket covered with pitch on the outside and clay on the inside.
GIRL 1: That was to make it waterproof. It was floating on the water of the Nile.
GIRL 2: It looks like a Hebrew boy.
PRINCESS: Poor baby. His mother must have put him in the basket to float on the river, trying to save him from Pharaoh's soldiers. You know girls, I think I will keep this boy.
GIRL 1: What will you do with him?
PRINCESS: He will be my son when he grows up.
GIRL 2: But what will you do until he grows up? He has to be nursed. He's only a little baby—maybe three months old.
MIRIAM: *(Enters)* Excuse me Princess. I heard what you said. I know a woman who will nurse the baby for you.
PRINCESS: That sounds just fine. What is your name?
MIRIAM: My name is Miriam.
PRINCESS: And who is this woman you know?
MIRIAM: Her name is Jochebed. She's my mother. She just lost her own son, so she'll be happy to nurse your son for you.
PRINCESS: Good! Run and call her at once.
MIRIAM: At once, Princess! *(She runs off)*
PRINCESS: Now, let me see, what shall I call my son? I have it! Since he is a Hebrew boy, I will give him a Hebrew name. In Hebrew the word *Moshe* means "to draw out." I will call him *Moshe* since I have drawn him out of the water. Ah, there comes Miriam with the nurse Jochebed. Don't cry, baby Moshe. Soon you will be fed . . . soon, Moshe.

CASIMIR THE GREAT

SCENE 1

SCENE *(Room in the house of Reb Moshe in Posen.)*

R. MOSHE: *(Enters, looks around and calls)* Malkah! Malkah!

MALKAH: *(Enters)* Moshe! My husband! When did you come back from Cracow?

R. MOSHE: Just a while ago.

MALKAH: Sit down. Rest. I will get you some food.

R. MOSHE: Thank you, Malkah. I am rather hungry.

MALKAH: I will tell the servant girl. She will have some food for you in a few minutes. *(She goes to the side and calls)* Esther! The master is home. Get some food ready, quickly. How was the journey, Moshe?

MOSHE: Hard. We had to change horses many times. The wagon broke an axle twice.

MALKAH: Thank God there were no robbers.

R. MOSHE: We had our share of those too. After all, a journey from Cracow to Posen is no small matter. It took us more than six weeks.

MALKAH: Thank God you are home now. Did you get everything settled?

R. MOSHE: Not everything. The Polish town merchants don't like us Jews. They're a hard lot.

MALKAH: Don't complain, my husband. Was it any better in Germany where they accused us of causing the Black Death, where mobs killed your mother and our two children? Thank God we were able to escape and come here to Poland. At least here we and our three remaining children are not afraid for our lives.

R. MOSHE: You are right of course.

MALKAH: Did the king accept your petition?

R. MOSHE: Casimir the Great, may his glory increase, is a noble monarch—not like the dukes and counts of Germany and France who rob our brothers and then let the mobs kill and burn all they want. Poland is fortunate in having such a king and we are fortunate to be under his protection.

MALKAH: I see he accepted your petition.

R. MOSHE: That he did. I told him I had been sent to him as a representative of the German Jews who have been living in Poland for a long time and those who just came. He listened very graciously.

MALKAH: And what did he answer you?

R. MOSHE: Nothing.

MALKAH: Nothing?

R. MOSHE: So far, nothing. These things take time. He has to think about it. He told me to come back in six months.

MALKAH: To Cracow?

R. MOSHE: Where else? Of course to Cracow. That's the capital of Poland. That's where the Polish king, Casimir the Great, may his glory be increased, has his residence—right in the great Wawel Palace.

MALKAH: So you will have to make the dangerous journey again.

R. MOSHE: What else can I do?
MALKAH: I'm afraid, Moshe.
R. MOSHE: Don't be afraid, my Malkah. The Talmud says: "*Shlihey Mitzvoh eynon nizokin*—Messengers for a righteous cause are protected from harm."
MALKAH: The highwaymen don't know any Talmud, Moshe.
R. MOSHE: Stop worrying. It will be another four months before I start out again.
MALKAH: And what if the king denies our petition?
R. MOSHE: God forbid!
MALKAH: What if he does?
R. MOSHE: Then the Jews in Poland might as well pick up and move on. If our rights are not confirmed by the king, it will be impossible for us to live in Poland. We will just have to move again.
MALKAH: Move again? Where to? To France, to England, to Germany? To the blood accusations? To the massacres? To the forced conversions? Where to?
R. MOSHE: That's right. We have no place left to run any more. Well, let's hope for the best. In the meantime I am hungry.
MALKAH: I nearly forgot. The food must be ready by now. Come, my husband.

(They both leave.)

SCENE 2

SCENE *(A room in Casimir's palace in Cracow. The king is seated. Near him stands Count Barski with a parchment in his hand.)*

CASIMIR: It is all still not too clear to me, Count Barski. Who are they who petitioned me?
BARSKI: Jews, glorious and mighty king.
CASIMIR: I know that they are Jews. But aren't they the descendants of the Hebrews of the Old Testament?
BARSKI: Yes, glorious and mighty king.
CASIMIR: Then why don't they speak Hebrew, Count Barski? Why don't they, ha?
BARSKI: Because for many years they lived in Germany, so they got into the habit of speaking German.
CASIMIR: But our German settlers say that what the Jews speak is not German at all.
BARSKI: Well—that's something for the scholars to argue. The Jews speak German to which they've added many Hebrew words, some French words, a lot of Slavic words until, well, it is now a lot different from German.
CASIMIR: But you just said that it was German.
BARSKI: It is and it isn't, glorious and mighty king.
CASIMIR: Count Barski! What kind of talk is that? It is and it isn't. What kind of talk is that? Ha?
BARSKI: Well the Jews call it Yiddish-German or just Yiddish.
CASIMIR: Then why didn't you say so right away? Now I understand. They began with German. Now it's so changed that the Germans have trouble recognizing it. It's a new language of the Jews. Yiddish! Now I understand.
BARSKI: Thank you, glorious and mighty king.
CASIMIR: What about this Jewish representative. Is he here?
BARSKI: Reb Moshe has been waiting for you to call him in, glorious and mighty king.

CASIMIR: Then call him in, Count Barski, call him in.

(Barski turns to the side, motions and R. Moshe enters.)

R. MOSHE: Blessed art thou, Lord God, King of the universe, who has given of Thy glory to mortals.

CASIMIR: That sounded like a prayer, Reb Moshe.

R. MOSHE: It is a blessing which we Jews say when we come face to face with the ruler of a country.

CASIMIR: That is very nice. I like that. So you have come for the answer to your petition?

R. MOSHE: If the glorious and mighty king will see fit to give it.

CASIMIR: The glorious and mighty king sees fit. Tell me, Moshka, you say the Jews have been living in Poland for many hundreds of years?

R. MOSHE: Yes, glorious and mighty king, many hundreds of years.

CASIMIR: Let us see if we cannot figure this out. We now have the year 1360. In what year do you say the Jews first settled in Poland?

R. MOSHE: No one can say for sure. We know for instance that in the year 1173 Mieczyslav the Third, duke of Great Poland, issued an edict forbidding attacks on Jews.

CASIMIR: You seem to have studied your history.

R. MOSHE: Yes, glorious and mighty king.

CASIMIR: What else did you find out?

R. MOSHE: During the first Crusade in 1096, many Jews escaped from France and Germany to Poland. And there is even a legend that the Jews have been in Poland since before the Poles came here, even before the Slavs.

CASIMIR: Is that a fact, Moshka?!

R. MOSHE: Not a fact, glorious and mighty king, only a legend.

CASIMIR: Tell me the legend.

R. MOSHE: They tell that when the Jews were driven out of the Land of Israel into exile by the Babylonians, a large group kept going northwest looking for a home. Finally they came to a lovely land of great forests, rushing rivers and green meadows. They loved this land. So their leader stuck his staff into the ground and said to them in Hebrew: "*Polin*—Here we will spend the night"—meaning the long night of exile, glorious and mighty king. From this came the name of the land in Hebrew—*Po-lin* or Poland.

CASIMIR: I am glad to hear that your first settlers loved this land. I hope you and your brother Jews will continue to love it always.

R. MOSHE: Glorious and mighty king! Does that mean that . . . ?

CASIMIR: That your petition is granted. The rights which were granted to the Jews of Poland by King Boleslav the Pious in 1264 will be ratified. Additional rights will be granted to you. You will be allowed to live any place you wish in Poland, to buy property, to carry on business, to travel freely, and at all times you will be under the protection of the Crown.

R. MOSHE: Glorious and mighty king! How can we ever thank you for your kindness to us?

CASIMIR: Thank me? Just keep on loving this land and working for its welfare. Give me the charter, Count Barski.

BARSKI: *(Hands him the parchment and pen and ink)* Here it is, glorious and mighty king. Here also are pen and ink.

CASIMIR: This charter, Moshka, sets forth your rights. I will sign it now. *(He signs and repeats what he signs)* "Casimir, Rex Polonia." Place this in the Royal Archives, Count Barski. Give a copy to my Moshka here. See that other copies are published all over Poland.

R. MOSHE: May our Heavenly Father grant you long life and healthy years, glorious and mighty king. *(He bows out.)*

CASIMIR: Well, well! *Po-lin*—Here we will spend the long night of exile. I like that, Count Barski. I like that very much. Come. *(They both leave.)*

CHAPTER 5

Choral Reading for Teaching Prayer

■ Choral Reading as a technique for teaching prayer was introduced by this writer in 1950. It has been tried out by many teachers in a number of day schools, talmud torahs, and afternoon congregational schools for teaching *Siddur*. Some teachers in afternoon and Sunday schools have also used the technique for teaching prayer in English. They have found the results very gratifying.

Choral reading is a dramatic technique which provides meaningful practice in reading, "drill without drudgery." Children find it stimulating and are eager to utilize it. Though at first, it appears to be a slow process, it is actually a "short cut" to learning the *Siddur* prayers—to the acquisition of knowledge of content, fluency in reading, and a desirable prayer attitude. Through choral reading, we can provide not only the necessary opportunities for drill but can simultaneously also teach our children the meaning of the prayer, and its place in the traditional ritual. Above all, it enables us to develop within them an emotional attachment to the prayer.

In the pages that follow, the procedures for the utilization of this technique will be developed, step by step. Any teacher, whether or not he has had previous experience with choral reading, should be in a position to use the technique by learning these procedures and following them.

At the very outset the following should be noted:

a. The teacher bears in mind that he is using choral reading as a technique for effective teaching of prayer and not for teaching language. Although an initial understanding of the words is essential to determine their proper interpretation, it is not to be expected that the children will thereafter retain this knowledge. Certainly there is no room here for word drill, exercises, sentence structure, and all the other devices generally used for teaching language.

b. Choral reading is based on an understanding of the inner meanings and purpose of the prayer. However, this understanding is conveyed to the children only in general terms. Overanalyzing the prayer will tire the children and dull their interest. It is to be avoided.

c. No matter how interesting the children will find this technique, they will eventually tire of it, if it is used too frequently or for too long a period of time. Experience has shown that it is unwise to devote more than one third of the time normally allocated for *Siddur* to the use of choral reading.

d. Choral reading has been effectively used with all age groups. However, an initial elementary knowledge of Hebrew reading and language is essential before it can be used with any degree of success. It is recommended for frequent use beginning with the third year and for occasional use in the second year of the afternoon schools. Some teachers have used this technique successfully with first year classes. Generally, however, this is to be avoided.

e. In introducing a prayer to the children, the teacher will usually read it aloud the first time. In this manner he brings before them an example of meaningful reading. However, he bears in mind that examples are not samples to be copied and reproduced. The teacher bewares of setting the pattern. At all times he encourages creativity on the part of the children in working out all the aspects of a choral reading arrangement.

f. The teacher is careful to allocate solo parts to as many children as possible. Making certain children the "stars" by repeatedly giving them solo parts is to be avoided.

g. Over-dramatization in the reading makes for artificiality. "Elocution" style reading is meaningless form without substance. The speech is kept simple, natural. Sincerity is the essence of effective reading of a prayer.

Before proceeding to a development of techniques, consideration of some basic principles will prove helpful and will set the subject in its proper frame.

■ PRAYER IN THE CURRICULUM

In most Jewish schools, prayer, both in Hebrew and in English, is an important subject of study. That is as it should be. Prayer is the overt expression of Jewish life as reflected in the social environment within which the child functions. Prayer is the strand which binds the Jewish child to the Jewish people. Properly used, prayer is a vehicle for emotional dialogue between the child and his Creator.

Traditionally, Jews have utilized prescribed forms of prayer. Even when feeling a pressing personal need for prayer as at a time of personal joy, stress or bereavement, the Jew utilizes traditional prayers, reading into them his own emotional needs of the moment. The prayer book, the *Siddur* or *Mahzor*, is therefore the one universal link between the Jew and his God.

In all Jewish schools, excepting perhaps those that are affiliated with secularist movements, prayer is an important subject of study. In schools affiliated with the Orthodox or Conservative movements *Siddur* study is basic in the curriculum. Whether or not we approve of it, in many schools *Siddur* is often the main subject of study.

Goals in Teaching Siddur

In teaching *Siddur* the Jewish teacher assumes a heavy responsibility. He must provide his pupils with the skill of reading the Hebrew of the *Siddur* with accuracy and facility. He must teach his pupils the order of service and the place of each individual prayer within the ritual. Above all, he must develop within his pupils an emotional attachment to the traditional prayer book and the prayers therein.

To the child's parents, the child's ability to read the prayers in the *Siddur* with fluency and accuracy is often the yardstick by which they measure the quality of Jewish education. This is something tangible, something which they can understand and evaluate. The ability of their child to participate in the synagogue ritual, his skill in "keeping up" with the rapid flow of the prayers in the adult service is the overt, the visible manifestation of their child's "Jewishness."

To the child, fluency in the *Siddur* means adult approval and, what is more important, it gives him a sense of belonging, of being on a par with other Jews, a part of the Community of Israel.

Siddur Not a Texbook

Teachers often make the mistake of using the *Siddur* as a textbook for teaching Hebrew reading. To do so is to undermine the role of our traditional prayer book in the life of the child. The *Siddur* must be holy in the eyes of our students. The *Siddur* is our inheritance from past generations, the companion of our people on its long and terrible road of exile, soaked in the tears and hopes of the Jew.

The *Siddur* is our road to God and not a tool for learning the mechanics of reading. In the study of the *Siddur*, we have the opportunity to develop in the heart of the child a feeling of exaltation, to stimulate an outpouring of the soul, to create an attitude of at-oneness with generations past. In teaching *Siddur*, we are able to train the child in the path of accepted prayer, of ritual handed down to us from generation to generation. In short, this is our chance to awaken within the child the need for prayer and to teach him its accepted and sanctified forms.

Surely we default on a sacred obligation when we reduce the *Siddur* to the position of a reading textbook, when we degrade it to the role of a mere tool-for-drill and thus create in the child's mind an association of drudgery with the prayer book.

Need for Practice

Nevertheless, practice is an essential aspect of *Siddur* learning. The child will utilize the *Siddur* in the Junior Congregation Service and will one day take part in the adult service. He will have to read the prayers with fluency and accuracy. Only familiarity with the prayers through long practice can give him these skills. We must, therefore, utilize a method of instruction which will on the one hand provide opportunities for the necessary drill and on the other hand preserve in the child's eyes the traditional status of the *Siddur* and establish and reinforce his emotional relationship to it.

Meaningful Practice

An awareness of certain basic educational principles and their application in the teaching process will help the teacher to attain these objectives.

It is to be borne in mind that if practice is to be effective, it must serve to satisfy the learner's own wants. If it does not, the result of the practice will be exactly the reverse of what is sought. The learner will develop negative attitudes and an aversion to that which he had practiced. Furthermore, it is to be expected that if a stimulus is pleasurable, the response too should be pleasant. Children who learn their prayers in a pleasurable manner may be expected in later life to enjoy a pleasurable experience from participation in prayer. Finally, it is important that the learning situation be clear to the learner and that he understand it fully so that he can clearly distinguish the right response from a wrong one.

Consequently, since our aim is that the learners, now as children and later as adults, participate in synagogue worship skillfully, intelligently, and sympathetically, it is important that the process of teaching the prayers and the practice for fluency be meaningful, that it be stimulating, emotional, pleasant, and respectful of the child's intelligence. All too often the process of *Siddur* practice is monotonous, boring, tiresome, following procedures which may be acceptable to teach tricks to an animal but not prayer to a child with a mind and a heart.

Goal Determines Method

It is a recognized principle in art that "form follows function." In education it is equally true that goal determines method. Each method carries with it its own psychological overtones and it must be chosen in the light of our ultimate goal. It is quite proper, for example, to teach language by means of games. The utilization of such devices for teaching prayer would be completely out of consonance. Prayer is not a game. It is an expression of emotional feelings. The method used to teach prayer should therefore be one that is charged with emotion. Choral reading is such a method. It is a creative emotional art form which offers us rich opportunities to attain our teaching-learning goals when applied to prayer.

■ WHAT IS CHORAL READING?

Choral reading is interpretative reading aloud of poetic writings by a group of people speaking together. It is quite similar to choral singing, except that no pre-composed melodic pattern is utilized. It may well be called orchestrated speech. The selection may be read by the entire group in unison, or the group may be divided into sub-groups or sub-choruses such as: high voices and low voices, or boys and girls. Solo parts are often provided. In arranging a selection for choral reading, the appropriate rhythmic pattern, pitch, melody and mood are determined, phrase by phrase. Thereafter, whenever the selection is read together by the members of the group, they each follow the identical, pre-determined rhythm, pitch and speech melody.

The technique of choral reading is of particular value in teaching *Siddur*. It may, however, be applied in toto to other subjects of the curriculum, especially Bible and Jewish literature.

■ VALUES OF CHORAL READING

Choral reading is a democratic form of art expression, accessible to anyone who is not altogether tone-deaf or dumb. Since the total effect of choral reading depends on the working together of every individual within the group, it develops a spirit of responsibility to the group. On the other hand, since the manner in which the prayer is to be interpreted is determined by the children themselves, the technique presents great opportunities for individual self-expression. Choral reading draws on the individual in determining melody, pitch, rhythm and group arrangement. Once these are determined, the individual becomes submerged in the group, working for the welfare of the group in adhering to the line of interpretation, once it has been fixed.

The self-conscious, the diffident, who have their hearts in their throats whenever called upon, gain courage in the anonymity of the speaking chorus. They have the support of the mass but are not lost in the mass since they know that each one contributes to the total effect. Teachers who have been utilizing the technique report that children who stutter speak quite normally when participating in a choral reading. One teacher, in reporting this phenomenon, described the following situation: During a choral reading by her class, she suddenly motioned to them to stop so as to correct an error. One child, normally a stutterer, missed the signal. For a few moments he continued to read aloud, clearly, distinctly and without hesitation. Suddenly he became aware that he was reading alone and began to stutter once more. This incident is offered not as a suggestion that choral reading would cure stuttering but rather to indicate the extent to which choral reading gives ego support to the diffident child.

Through choral reading, the child learns that prayers are not "magic formula" with which to propitiate the Almighty; that the words in the prayers are not meaningless gibberish. The words have meaning. The words have beauty. The words are charged with emotion. The words are related to him. They are part of him. They are his personal speech to the Almighty. Through choral reading, the words are embodied with meaning, even when the literal meaning is not always understood.

The syllable by syllable, sing-song *Siddur* reading so often heard in many classrooms has no place in a choral reading rendition of a prayer by the class. Because choral reading depends so much on proper interpretation of the words and phrases of the prayer, it helps develop correct Hebrew speech patterns. It might be expected that children who are trained to interpret Hebrew prayers in a meaningful manner, will carry over such speech patterns into other areas of Hebrew reading.

■ IN HARMONY WITH TRADITION

The utilization of choral reading in prayer is in harmony with Jewish tradition. The Jew has always been enjoined to recite most of the prayers aloud. The Talmud, Tractate Berakhot, 13A, declares that in reciting the *Sh'ma*, one must hear what one says. Responsive reading, a form of choral reading, is used in many synagogues. Furthermore, from time immemorial Jewish tradition has frowned upon the rote recitation of prayer. Rabbi Simeon is quoted in *Ethics of the Fathers*, 2:18, as follows: "When thou prayest, regard not thy prayer as a fixed mechanical task but as an appeal for mercy and grace before the All-Present . . ." Choral reading is within the spirit of these traditions. Prayers are recited aloud; prayers are interpreted meaningfully.

Jewish tradition has always preferred congregational prayer to prayer in isolation. The very form of most prayers is cast in the plural—"With abounding love has Thou loved *us* . . . ," "Heal *us*, O Lord . . . ," "It is *our* duty to praise Thee . . . ," "Cause *us*, O Lord *our* God, to lie down in peace . . ." Through choral reading, patterns for group prayer are established early in the child's experience.

Finally, certain forms of choral reading have long been an accepted part of Jewish worship. The repetition of *Hodu . . . ki le-olam hasdo* and *Ana . . . ho-shiah na* in the *Hallel* is a form of choral reading which we will consider later under "Refrain Reading." The responsive reading of *Ashrei* and *Anim Z'mirot* is a form of antiphonal choral reading. If one wanders on a late Sabbath afternoon into a synagogue whose members are of Lithuanian origin, one is moved by the soulfull chanting of Psalms. A solo voice reads a sentence, the congregation reads another, alternating solo and chorus—antiphonal choral reading—a traditional aspect of Jewish worship.

How to Do It

■ THE TEACHER PREPARES

Developing a choral reading in the classroom is a creative process on the part of the teacher and the children working together. The teacher will therefore thoroughly prepare in advance so as to be able to guide the process competently.

The teacher bears in mind that he is the model for the class, his own manner of reading, the quality of his voice, his diction, his pronunciation, his emphasis, his phrasing, may unconsciously be imitated. Furthermore, his presentation of the prayer to the children will determine in a large measure their interest and the degree of enthusiastic participation. A competent teacher consequently prepares a plan of operation in advance—not a fully detailed "blueprint" to be slavishly followed, but rather a generalized plan of operation from which the teacher deviates whenever necessary. The following suggestions may prove helpful:

1. The teacher reads the prayer carefully, familiarizing himself with the prayer—its meaning, its rhythm patterns, its emotional implications, its ideals and values.

2. The teacher, utilizing reference works, finds out as much as possible about the prayer—the history of its origin, its development, its use and its place in the liturgy.

3. The teacher develops a motivation which he will utilize to introduce the prayer to the class. These are limited only by the imagination and ingenuity of the teacher. Following are a few suggestions:

a. The historical background and significance of the prayer—

Aleynu proclaims God as the Ruler of all humanity. This prayer was on the lips of Jewish martyrs as they went to their death "*al kiddush ha-shem*—to sanctify the Name of God."

L'olam Y'hey Adam ("At all times let a man revere God in private") is the beginning of a group of prayers in the *Shaharit* (Morning) Service composed in the 5th Century C.E. They were intended to be said in private, secretly, and to serve as a substitute for the whole *Shaharit* Service. This was a result of the edict promulgated by the Persian Yazdegered II in 456 C.E. forbidding Jewish public worship and the recitation of the *Sh'ma*.

Av Harahamim, the Prayer for the Martyrs recited on the Sabbath after the Torah reading, was composed after the First Crusade in 1096 C.E. to memorialize the many communities in Germany that were destroyed by the Crusaders when the Jews refused to accept baptism.

b. A biographical sketch of the author of the prayer, when known—

Adon Olam is attributed to Solomon ibn Gabirol, the great Spanish-Jewish philosopher and poet of the 11th Century C.E. There are many fascinating legends about him which the children would want to hear.

Nishmat ("The breath of every living being shall bless Thy Name . . .") in the Sabbath morning service is attributed to Rabbi Simeon ben Shetah of the 1st Century B.C.E. This statesman and sage was the brother of Queen Salome Alexandra, widow of King Jannai. Both his life story and many legends about him will evoke great interest among the children.

Shir Hakavod, Hymn of Glory was written by the philosopher, poet, saint and mystic of the 13th Century C.E., Judah the Pious. The folk imagination has woven many legends about his personality.

c. A folk tale connected with prayer, its author or the ideas expressed in it—

Ashrei has the line "His tender mercies are over all His works." In connection with this the tale is related that Rabbi Judah the Prince suffered great physical affliction as a punishment. It seems that once a calf, while being led to the slaughter, ran to him for protection. The Rabbi repulsed the animal with the words, "Go, for such is your destiny." He was healed from his ills when he saved a field animal from a servant who was about to kill it with the words, "Let the creature live, for is it not written, 'His tender mercies are over all His works.' "

Sh'ma enjoins us to love God "with all thy soul." Rabbi Akiba, when martyred by the Romans for his part in the Bar Kokhba revolt, comforted his weeping disciples by saying, "I have loved God *with all my heart,* and I have loved Him *with all my might;* now that I can love Him *with my whole soul,* I am completely happy."

d. A discussion of the place of the prayer in the liturgy or in the children's daily lives.

4. The teacher, in the privacy of his home, reads the prayer aloud several times so as to accustom himself to read it in a meaningful manner.

■ THE CLASSROOM PROCESS

Introducing Choral Reading

When Choral Reading is to be used in the class for the first time, the teacher will find it necessary to introduce the idea to the students. Often this may be done very briefly. The teacher might ask whether any of the children have ever participated in or heard choral reading. Since this technique is widely used in the public schools, it is quite possible that many, if not all of the children, may be familiar with the technique and reply in the affirmative. In that event, a suggestion by the teacher, "Suppose we arrange this prayer for choral reading," might be sufficient to enlist the enthusiastic assent of the class.

Sometimes only a few of the children are familiar with the technique. The teacher might then ask these children to tell the class what choral reading is. Usually, they will discuss the process quite clearly. A suggestion to the class to utilize it for the prayer then follows.

In some classes, particularly the younger ones, the children may never have heard about choral reading. The teacher may find it necessary to present the idea of choral reading in more detail. This might be done somewhat along these lines:

TEACHER: How many of you have ever heard a choir singing? Did you notice how much nicer a song sounds when many voices sing it together, in chorus? Notice how interesting the music is when it is sung in different ways—first by the whole chorus, then only by high voices, or only by low voices, now a solo voice is heard and again the full chorus swells out in song? Reading too, may gain in beauty when a number of voices read together, in chorus.

The singing choir sings the words of the song with the melody set for them by the composer. But, not only songs—all words, all speech has melody. Every time we utter a word, every time we read a phrase, we use melody—melody which the speaker or reader composes, often without even knowing it. Just listen to the way I speak the following: "Give me this book."

The teacher proceeds to say the statement, "Give me this book," in many different ways—pleading, commanding, angry, etc. Each time he makes the statement he asks the children to tell how he sounded. He then proceeds to explain:

TEACHER: Notice how the melody changes every time the meaning changes? When I demanded the book angrily, I used an altogether different speech-melody than when I pleaded with you. In all speech the meaning of the words determines the melody we use.

Now, when we read a phrase in chorus, every member of the chorus must read the phrase with the same melody. Why?——— Of course! Otherwise there would be confusion. The listener would not get the meaning of what we read. So, when we arrange a selection for choral reading, we first determine the melody of each phrase according to its meaning. Then we all read the phrase together, using the melody upon which we decided.

Now suppose we try something. Let us all read together a few sentences of the prayer ———. You will find it on page —— of your *Siddurim*.

The class reads a few sentences. The teacher points out how sing-songy and monotonous the reading was. Naturally! Since they did not know the meaning of the words, they could not use the proper melodies which would convey the meaning and give interest and variety to the reading.

The teacher reads the same phrases from the prayer with meaningful melody and intonation. The contrast between his meaningful reading and their sing-song is now more than obvious. Once again the point is made how much more pleasant meaningful reading sounds.

The suggestion now ensues that the prayer be arranged for choral reading, with the children themselves determining the proper melodic pitch, tempo, and group arrangements to be used.

The Process, Step by Step

The utilization of choral reading for teaching prayer follows a process consisting of a series of well-defined steps. The length of time devoted to each step will depend on the individual teacher as well as on the time allotted for *Siddur* reading in the individual school. In some instances, for example, the teacher will devote a relatively great deal of time to developing the background of the prayer—its history, its inner meaning, its use in the liturgy. At other times, this aspect may be glossed over in just a few brief statements. The teacher proceeds directly to reading and interpretation. Bearing this caution in mind, the process will develop according to the following steps:

1. Motivation

The teacher will introduce the prayer to be learned by placing it in a relationship with the needs of the child, a community event, a historical occurrence, etc. For example:

a. The Needs of the Child

In motivating *Ha-zan et Ha-olam*, the first prayer of the *Birkat Ha-mazon* (Grace After Meals), the teacher will bring out, by a series of questions, that the children have often felt the need and desire to say "thank you" for favors received—to parents for care and help, to friends for kindness or for gifts, to acquaintances for consideration, to total strangers for casual courtesies. The teacher encourages the children to describe actual instances when they have felt the need to thank someone. The point is then made by eliciting the response from the children, if possible, that similarly we have the need to thank the Almighty for giving us life and for providing us with the food and other necessities to sustain life. The prayer which the class is about to study is man's "thank you" to the Almighty.

b. A Community Event

The class may want to arrange *Mizmor Shir Hanukat Habayit* for choral reading, to be recited in connection with the dedication of a new synagogue building, a new wing to the local hospital, or even moving into a different classroom. The motivation might consist of a brief discussion with the children regarding the manner in which people celebrate moving into a new house:—They attach a *M'zuzah*, giving the new home a specifically Jewish character; they recite the blessing *Sh'-he-he-yanu*, thanking the Almighty for having kept us in life to reach this occasion, etc. Similarly, we thank God when we dedicate a new community building by reciting *Mizmor Shir Hanukat Habayit.*

c. A Historical Occurrence

Many prayers lend themselves to correlation with historical events. All holiday prayers may be introduced by recall of the historical occurrence with which the festival is associated. A prayer from *Hallel* might be connected with the celebration of Israel Independence Day. In motivating *Avadim Hayinu* from the Passover *Haggadah* a discussion elicits the fact that a nation gains strength from recalling its difficult days. American children sing the "Star Spangled Banner" and recall the heroic defense of liberty during the War of 1812, when our nation was in its early childhood. We study the Gettysburg Address and recall the mortal danger that confronted our Union in its adolescence. The Jew gains strength in remembering his beginnings. He treasures liberty when he recalls the slavery of our ancestors in the Land of Egypt. The recital of *Avadim Hayinu* ("Once We Were Slaves Unto Pharaoh") recalls our beginnings during our annual celebration of the historic event of our liberation.

d. A Personal Event

Motivating a prayer by connecting its study with an event in the children's personal lives is especially rewarding. The teacher is ever alert for such opportunities. For example, the parents of one of the children are about to leave on a visit to Israel. A child is about to be taken on a pilgrimage to Israel by his parents. The teacher can use an event of this nature to motivate the study of any one of the many prayers which deal with the Jewish yearning for return to Zion. *V'lirushalayim Irkha B'rahamim Tashuv* ("And to Jerusalem, Thy City, Return in Mercy") from the weekday *Amidah* may well be motivated in this manner. The prospective pilgrim-child might be asked to tell briefly about his planned trip. Teacher then brings out through class discussion that Jews, in their lands of exile, always yearned to return to the Land of Israel. Jerusalem especially was cherished in their hearts. In the daily devotions they prayed for the Return. *V'lirushalayim* . . . is one of these prayers. The suggestion might even be made that the prayer be arranged for choral reading and recited at a class farewell party to the pilgrim-child.

2. Background

The teacher provides the children with a background for the prayer to be studied. In this connection some of the following areas are explored:

a. Its Place in the Liturgy

It is important that children be familiarized with the actual use of the prayer in Jewish worship. They learn whether it is a home prayer as "Grace After Meals" or a synagogue prayer as "*Ki Mitziyon*"; whether it is part of the daily, Sabbath, or festival services; its relative place within a given service as part of the *Amidah,* the Torah service, Hallel, etc.

b. Its History

The teacher reviews for the children the historical events, when these are known, which gave rise to the composition of the prayer or in connection with which the prayer was used in the past. Several have been indicated under "The Teacher Prepares." Other examples:

Sh'ma—Enunciated by Moses in the desert.

V'lamalshinim—The struggle against renegades during the Roman period.

Ani Ma'amin—Sung by the Jewish martyrs during the Nazi holocaust.

Standard reference works on the *Siddur* and prayers contain much information about the origin of specific prayers and their use.

c. Biographical Material

A brief biographical sketch or some interesting incidents in the life of the prayer's author, if known or attributed, will not only add to the interest of the lesson, but also broaden the children's knowledge. Some suggestions have been given under "The Teacher Prepares." Some other possibilities are:

Elohai N'tzor—Composed by Mar, the son of Rabina, a famous sage of the 4th Century C.E.

Un'tane Tokef—Attributed to Rabbi Amnon of Mainz. The story of his martyrdom and composition of the prayer has moved generations of Jews who read it in their High Holy Days prayer books.

Hodu . . . Kiru Vishmo (From the *Shaharit* Service)—This song of thanksgiving is from I Chronicles 16:8-36. It was recited when the Ark of the Covenant was brought by David to Zion. Incidents in the biography of David are heroic and usually appeal to the children.

When the teacher ascertains the name of the person to whom the prayer is attributed, he will do well to examine the *Jewish Encyclopedia*, a good history book and other standard reference works to learn as much as possible about this person. However, the teacher will be highly selective in the presentation of the material to the children. The teacher will never lose sight of the fact the major goal is to teach the prayer itself and not everything that is known about its background, author, etc.

d. Folk Tales

The teacher will bring to the children interesting folk tales which may be current in connection with a given prayer or which may be correlated with some of the thoughts and ideas expressed in the prayer. This may be done as part of the introduction of the prayer to the class, or it may be utilized in later lessons to add interest and variety. Several such folk tales have already been indicated. A few others follow:

V'lirushalayim—The study of this prayer may be reinforced with any folk tale dealing with extraordinary devotion to Zion. The story about Yehudah Halevi, his yearning for Zion, his defiance of all danger to make the pilgrimage in his old age, his arrival before the walls of destroyed Jerusalem, weeping and kissing the soil of the Holy City and dying under the hoofs of a Saracen horse—this tale is most appropriate for telling in connection with *V'lirushalayim.*

Sim Shalom—This is a prayer expressing the Jew's yearning for and love of peace. In this connection the children might enjoy hearing the story of The Two Brothers. Briefly, it is the story of two brothers, one single, the other married and a father of a brood of children. Their fields adjoined. During the harvest the single brother began to think how much greater are the needs of his brother with his large family and he proceeded, in the dead of night to bring a bundle of grain from his field to his brother. The married brother too considered that he, with his family, is more fortunate than his brother who is all alone, with no one to care for him when he will grow old. He too, proceeded, in the dark of night, to bring a bundle of his grain to add to his single brother's harvest. For two nights they did this. On the third night, they met in the open field, each carrying his bundle of grain as a gift for his brother. On the field where they met and embraced in brotherly love was later established the City of Jerusalem, the City of Peace.

3. Understanding of Content

The class discusses the content of the prayer to arrive at an understanding of the basic ideas expressed in it, such as: Thanksgiving, glorification of the Almighty, a plea for health, a plea for peace, a prayer for Zion, a prayer for aid in study of the Torah, etc.

When the available time is limited, the teacher will explain the content without devoting much time to discussion.

As indicated previously, the teacher will try to relate the prayer to the needs and experiences of the children by connecting it, whenever possible, to parallel situations in the lives of the children as:

Yearning for Zion—A child's trip to Israel.

Prayer for healing—A previous illness in the family.

Elohai N'tzor—Children's natural abhorrence of tattling.

Hashkivenu—The sense of mystery felt in connection with darkness and night. This will be brought out either through a statement of the relationship by the teacher or by means of question and answer, discussion, socio-drama, etc.

4. The Prayer Is Read

The teacher reads the prayer aloud with understanding, with honesty, with sincerity. This is done not in order to set the pattern for reading by the students, but to convey the idea that the prayer is living and vital, that it is charged with meaning and emotion.

The teacher is careful not to fall in love with his own interpretation. At best, his reading of the prayer may serve as an example. It definitely is not to become a model which the teacher expects to be copied and reproduced.

5. Function of Speech-Melody

The teacher once again calls to the attention of the children the fact that all words have melodies; that the melody used often determines the variations of meaning. The teacher points out that the children themselves will determine the proper melody with which each phrase of the prayer will be read by the class chorus. The class is informed that suggestions for correct melodic interpretation is now in order. However, in order to give the phrases the melody which will convey their proper meaning, an understanding of the phrases is now necessary. The class will therefore discuss the meaning of each phrase and determine its correct melody line.

6. Understanding the Meaning

The prayer is gone over, sentence by sentence, or phrase by phrase, to discover the meaning of each word within the phrase and the entire phrase or sentence.

In studying each phrase the teacher begins by asking the children the meaning of those words which they may be expected to know from previous study. The words within the phrase which the children may have learned earlier in different forms are considered next. Thereafter the teacher helps the children to discover the meaning of the unfamiliar words by their context within the phrase, using the known words as aids. Finally, the meaning of the entire phrase is ascertained. The following is an example:

HASHKIVENU ADONAI ELOHENU L'SHALOM, ETC.

TEACHER: Now, let's see. If any of you recognizes a word you know, please raise your hand. Yes?

CHILD 1: *Adonai*—God

CHILD 2: *Elohenu*—our God

TEACHER: Very good. *Adonai Elohenu*—God our God or O Lord our God. Where did you come across these words before?

CHILD 3: In the prayer over bread.

CHILD 4: In the prayer over fruit.

TEACHER: Very good. Many blessings begin this way. Would you want to say for us the beginning of such a blessing?

CHILD 5: *Barukh ata Adonai Elohenu Melekh haolam . . .*

TEACHER: Fine. And what does that mean?

CHILD 5: Blessed are you, O Lord our God, King of the world . . .

TEACHER: Very, very good. Let's see now, you said before that *Elohenu* means *our* God. We have this very often in our prayers—*Elohenu, our* God, *Avinu, our* Father, *malkenu . . .*

CHILD 2: *Our* king?

TEACHER: Exactly. In Hebrew the ending *nu* means "our" or "us." What other word here ends this way?

CHILD 3: *Hashkivenu*
TEACHER: That's right. What do you think it means? What does it look like? You remember *shokhev?*
CHILDREN: Lies!
TEACHER: Right! *Shokhev*—lies down. *Hashkev*—make to lie down. *Hashkivenu?*
CHILD 4: Make *us* to lie down?
TEACHER: That's it. Now read the first three words.
CHILD 5: *Hashkivenu Adonai Elohenu. . . .*
TEACHER: Which means . . . ?
CHILD 5: Make us to lie down, O Lord our God
TEACHER: . . . and the next word?
CHILD 5: *L'shalom*
TEACHER: Yes . . . ?
CHILD 5: To peace?
TEACHER: Almost. *L'* in front of a word may mean "to" or "at." Here it means "in."
CHILD 5: In peace?
TEACHER: That's it. Now, let's all read the whole phrase.
CLASS: *Hashkivenu Adonai Elohenu l'shalom*
TEACHER: And the meaning . . . ?
CHILD 3: Make us to lie down, O Lord our God, in peace
TEACHER: Or, "Cause us to lie down, O Lord our God, in peace." Now, how would you read this phrase to best express its meaning? What speech melody would you use for it? Any suggestions? . . .

It must be emphasized again that the prayer lesson is not expected to serve as a lesson in Hebrew language. The purpose of this step is to provide sufficient *initial* understanding of the phrases so that the children may be able to determine with intelligence their proper oral interpretation. It is not to be expected that the children will thereafter continue to remember the Hebrew meanings. Consequently, only the barest minimum of time is devoted to this step—avoiding the usual drill, utilization and other techniques normally used in a language lesson. Experience has shown that there is some carry-over learning of Hebrew. However, the basic purpose of this step is to enable intelligent and meaningful interpretive reading. At the same time, while selecting for the meaning of the words, they are incidentally practicing their correct reading.

7. Determining the Speech-Melody

As the meaning of each phrase is learned, the children are asked to suggest the proper melody with which it is to be read. Children volunteer suggestions, each reading the phrase in a manner that seems to him most suitable, giving his reasons. For example:

CHILD 1: *Hashkivenu Adonai* ELOHENU *l'shalom* (Emphasizing *Elohenu*)
TEACHER: Why did you read it this way?
CHILD 1: Because the Lord *our God* will cause us to lie down.
TEACHER: Anyone think it should be read differently?
CHILD 2: HASHKIVENU *Adonai Elohenu l'shalom*

TEACHER: Why?
CHILD 2: Because we are asking God to cause us to *lie down.*
TEACHER: Is this the main idea of the phrase? How many agree with Child 2? How many agree with Child 1? Anyone have a different way of saying it?
CHILD 3: *Hashkivenu Adonai Elohenu* L'SHALOM. The whole idea here is that we are asking God to cause us to lie down in *peace.*
TEACHER: How many agree with this? . . .
CHILD 4: It's not the lying down that's important but that we have peace when we lie down.
TEACHER: Very good. It seems most of you like the way Child 3 read it. Now, let us hear it again your way, then we will try it together.
CHILD 3: *Hashkivenu Adonai Elohenu* L'SHALOM.
TEACHER: All together now . . .
CLASS: *Hashkivenu Adonai Elohenu l'shalom.*
TEACHER: Not quite. Let us hear it again, Child 3.
CHILD 3: *Hashkivenu Adonai Elohenu* L'SHALOM
TEACHER: Class. . . .
CLASS: *Hashkivenu Adonai Elohenu* L'SHALOM
TEACHER: Good! Now, once more to make sure we have it.
CLASS: *Hashkivenu Adonai Elohenu* L'SHALOM
TEACHER: Now, let's try to remember it. From now on, every time we will read this phrase we will read it how . . . ?
CLASS: *Hashkivenu Adonai Elohenu* L'SHALOM.
TEACHER: Fine. Now let's go on to the next phrase. We already know that *malkenu* means "our king." What other word do you recognize? . . .

Again the process of learning to understand the meaning and of determining the speech-melody is repeated, until a sizable section of the prayer has thus been arranged. Each time a new phrase is completed, the entire prayer, from the beginning up to that point, is read again to make sure that the agreed melody is adhered to. If an error is made, the child who originally suggested the correct interpretation is asked to repeat it and the error is rectified.

There is no need for this process to be completed in one lesson. It is suggested that the teacher be keenly aware of the reaction of the children and stop before there is any flagging of interest. The process may be continued in one or more subsequent lessons, as needed.

It now becomes apparent that inherent in this process are two major educational values. Utilization of these techniques results in:

a. Democratic Learning

It allows every child to participate equally in the learning process. It permits many children to contribute original ideas toward a class learning project. The teacher is the leader, the guide. The children determine the pitch, tempo, group arrangement, rhythm, etc. Children volunteer their ideas about the interpretation of each phrase. The class expresses its preference on the basis of sense and reason. Each interpretation is the creative contribution of an individual child. It is rejected or accepted by the class in a democratice manner. Once it is democratically stamped as "authoritative," every individual accepts it and adheres to it as a member of the classroom democracy.

b. Meaningful Practice

This has been referred to earlier. Now it becomes clear in its operation. Every step in the process offers many opportunities for meaningful practice of reading with fluency and accuracy.

If children were asked to repeat a phrase ten to fifteen times, until they could read it quickly and accurately, they would soon become bored and annoyed with the lesson, the teacher, and the subject matter. The reading lesson would degenerate, as it often does, to a monotonous and trying experience. However, it is to be noted that in the choral reading process each phrase is repeated ten, fifteen, and twenty times by individual children and by the class as a whole and the children are not even aware of the fact that they are practicing reading and gaining fluency and accuracy in the process.

As the children work to discover the meaning of each phrase, they "meet" each word in the phrase as a word and not as a composite of syllables-without-meaning. As each child offers a suggestion regarding the manner in which the phrase is to be read, he must of necessity read the phrase aloud in order to demonstrate his proposed interpretation. As this child reads the phrase, the class follows along in the *Siddur*. They do this naturally, while listening to the interpretation, meanwhile making up their minds whether or nor to accept the proposed interpretation. If the teacher wants, he might ask the class to try out each suggestion by reading the phrase aloud with the proposed speech-melody. When an interpretation is ultimately accepted, the child who suggested it is asked to read it aloud, once and again, to fix it in the minds of the children. Finally, the class reads it several times with the melody which they have just accepted to "get the feel of it." They read it again a number of times as interpretations of additional phrases are determined.

The result is that each phrase is read many times, by individuals and by the class as a whole. They are constantly practicing reading of the prayer. It is meaningful practice—reading with a purpose, for a goal which is clear to the children. The result is meaningful reading, accurate, and fluent. During the steps which follow in the process of arranging a prayer for choral reading, the children have many more opportunities for meaningful practice of reading.

The teacher may wait until the melody for the entire prayer has been determined before proceeding to the next step. In some instances, however, it might be advisable to do so after the speech melody has been determined for a small section of the prayer only, returning to the earlier steps later on.

8. *Dividing the Group*

Choral speaking depends for its effectiveness in large measure on the arrangement of words and phrases. Some are said by the entire chorus, some by half the the chorus, some by soloists. Consequently it is necessary that the class be divided into sections or sub-choruses.

a. The Sections

The class is divided into sub-choruses, at least two, according to the pitch level of the children's voices. All children with higher pitched voices are placed together in one sub-chorus. In the other sub-chorus are placed the children with low pitched voices. Since among children of elementary school age there is no great variety of pitch level, the division into sub-choruses may be done rather arbitrarily—half the class forming sub-chorus 1, the other half of the class sub-chorus 2, or all boys in sub-chorus 1 and all girls in sub-chorus 2.

b. Size of Groups

Any size class may be organized as a speaking chorus. Even a group consisting of as few as six children can be used for this purpose. As far as possible, sub-choruses should consist of an equal number of children so as to be able to produce balanced sound. As few as three children and as many as twenty or more may constitute a sub-chorus. The determining factor is the number which the teacher or leader can keep in view and conveniently control.

c. Placement of Groups

The children of each sub-chorus are seated together. In a classroom in which seats are arranged in rows, the children of sub-chorus 1 might all be placed at the right side of the room, the children of sub-chorus 2 at the left side of the room. When children are arranged in an open semi-circle, the children of one sub-chorus would be together in the right half of the semi-circle, the children of the second sub-chorus would constitute the left half of the semi-circle.

During the process of arranging the prayer for choral reading the children are seated. If the choral reading selection is ultimately performed publicly, either before another class, as part of the Junior Congregation service, or at an assembly program, the children stand in an open semi-circle with the teacher or leader in the center facing the group much as the conductor of a singing choir faces his ensemble and directs their tempo, dynamics, etc. It is also possible to have the children stand in wedge formation forming a triangle, the apex of the triangle being closest to the listeners and the base furthest away. In this arrangement, also, all children of a particular sub-chorus are kept together.

9. Arranging the Selection

The class decides, as a result of discussion, how the prayer is to be arranged—which words and phrases are to be said by the entire group, which by the sub-chorus of low voices, which by the sub-chorus of high voices, and which by soloists. The teacher stimulates the children to decide on proper arrangement on the basis of the meaning of the words and phrases and their relationship to the rest of the prayer. For example: in arranging the prayer *Modim*, the children might feel that the first sentence, *Modim anahnu lakh* . . . "We thank Thee, O Lord, etc.," should be said by the entire class-chorus since it speaks in the plural, on behalf of the entire congregation. In *Modeh Ani* they may feel that each phrase should be said by a soloist since this prayer of thanksgiving to the Almighty for allowing us to awake in the morning speaks in individual, personal terms. In one arrangement of this prayer, it was felt that each phrase should be given by a soloist, but thereafter repeated by the entire group because, while personal in form, it also concerns every single individual in the group.

The analysis of the arrangement of a brief section of *Mah Tovu* with the reasons for its arrangement will prove enlightening.

CHORUS:	המקהלה:
How goodly are They Tents, O Jacob,	מַה טֹּבוּ אֹהָלֶיךָ, יַעֲקֹב,
Thy dwelling places, O Israel,	מִשְׁכְּנֹתֶיךָ יִשְׂרָאֵל.

The above opening statement was allocated to the entire class chorus since it speaks about the entire community of Israel. Furthermore it was felt that it would make an effective dramatic opening to the choral reading.

HIGH VOICES:	קולות רמים:
As for me in Thy great loving kindness	וַאֲנִי, בְּרֹב חַסְדְּךָ,
I will come into Thy house,	אָבֹא בֵיתֶךָ,

LOW VOICES:	קולות נמוכים:
I will worship at Thy Holy Temple,	אֶשְׁתַּחֲוֶה אֶל הֵיכַל קָדְשְׁךָ
In the fear of Thee,	בְּיִרְאָתֶךָ.

The idea is first stated by the high voices and then echoed by the low voices. This was done since the thoughts and sentiments of the second phrase parallel and echo those of the first phrase. Also, this arrangement provides an opportunity early in the prayer to introduce the variety inherent in the use of sub-choruses.

SOLO 1:	סולו א׳:
O Lord, I love the habitation of Thy house	יְיָ, אָהַבְתִּי מְעוֹן בֵּיתֶךָ,

Here the thought is expressed by the individual. It is an intimate thought of love and attachment to the Sanctuary. Consequently it was assigned to be read by a single child, a solo voice.

SOLO 2:	סולו ב׳:
And the place where Thy Glory dwells	וּמְקוֹם מִשְׁכַּן כְּבוֹדֶךָ.

This is a restatement in different words of the sentiments expressed in the phrase immediately preceding it.

It follows the pattern so often found in biblical poetry—repetition of ideas line by line. It was assigned to a soloist for the same reason as the previous statement. However, since it repeats the previous idea and therefore emphasizes it, the instructions were that in reading this line, the soloist do so with greater emphasis than Soloist 1.

10. Types of Arrangements

There are many types of choral reading arrangements possible. Some of them, like refrain or antiphonal arrangements, are familiar to us from accepted synagogue practice. In arranging a prayer for choral reading it is not necessary that the class adhere rigidly to any one form for a given selection. The teacher and class have the option to decide whether to do so or to utilize a combination of differing forms. The types of choral reading arrangements which the teacher may find useful are as follows:

a. Refrain

In refrain arrangements a soloist states a line and the chorus repeats it; a group says a line and the second group repeats it; a soloist states each line with the chorus repeating a recurring word, phrase, or line after each statement by the soloist.

This form is often used in Jewish public worship. During *Hallel*, the *Hazzan* (Soloist) recites or chants *Ana ha-Shem hoshia na* and the Congregation (Chorus) responds, repeating the phrase as a *refrain*. On the Day of Atonement, the recital of the *Avodah* concludes with the following:

HAZZAN: *K'ohel hanimtah b'darey malah—*
CONGREGATION: *Mareh Kohen!*
HAZZAN: *Kiv'rakim hayotzim miziv hahayot—*
CONGREGATION: *Mareh Kohen!*

The refrain *Mareh Kokhen* (Was the countenance of the Priest) is a recurring repetition by the Congregation (Chorus) after each line by the *Hazzan* (Soloist) describing the radiance of the High Priest at the Temple service in ancient Jerusalem on the Day of Atonement.

The following arrangement of *Modeh Ani* illustrates a refrain arrangement in which the soloist states the ideas, line by line, and the chorus repeats each solo statement.

מוֹדֶה אֲנִי

SOLO 1 *(Joyously):* מוֹדֶה אֲנִי לְפָנֶיךָ, סולו א׳ (בשמחה):

CHORUS *(Softly):*	מוֹדֶה אֲנִי לְפָנֶיךָ,	המקהלה (בקול נמוך):
SOLO 2 *(With rising volume):*	מֶלֶךְ חַי וְקַיָּם,	סולו ב׳ (בהגברת קול):
CHORUS *(Louder):*	מֶלֶךְ חַי וְקַיָּם,	המקהלה (בהגברת קול יתירה):
SOLO 3 *(With emphasis):*	שֶׁהֶחֱזַרְתָּ בִּי נִשְׁמָתִי בְּחֶמְלָה.	סולו ג׳ (בהדגשה):
CHORUS *(Echoing):*	שֶׁהֶחֱזַרְתָּ בִּי נִשְׁמָתִי בְּחֶמְלָה,	המקהלה (הד קול):
(Drawn out tempo)	רַבָּה אֱמוּנָתֶךָ.	(בקצב ממושך)

In the following arrangement of part Psalm 150, the repetition by the chorus of the phrase "Praise Him" is typical of a refrain arrangement

PSALM 150

SOLO:	*Halleluyah!*	*(A clarion call)*
LOW VOICES:	Praise God in His sanctuary	*(Joyously)*
CHORUS:	Praise Him!	*(Softly)*
HIGH VOICES:	Praise Him in the firmament of His Power	*(In fast tempo)*
CHORUS:	Praise Him!	*(Softly)*
LOW VOICES:	Praise Him for His mighty deeds;	*(Strong)*
HIGH VOICES:	Praise Him according to His abundant greatness	*(A quick answer)*
CHORUS:	Praise Him!	*(Softly)*
	Praise Him!	*(Louder)*
	Praise Him!	*(Louder)*

b. Antiphonal

Antiphonal reading literally means the placing of "sound against sound." In this form of arrangement, two sections of the chorus respond to each other. It is a form of choral speaking that is most familiar to us from the synagogue service. The responsive reading for *Ashrei* or *An'im Z'mirot* are forms of antiphonal reading. It was widely used in ancient times. *Mi Ya'aleh* with its questions and responses was probably recited in that fashion—the chief Levite stating the question, the Levite chorus giving the response. We can visualize this same psalm being chanted by groups of pilgrims on their way to the Temple in Jerusalem. As they approach the Temple Mount, Group 1 calls out the question: "Who will ascend the mountain of the Lord . . . ?" Group 2 fervently responds antiphonally: "He who has clean hands and a pure heart, etc."

Much of biblical poetry is written in the style known as "parallelism"—statement and restatement or statement and echo. A thought is expressed in one line and repeated in the next line using different words. Many selections from the Prophets and Psalms, written in this style, are to be found in the prayer book. They lend themselves admirably to antiphonal arrangement. The first statement is allocated to one sub-chorus, the second to the other. Antiphonal arrangements are also used where the prayer is one of plea and response.

In this type of arrangement, the element of tonal contrast is of great importance. For example: one line or phrase is stated by the high voices. The succeeding line or phrase, paralleling the thoughts of the first is allocated to the low voices. Or, there may be a strong, loud statement which is followed immediately by a soft echo. A line spoken rapidly might be followed by a line delivered in slow, lingering fashion.

The prayer *Ki Anu Amekha* from the High Holiday service is a typical synagogal antiphonal arrangement. It states the relationship which exists between the Almighty and the people of Israel in its many aspects. As used in the synagogue, the *Hazzan* takes every statement dealing with the relationship of the Almighty to Israel. The Congregation responds with the statements describing Israel's relationship to the Lord, thus:

HAZZAN: Our God and God of our fathers
Forgive us, pardon us, and grant us atonement.
CONGREGATION: We are thy people,
HAZZAN: and Thou art our God;
CONGREGATION: We are Thy children
HAZZAN: and Thou art our Father.
CONGREGATION: We are Thy servants,
HAZZAN: and Thou art our Master.

In this example, the lines are divided between a soloist—the *Hazzan* and the chorus—the congregation. It borders also very close on refrain arrangement. In pure antiphony, the lines or phrase are divided between two equally balanced choruses——high voices—low voices, boys—girls, etc. The following setting of *Ki Anu Amekha* in Hebrew illustrates such an antiphonal arrangement with a unison opening and closing:

כִּי אָנוּ עַמֶּךָ

CHORUS *(Prayerful):* אֱלֹהֵינוּ וֵאלֹהֵי המקהלה (בנעימת תפלה):
אֲבוֹתֵינוּ
סְלַח לָנוּ,
מְחַל לָנוּ,
כַּפֶּר לָנוּ:

		(קול קורא וקול עונה כהד)
HIGH VOICES *(A call!):*	כִּי אָנוּ עַמֶּךָ	קולות רמים:
LOW VOICES *(Echoing):*	וְאַתָּה אֱלֹהֵינוּ.	קולות נמוכים:
HIGH VOICES:	אָנוּ בָנֶיךָ	קולות רמים:
LOW VOICES:	וְאַתָּה אָבִינוּ.	קולות נמוכים:
HIGH VOICES:	אָנוּ עֲבָדֶיךָ	קולות רמים:
LOW VOICES:	וְאַתָּה אֲדוֹנֵינוּ.	קולות נמוכים:
HIGH VOICES:	אָנוּ קְהָלֶךָ	קולות רמים:
LOW VOICES:	וְאַתָּה חֶלְקֵנוּ.	קולות נמוכים:
(Continuously rising tempo)		(הקצב הולך ומתגבר)
HIGH VOICES:	אָנוּ נַחֲלָתֶךָ	קולות רמים:
LOW VOICES:	וְאַתָּה גוֹרָלֵנוּ.	קולות נמוכים:
HIGH VOICES:	אָנוּ צֹאנֶךָ	קולות רמים:
LOW VOICES:	וְאַתָּה רוֹעֵנוּ.	קולות נמוכים:
		(הקצב הולך ומתגבר)
HIGH VOICES:	אָנוּ כַרְמֶךָ	קולות רמים:
LOW VOICES:	וְאַתָּה נוֹטְרֵנוּ.	קולות נמוכים:
HIGH VOICES:	אָנוּ פְעוּלָּתֶךָ	קולות רמים:
LOW VOICES:	וְאַתָּה יוֹצְרֵנוּ.	קולות נמוכים:
HIGH VOICES:	אָנוּ רַעְיָתֶךָ	קולות רמים:
LOW VOICES:	וְאַתָּה דוֹדֵנוּ.	קולות נמוכים:
HIGH VOICES:	אָנוּ סְגֻלָּתֶךָ	קולות רמים:
LOW VOICES:	וְאַתָּה קְרוֹבֵנוּ.	קולות נמוכים:
HIGH VOICES:	אָנוּ עַמֶּךָ	קולות רמים:
LOW VOICES:	וְאַתָּה מַלְכֵּנוּ.	קולות נמוכים:
HIGH VOICES:	אָנוּ מַאֲמִירֶךָ	קולות רמים:
LOW VOICES:	וְאַתָּה מַאֲמִירֵנוּ.	קולות נמוכים:

(ברגש ענוה ובקול הולך ונמוך)

CHORUS *(With humility, softer and softer)*:

המקהלה:

אָנוּ עַזֵּי פָנִים
וְאַתָּה רַחוּם וְחַנּוּן.
אָנוּ קְשֵׁי עֹרֶף
וְאַתָּה אֶרֶךְ אַפַּיִם.
אָנוּ מְלֵאֵי עָוֹן
וְאַתָּה מָלֵא רַחֲמִים.
אָנוּ יָמֵינוּ כְּצֵל עוֹבֵר,

(Strong and emphatic)

(בהרמת קול ובהדגשה)

וְאַתָּה הוּא
וּשְׁנוֹתֶיךָ לֹא יִתָּמּוּ.

Psalm 93 is an example of biblical poetry utilizing statement and restatement. It has been arranged for antiphonal reading with unison ending, the full chorus summing up the basic truths of the poem.

PSALM 93

HIGH VOICES:	The Lord reigneth;	*(With awe)*
LOW VOICES:	He is robed in majesty.	*(Echoing)*
HIGH VOICES:	The Lord is robed,	*(As before)*
LOW VOICES:	He hath girded himself with strength.	*(Strong)*
HIGH VOICES:	Now is the earth firmly established	*(With emphasis)*
LOW VOICES:	It shall not be moved.	*(Slow, definite)*
HIGH VOICES:	Thy throne is established of old;	*(Fast tempo)*
LOW VOICES:	Thou art from everlasting.	*(Broad, all encompassing)*
HIGH VOICES:	The waters lift up their voices, O Lord, The waters lift up their roaring.	*(The volume rises)*
LOW VOICES:	Yet above the voices of many waters, Above the breakers of the sea, Thou, O Lord, art mighty.	*(Tempo and volume rise to a climax)*
CHORUS:	Thy law is true and unfailing; Holiness is becoming to Thy house, O Lord, Forevermore.	*(Fervent, growing softer and softer)*

c. Part Speaking

This is a form of choral reading arrangement which builds up a cumulative effect by using a combination of various approaches. In this type of arrangement we might utilize, in varying combinations, refrain, antiphonal and unison reading.

Solo and combinations of two, three, and four voices alternate with readings by the massed chorus. In short, part speaking choral reading is very like the rendition of a musical selection by an orchestra: some sections are stated by the massed violins and echoed by the cellos; a thin flute solo comes in with several musical phrases and is overwhelmed by a climax of sound from the entire orchestra; brasses play against woodwinds; the tinkling sound of the triangle is swallowed up by the crash of cymbals and the thunder of kettledrums, etc. In choral reading arranged for part speaking, a similar use is made of all the personnel composing the reading chorus. The selection might be introduced by the entire chorus reading the opening sentence. Then may follow a phrase read by the high voices and a phrase echoed by the low voices. Thereafter three soloists in succession may each read a word with the entire chorus coming in with the succeeding phrase.

The arrangements are not made arbitrarily. The children, with the guidance of the teacher, decide on the allocation of parts to chorus, sub-groups, or soloists, after giving due consideration to the prayer as a whole and to the meaning of each part. Certain parts may be personal, introspective, soft—best suited for low voices or soloists. Other phrases are powerful and need powerful statement by the entire group.

A phrase such as "Out of the depths I called to Thee . . ." is a personal statement of need which might be most effective if read by a solo voice. On the other hand, the class may feel that, although the phrase is stated in the singular, it is a yearning call which comes from the heart of *every one*. They may want it said by the entire group, in unison, humbly, movingly, softly. They may well be right.

The phrase, "Let all flesh bless His Name for ever and ever" is a statement that is all-embracing, all-pervading. It speaks for the community. Its allocation to the entire chorus seems to be indicated. Nevertheless, the class may feel that this phrase is in the nature of a call by the leader to the community; they may feel that it is similar to the call of the *Shamash* in the hamlets of Eastern Europe long ago, walking the streets at dawn, waking the householders with his cry, "Arise, arise to worship your Creator!" Consequently they may decide to allocate the sentence to a solo voice that would state it strongly, challengingly.

What is decided, then, is not nearly as important as why it was decided.

The Sabbath morning prayer *Nishmat*, is quite complex in its structure. It combines long phrases, calling for slow rhythms with short statements, repeating parallel ideas over and over in different words, in quick, choppy rhythm. Only a combination of forms can adequately express the theme and its emotional rhythms. Part speaking would seem to be the desired type of arrangement for this selection. The details of the arrangement will of course vary with each class. The following is an example:

	נִשְׁמַת	
CHORUS (*softly, devotionally*):	נִשְׁמַת כָּל חַי תְּבָרֵךְ אֶת שִׁמְךָ יְיָ אֱלֹהֵינוּ.	המקהלה: (בקול רך ובחרדת קדש)

TWO VOICES *(Louder):*	וְרוּחַ כָּל בָּשָׂר	שני קולות (בהגברת קול):
SOLO 1 *(In cadence. The volume rises):*	תְּפָאֵר,	סולו א׳ (בקצב לכת הולך וגובר):
SOLO 2:	וּתְרוֹמֵם	סולו ב׳:
SOLO 3:	זִכְרְךָ	סולו ג׳:
SOLO 4:	מַלְכֵּנוּ	סולו ד׳:
TWO VOICES *(With emphasis):*	תָּמִיד.	שני קולות (בהדגשה):
SOLO 1 *(All embracing):*	מִן הָעוֹלָם	סולו א׳ (בהטעמה):
SOLO 2:	וְעַד הָעוֹלָם	סולו ב׳ (בהטעמה יתירה):
TWO VOICES *(A clarion call):*	אַתָּה אֵל,	שני קולות (בקול תרועה):
THREE VOICES *(With ecstasy):*	וּמִבַּלְעָדֶיךָ אֵין לָנוּ מֶלֶךְ	שלשה קולות (בהתלהבות):
		(קול קורא וקול עונה כהד)
HIGH VOICES *(Calling):*	גּוֹאֵל	קולות רמים:
LOW VOICES *(Echoing):*	וּמוֹשִׁיעַ	קולות נמוכים:
HIGH VOICES:	פּוֹדֶה	קולות רמים:
LOW VOICES:	וּמַצִּיל	קולות נמוכים:
HIGH VOICES:	וּמְפַרְנֵס	קולות רמים:
LOW VOICES:	וּמְרַחֵם	קולות נמוכים:
CHORUS *(Rising volume):*	בְּכָל עֵת צָרָה וְצוּקָה,	המקהלה (בהרמת קול):
SOLO 1 *(Joyously):*	אֵין לָנוּ מֶלֶךְ אֶלָּא אָתָּה.	סולו א׳ (בהתרוננות):
CHORUS *(Continuously rising volume and tempo):*	אֱלֹהֵי הָרִאשׁוֹנִים וְהָאַחֲרוֹנִים, אֱלוֹהַּ כָּל בְּרִיּוֹת, אֲדוֹן כָּל תּוֹלָדוֹת, הַמְהֻלָּל בְּרוֹב הַתִּשְׁבָּחוֹת, הַמְנַהֵג עוֹלָמוֹ בְּחֶסֶד, וּבְרִיּוֹתָיו בְּרַחֲמִים.	המקהלה (בקול ובקצב הולכים ומתגברים):
SOLO 1 *(With emphasis):*	וַייָ לֹא יָנוּם וְלֹא יִישָׁן,	סולו א׳ (בהדגשה):
HIGH VOICES *(Exclamation!):*	הַמְעוֹרֵר	קולות רמים (בסמן הקריאה):

LOW VOICES *(Punctuate!)*:	יְשֵׁנִים,	קולות נמוכים (בהדגשה):
HIGH VOICES *(Exclamation!)*:	וְהַמֵּקִיץ	קולות רמים (בסמן הקריאה):
LOW VOICES *(Emphasize!)*:	נִרְדָּמִים,	קולות נמוכים (בהדגשה):
HIGH VOICES *(Exclamation!)*:	וְהַמֵּשִׂיחַ	קולות רמים (בסמן הקריאה):
LOW VOICES *(Broadly)*:	אִלְּמִים,	קולות נמוכים (בהדגשה):
(Fast tempo)		(בקצב מזורז)
SOLO 1:	וְהַמַּתִּיר אֲסוּרִים,	סולו א׳:
SOLO 2:	וְהַסּוֹמֵךְ נוֹפְלִים,	סולו ב׳:
SOLO 3:	וְהַזּוֹקֵף כְּפוּפִים.	סולו ג׳:
CHORUS *(Fervent, in slow tempo)*:	לְךָ לְבַדְּךָ אֲנַחְנוּ מוֹדִים.	המקהלה (בחרדת קודש ובקצב מואט):

Here is another example of a prayer arranged for Part Speaking:

THE LORD IS MY LIGHT (PSALM 27)

SOLO:	The Lord is my light and my salvation. Whom shall I fear? The Lord is the stronghold of my life; Of whom shall I be afraid?	*(Broadly, with conviction)*
CHORUS:	When evil-doers came upon me to consume my flesh, Even mine enemies and my foes, They stumbled and fell.	*(With wonder)*
HIGH VOICES:	Though a host should encamp against me,	*(With assurance)*
LOW VOICES:	My heart shall not fear;	*(Emphatic)*
HIGH VOICES:	Though war were waged on me,	*(In cadence)*
LOW VOICES:	Even then would I be confident.	*(Emphatic)*
SOLO:	One thing have I asked of the Lord,	
CHORUS:	That I may dwell in the house of the Lord, all the days of my life, To behold the graciousness of the Lord And to enter in His Temple;	*(Simply)*
HIGH VOICES:	For He concealeth me in His pavilion in the day of evil. He hideth me in the shelter of His tent; He lifteth me up upon a rock.	*(Fervent)*
LOW VOICES:	And now shall my head be lifted up to victory,	*(With assurance)*
	And I will bring to His tabernacle offerings with trumpet sound.	*(Strong)*

SOLO:	I will sing, yea, I will sing praises unto the Lord;	*(Fervent)*
CHORUS:	Hear, O Lord, when I cry with my voice,	*(Pleading, softly)*
	And be gracious unto me, and answer me.	*(Softer)*
	Thou hast been my help; Cast me not off, neither forsake me, O God of my salvation.	*(Almost whispering)*

d. Unison

This is undoubtedly the most difficult form of choral reading arrangement. It is the reading of a complete selection by the entire chorus. Few groups have the requisite experience to read effectively a prayer arranged for unison rendition.

Unison reading is quite different from "concert reading" which we often hear in our classrooms during the *Siddur* lesson. In concert reading all the children read the prayer together. It is not an outgrowth of understanding, nor is any attempt made at interpretation. At best the teacher sees to it that all the children read at the same rate of speed, all pausing in the same places. Usually concert reading slips into sing-song. It can easily become monotonous and boring. Certainly, since the children do not feel that their individual contribution adds to the total effectiveness of the prayer, there is room for malingering, reinforcement of errors in reading, etc.

Unison reading is interpretive reading by the entire group reading together. It depends for its effect on variety of pitch, tone, rhythm, rate of speech, volume, etc. All must read together—beginning together, pausing together, ending together, using the same speech melody for every word and phrase.

Let us take, for example, the prayer *Mah Tovu* ("How goodly are Thy tents"). If the class has determined that the opening phrase be read with a rising tone and strong accent on the word "goodly," every child in the group must raise his tone and accent that word together, otherwise confusion would result in the reading. This requires a good deal of skill. The teacher will therefore use unison arrangements for complete prayers sparingly, and only after the class has had a good deal of previous experience in choral reading.

Following are examples of two prayers arranged for Unison Reading:

וּבְמַקְהֲלוֹת

CHORUS:	וּבְמַקְהֲלוֹת רִבְבוֹת עַמְּךָ	המקהלה (בשמחה, בהדגשה):
(Joyous, emphatic)	בֵּית יִשְׂרָאֵל,	
	בְּרִנָּה יִתְפָּאַר שִׁמְךָ מַלְכֵּנוּ	
(Drawn out)	בְּכָל־דּוֹר וָדוֹר.	(בקצב ממושך)
(With conviction)	שֶׁכֵּן חוֹבַת כָּל־הַיְצוּרִים	(בהטעמה)
	לְפָנֶיךָ,	
	יְיָ אֱלֹהֵינוּ	
	וֵאלֹהֵי אֲבוֹתֵינוּ.	

(In rising cadence)	לְהוֹדוֹת לְהַלֵּל	(בקצב מנין הולך וגובר)
	לְשַׁבֵּחַ לְפָאֵר	
	לְרוֹמֵם לְהַדֵּר	
	לְבָרֵךְ	
	לְעַלֵּה	
	וּלְקַלֵּס,	
(Fervent, strong)	עַל כָּל דִּבְרֵי שִׁירוֹת	(בהתרוננות,
	וְתִשְׁבְּחוֹת	בהטעמה יתרה)
	דָּוִד בֶּן־יִשַׁי,	
(Emphatic)	עַבְדְּךָ	(בהדגשה)
(Softly, ecstatic)	מְשִׁיחֶךָ.	(בהתרגשות, ברוך)

BLESSED BE THE LORD BY DAY

(From the Weekday Evening Service)

CHORUS:	Blessed be the Lord by day;	*(Joyfully)*
	Blessed be the Lord by night;	*(Softly)*
	Blessed be the Lord when we lie down;	*(Slowly)*
	Blessed be the Lord when we rise up.	*(Loudly)*
	For in Thy hand are	*(Humbly)*
	the souls of the living	
	and the dead,	
	As it is said:	*(Simply)*
	"In His hand	*(Emphatically with rising*
	is the soul of every living thing,	*pitch and tempo)*
	and the spirit	*(Very softly)*
	of all human flesh."	*(Fervently)*
	Into Thy hand I commend my spirit;	*(Exultantly)*
	Thou hast redeemed me,	
	O Lord God of truth!	

Unison reading of certain words, phrases, or sentences is, of course, constantly used as part of other types of arrangements. Note, for example, the following setting of *Sh'ma*. It is arranged for antiphonal reading. However, there is a unison statement of the theme as an opening and a unison closing of the prayer which is in the nature of a clarion call and summation.

שְׁמַע

CHORUS:	שְׁמַע יִשְׂרָאֵל, יְיָ אֱלֹהֵינוּ, יְיָ אֶחָד. בָּרוּךְ שֵׁם כְּבוֹד מַלְכוּתוֹ לְעוֹלָם וָעֶד:	הַמַּקְהֵלָה:
HIGH VOICES:	וְאָהַבְתָּ אֵת יְיָ אֱלֹהֶיךָ,	קוֹלוֹת רָמִים:
LOW VOICES:	בְּכָל לְבָבְךָ,	קוֹלוֹת נְמוּכִים:
HIGH VOICES:	וּבְכָל נַפְשְׁךָ,	קוֹלוֹת רָמִים:
LOW VOICES:	וּבְכָל מְאֹדֶךָ.	קוֹלוֹת נְמוּכִים:
HIGH VOICES:	וְהָיוּ הַדְּבָרִים הָאֵלֶּה, אֲשֶׁר אָנֹכִי מְצַוְּךָ הַיּוֹם, עַל לְבָבֶךָ.	קוֹלוֹת רָמִים:
LOW VOICES:	וְשִׁנַּנְתָּם לְבָנֶיךָ,	קוֹלוֹת נְמוּכִים:
HIGH VOICES:	וְדִבַּרְתָּ בָּם, בְּשִׁבְתְּךָ בְּבֵיתֶךָ,	קוֹלוֹת רָמִים:
LOW VOICES:	וּבְלֶכְתְּךָ בַדֶּרֶךְ, וּבְשָׁכְבְּךָ, וּבְקוּמֶךָ.	קוֹלוֹת נְמוּכִים:
HIGH VOICES:	וּקְשַׁרְתָּם לְאוֹת עַל יָדֶךָ,	קוֹלוֹת רָמִים:
LOW VOICES:	וְהָיוּ לְטֹטָפֹת בֵּין עֵינֶיךָ.	קוֹלוֹת נְמוּכִים:
CHORUS:	וּכְתַבְתָּם עַל מְזֻזוֹת בֵּיתֶךָ וּבִשְׁעָרֶיךָ.	הַמַּקְהֵלָה:

11. Aspects of Interpretation

Having determined the arrangement of a prayer, attention is now given to certain other details which will make for an effective reading. The tone, the tempo, the rhythm are carefully determined as a result of cooperative planning by the children with stimulating teacher guidance. Once more it is to be noted that in settling on these aspects of the reading, the children, again and again, must read the words, the phrases, the sentences in order to demonstrate how, in their opinion, they are to be read. While doing so they gain further meaningful practice leading to fluency in the reading. Some of the elements to be considered are:

a. Tone

This concerns the quality of the voice used in the reading. In determining the tone we establish the *pitch* with which the phrase is read—using high notes or low. The proper pitch is often a determining factor whether a word or phrase is assigned to the sub-chorus of high voices or low voices; the *inflection* to be used—whether, in reading a word or phrase, the voice is kept at an even level, rises upward or slides downward on the scale; and the *volume* of sound—whether the word or phrase is read loudly or softly. The volume needed will also influence the decision whether the word or phrase is to be assigned to a solo, a sub-chorus, or the entire chorus.

b. Rhythm

This is the orderly flow of the words in time, determined by the regular stress or beat which recurs over and over again in a definite pattern. Often the rhythm is the same for the entire prayer. At other times the rhythm changes during the selection.

The meaning of the selection is the major factor determining its rhythm. One selection may call for march rhythm, another for flowing, waltzlike rhythm.

In the "Song of Moses" the march rhythm is obvious for lines such as the following:

The Lord is a man of war,
The Lord is His name.
Pharaoh's chariots
and his host
hath He cast
into the sea.

The words breathe action. There is a choppiness, a strength in the lines, a rhythmic pattern of marching feet calling for a reading in a definite, march-like rhythm.

In contrast to this selection one might mention the Twenty-third Psalm. This is an outpouring of the soul—romantic and lyrical. The words flow peacefully like the "still waters" of which they speak. A waltzlike, flowing rhythm is obviously called for when reading in chorus:

The Lord is my shepherd;
I shall not want.
He maketh me to lie down in green pastures;
He leadeth me beside the still waters.
He restoreth my soul.

The teacher will give careful consideration to developing within the children a feeling for the rhythm inherent in the prayer. This may be done by having the children beat out the rhythm silently by tapping their index finger against the open palm as the teacher or a child reads the selection in the rhythm which the class has determined as appropriate for the selection.

Making the children conscious of the rhythm inherent in each prayer will do much to overcome the characteristic monotonous sing-song, so often heard during *Siddur* reading in our classrooms. Also, it will tend to improve the children's grouping of words, so as to express properly the sense and meaning of the prayer.

c. *Tempo*

This is actually an aspect of rhythm. It is the rate of speed with which a selection or a section of a selection is read.

The example given above from the "Song of Moses" is heroic in nature. The tempo in which it is read would be fast, choppy, exciting. The class might even decide to emphasize the mounting excitement of the lines by increasing the speed with each line that is read, beginning somewhat slowly, the tempo grows faster and faster until the selection reaches a climax.

The lines from the Twenty-third Psalm speak of calm faith, of spiritual tranquility. It would seem appropriate that they be read in a contemplative tempo, slowly, with long pauses between certain phrases.

In general, it is well to note that when a selection is read aloud, the tempo is to be somewhat slower than when it is read silently. This is necessary in order to avoid overlapping sounds causing the words to be heard as a jumble. Also, the listener is given an opportunity to assimilate the thoughts expressed.

d. *Emphasis*

A selection gains in interest when certain words are stressed.

These are the key words which have the chief meaning in a phrase or sentence. The children will determine on the words to be stressed, thus getting yet another opportunity for practicing reading with a purpose.

Emphasis is accomplished by using slightly louder tones or stronger beat on the key words as:

O *come,*
let us *sing* before the Lord,
let us *shout* for *joy*
to the *Rock* of our *salvation.*

e. *Contrast*

This is another element which makes for better interpretation and for more interesting reading. A line spoken loudly is followed contrastingly with a line rendered softly. A fast phrase is succeeded by a slow one. The full chorus takes up the reading following a solo voice. Etc.

While the teacher bears in mind the undoubted value of contrasts, he is careful not to establish a regular pattern, alternating slow-fast, slow-fast, or, soft-loud, soft-loud, and so on. This would make for artificiality. It would tend to defeat the end goal toward which we are striving—reading of prayer with understanding, with feeling, with beauty, with devotion.

f. Mood

Mood is the inner feeling of the prayer—joy, sadness, contemplation, humility, faith, tranquility, etc. The mood is determined by the meaning of the prayer. It is conveyed to the listener by means of a combination of all the elements discussed above: the tone, the rhythm, the tempo, etc.

The teacher elicits from the children their opinions regarding the mood which is to be created with the reading of a given prayer. Once this is agreed upon, the teacher helps them to maintain this mood by calling their attention to it from time to time. Thus, when there is a tendency to speed up, the teacher might remind the children, "the mood of this prayer is one of sadness." Let's slow it up a bit, shall we?" or, "the mood is one of triumph. Don't you think a little more volume would help?"

■ PRAYER IS FOR WORSHIP

Although we have been stressing "meaningful prayer," the teacher will bear in mind that prayers are not intended as vehicles for intellectual exercises. Prayers are for worship. The teacher will therefore provide worship experiences during which the children will pray, utilizing whenever possible, the choral reading arrangements which they have developed in the classroom. For example:

a. It is altogether proper to begin each class session with a brief worship service. A choral reading of one of the Psalms would be most suitable for this purpose.

b. During the last few minutes of each session or once a week for a longer period of time, the children might participate in an abbreviated class *Minha* (Afternoon) or *Maariv* (Evening) service. The inclusion of prayers arranged for choral reading would, on the one hand, add interest and beauty to the service and, on the other hand, lend reality and purpose to their efforts in arranging the prayers for choral reading as part of their *Siddur* lessons.

c. Special calendar occasions lend themselves to special class worship services of which choral reading is a part. *Rosh Hodesh* (the first of the Hebrew calendar month), minor Jewish festivals, American national holidays are proper occasions for special class services.

d. Choral reading may be made a significant part of the Junior Congregation services on Sabbath and on festivals. At every service a different class might read a prayer which was especially arranged for choral reading at the service. More than one selection might be read chorally, with classes alternating in reading the prayers which they had prepared. It is also possible that certain prayers be read chorally at every service just as certain prayers are normally sung at every service.

■ IN THE ADULT SYNAGOGUE

Just as many congregations use choral singing to add beauty to the services, choral reading, too, may well be considered for use for that purpose. Its utilization would add an emotional quality to synagogue worship, particularly in synagogues having late Friday evening services.

The singing choir, or a special reading chorus organized for that purpose with volunteers or professionals, might be trained in choral reading of selections from the services. Prayers such as *Lekhu N'ran'nah* (Come, let us sing), *Ahavat Olam* (With everlasting love) or *Hashkivenu* (Cause us, O Lord, to lie down in peace) are particularly suitable for this purpose. The example set by the reading chorus might even influence the quality of the congregational reading of responsive prayers such as *Ashrei* (Happy are they that dwell in Thy house) or unison prayers such as *Sh'ma Yisrael* (Hear, O Israel).

Several synagogues have tried this and found it successful. Others may find it worthwhile experimenting with choral reading.

CHAPTER 6

Teaching Hebrew Language

■ In this section we will deal in detail with some dramatic techniques which are particularly suitable for Hebrew language instruction. A number of other techniques, such as "Story Dramatization" and the like, which have been fully developed in connection with other subjects, will be indicated here by reference only. Where such a technique has particular modes of use in connection with Hebrew language, these specialized uses will also be indicated.

The choice of the proper dramatic techniques for Hebrew language learning is beset with greater difficulties than are to be found in connection with other subjects. There are many factors which complicate the teacher's task. Not the least of these is the fact that Hebrew language is asked to play so many different roles in the curriculum of the Jewish school.

■ HEBREW IN THE CURRICULUM

About no other subject is there so much agreement and at the same time so much disagreement as there is about Hebrew language study. Its position would seem to be akin to that of democracy—nearly everyone is for it but interprets it differently.

There is almost universal agreement about the importance of Hebrew language in Jewish education. But this is as far as the agreement goes and now the cleavages begin.

Educators differ greatly as to the purpose for Hebrew language study. Some want Hebrew language taught so as to prepare the students for Bible study. Some see as its purpose to orient the pupil toward reading of Hebrew literature. There are those who place the emphasis on spoken Hebrew. Others argue that Hebrew language study in the elementary school is to be geared toward ritual function. There are even proponents of so-called "social Hebrew" whatever that may be.

The differences of opinion regarding our objectives in teaching Hebrew naturally result in basic differences in methodology. There are the proponents of *Ivrit b'Ivrit* or the Natural Method, the partisans of translation, the devotees of the aural-oral approach, and a host of others. There is even a growing coterie of educators who put their faith in teaching machines of all sorts.

■ THE TEACHER'S PROBLEM

All of these divergencies complicate infinitely the task of the teacher who is generally removed from the rarified atmosphere of the theorists. All he knows is that Hebrew is *the* major subject in most Jewish schools where he is called upon to teach. He must move ahead, doing as best as he can. To him the proper methodology is of deep concern, in more than a theoretical manner. If he makes a mistake with a generation of pupils it is an error that is generally beyond rectifying. The damage is done and there is nothing the teacher can do about it after the pupil has left the class and the school.

So the teacher seeks for help in the writings of the experts. And he finds, often to his great dismay, that suggestions are offered all too often in the most general terms, so that the teacher is at a loss to implement them. He is advised to use filmstrips but the "experts" do not indicate which filmstrips, where they are to be gotten, nor even whether such filmstrips actually exist. He is told to expose his students to Hebrew language experiences within the community without taking into account that in most communities such opportunities simply do not exist. Even metropolitan New York, with the greatest concentration of Jewish population anywhere in the world, has not been able to maintain a Hebrew theatre for children where they might hear Hebrew spoken in a living manner outside the walls of their school building. Every curriculum suggests "dramatization" taking it for granted that the teacher will thereafter go ahead and use dramatization for more effective Hebrew teaching, but the teacher is bewildered about its implementation.

■ DRAMATICS FOR LANGUAGE TEACHING

Much of the teacher's difficulty in using dramatization stems from the fact that he has the feeling that he is being asked to "make bricks without straw." Dramatics is basically a language art form. As the painter is dependent on canvas, paints and brushes, as the musician's art is expressed through voice or instrument, so the dramaturgist depends on words and sentences. Words are the bricks and the timber out of which the edifice is built to house the dramatic idea. Lacking these bricks and timber because of the students' initial ignorance of the language, the teacher feels himself severely handicapped in the creation through dramatization of simulated reality situations for making Hebrew language study meaningful and vital.

This is a real difficulty and a real problem, but it is not altogether insurmountable. Granted that the teacher cannot use, particularly in the early stages of language instruction, creative dramatic techniques which call for free expression of ideas, such as are possible with subjects like history, current history and others that are generally taught in the vernacular. Nevertheless, there are some dramatic forms which call for a minimum use of language—games, pantomimes, and the like—which the teacher can utilize to advantage with beginners. Their function will be limited, in the beginning at least, to motivation and practice rather than to initial learning. As the pupils' vocabulary and their skill in its use expands, the teacher will begin to use more complex dramatic forms, such as call for creative language use. In time the teacher will be able to resort to dramatic techniques requiring original composition of story and text, and spontaneous development of character and dialogue, providing the pupils with reality experience in the use of Hebrew language that are living, pleasurable and meaningful to the students.

Dramatic Language Techniques

The techniques which follow are being set down in the order of their complexity. We begin with the fairly simple and go on to the more difficult, calling for greater experience with dramatization and more extensive language knowledge. The teacher will of course use them as the need may arise.

■ GAMES

The dramatic game is by far the simplest technique. It calls for a minimum of dramatization and language skill. Generally it is most suitable as a drill technique.

Dramatic games have been fully discussed in Chapter 1, "Games for Teaching and for Developing Dramatization Readiness." The reader is referred to that chapter for details. The following are especially suitable:

Concentration	For drill, review, testing, motivation.
The Lost Word	For initial presentation of new material, review, testing.
Double Up	For vocabulary drill, sentence comprehension practice.
Ani	Similar to "Double Up."
Alert	For vocabulary drill suitable only where translation is not frowned upon.
Animal Farm	For story comprehension practice, especially good for younger children.
Sounds I Hear	For comprehension practice, especially suitable for "functional Hebrew."
Shimon Omer	For drill, review, testing.
Bankers	For practice with Hebrew numbers.
Dreidle Grab	For practice with Hebrew calendar, alphabet, numbers, or other vocabulary dealing with a category or central theme.
Numbers Change	An active game for drill in Hebrew numbers. The game may be adapted to vocabulary drill of any group of words dealing with a unified theme.
Catastrophe	For motivating a new lesson. For drill, review, testing.
Down You Go	For teaching Hebrew Alphabet. For spelling practice, and writing.
In the Manner of the Word	For drill and review.
Detective	Practice in speaking, review.

The following games require greater knowledge of Hebrew and are suitable only for groups that can carry on with simple Hebrew conversation:

Close Your Eyes And See	Practice in simple conversation. The game requires adaptation if it is to be used for Hebrew language.
Story Chain-Reaction	Review of Hebrew story, vocabulary use.
Original Story Chain-Reaction	Similar to the above but requiring a more advanced knowledge of Hebrew. Probably useful in a 3rd year Hebrew class.

Pairs	Review, original language use. Suitable only with advanced class, learning *Humash* or history in Hebrew.
I Did It!	Practice in language use.

The teacher will do well to examine some of the standard books of games. Many of the general party games may, with minor adaptation, be utilized as aids in language teaching. Also, the games given here are basically dramatic in nature. There are many others calling for non-dramatic activities such as word-matching, writing, etc., with which the teacher should become familiar and utilize to add the element of "fun" to language learning.

Talking Mirror

In the early stages of learning a language there is an element of strangeness in the new combinations of sounds which require practice by the learner. Also, it is desirable that from the very outset the pupils learn to pronounce the new words properly. The following technique utilizes children's well known propensity for mimicry to help them to learn to speak Hebrew correctly.

"Talking Mirror" is basically a game. The teacher speaks a Hebrew sentence, accompanying his speech with interpretive movements. The class repeats the sentence and the movements, trying to mirror exactly the teacher's pronunciation, intonation and movements. The teacher then repeats the sentence, one or more times. Each time the sentence is repeated the teacher changes the intonation, rate of speed, emphasis, etc. After each repetition by the teacher, the class tries to imitate the teacher exactly.

■ REALITY SITUATIONS

Even with the limited vocabulary of the first year, the pupils can participate in reality situations—actual or simulated—in which they have opportunities to utilize Hebrew language in a purposeful manner. Here are a few suggestions:

Newscaster

At the beginning of each session, a pupil who has been appointed in advance to be the class Newscaster for that day, comes to the front of the room. He presents to the class the news of the day which is important such as: he announces the day of the week, the date, the weather report, the weekly *Sidrah,* special class and school activities, etc. Even in a first year class the following is possible:

NEWSCASTER: *Hayom yom sheni.*
Parashat hashavua "B'shalah".
L'Yaakov Katz yesh beged hadash.
Hayom yom huledet shel Hannah Pearl.
Hayom anahnu lomdim ivrit, historiah u-t'filah.
Hayom kar bahutz. Yesh shemesh bashamayim.
Mahar-sheleg.

Making the class newscast a regular feature of class life takes it out of the category of "stunt" or lesson and sets up an actual reality situation within which Hebrew language is functional for the students.

As the class learns more Hebrew, more news items are added to the newscast. In older classes it is actually possible to have the Newscaster present summaries of Jewish news and general news items of major significance in addition to the class and school news.

The role of Newscaster is assumed each session by a different student, so that all will eventually have an opportunity to participate. It is also possible to divide the task among several students each time. The Newscasters are told in advance when their turn will come so that they can prepare their newscast at home or ask for the teacher's help where necessary. The teacher of course encourages the Newscasters to elaborate their reports as much as their vocabulary limits will permit.

Exhibition Guides

Once in two weeks, or oftener if desired, the pupils arrange an exhibition in class of reproductions of paintings of Jewish interest, ceremonial objects, the pupils' own art work, and the like. The exhibitions might center about themes that are determined in advance such as: Shabbat, Israel, a festival, etc.

Several pupils are appointed to the Exhibit Committee. They plan the exhibition, obtain the pictures or objects and set them up about the room. On the day of the exhibition, the class views the exhibit while the committee members act as Exhibition Guides. Each of the guides explains in Hebrew one or more of the items on exhibition. The guides are of course given an opportunity to prepare their guide-talks in advance, either at a committee meeting outside of class or at home. Even in a fairly elementary class this might proceed as follows:

GUIDE 1: *(Pointing out an Ilyah Schor woodcut of the Sabbath)*
Hineh t'munah.
Ba-t'munah bayit.
Zeh bayit Ivri.
Ba-bayit yesh shulhan.
Hashulhan omed etzel halon.
Al hashulhan sh'ney nerot, kos, bakbuk yayin.
Etzel hashulhan omdim imma, yeled, yaldah.
Aba ba mibeyt hak'neset.
Etzel aba sh'ney malakhim.
Shabbat babayit.

GUIDE 2: *(Pointing to a Kiddush cup)*
Hiney kos.
Zeh kos l'kiddush.
Hakos kesef.
Hakos ba meEretz Yisrael.
Zeh kos shel Shabbat.

As their vocabulary increases, the guides make their talks more elaborate adding details about the artists, the places where the objects come from, their history, etc.

From the outset the class is encouraged to ask questions which the guides answer to the best of their abilities. In the beginning the questions are simple, limited to such matters as to whom each item belongs, what is the name of the painter, and the like.

Shel mi hat'munah?
Mah shem hatzayar?
Kamah shanim lakos?

Later, more complex questions are added. The teacher stimulates the class in this direction by setting the example and asking questions himself. There are two cautions which must be observed in this connection: (1) The questions should be such as will permit the guides to answer within the limits of their Hebrew knowledge. (2) The questions should be, as the children say, "for real," for the purpose of actually eliciting information about the exhibit and not purely for language exercise.

If desired, the exhibit is allowed to remain for a while, other classes being invited to see it and hear the guides' Hebrew explanations.

Song-Master

This is another reality situation that is possible in a class, providing the students with opportunities for utilizing their Hebrew vocabularies.

Whenever a new song is to be taught, a pupil, who has been especially appointed for the task, acts as the Song-Master. He introduces the song to the class for the first time by saying a few words about the occasion for the song, the writer of the words or the composer of the music, the content of the song, etc. The Song-Master then recites the words of the song, reading it aloud meaningfully or singing it if he has managed to learn it in advance.

Following is an example:

SONG-MASTER: *Shalom yeladim.*
Hayom yom huledet.
Hayom yom huledet shel Hayim Nahman Bialik.
Hineh shir yafeh.
Bialik katav et hashir.
Shem hashir "Ken Latzipor."
(He sings or reads)
Ken latzipor ben haetzim.
Uvaken lah shalosh betzim.
Uv'khol betzah—has, pen ta'ir!
Yashen lo efroah za'ir.

Come to a Party!

This is a form of dramatization which is especially suitable for practicing the use of vocabulary dealing with the home, food, festival observance, and similar areas.

The custom is established in the class that once a week, generally the last session of the week, the children are given a little party. The party takes place during the last few minutes of the session. Each week the party is prepared by a different Party

Committee which is appointed in advance for this purpose. Such a party can be centered each time about a different occasion—Shabbat, Rosh Hodesh, a festival, honoring a new student, or a pupil with a birthday, etc. Such parties are especially valuable in that they can be utilized to provide reality practice in the use of Hebrew blessings, Grace after Meals, songs, etc.

The Party Committee obtains the refreshments and sets them up, ready to be served. The Committee elects one of its members to be the Inviter. He appears before the class, just before the party is about to begin, and issues an invitation on behalf of the Party Committee. The class is encouraged to try to find out what they may expect before they accept the invitation, as well as the occasion for the party. The Inviter tries to get them to accept by describing enticingly the party, the refreshments, etc. When the teacher feels that he has done as well as might be expected, he accepts on behalf of the class. Here is a sample:

INVITER: *Bou lamishteh, b'vakashah.*
STUDENT 1: *Mah atah noten bamishteh?*
INVITER: *Ani lo noten. Hahaverim notnim perot.*
STUDENT 2: *Eizeh perot notnim hem?*
INVITER: *Hem notnim tapuz, t'enah, sh'kedim, v'od perot.*
STUDENT 3: *Madua yesh mishteh hayom?*
INVITER: *Ki hayom hag. Hayom Tu Bishvat.*
TEACHER: *Tov m'od. Todah. Anahnu ba'im lamishteh.*

■ DIALOGUES

These are simulated reality situations which are set up to give the pupils practice in the use of language. These simple dramatizations involve the use of dialogue on an elementary level. They are very close to the games which children generally play when they are young.

At the Telephone

Pupils telephone each other for various purposes such as to discuss the homework, to plan an outing, to decide on a purchase, to discuss a class event, to talk of a holiday that is approaching, to plan a party, etc.

The teacher selects two students to be at the telephone. The telephones are imaginary or toy telephones are used. He announces the subject of their conversation. They then go ahead and talk as long as they are able or until the teacher signals them to end the conversation. The first time this is tried, the teacher himself might be one of the telephone callers so as to give the pupils an idea of what is possible within the limits of their Hebrew knowledge. Following is an example of a dramatized telephone conversation on the subject of "a trip."

STUDENT 1: *Shalom. Ani hafetz l'daber el Moshe.*
STUDENT 2: *Ani Moshe. Mi m'daber?*
STUDENT 1: *Zeh Yosef. Mah shlomkha Moshe?*
STUDENT 2: *Shalom li. Todah. Umah shlomkha?*

STUDENT 1: *Shalom li. Moshe!*
STUDENT 2: *Ken?*
STUDENT 1: *Mahar ani nose'a.*
STUDENT 2: *L'an atah nose'a, Yosef?*
STUDENT 1: *Ani nose'a l'Washington.*
STUDENT 2: *Yafeh! Yafeh m'od!*
STUDENT 1: *Moshe, hanasi yoshev b'Washington.*
STUDENT 2: *Ken. Ani yode'a. Mah atah loke'ah el Washington?*
STUDENT 1: *Ani loke'ah beged hadash, s'farim, v'kadur sheli.*
STUDENT 2: *Yafeh m'od.*
STUDENT 1: *Shalom Moshe. B'hamesh ani m'tzaltzel od hapa'am.*
STUDENT 2: *Tov m'od. Todah. Shalom Yosef.*

Shopping

This is similar to the well-known children's game of playing store. A student assumes the role of storekeeper and another becomes the customer. The customer asks for a suit, dress, shoes, or food, depending upon the vocabulary which the teacher wants practiced. The storekeeper tries to sell the merchandise, praises it, etc. In the end the sale is made and the dramatization ends.

Following is an example of "Shopping" in a grocery on Friday:

GROCER: *Mah atah hafetz?*
CUSTOMER: *Ani hafetz halah.*
GROCER: *Madu'ah atah hafetz halah hayom?*
CUSTOMER: *Ki hayom erev Shabbat.*
GROCER: *Tov. Hineh halah g'dolah.*
CUSTOMER: *Hahalah tovah?*
GROCER: *Ken. Hahalah tovah m'od. Mah od atah hafetz?*
CUSTOMER: *Ima sheli hafetza shnei nerot.*
GROCER: *Madu'a shnayim?*
CUSTOMER: *Ki b'shabbat hi madlikah shnei nerot.*
GROCER: *Tov. Madu'ah lo shtei halot? B'shabbat m'varkhim al shtei halot.*
CUSTOMER: *Ken?*
GROCER: *Ken. Atah hafetz od hallah?*
CUSTOMER: *Tov. Ten li od halah ahat.*
GROCER: *Hineh od halah. Et hab'rakhah al halah atah yode'a?*
CUSTOMER: *Ken.*
GROCER: *Tov. Emor et habrakhah b'vakashah.*
CUSTOMER: *Barukh atah Adonai, Elohenu melekh haolam, hamotzi lehem min haaretz.*
GROCER: *Tov m'od. Atah yeled hakham. Hineh hahalot v'hanerot. Ten li dolar v'hamishah cent. V'hineh l'kha tapuah. Zot matanah l'kha.*
CUSTOMER: *Todah. Shabbat Shalom.*
GROCER: *Shabbat Shalom. Bo od hapa'am.*

Ringing Doorbells

In this simple dialogue dramatization a pupil assumes the role of a charity volunteer. He rings the door bell of a householder and asks for clothes for a rummage sale, or contributions for the charity fund. The householder wants more information before contributing.

Late for Synagogue

A pupil assumes the role of a boy who comes late for services on Sabbath morning. The man at the door asks him to wait outside. He informs him that they are taking out the Torah scrolls from the Ark. He questions the boy about the *Sidrah* they are about to read. Finally the Torah scrolls are placed on the pulpit and the boy is allowed to enter.

■ PANTOMIMES

It is generally accepted that in language learning the students' passive vocabulary is substantially greater than their active one. They understand a great deal more than they speak. In guiding the pupils toward dramatization for more intensive language use, the pantomime is a first step, since it takes advantage of their greater passive vocabulary. Also the fear of appearing before their classmates in an unfamiliar role is minimized when, at the beginning, they are freed from the actual verbalization of the dialogue.

Group Action Pantomime

This is the very simplest form. It is similar to the games "*Shimon Omer*" or "In the Manner of the Word." A leader is chosen. He gives a series of action words and phrases. The whole class acts them out. Example:

> *Mabit. Mistovev. Ima madlikah nerot. Y'ladim okhlim halah. Y'ladim okhlim sh'kedim. Etc.*

Pantomime With Narration

Pupils are selected to represent the characters in the Hebrew story being studied. One student reads or tells the story while the "characters" act it out in pantomime. For example, in the story "*Havdalah*" on page 71 of *Shalom Yeladim*, Book One, pupils are selected to pantomime the roles of *Aba*, *Hanah* and *Moshe*. As the Narrator reads the story, *Aba* takes the candle, lights the candle, *Hanah* asks him for the candle, *Aba* gives it to her, etc.

This is a simple way of leading the pupils toward dramatization. The teacher will find, however, that the pupils will soon tire of it since it does not offer enough of a challenge.

Creative Story Pantomime

This is a variant of "Pantomime With Narration" which offers a great deal more challenge to the students. It is particularly suitable in a class where the aural-oral approach is stressed. In other classes it may be used in connection with material studied earlier and is now to be reviewed without the use of the book.

The teacher announces a theme such as: "*Nerot Shel Shabbat*" or "*Navhan Holekh el Bet Haknesset*."

If it is a familiar story which has been previously studied, the class recalls the characters which will be needed. Students are selected to play these roles. One is chosen Narrator. The group is given a few moments to decide what they will do. Then the Narrator tells the story in his own words while the others act it out.

If the story is to be made up orally by the students on a theme announced by the teacher, the pupils create it through class discussion. Students are then selected to play the characters and the Narrator. Then the Narrator tells the story which has been developed by the class in his own words while the others pantomime the action.

■ PUPPETS

Puppets are prime favorites of children and they can be used to great advantage in language teaching in a variety of ways.

There are many books which deal with the techniques of making puppets. They are readily obtainable in the local public library so that there is no need to give here detailed information about puppet construction and operation. Basically, a hand puppet consists of a head attached to a skirt with two arms protruding at either side. The head and arms have holes for the manipulator's fingers. The manipulator slips the skirt over his hand and forearm like a sleeve. He inserts his index finger into the head and his thumb and second finger into the arms of the puppet, thus being able to manipulate with his fingers the head and each arm independently. The desk top becomes the stage and the teacher is ready for the puppet presentation.

Puppet heads can be made from very simple materials: A rubber ball on which are painted eyes, nose and mouth; a small potato; a blown up small paper bag; a balloon; etc.

The teacher will find that generally some of the students own puppets and are only too glad to bring them in to be used in their Hebrew lessons.

Presenting New Material

In presenting new material, the teacher can utilize hand puppets to represent the different characters in the story. The teacher, in his role as teacher, presents the narrative portions, while the active sections and the dialogue are done by him using hand puppets for the characters. The teacher speaks the dialogue for the puppets, changing his voice slightly for each: heavy voiced for *Aba*, light-toned for *Yeled*, etc.

This form of presentation of new material serves as a welcome change of pace in the classroom routine. It also helps to clarify the presentation when the lesson is distributed among teacher and puppets with the puppets making much of the story concrete, thus minimizing the need of labored explanations of many new words in the lesson.

Dolls

Some teachers have found small dolls very useful as impersonators of characters in the simple Hebrew stories of the elementary texts. They collect dolls which assume distinct personalities. One doll is always *Aba,* another is *Ima, Hanah, David, Navhan* the Dog, etc. Each time one of these characters functions in a story, the teacher presses his doll-character into service to go through the actions described in the story.

Later, when the children are called upon to tell the story, they are permitted to use the dolls as their actors. The student retells the story, while he manipulates the doll-characters, putting them through the action described.

Enacting the Story With Puppets

This is a step ahead of story-pantomime and yet simpler than story dramatization. After a new story has been presented to the class by the teacher, the students are called upon to act it out with the aid of the puppets, thus gaining necessary practice and drill with the new lesson.

One pupil is selected to be the Narrator. Puppets represent the characters, and students are selected to manipulate each character-puppet. The Narrator reads or tells the narrative portion of the story. The puppet-characters do the action called for by the story, while the pupil-manipulators speak the lines for the puppet-characters.

Inter-Class Teaching With Puppets

In many schools there are a number of parallel classes for each grade studying the same material at the same time. Where this is the case, teams in one class can prepare a puppet show of a lesson which they then present to the other class, thus teaching each other. Teachers will find the students to be very eager for such an activity, and consequently ready to learn the material willingly and thoroughly so as to be able to present it with their puppets to the other class. The other class is encouraged to do likewise and to repay with a return teaching visit.

■ TV SHOW

This is another intermediate step in classroom dramatization providing Hebrew language practice opportunities. This form, although it requires a great deal of creative participation on the part of the students, still provides them with some form of mechanical aid to serve as a psychological prop before they are quite ready for full creative dramatization.

TV Show combines art work and dramatics in providing language practice for the students. It is best suited for a class with a fairly good Hebrew vocabulary that is able to create a longer story.

A story is developed in class by the students together with the teacher, or a story is selected from the textbook or other source. A committee is then appointed to prepare the "TV Show." The committee draws or paints the incidents on sheets of paper. The sheets are then pasted together so that they make a continuous roll which is then put on two rollers. The rollers are placed on top and on the bottom of an opening in a cardboard box so that when the rollers are turned individual pictures are seen in the opening as on a TV screen. One student is the Narrator. The other members of the committee are the voices of the different characters of the story.

During the presentation of the TV Show, the rollers are turned, exposing the pictures of the incidents in sequence. The Narrator describes the scene and the others speak the dialogue needed, thus presenting a "television" show of pictures and voice-over narration and dialogue.

■ STORY DRAMATIZATION

This is the most difficult and at the same time educationally the most rewarding dramatic technique for language learning. Whether the pupils dramatize a story in the textbook or from collateral reading, or they create the entire story themselves, they are called upon to draw on their full store of language-knowledge and put it to use in the creation of dialogue and action. In this way they engage in meaningful practice which helps them to use their language skills freely and naturally.

The technique of story dramatization is fully described under the special section devoted to it and repetition here would only be superfluous. We will however indicate here some special uses for story dramatization for language learning in addition to its ongoing use as a part of the classroom routine.

Reading Club Dramatization

All schools, regardless of their specific objective in teaching Hebrew language, are eager to implant in their students the desire and the habit of reading Hebrew books. Fortunately there now exist in the *Lador* and the *Oneg* series a large selection of Hebrew stories that are appealing to the American elementary and junior high school student.

It is suggested that Hebrew reading clubs be formed in the upper grades whose pupils have a sufficient knowledge of Hebrew to read these stories independently or by helping each other without the aid of the teacher. Each such club is to consist of a maximum of six members so that in a large class there would be several such clubs.

The function of the club would be to read a selected story and then dramatize it with a view to presenting the play in class. Each reading club would have as its culminating activity the preparation and presentation of such a dramatization. In that way the club members would gain valuable practice with Hebrew language during the process of dramatization while the class would have an experience with Hebrew as a living language in watching the dramatization as it is presented.

If the quality of the dramatization warrants it, the teacher might arrange for its subsequent presentation before another class, an assembly program, or even before the parents during open school week, or a similar occasion.

■ HEBREW THEATRE

The techniques of story dramatization can be applied to the development of a Hebrew theatre within the school. It is generally agreed that the more opportunities the students have of speaking and hearing Hebrew as part of a vital experience, the better their attitude will be toward Hebrew language study and the more efficient their learning will be.

Unfortunately there are all too few opportunities for the students in the American Jewish school to hear Hebrew under functional cricumstances, particularly on their own level of interest. Hebrew theatre might provide such an opportunity and whenever possible schools should encourage the formation of such a theatre on a community level so that their students might come to the presentations and hear Hebrew spoken under artistic and stimulating circumstances. Lacking such theatre or as a supplement to it, each school might foster the formation of a Hebrew theatre of its own, with the participation of its own students.

The plays which such school Hebrew theatre groups will present will, of necessity, be short. They will be creative dramatizations of stories and legends or enactments of Hebrew skits and simple one act plays. Such a project might well become the province of the graduating class. Their Hebrew language study in class would center about these dramatizations. They would then present them on special occasions such as Rosh Hodesh, before a festival, Open School Week, etc.

■ SCHOOL RADIO STATION

Many schools have intercommunications systems which connect the classes with a central place like a principal's office. Some schools have utilized these systems for school "radio" broadcasts. The Forest Hills Jewish Center in Queens, New York, has for a number of years utilized its intercom system in this way with notable success. The school dramatic group and occasionally some classes prepare special radio programs consisting of news, music and dramatization. The programs are broadcast over the intercom system and heard by the children in their classrooms. The teachers conduct preparatory and follow-up activities in connection with the broadcasts.

As an aid toward lending vitality to the school's language program, a regular Hebrew radio program has great merit. Even the younger children, whose Hebrew knowledge may be too limited to understand the programs, will gain from their regular exposure to Hebrew as a functioning aspect of their school life. Hebrew broadcasts will help create a Hebrew atmosphere in the Jewish school and give it a specific character all its own.

The programs would be prepared either by a special radio workshop group, by different classes each time, or a combination of both. A School Hebrew radio program might consist of the following:

1. Opening announcement.
2. Newscast (Utilizing any one of the techniques discussed in the section *Current History*).
3. Weather report.

4. Song or instrumental selection.
5. Story dramatization or skit.
6. Closing announcement.

In schools that do not have an intercom system, the radio broadcasts might be given as part of an assembly program or presented by the radio workshop group "traveling" to the individual classes.

It is to be noted that the greatest value of this activity is the fact that it is a regular, ongoing one; a foreseeable and expected aspect of school life. To get its full benefit it must be planned that way and not as a sporadic undertaking.

■ IN SUMMARY

These are but a few suggestions of what is possible to do with dramatic techniques to vitalize Hebrew language learning in our schools. Whatever the official school objective may be in offering Hebrew language instruction to its students, it will be more easily and efficiently achieved if the pupils are given opportunities for continuous, meaningful use of the language in stimulating situations. It has been rightly said about language: "Use or Lose!" Dramatization provides "*Derekh arukah shehi k'tzarah*"—"the long way that is the short way in the end" to help us achieve our objectives.

CHAPTER 7

Socio-Drama in Teaching Bible or *Ḥumash*

■ Thoughtful educators have long been concerned with the manner in which Bible or *Humash* (the Pentateuch in Hebrew) is being taught by many teachers. In classroom after classroom one may observe the intense concentration upon the linguistic or "historical" aspects of the subject. Little or no attempt is made to underline the relatedness of the Bible to the day-to-day problems of personal conduct and human relations with which the students are constantly confronted.

In an attempt to overcome this difficulty this writer proposed in 1950 a procedure for applying socio-dramatic techniques to the teaching of Bible. It was introduced at a number of teachers' conferences in Chicago, Detroit, Buffalo, New Haven, Providence, Betterton, and Ste. Agathe, Quebec. The methodology was refined in the course of time as a result of experimentation in numerous classrooms by this writer and many teachers who have attended his in-service workshops in educational dramatics under the sponsorship of the Jewish Education Committee of New York. A brief resume was published in the June, 1953, issue of *Jewish Center Program Aids* of the Jewish Welfare Board and a more complete summary in the March, 1954, issue of the *JEC Bulletin*, published by the Jewish Education Committee of New York. Since then, further experimentation has given convincing evidence of the effectiveness of the technique as an aid in teaching Bible.

Socio-drama is an extremely simple form of creative dramatics. It requires little or no previous experience in dramatization on the part of both students and teachers. When applied to teaching Bible, it brings into focus the morality and ethics in the Scriptures, and relates them in an organic manner to the value system of the students. In the pages which follow, the manner of utilization of this technique will be indicated in detail and illustrated by examples of actual class procedure.

■ BIBLE IN THE CURRICULUM

Bible study is part of any religious course of study almost by definition. For three world religions the Bible is the foundation upon which they rest. It is the hub from which radiates the complex of Judaeo-Christian morality which, theoretically at least, guides the ethical conduct of unnumbered millions.

To the Jew the Bible has been the standard of his behavior, the mold of his way of life, the very pattern of his culture. This has been true for nearly all Jews until fairly recent times and for masses of Jews to this very day. Hundreds of generations studied the Bible and built upon it, expanding it, interpreting it, seeking its innermost meanings. Some groped for its mystic implications. Others searched for its practical applications. Rabbi Akiba, they say, interpreted even the *tagin*, the little ornaments, curlicues, and embellishments upon certain of the Hebrew letters as they appear in the Torah scrolls. The *Sefer Hatagin*, the *Book on Letter-Ornaments*, a Midrash dealing with the letters and letter-ornaments, as well as with the single letters which are found in the Hebrew text of the Bible in a different size from the others, has been ascribed to this martyr-sage. Thus humility is taught through the form of the Hebrew letter *Lamed* (L):

> *Lamed,* the tallest letter, has its head bent downward, thus representing God, who is exalted above all and still looks down upon us.

The universality of the Almighty is derived from the size of the letter *Yod* (Y) in the word *Yigdal* in Numbers XIV:17, "And now, I pray Thee, let the power of the Lord *be great,* according as Thou hast spoken. . . ." The *Sefer Hatagin* states:

> Why is the *Yod* in *Yigdal* written large? In order to indicate that God's mercy is so great that it extends over all the inhabitants of the earth.

It is quite impossible to conceive of a religious school which does not accord Bible study a central and dominant position in its curriculum. In the elementary Jewish religious school Bible or *Humash* is a basic subject in the curriculum. In most Jewish schools—religious or secular—regardless of linguistic or ideological orientation, the Bible is taught in varying degrees of intensity.

Purpose for Bible Teaching

In the light of the importance of Bible study in our schools it is only natural that we be concerned with the improvement of the methodolgy for the teaching of this vital subject. It is a truism that in teaching any subject, the *goal* in a large measure determines the *method.* In order to determine which method will best help us to accomplish our educational purpose, it must be clear to us exactly what our purpose *is* in teaching the particular subject, or even the individual lesson. What then is our goal in teaching Bible?

Quite obviously we do not teach Bible primarily in order to convey a knowledge of the early history of the Jews. Our modern, graded history texts are much better suited for that purpose. Nor do we utilize the *Humash* chiefly as a text for the teaching of Hebrew language. The words in the *Humash* are not graded, the sentence structure is complex—in short, a good language text is much more suitable for the purpose of Hebrew language instruction then the Pentateuch in Hebrew. The learning of early Jewish history and Hebrew language are some of the products of Bible study. They are important products and not to be lightly dismissed. They must not however become the only or even the major goal toward which all the teacher's efforts will be bent, to which will be devoted the bulk of the allotted class time. Our true goals concern the very essence of human behavior within the social organism.

The teacher bears in mind at all times that the basic reason for including Bible in our curriculum is that it is our *Torah,* in its most literal sense. It is *tor*—a path, a guide for living. The traditional way of studying the Bible throughout the centuries reflected this outlook. Language was important. Story was vital. But its potential as a guide for every day living—the moral and ethical values inherent in biblical text—that was the overriding reason for the study of Scriptures. The search for these values within the text was an integral part of this study. Thus, when a Jewish child, until fairly recent times, studied the Bible, interpretation of text was part of the methodology from the very outset. Alongside biblical text, Rashi's moralistic-philological commentary almost immediately became part of the child's Bible course of study. When a Jewish child would be asked, "What do you study?"

the answer would be, "Humash with Rashi"—not "Bible" but "Bible with commentary." Text and its interpretation were a unity.

Those whose memories go back to East European backgrounds will recall the emotionally charged manner in which, as very young children, the yearning for Messianic redemption was kindled in their hearts by the manner in which they were taught the text of Genesis 48:7:

> And as for me, when I came from Paddan, Rachel died unto me in the Land of Canaan in the way, when there was still some way to come unto Ephrath; and I buried her there on the way to Ephrath—the same is Bethlehem.

The Patriarch Jacob, sick unto death, says a last good bye to his favorite son Joseph and to Joseph's sons, Ephraim and Menasseh whom he had just accepted as his very own. Suddenly he recalls the tragic death of Joseph's mother, his beloved wife Rachel, so very long ago. As taught to Jewish children, the sad memories of a dying man became the prophetic vision of Israel's downfall and promise of ultimate redemption in a far distant future. Text translation and interpretation were interwoven into a prophetic fantasy, and the deathbed scene in ancient Egypt became charged with personal meaning for the Jewish child living under the oppressive conditions of the Pale of Settlement. Seated around the long table in the winter twilight, teacher and students chanted:

> *Va'ani*—and I, even though I am troubling you to bring me for burial to the land of Canaan, *B'vo-i miPaddan Aram,* when I came from Paddan Aram, I did not do the same for your mother Rachel, *Meyso olai Rohel,* when Rachel died unto me, *beEretz K'naan baderekh*—in the land of Canaan in the way, *b'od kivras-eretz lovo Ephroso,* even though there was only a little way to Bethlehem. Do not think that the rains stopped me from bringing her body for burial in our ancestral graves in Hebron. It was the dry season in the land so that the earth was porous as a sieve. *V'ekb'reho shom b'derekh Ephros*—and I buried her there beside the road to Bethlehem. I did not even bring her into Bethlehem for burial. I know that you hold this against me in your heart. Know then that I buried her there according to God's command so that she may one day come to the aid of her children when they will be in great trouble. When Nebuzradan will drive the Jews into exile and they will go by way of Mother Rachel's grave, Rachel will come out of her grave and raise her voice, weeping, begging mercy for her children, as it is written "*Kol b'romoh nishma*—a voice is heard in Ramah," and the Holy One, blessed be He will give ear to her pleas and answer her, "Cease your weeping. Your efforts will be rewarded and your children will one day return to their own land."

Generation after generation, Bible lessons such as these kept alive the Jewish love for the Land ot Israel, fanned the hope for an end of exile, held forth the promise of ultimate redemption.

Many learned moderation and the limits of expectancy imposed by human fallibility in Rashi's commentary to Deuteronomy 21:10-11. The Bible prescribes what a soldier is to do if he wants to marry a woman whom he took captive in war. On this Rashi comments:

> The Torah knew man's evil inclinations. If the Holy One blessed be He had not made it permissible to marry her, he (the soldier grown gross in war) would take her anyway, even though it be forbidden.

The Jewish Bible student learned very early to set limits on what one may expect from other human beings.

Today, the methodology may be different. The purpose for Bible study remains the same. The Almighty, speaking of the words of the Scriptures is quoted as proclaiming: "*V'hai bahem*—and you shall live according to them!"

Teaching Moral Values

It is clearly the goal and the task of the teacher to draw out of every *Humash* or Bible lesson insofar as is possible, the moral rules of conduct, the ethical principles which are inherent in it and help the students to apply them to their own lives. How? How does one teach moral values? Certainly not by introducing or summarizing the Bible lesson with a statement, "The moral of this story is . . ." Certainly not by preaching to the students and exhorting them to right moral conduct. With diligent searching, nearly every Bible lesson may yield its harvest of moral values, nearly every Bible incident can be seen to involve ethical problems. How is the teacher to help the students to recognize them, to understand them, to accept them?

The most effective way is to guide the students not only into a clear recognition of the question at issue, but to help them immerse themselves emotionally in the problem at hand, to relate to it in a personal manner and to strain their intellectual faculties in the search for an ethical solution. The students are stimulated to distill the moral and ethical precepts by themselves, through their own mental groping and searching. Furthermore, they are helped to relate these to their own lives, on their own level of maturity, in their own social terms and to arrive, on their own, at socially acceptable solutions which will function for them in their own sphere of activity. In that fashion they absorb the values inherent in their Bible lessons into their life-stream of remembered experience.

■ THE USE OF SOCIO-DRAMA

This kind of Bible teaching requires the conversion of each lesson into an experience-situation within which the students can become personally involved, which they may actually live through. Socio-drama offers us the opportunity to do this. This dramatic technique permits the transposition of biblical incidents and problems into contemporary situations and problems—situations within which the students can become personally involved and problems which they can solve with their own mental and emotional resources. Thus, the biblical lesson of Abraham and Lot highlights love of peace, compromise, sharing. The story of sheep and pasture lands in ancient Canaan transposed into a contemporary situation familiar to the students and involving the same problems, becomes a vehicle for a socio-dramatic enactment which affords the students an opportunity to actually experience the feelings of Abraham and Lot and to arrive at the ethical solution as a result of their own efforts at problem solving.

What Is Socio-Drama?

Socio-drama is creative dramatics applied to the area of social relations. It is a spontaneous acting out of situations of every day life which bring to the fore problems in human relations. For example:

> The crucial game of the season is about to be shown on television. The student had been given permission to watch it on the set which is located in the parents' bedroom. Now mother has a headache and is lying down. Father tells the boy, "I know I promised to let you see the game, but . . ."
>
> It is the beginning of the school year and the student is the only one who knows the melodies well enough to act as cantor of the Junior Congregation. He comes home and tells his parents that he will serve in this capacity next Sabbath. The parents inform him that they had long ago accepted for the entire family to attend a relative's Bar Mitzvah at another synagogue.
>
> Playing ball with a group of friends, one of them bats the ball into a neighbor's window, breaking it. The neighbor is not at home. The boys are divided—some want to forget about the incident while others feel that they should tell the neighbor about the damage when he returns.

Problems such as these are the counterparts of similar problems faced by biblical characters but are much closer to the level of experience of the students. Acting out such problem situations affords the students an opportunity to deal with such problems on the level of make-believe. They are not exposed to the social sanctions which might be applied to them as a result of a socially unacceptable solution in real life. In the socio-drama they are "trying on" situations, acts, and emotions which they may meet, or are meeting daily, learning by actual experience, how to deal with them when confronted by them in real life.

Students volunteer or are chosen to assume roles of the characters in the real life story, acting out the situation before the rest of the class. There is no previously prepared script. There is no definite dialogue for the players. Only the barest outlines of the situation to be enacted are structured in advance. Just a mere suggestion of characterization for each participant is determined. The dramatization grows as it is acted out. The characters develop as they are played. The dialogue is created spontaneously. The dramatization is brief, lasting but a few minutes. When the problem involved has been brought into a focus and a solution proposed, the dramatization is concluded.

The rest of the class now takes over and becomes actively involved. Through discussion, the problems which were raised are analyzed. The opinions expressed by the players are carefully examined. The solutions offered in the dramatization are critically evaluated. Free opportunities are offered for the expression of opposing points of view and solutions.

Additional opportunities for re-enactment of the same situation in the light of the discussion may be offered. Finally an attempt is made to arrive at a consensus of opinion. Out of the enactments and the discussion, general principles are arrived at which relate to the biblical lesson to be studied and have application to the life problems of the students.

Its Roots Are in the Bible

The use of socio-drama as a means of bringing ethical problems to the fore has its roots in the Bible itself. Utilizing the parallel problem story is traditional in Jewish education. As a non-dramatic technique it is familiar in the Midrashim, or the preachers' parables. The famous preacher, the Dubner Maggid for example, made extensive use of the parallel story—the *mashal* to bring his moral lessons to his audiences. The Bible uses it extensively:

Let me sing of my well-beloved,
A song of my beloved touching his vineyard.
My well-beloved had a vineyard
In a very fruitful hill;
And he digged it, and cleared it of stones,
And planted it with the choicest vine,
And built a tower in the midst of it,
And also hewed out a vat therein;
And he looked that it should bring forth grapes
And it brought forth wild grapes.

Thus the prophet Isaiah states a parallel problem story to his listeners, the inhabitants of Jerusalem whom he is seeking to teach righteousness and justice. Now, having stated the basic situation and brought the problem to the fore, the prophet figuratively turns to his audience and asks his listeners to enact the roles of judges in the case:

And now, O inhabitants of Jerusalem and men of Judah,
Judge, I pray you, betwixt me and my vineyard.
What could have been done more to my vineyard,
That I have not done in it?
Wherefore, when I looked that it should bring forth grapes,
Brought it forth wild grapes?

One can almost hear the inhabitants of Jerusalem and the men of Judah, their emotions aroused by the tale of the faithless vineyard, assume the roles of judges and respond in judgment the sentiments set down by the prophet in the lines that follow:

And now come, I will tell you
What I will do to my vineyard:
I will take away the hedge thereof,
And it shall be eaten up;
I will break down the fence thereof,
And it shall be trodden down;

And I will lay it waste:
It shall not be pruned nor hoed,
But there shall come up briers and thorns;
I will also command the clouds
That they rain no rain upon it.

Now the final step! The prophet draws his parallel and applies the solution to the real problem at hand—the transgressions of his listeners, their abandonment of righteousness and justice:

For the vineyard of the Lord of hosts is the house of Israel,
And the men of Judah the plant of His delight;
And He looked for justice, but behold violence;
For righteousness, but behold a cry.

—Isaiah, v: 1-7

A true dramatization, having nearly the same form as our modern socio-drama is used by the prophet Nathan to teach an ethical lesson to King David. First he states the problem story:

NATHAN: There were two men in one city: the one rich, and the other poor. The rich man had exceeding many flocks and herds; but the poor man had nothing, save one little ewe lamb, which he had bought and reared; and it grew up together with him, and with his children; it did eat of his own morsel, and drank of his own cup, and lay in his bosom, and was unto him as a daughter. And there came a traveler unto the rich man, and he spared to take of his own flock and of his own herd, to dress for the wayfaring man that was come unto him, but took the poor man's lamb, and dressed it for the man that was come to him.

King David, carried away by the tale of the rich man's perfidy, assumes the role of judge, offering a characteristically royal solution to the ethical problem posed by the prophet:

DAVID: As the Lord liveth, the man that hath done this deserveth to die; and he shall restore the lamb fourfold, because he did this thing, and because he had no pity.

With this, the enactment is over and Nathan draws his parallel:

NATHAN: Thou art the man!

And the prophet compares the act of the king in relation to Uriah the Hittite and Bathsheba. The lesson strikes home:

DAVID: I have sinned against the Lord . . .

—Second Samuel, XII: 1-13

The Bible even relates an incident of the use of the parallel problem story in a form of socio-drama, actually employing the acting talents of a professional actress. Again, the matter concerns King David. The king's sons became embroiled in a blood feud and Absalom, David's beloved son is forced to flee. Joab, aware of the king's longing for his son, seeks to bring to the king's attention the principle that "two wrongs do not make a right" and consequently Absalom should be permitted to return home and the blood feud brought to a halt. Joab does this by resorting to a parallel problem story which is to be enacted before the king, thus bringing home to him the desired lesson. For this purpose Joab sends to Tekoah and fetches from there *isha hakhamah*—a wise woman, variously translated "a skilled woman—an actress." He tells her to put on costume and makeup and assume the role of a mourner. He outlines a script for her. Thus prepared she appears before the king. Second Samuel, Chapter XIV, describes the enactment in detail. With minor changes in form to conform with modern usage in playwriting, the scene reads:

WOMAN: Help, O king!
DAVID: What aileth thee?
WOMAN: Of a truth I am a widow, my husband being dead. And thy handmaid had two sons, and they two strove together in the field, and there was none to part them, but the one smote the other and killed him. And, behold, the whole family is risen against thy handmaid, and they said: "Deliver him that smote his brother, that we may kill him for the life of his brother whom he slew, and so destroy the heir also." Thus will they quench my coal which is left, and will leave to my husband neither name nor remainder upon the face of the earth.
DAVID: Go to thy house, and I will give charge concerning thee.
WOMAN: My lord, O king, the iniquity be on me and on my father's house: and the king and his throne be guiltless.
KING: Whosoever saith aught unto thee, bring him to me, and he shall not touch thee any more.
WOMAN: I pray thee, let the king remember the Lord thy God, that the avenger of blood destroy not any more, lest they destroy my son.
DAVID: As the Lord liveth, there shall not one hair of thy son fall to the earth.

The parallel problem story is completed. The enactment is finished. The actress has made her point with the king through the role she assumed. Now she draws the parallel, applying the principle brought out via the socio-drama to the actual problem with which the king is faced:

WOMAN: Let thy handmaid, I pray thee, speak a word unto my lord the king.
DAVID: Say on.
WOMAN: Wherefore then hast thou devised such a thing against the people of God? for in speaking this word the king is as one that is guilty, in that the king doth not fetch home again his banished one. . . .

Somewhat expanded, the methodology of Nathan the Prophet and Joab the son of Zeruiah, may well be followed by us in transmitting to our students the morality inherent in the Bible; in setting their feet upon the *tor*, the path, which Scriptures provide for their ethical conduct.

The following schematic design for the use of socio-drama in teaching Bible is offered by way of introduction to the use of the technique. Teachers will of course develop variants as they gain experience and skill in its application:

The Process Step by Step

■ THE TEACHER PREPARES

The use of socio-drama in teaching Bible calls for special advance preparation on the part of the teacher. He is required to examine the Bible lesson from what may have been a hitherto neglected point of view—its moral and ethical implications. He must also draw on his creative resources to develop the necessary problem story that is to be dramatized. We will consider these two aspects of the teacher's advance preparation in detail:

1. Determine the Values Involved

The teacher analyzes the biblical lesson to be taught for its inherent moral and ethical values. Thus the teacher might find that the following values may be taught through these stories:

Creation: The importance of order, of planning.

Creation of Man: Human equality. No man is more important than another since all were created "in the image of God."

The Forbidden Fruit: Obedience, self-control, value of truthfulness.

Cain and Abel: Evil of jealousy, assumption of responsibility.

Abraham and Lot: Love of peace, compromising, sharing.

Abraham and the Kings: To do what is right without material rewards.

Purchase of Machpelah: Courtesy, tact, honesty.

Jacob's Blessings: The importance of merit over age or position.

The search for moral values may seem difficult at first, particularly for some lessons which seem at first blush to be pure narrative. Some hard thinking aided by some research will yield surprising results. The search for inherent moral values will take the teacher into very interesting by-paths of Jewish creativity throughout the ages. First and foremost will come the commentary of Rashi. Then follow some of the ancient commentaries to be found in a Hebrew Bible text such as *Mikra'ot Gedolot* and the English Commentary to the Pentateuch edited by Dr. J. H. Hertz. Midrashim will yield a rich harvest and not to be scorned are some of the Yiddish Bible commentaries, particularly the faithful companion of generations of Jewish women the *Tsenah Urenah.* Books of sermons, too, often highlight moral values which are not readily apparent in biblical text.

Thus there is no paucity of sources to aid the teacher in determining what values to emphasize with each biblical lesson. The teacher will however have to make certain that the values are such as will have meaning for the students at their particular state of maturity. Often adaptation will be necessary to apply the suggestions found in the sources to the needs of the class.

2. Develop a Problem Story

The teacher develops a problem story of contemporary nature which will parallel the biblical story about to be taught. The story need not be elaborate. On the contrary, the simpler it is the more effectively will it serve its purpose. Chiefly the story is to deal with a conflict situation revolving about an ethical problem that is the subject of the particular lesson. For example, in teaching the values of obedience, truthfulness, self-control, and assumption of responsibility for one's acts, inherent in the story of the Forbidden Fruit, the following problem story might be developed:

> Jack's birthday will be next week. He has just come home from school. As he is putting his books away, mother comes in very breathless. She is carrying a package. While she tells Jack that she was delayed shopping and now she is late for her meeting, she places the package on a shelf high up in the closet. Jack asks her what is in the package. Mother replies "Never mind the package, you leave it alone, Jack. I don't want you to even touch it. Promise?" "All right mother," Jack answers. "Good. Now you have some milk and cookies and then hurry off to Hebrew school." With that mother hurries off to her meeting.
>
> A moment later, Jack's friend Billy comes in. He had seen Jack's mother carrying the package and asks Jack what's in it. When Jack replies that he does not know, Billy urges him to open it. "I'll bet it's a birthday present for you. Go on. Open it." At first Jack refuses. "I promised mother not to touch it." Finally, after repeated urgings Jack gives in. He gets up on a kitchen chair and reaches for the package. Just as he gets it in his hands, the chair under him rocks a little and in trying to regain his balance Jack drops the package and it falls to the floor.
>
> As he picks up the package from the floor, he hears a tinkling inside. Afraid that he broke something inside the package, he quickly puts it back on the shelf.
>
> Jack's birthday arrives. Smilingly, mother and father wish him a happy birthday and hand him the package—his birthday gift. Jack opens it and finds the microscope for which he had been yearning—broken. Mother tries to determine who is at fault. Did they sell her a broken microscope or did Jack disobey her and . . . ?

This is as far as the teacher goes in developing the parallel problem story. The story is brought to the point where the problem is stated. Under no circumstances does the teacher continue with the story to a solution. To do so would rob the process of its chief value—the fact that it offers the students the opportunity to wrestle with the problem and arrive, through their own efforts, at the solution—a solution which is their very own and consequently tends to become a part of their behavior pattern in the future.

■ THE CLASSROOM PROCEDURE

1. Warming Up

This is a necessary preliminary step in the process. It is the motivation which arrests the interest of the students and involves them actively in the presentation which is to follow.

The warm-up begins with an attention arresting device. This may be almost anything which will capture the interest of the students and stimulate them to become involved by expressing opinions, commenting, discussing, etc. The teacher may use, for example:

a. A *picture*—the teacher displays a photograph or a painting that is large enough to be seen by every child, meanwhile speaking to the class:

TEACHER: Look at this picture of the old man with the little boy. Isn't it a lovely, heart-warming sight? Do you think they may be related? What do you think, Joan?

JOAN: I think so.

TEACHER: How?

JOAN: They're probably grandfather and grandson.

TEACHER: From the way they are walking together, would you say, Anne, that they have just quarreled?

ANNE: O no. They seem to love each other very much.

TEACHER: And yet, it often happens that older people and children as these, even though they love each other, do things which irritate one another, that are annoying. For example, that very afternoon this little boy may have wanted to practice beating his drum just when his grandfather wanted to take a nap. Or maybe grandpa here wanted his daughter to drive him to his other son's home, thirty miles away, just when his daughter finished arranging to meet her friends for dinner. Such differences often arise between people, no matter how close they are. Has it ever happened to any of you? Tell us about it. . . .

b. *Personal reminiscences*—Childhood reminiscences by the teacher are a good attention-getting device:

TEACHER: When I was a little boy, I managed to get myself into more trouble than any ten people I know. I remember once, coming home from school and being greeted by a very angry mother. She had found her favorite English bone china cup and saucer broken. I knew that my father had dropped it that morning. But she was convinced that I had done it. What could I say—really? What would you have done in my place?

With this, pupils are encouraged to express opinions, argue, discuss, offer their own reminiscences, etc.

c. A *game*—Games are ever popular in class. They can be used to advantage for our present purpose. For example, the teacher plays with the class the well-known "telephone" game. She whispers a phrase to a student. This student whispers the phrase to the student seated next to him, and so on, until the phrase has passed in whispers through all the pupils. Then the last one is asked to state the phrase. Almost invariably it will come out substantially different from the phrase which the first student is now asked to repeat. The teacher then goes on with:

TEACHER: You see, people often have this trouble. You are sure you heard something, when actually it was quite a different thing. You watch a baseball game. The batter is sliding into first. From your position you are sure he's safe. The umpire, from his position, saw him tagged before his foot touched the base. It happens very often. Has it ever happened to any of you?

d. A *newspaper item*—Often, an item in the news will involve a problem in human relations which may serve as a stimulant for a warm-up discussion. This is particularly suitable for older classes. For example:

TEACHER: Who read the item in the newspaper about the 16 year old boy who took his father's car without permission and then had that awful accident? Tell us about it.

STUDENT: *(Tells the details of the news item)*

TEACHER: That young driver wasn't very smart, was he? In a family everybody usually shares everything. However, there may be some limits, where each member of the family can say, "This is mine, and mine only." What do you think about this?

(The students then express opinions, offer examples from personal experiences, etc.)

The newspaper item need not necessarily concern itself with local or personal problems. Items of international significance may well be used to stimulate a discussion which would lead to an examination of purely personal ethical problems which at the same time have wider and more general applications. For example, fairly recently the attention of the world was focused on the problem of underdeveloped nations emerging from colonialism to national independence. Some, at the very beginning of their independence, had a corps of trained native administrators, public servants and statesmen who quickly grasped the helm of leadership and got their ship of state under immediate control. Others had only a minute number of the native population with any sort of higher education or training in public administration or statesmanship. This gave rise to very difficult situations and to speculation in the world press about the wisdom of granting independent national existence to such peoples. The problem arose: Is independence the inherent right of every nation that wants it, whether it is ready to handle its own destinies or not, or does the world have an obligation to be the caretaker of such peoples, withholding independence from them until they are ready for it according to the standards of nationhood as currently understood by the rest of the world? Carried over on a personal level, this problem has application to parent-child relations, to teacher-pupil situations, etc. To what extent does each human being have the right to determine his own course of action? Carried further: to what extent is each human being *responsible* for his own acts? Do the people with greater experience, such as parents or teachers have the right and obligation to guide and impose limits on the act of those with more limited experience, knowledge, or training, such as their children or students? If so, are there any limits to such controls? What are those limits?

These are examples of problems which come to the fore in Bible lessons:

> Is Esau altogether guilty in his conduct regarding the birthright or is Isaac to share part of the guilt for not training and controlling his son?
>
> Is the guilt of Cain inherent, or is his act to be partly condoned on the basis that he had not been forewarned about the evil of murder?
>
> Wherein lies the guilt of the "Hebrew slave" whom the Bible condemns to life-long disgrace for refusing to abandon the security he finds in slavery, who pleads: "I love my master, my wife, and my children; I will not go out free?"

The teacher may begin by reading the news item:

TEACHER: Here's something which was in all the newspapers today. Just listen. "The Premier of X accuses UN—: John Doe, Premier of the newly-independent African state X, today accused the United Nations of undermining its independence and trying to control its freedom of democratic action . . ."

The teacher finishes reading the item and then continues:

TEACHER: You'll notice that the Secretary General of the U.N. claims that until the people of country X have more training in nationhood, some controls by the U.N. will be necessary. Do you think he is right? If X is independent, can any other body, national or international, control its actions?

The class is thus encouraged to discuss the ethics of the international situation. Then the teacher slowly guides the discussions into more personal channels of parent-child relations. This goes on for several minutes. The teacher then proceeds to the next step—the telling of the parallel story which will serve as the framework for the socio-drama.

e. A *direct beginning*

The teacher begins by posing the problem at the very outset:

TEACHER: Often it happens that two people want the same thing. Has it ever happened to any of you? Tell us about it.

Or in this fashion:

TEACHER: I am sure you have often been faced with a situation where you were blamed for something that was not your fault. Tell us about it.

Having begun the warm-up with any of these devices, or others which will occur to the teacher, the students are encouraged to develop the general problem posed through personal reminiscences, discussion, and expressions of opinion. Only a very few minutes are devoted to this first step. As soon as the teacher feels that the students are sufficiently involved, it is time to proceed with the next step.

2. *Telling the Problem Story*

This step flows right out of and is a continuation of the warm-up process:

TEACHER: So you see, many of us face this kind of a problem: If we tell the truth, punishment is sure to follow. If we keep quiet—we don't even have to tell a lie—there's a very good chance we might get away with it. There's a story along these lines which I would like to tell you. Jack was a normal, average boy who was very interested in science. His greatest hope was to . . .

The teacher then proceeds to tell the problem story which parallels the Bible lesson to be taught that day, that the teacher had prepared in advance, bringing it up to the point of problem. Using the example which we gave earlier, the teacher would proceed to:

TEACHER: . . . Jack opened the package. He saw the microscope for which he had yearned these many months—broken! Jack was heartbroken. Mother was aghast. She just couldn't understand it. Did the storekeeper put a broken microscope in the package? Then another thought flashed through her mind—maybe Jack disobeyed her, opened the package, and broke the microscope. She turned to Jack and said . . .

The problem has been posed. The teacher stops the story right at this point. No attempt is made to offer a solution, or even to hint at it. Is Jack to confess that he dropped the package? Is he to deny handling it? Should he just keep quiet and let mother draw her own conclusions from an evasive answer? The students themselves will have to determine the end of the story—the solution to the problem.

3. *Selecting the Role Players*

Having stopped at the "problem point" the teacher suggests that the balance of the story be acted out by the students and asks for volunteers to assume the necessary roles:

TEACHER: She turned to Jack and said . . . Suppose, class, instead of me telling you the end of the story, we figure it out by acting it out to the end. Who would like to be Jack? Who would like to play the mother? The father?

For the first enactment, the teacher chooses students who have revealed in the warm-up discussion that they have identified with some of the characters in the story, or who have taken strong positions, pro or con, regarding the problem under consideration. This not only helps to achieve a fairly smooth enactment but sets up the arguments on both sides of the question in a manner which provides opportunities for a lively discussion to follow.

4. The Enactment

The students chosen for the roles come to the front of the room. Standing, or seated at a table or desk, they act out the end of the story beginning at the point where the teacher stopped:

FATHER: Look Mother, the microscope is broken!
MOTHER: Broken? How could that be? Jackie, did you break it?
JACK: Me?
FATHER: Why blame Jack? Maybe the storekeeper put in a broken microscope.
MOTHER: It's possible.
FATHER: I think you ought to go back to the store and demand a new one. What do you think, Jack?
JACK: Who, me? Oh, sure, sure.
MOTHER: But still, why should they give me a broken microscope? Jack, are you sure you didn't open the package?
JACK: I didn't open it. Honest. I never opened it.
MOTHER: Well, I'm sure if you didn't open it, it's the storekeeper's fault. He'll just have to take the loss. Unless . . . Jack did you handle the package at all?
JACK: Well . . .
MOTHER: Did you?
JACK: Yes, mother. I did.
MOTHER: And did you drop it?
JACK: Yes, mother.
TEACHER: Thank you very much. Each of you acted very well. You may go back to your seats. Now class, do you think that Jack should have . . .

The enactment is usually brief—several minutes at most. As soon as the problem is resolved—affirmatively or negatively—by Jack's admission of fault or by his categorical denial, as the particular role player may choose to do, the enactment is at an end.

Sometimes an impasse is met. The role players find themselves unable to continue. The teacher then helps the dramatization along by posing questions such as: "Are you going to take this answer from Jack?" "How about it Mother, maybe he dropped it?" At times, even this stimulation does not help. The role player who has to offer the solution—Jack in this case—just does not come up with anything. The teacher might then select another student who feels he has a solution to play the role, or, the enactment is ended at this point and the discussion proceeds.

5. Discussion and Evaluation

The class is asked to express opinions on how well the problem was solved. A free expression of opinions is encouraged, even though they may not be of a socially acceptable nature. It is far more helpful to permit the vocal expression of anti-social attitudes than to submerge them under a cover of silence resulting from teacher disapproval. Openly expressed, such anti-social attitudes will be critically discussed by the other students and placed in their proper perspective. The teacher is of course on the alert to encourage such criticism so that the anti-social solution does not remain unchallenged and in a sense become the consensus of opinion of the class as a whole. At the same time the teacher sees to it that the discussion remains on a plane of evaluating the role and not the student who played the role. It is always "Jack should not have denied his guilt" and never "student X should not have denied his guilt."

Many ethical problems are open to more than one solution, each of which is equally acceptable under the circumstances. The teacher encourages the expression of alternate solutions thus helping the students to see the problem in all its aspects.

In our current example, the discussion might proceed somewhat as follows:

TEACHER: What did you think of Jack's answers? Was it right for him to deny that he opened the package?

STUDENT 1: Sure. He didn't open it. That was the truth.

TEACHER: Does any one feel differently?

STUDENT 2: Maybe it was true that he didn't open it. But he knew that's not what his mother wanted to know. She was trying to find out if he broke it and he broke it all right.

STUDENT 3: That's not so. He dropped the package. But no one really knows if he broke the microscope when it fell or if it was broken to begin with.

STUDENT 4: It stands to reason that he broke it. The storekeeper wouldn't deliberately pack in a broken one.

STUDENT 5: Oh yeah? Didn't your mother ever get a delivery of broken articles?

STUDENT 6: This package wasn't delivered. The mother carried it home.

STUDENT 7: She might have busted it herself by bumping into something.

TEACHER: Then, do you think Jack was right in confessing?

STUDENT 8: He shouldn't have taken the blame. There were too many other possibilities of how the microscope was broken.

TEACHER: Then what should he have done?

STUDENT 9: He should have denied everything.

TEACHER: Anybody think differently?

STUDENT 10: He was guilty all right of disobeying his mother. But no one can say that he was really guilty of breaking the microscope.

TEACHER: Therefore?

STUDENT 10: Therefore, he had to admit that he dropped it. But his mother should not let it go at that. She should still go back to the store and see if she couldn't get it exchanged.

TEACHER: I see you don't agree, Student 11.

STUDENT 11: No, I don't. Why should the storekeeper suffer? Jack dropped it. He disobeyed his mother. He should be punished.

STUDENT 12: He should be punished for disobeying his mother, but not for breaking the microscope. Nobody can say he did it.

TEACHER: I see you are bringing up an entirely new problem—assuming this boy is guilty of one thing how are we to handle the rest of the problem? Is he also to suffer for the broken microscope? If not, is the storekeeper to stand the damage? Is there another way to handle the problem? Supposing we act this scene out once more. This time we will let it go a little further. Maybe father, mother and Jack can come up with a good way out.

6. The Re-Enactment

In the light of the discussion, the scene is enacted again, one or more times, if time permits. Other students, particularly those who have indicated alternate solutions, are given an opportunity to play the roles. After each enactment some time is allocated for discussion and evaluation.

It is most desirable that the original role players be given another opportunity to re-enact their roles in the light of the discussion. This is one of the truly great values of socio-drama. In real life we often yearn for a second chance which we rarely get. We make a decision, act on it, and then learn new facts which make us wish with all our heart that we could undo what we did. But it is too late. What is done, is done. The best we could usually hope for is that we will act differently if confronted again by the same circumstances. Socio-drama permits us to make mistakes without incurring the social sanctions which usually follow such errors. It allows us to practice life roles many times, to make error after error, until ultimately socially useful and desirable patterns are worked through.

7. Role Reversal

People see things from where they sit. Jack reacts out of his desire for the microscope, fear of punishment, training to tell the truth. Mother is motivated by eagerness not to spoil her son's birthday, hurt at her son's disobedience, reluctance to lose the money she spent, consideration for the storekeeper. Father is eager to train his son in the right path but is affected by his understanding the temptation placed before his son. In real life the child can not feel the same as his parents. The parents can only approximate an understanding of the motivations of their child—and often they fail miserably even at reaching an approximation.

In socio-drama we have an opportunity of being, so to speak, "on both sides of the fence" by means of role reversal. In our current socio-drama the students who took part in the enactment are asked to reverse roles. The pupil who played Jack, now assumes the role of the mother. The one who was the mother now plays Jack. This gives each role player an opportunity to learn how others feel in a given situation. For the students, this aspect of socio-drama helps develop the habit of examining a problem from every aspect and from more than one point of view.

8. Sharing Experiences and Generalizing

The dramatization is always followed by a discussion which brings the situation and the problem within the framework of the students' own personal experiences. Such a discussion might begin with the teacher saying: "Can you think of a similar experience which happened to someone you know? Tell us about it." The students are then encouraged to describe similar problems faced by some one they know, or by themselves if they wish it. As many students as possible are encouraged to take part in this. In that way they not only feel that they are important participants in the process, but also learn to apply the solutions arrived at through the enactment and discussion.

The students are encouraged to think of the problem and its solution in general terms. Now it is no longer, "Jack should face up to his punishment," but "a person should face up . . ." The students no longer speak of, "The mother should not have put the package in the closet while Jack could see it," but "No one should expose another to strong temptation." If this general application is not arrived at by the students, the teacher points it out:

TEACHER: From what most of you have said it would seem that we are in agreement about one thing: When a person commits a wrong, it is his duty to admit it—especially when some one else might be blamed for it. Most of us also seem to agree that it is not fair to put temptations before people and then expect them to resist them—unless of course there is no other way. For example, in today's *Humash* lesson . . .

9. Drawing the Parallel

The teacher now draws the parallel between the problem story just enacted and the *Humash* or Bible lesson they are to study:

TEACHER: Today's *Humash* lesson deals with a similar situation . . . or

TEACHER: Now, let us see what we can find in today's Bible lesson that is very much like the story we acted out.

The teacher then proceeds to teach the Bible lesson in the usual manner. However, after the lesson is presented, a discussion of the ethical questions involved in the Bible lesson takes place. The students are now more keenly attuned to the problem and have acquired certain guides which they can apply intelligently to its evaluation and to its solution.

Time Allocation

Time is always of the essence, particularly in a supplementary Jewish school. The teacher is therefore cognizant of the time element in utilizing any teaching technique. How much time then is to be devoted to the use of socio-drama in teaching Bible? It is difficult to gauge each step exactly. At one time a step may take longer, another time it may take less. Once the discussion may consume only two minutes and the enactment five. Another time the scene may be acted out in less than a minute and the discussion may consume six minutes. It is possible however to offer a general guide.

Within the framework of the afternoon school, the very maximum allotted to the entire process, from the beginning of the warm-up until the beginning of the *Humash* or Bible lesson itself should be no more than twenty minutes. A reasonable allocation of time for each individual step in the process might be as follows:

1. Warming up	3 minutes
2. Telling the problem story	2 minutes
3. Selecting the role players	1 minute
4. The enactment	2 minutes
5. Discussion and evaluation	4 minutes
6. The re-enactment	3 minutes
7. Role reversal	2 minutes
8. Sharing experiences and generalizing	3 minutes
Total	20 minutes

It must be emphasized again that flexibility is an important ingredient of the process as it is in teaching generally. There are no hard and fast rules. On certain occasions, for instance, it is possible to develop a complete role-playing session in half the time here indicated, or even less. Also, it is not at all necessary that the entire eight steps of the process be followed through in a single, continuous session. If the teacher deems it advisable, the process may be carried over to two or even more sessions. Thus, the first session may end in the middle of step 5, during the discussion and evaluation. The teacher, if pressed for time, might say, "This is all the time we can give to this problem today. Let us think about it and continue the next time we meet," or, "we have Bible study scheduled. In the meantime we will go on with . . ."

What Do We Accomplish?

What do we accomplish by utilizing socio-drama in our teaching of Bible? What additional positive factors do we add to our study of Scriptures to warrant devoting up to twenty minutes of the limited time at our disposal? Let us summarize briefly:

1. It induces the teacher to be continuously aware of a basic goal in Bible teaching. It stimulates the teacher to search for the ethical content, for the human problems in each Bible lesson, and to try to transmit them to the students.

2. It makes for creative teaching. The give-and-take of pupil participation, reminiscence, discussion, etc., is insurance against pattern-teaching and a humdrum classroom atmosphere.

3. It brings to the fore the timelessness, the immediacy, the vitality of the Bible.

4. It gives the pupil an opportunity to live through the very same emotions and conflict situations in which the biblical heroes were involved. Thus he learns to understand them, not as shadowy figures, but as human beings acting out of recognizable human motivations.

5. Through an activity which is meaningful to him and is on his own level of experience, the pupil learns to understand the social and ethical values inherent in the Bible lessons.

6. By having been vicariously involved in the enactment of a similar role, these values become part of his own experience-pattern and possibly a motivating force for future conduct.

7. It develops in the students the awareness of the value of sub-surface exploration in biblical texts. It sensitizes him to the moral overtones which may be heard within even the most prosaic biblical narrative.

8. It creates a personal relationship between the pupils and the Book of books —it helps to form a habit of turning to the Bible, not only for comfort in moments of stress but, for guidance and wisdom in moments of personal decision.

■ ABSTRACT OF A SOCIO-DRAMA IN TEACHING BIBLE

The following is an abstract of a class session utilizing socio-drama for teaching *Humash*. It is somewhat abbreviated and edited to eliminate repetitions. The dialogue is not a verbatim transcript, but rather a reconstruction from notes, indicating what might be expected in a class of eleven year olds.

This abstract is included here only for the purpose of acquainting those who have never witnessed a socio-drama session, with its actual operation. At best, it may be a guide. Under no circumstances is it to be considered as a model to be copied.

■ THE LESSON TO BE STUDIED

ABRAHAM AND THE ANGELS

Genesis, 18:1-8

And the Lord appeared unto him by the terebinths of Mamre, as he sat in the tent door in the heat of the day; and he lifted up his eyes and looked, and lo, three men stood over against him; and when he saw them, he ran to meet them from the tent door, and bowed down to the earth, and said: "My lord, if now I have found favour in thy sight, pass not away, I pray thee, from thy servant. Let now a little water be fetched, and wash your feet, and recline yourselves under the tree. And I will fetch a morsel of bread, and stay ye your heart; after that ye shall pass on; forasmuch as ye are come to your servant." And they said: "So do, as thou hast said." And Abraham hastened into the tent unto Sarah, and said: "Make ready quickly three measures of fine meal, knead it, and make cakes." And Abraham ran into the herd, and fetched a calf, tender and good, and gave it unto the servant; and he hastened to dress it. And he took curd, and milk,

אַבְרָהָם וְהַמַּלְאָכִים

בראשית, י״ח, א׳–ח׳

וַיֵּרָא אֵלָיו ה׳ בְּאֵלֹנֵי מַמְרֵא, וְהוּא יֹשֵׁב פֶּתַח־הָאֹהֶל כְּחֹם הַיּוֹם. וַיִּשָּׂא עֵינָיו, וַיַּרְא, וְהִנֵּה שְׁלֹשָׁה אֲנָשִׁים נִצָּבִים עָלָיו. וַיַּרְא, וַיָּרָץ לִקְרָאתָם מִפֶּתַח הָאֹהֶל. וַיִּשְׁתַּחוּ אָרְצָה. וַיֹּאמַר: „אֲדֹנָי, אִם־נָא מָצָאתִי חֵן בְּעֵינֶיךָ, אַל־נָא תַעֲבֹר מֵעַל עַבְדֶּךָ. יֻקַּח־נָא מְעַט־מַיִם; וְרַחֲצוּ רַגְלֵיכֶם, וְהִשָּׁעֲנוּ תַּחַת הָעֵץ. וְאֶקְחָה פַת־לֶחֶם, וְסַעֲדוּ לִבְּכֶם, אַחַר תַּעֲבֹרוּ כִּי־עַל־כֵּן עֲבַרְתֶּם עַל עַבְדְּכֶם.״ וַיֹּאמְרוּ: „כֵּן תַּעֲשֶׂה כַּאֲשֶׁר דִּבַּרְתָּ.״ וַיְמַהֵר אַבְרָהָם הָאֹהֱלָה אֶל־שָׂרָה וַיֹּאמֶר: „מַהֲרִי שְׁלֹשׁ סְאִים קֶמַח סֹלֶת. לוּשִׁי וַעֲשִׂי עֻגוֹת.״ וְאֶל־הַבָּקָר רָץ אַבְרָהָם, וַיִּקַּח בֶּן־בָּקָר רַךְ וָטוֹב וַיִּתֵּן אֶל־הַנַּעַר, וַיְמַהֵר לַעֲשׂוֹת אֹתוֹ. וַיִּקַּח חֶמְאָה וְחָלָב וּבֶן־הַבָּקָר אֲשֶׁר

and the calf which he had dressed, and set it before them; and he stood by them under the tree, and they did eat.

עָשָׂה, וַיִּתֵּן לִפְנֵיהֶם. וְהוּא־עֹמֵד עֲלֵיהֶם תַּחַת הָעֵץ, וַיֹּאכֵלוּ.

Values Involved

Hospitality. Welcoming strangers.

The Problem Story

Miriam and Joseph were twins. Their parents lived in a small, four room apartment consisting of a kitchen, a living room, a bedroom for the parents, and a bedroom shared by the twins.

Miriam had a hobby of collecting dolls of all nations. Joseph was interested in rocks and minerals and he had a substantial collection of specimens. The bedroom which the twins shared was barely large enough for their double-decker bed and their two small desks. The result was that there was always trouble about their collections. Joseph and Miriam kept getting in each other's way. They dreamed of the day when they each might have a bedroom of their own. Finally their dream came true. Their parents bought a three bedroom house on a quiet, residential street. Now Joseph and Miriam had the privacy they always longed for. If Miriam wanted to work on her doll collection, all she had to do was close her door and spread out the dolls on the bed, on the desk, on the floor, and no one bothered her. If Joseph wanted to study his specimens, or read a book, or listen to a favorite radio program, he closed his door and nobody bothered him and he got in no one's way.

One summer, when the children were eleven years old, their parents took them on a wonderful trip to Israel. In Jerusalem, in Haifa and other cities they stayed in hotels but not in Tel Aviv. There, their uncle Jacob turned over his bedroom to them and insisted that they stay in his house. The children grew very fond of their uncle Jacob, who took them around Tel Aviv, showed them the sights and generally saw to it that they had a good time. The children were sorry when the trip finally ended and they had to return home. They missed the fun, the excitement of the trip. But one thing made up for it—now they could have their privacy once again. They came back to their own rooms, to their own things and they greeted every little thing like a long lost friend—their hobbies, their books, even their beds.

They kept up a correspondence with their uncle Jacob and they were delighted when he wrote them he was coming to visit them and would stay in America for three months. The twins and their parents made all kinds of plans: they would take uncle Jacob on trips, sightseeing, to shows, etc. As they were talking, mother remarked casually: "Naturally Jacob will stay in our house." "Of course," father agreed. "He will want his privacy, so we will put him in one of the children's bedrooms. The children will share a room while he is with us. Miriam will move into Joseph's room and . . ."

"Why should I be the one to move? Why not Joseph?"

"Why pick on me?" Joseph answered. "I have all my things arranged and I'm not going to mess them up."

"Now look children," mother turned to them, "don't you want to have uncle Jacob visit us?"

"Sure we do," Joseph answered, "but why kick us out of our rooms and . . ."

Father now lost his patience. "Ho, hold on there," he said. "When you were in Tel Aviv, your uncle Jacob gave up . . ."

The Classroom Procedure

1. Warming Up

TEACHER: When I was a little girl, I hardly ever slept in a bed. I almost always slept on chairs. Did any of you ever sleep on chairs?

STUDENT 1: Once I fell asleep sitting in a chair while I watched TV.

TEACHER: I don't mean sleeping in a chair sitting up. I mean using chairs for a bed and sleeping on them all night. We always had relatives visiting us from out of town. We weren't very rich in those days. But my mother loved to have visitors. She used to say: "Feeding guests? That's no problem. I just add another glass of water to the soup. As far as sleeping over? We can always give them Laura's bed. As for Laura (meaning me), I put three chairs together, place some pillows on them and Laura has a bed fit for a queen." That's how we took care of our house guests. Did any of you have any house-guests in your home recently?

STUDENT 2: My aunt from Chicago visited us.

TEACHER: How long did she stay?

STUDENT: 2: About a week.

TEACHER: Where did she sleep?

STUDENT 2: In the guest room.

TEACHER: Did any one here have to give up his bedroom for a house guest?

STUDENT 3: I did. My cousin came from Philadelphia so we put up a cot for him in my room.

TEACHER: But what about giving up the room completely? Did any one here have to do that?

STUDENT 4: I did. Grandma came to visit with us for two weeks so she slept in my room.

TEACHER: And where did you sleep?

STUDENT 4: In my brother's room.

TEACHER: Was it very convenient for you?

STUDENT 4: Well . . . I had to wait sometimes for grandma to get up from her nap before I could do my homework, because all my books were in the room and . . .

TEACHER: Did you mind very much?

STUDENT 4: Well . . . sometimes . . .

TEACHER: You see, we all love company. But sometimes, it isn't very convenient to receive them . . .

2. *Telling the Problem Story*

TEACHER: . . . There's a story I'd like to tell you. We'll see what you'll make of it. It involves the question of hospitality.

Miriam and Joseph were twins. Their parents lived in a small, four room apartment consisting of . . .

(Teacher tells the story previously prepared until:)

3. *Selecting the Role Players*

TEACHER: . . . "Why should I be the one to move?" Miriam complained. "Why shouldn't Joseph move?"

I won't tell you what happened. We will decide how to finish this story by acting out the ending. We will need someone to play the role of mother. Who would like to take that role? I see four hands. Student 5, you haven't played a role for some time. You be the mother. Who else hasn't played a role recently?

STUDENT 6: I didn't.

TEACHER: Good. You be the father. Now, Student 4, you had almost a similar problem when your grandma came to visit you. Supposing you be Joseph. Student 7, you seem to be very anxious to play a part. We'll let you be Miriam. Now, you four role players may leave the room for two minutes so you can talk things over and decide how to play the scene. Remember—two minutes only. Go ahead. *(Role players leave the room. Meanwhile teacher speaks to the class)* Class, I want you to watch the enactment very carefully. Listen attentively to what each role player has to say. When they have finished, we will have to decide whether or not we agree with them and what we would have done if we were in their place. Keep in mind that problems such as these come up in all our lives at one time or another. Each of us solves it as we think best . . .

I see that our role players have returned and are ready to begin. Come up to the front of the room, please. Now begin.

FATHER: Look, mother. A letter from Jacob in Tel Aviv.

MOTHER: What does he write?

FATHER: He's coming to visit us.

MIRIAM: Wonderful! I love uncle Jacob.

JOSEPH: He's a swell guy! Remember how he took us around every place when we visited Tel Aviv last year?

MOTHER: How long will he stay?

FATHER: Three months.

JOSEPH: That's swell. We'll be able to take him all over.

MIRIAM: We'll show him the amusement park.

JOSEPH: I'll take him to the Museum of Natural History.

MIRIAM: It'll be lots of fun.

MOTHER: We'll write him right away that he has to plan on staying with us while he's in the United States.

FATHER: Naturally.
JOSEPH: Sure, we stayed in his house when we were in Tel Aviv.
MOTHER: We'll give him Miriam's bedroom.
MIRIAM: And where will I stay?
MOTHER: You'll move into Joseph's room.
MIRIAM: Why should I be the one to move? Why not Joseph?
MOTHER: I thought you'd like to give up your room for uncle Jacob. If you don't, I'm sure Joseph won't mind giving up his room.
JOSEPH: Well . . . I don't know . . . I have all my mineral specimens, and my books and . . .
FATHER: I'm not very proud. When we were in Tel Aviv, uncle Jacob gave up his room for you.
MIRIAM: Why can't he stay one week in my room and one week in Joseph's room. We could change off.
JOSEPH: That's a good idea. We could change off.

TEACHER: Thank you very much. Each of you played your role very convincingly. You may go back to your seats now.

5. Discussion and Evaluation

TEACHER: Did you think that Miriam's solution was a good one?
STUDENT 1: Yes. I thought it was very fair.
STUDENT 2: I don't think that's such a hot idea. You can't move a person around one week here and one week there.
TEACHER: What would you have done?
STUDENT 2: One of the kids should have given up his room for the duration.
TEACHER: Who else thinks that way?
STUDENT 3: I do. After the way their uncle treated them in Tel Aviv they should have been anxious to give up their room for him.
TEACHER: Yes, but whose room? How were they to decide that?
STUDENT 8: They could have tossed a coin.
TEACHER: Do you think that was really necessary? Or do you think the children should not have raised the question to begin with?
STUDENT 9: I don't think so. They should have both offered their rooms. The way their uncle treated them, it was no more than fair.
TEACHER: Is that what you would have done?
STUDENT 9: Sure.
TEACHER: Very well. Suppose we play the scene again. Now, you, Student 9, be Joseph. Student 10 will be Miriam. Student 11 will be the mother and Student 12 the father.

6. The Re-Enactment

TEACHER: Will you please come up front and we will play the scene once again—your way.

I

FATHER: Look! A letter just came from Jacob in Tel Aviv.
MOTHER: What does he write?
FATHER: He's coming for a visit to America.
JOSEPH: Hooray!
MIRIAM: Wonderful!
MOTHER: How long will he stay?
FATHER: Three months.
MOTHER: We will write him tonight that he'll have to stay in our house.
MIRIAM: He can have my room.
MOTHER: And where will you sleep, Miriam?
MIRIAM: I'll move in with Joseph.
JOSEPH: Oh, no. I'll give him my room.
MIRIAM: Why yours?
JOSEPH: Because uncle Jacob is a man so its more proper that he sleep in a man's room. I'll sleep on the couch.
MOTHER: You'll be uncomfortable there.
JOSEPH: I don't mind. Uncle Jacob gave up his room when we were in Tel Aviv, so it's no more than fair . . .
TEACHER: Thank you. Very, very nice. You may go back to your seats now.

(Students go back to seats. Further discussion follows.)

What did you think of the children's actions now?
STUDENT 1: Much better.
STUDENT 2: I guess now they would have to toss a coin to see who would get the privilege of giving up his room.
TEACHER: What about Joseph's reason for offering his room? Do you think that was a good reason?
STUDENT 3: Sure. If the uncle gave up his room—it's fair exchange.
TEACHER: Supposing the uncle hadn't done this? Supposing the family had stayed in a hotel in Tel Aviv, would you say that the uncle should also be asked to stay in a hotel?
STUDENT 3: Oh no. They had the room. They should be glad to have him.
TEACHER: Then do you think some one should have pointed this out to Joseph? The mother maybe?
STUDENT 4: That's the father's job to teach children things like that.
TEACHER: In most families the father *and* mother both feel responsible for teaching their children. Supposing we try the scene once more with our original role players—the same students who took the parts the very first time. Come ahead now.

II

FATHER: Look! A letter from Jacob in Tel Aviv.
MOTHER: What's he write?
FATHER: He's coming to the United States for three months.
MIRIAM: Wonderful!
JOSEPH: He'll stay in our house. Write him that, Dad.

MIRIAM: Sure, I'll give him my room. I'll move in with Joseph.
JOSEPH: Oh, no, you won't. I'll sleep on the couch and he'll take my room.
MOTHER: You'll be uncomfortable on the couch.
JOSEPH: So what? Uncle Jacob was uncomfortable when he gave up his room for us.
FATHER: Is that your reason for giving up your room?
JOSEPH: Sure. It's a good reason.
FATHER: Suppose we had stayed in a hotel in Tel Aviv, would you not give up your room for him now?
JOSEPH: Well . . . I don't know.
MOTHER: Hospitality doesn't mean that we only pay back for what we got before.
FATHER: Sure. When uncle Jacob gave up his room, he didn't do it because he owed us something. We were guests and he welcomed us as guests should be welcomed.
TEACHER: *(Prompting to keep the enactment going)* How about it, mother? Do you agree with father?
MOTHER: Father is right. We should welcome our guests even if they never did anything for us.
TEACHER: How about it, father? Supposing the guest were a stranger in need of food or a place to sleep?
FATHER: Even if it wasn't your uncle, even if it was an absolute stranger, we should take him in and make him comfortable.

TEACHER: Thank you. I see that now you played the scene quite differently from the first time. Why?
MIRIAM: Well, the first time we followed the story. After we discussed it, naturally things looked different.

7. Role Reversal

TEACHER: They sure did. Now you were even ready to take in a stranger. That was father's idea. Would the children agree with him? I wonder. Suppose we try the scene once more with the original cast but, this time, we will reverse roles. The student who played Father will now be Joseph and Joseph will be Father. Mother and Miriam will also switch roles. Go ahead!

(The scene is enacted once more with the roles reversed)

8. Sharing Experiences and Generalizing

TEACHER: Father suggested that even for a stranger we should be ready to extend our hospitality. Who knows of someone who was hospitable to a stranger?
STUDENT 1: My brother brought home a friend from school.
STUDENT 2: That wasn't a stranger. Billy's parents put up his Hebrew teacher when he had to stay over because his class conducted the Friday night service.
TEACHER: Hospitality doesn't mean necessarily giving someone a meal or a place to sleep. Supposing a stranger moves into your block and you make him feel at home, or a new boy moves into the neighborhood and you take him into your games. That's hospitality to strangers too. Have you had such experiences? What did you do?

STUDENT 3: A new kid moved into our block last month. He's a good ball player and we made him pitcher on our team.

STUDENT 4: There was this new girl in my class. She didn't know the work. So I met her after class and showed her what we had studied before she came.

STUDENT 5: There was this couple moved in next door to us. They had a little baby and by the time the movers were finished it was pretty late, so my mother made them come in and have supper with us.

TEACHER: So you see, hospitality is not reserved for relatives only and one can practice hospitality in many ways. Hospitality is making grandma feel at home, inviting a new neighbor for supper. Hospitality is helping a new kid in the block to make friends and feel at home. Hospitality is not reserved for people of your own family, or your own age, or your own religion or your own race. Hospitality is practiced towards any one who needs it. To practice hospitality is to fulfill one of the great commandments of our religion. Let us just turn to *Shaharith,* the Morning Service in our prayer book, and read on page —— Will you read, please?

STUDENT 6: *E-lu d'va-rim she-a-dam o-khel pe-ro-te-hem ba-o-lam ha-zeh, v'ha-ke-ren ka-ye-met lo l'o-lam ha-ba, v'e-lu hen: ki-bud av va-em, ug-mi-lut ha-sa-dim, v'hash-ka-mat bet ha-mid-rash sha-ha-rit v'ar-vit, v'hakh-na-sat or-him. . . .*

TEACHER: That will be enough. Student 7, will you read the translation, please.

STUDENT 7: These are the things, of which a man enjoys the fruits in this world, while the stock remains for him in the world to come: honouring father and mother, deeds of lovingkindness, timely attendance at the house of study morning and evening, hospitality to wayfarers . . .

TEACHER: Thank you. So you see, our Sages considered hospitality to wayfarers just as important as what?

STUDENT 8: Attendance at services.

STUDENT 9: Honoring father and mother.

STUDENT 10: Acts of lovingkindness.

TEACHER: That means helping people in need, contributing to important causes like Federation or the United Jewish Appeal. Now, where do you think we Jews learned this great commandment of *Hakhnasat Orhim,* hospitality?

STUDENT 11: In the Bible?

TEACHER: That was a safe try. Most of our *Mitzvot,* our commandments, have their source in the Bible. The *Mitzvah* of *Hakhnasat Orhim,* of hospitality, is one of our most ancient and we learn it from our Father Abraham himself. In our new lesson in the Bible we see how Abraham practiced *Hakhnasat Orhim,* hospitality to wayfarers who were complete strangers to him. This he did at a time when he was not well himself, and most people would have lain in bed. Abraham, however, sat under a tree in front of his tent, ready to welcome tired travelers, to give them food, and rest from the heat of the day. Let us turn to our new lesson. Chapter 18 in Genesis—*Sidra Vayera* in the Book of *Bereshit* in our *Humash.* We will read the first sentence . . . .

Additional Examples

As has been previously indicated, many Bible lessons may serve to demonstrate moral and ethical principles by which human beings in general and Jews in particular order their lives. That is not to say that *every* lesson in the Bible must be contorted until it yields ethical fruit. There are quite a few biblical lessons which it would be best to teach in the conventional manner. There are others which might well be skipped with younger children. Their immaturity makes it difficult if not impossible for them to learn certain parts of the Bible which may only be studied in the light of the stage of civilization in which the world found itself at the time that the biblical incident describes; others which only have validity by interpretation—a fact long recognized by our Sages.

Some sources were indicated earlier for the teacher who finds it difficult at first to elicit the inherent ethical principles. After resorting to these sources a number of times, the teacher will find it a great deal easier to discover and formulate these principles on his own.

Some teachers may find it hard to develop problem stories for socio-dramatization, particularly in the beginning. It is to be emphasized again that these stories need not be "masterpieces of fiction." Simple incidents of daily life are best suited for our purpose. To stimulate the teachers' thinking in this direction—and definitely not as models to be copied—we offer the following few examples:

SABBATH

Genesis, 2:1-3

And the heaven and the earth were finished, and all the host of them. And on the seventh day God finished His work which He had made; and He rested on the seventh day from all His work which He had made. And God blessed the seventh day, and hallowed it; because that in it He rested from all His work which God in creating had made.

שַׁבָּת

בראשית ב׳, א׳–ג׳

וַיְכֻלּוּ הַשָּׁמַיִם וְהָאָרֶץ וְכָל צְבָאָם. וַיְכַל אֱלֹהִים בַּיּוֹם הַשְּׁבִיעִי מְלַאכְתּוֹ אֲשֶׁר עָשָׂה, וַיִּשְׁבֹּת בַּיּוֹם הַשְּׁבִיעִי מִכָּל מְלַאכְתּוֹ אֲשֶׁר עָשָׂה. וַיְבָרֶךְ אֱלֹהִים אֶת־יוֹם הַשְּׁבִיעִי, וַיְקַדֵּשׁ אוֹתוֹ; כִּי בוֹ שָׁבַת מִכָּל מְלַאכְתּוֹ, אֲשֶׁר בָּרָא אֱלֹהִים לַעֲשׂוֹת.

Values Involved

We must take time out from work for rest and meditation, not only to refresh the body and spirit, but also to take stock of what we have done. All week we do our work. On the Sabbath we sit back and examine our accomplishments to see what has been worthwhile, where we have succeeded, and where we have failed. (The act of examination and evaluation is as much a part of the process of creation as is the work itself. That is why, according to the biblical account, although the actual work of creation was done in six days, there is the statement, "And on the seventh day God finished his work." On this day He examined what He had made and the examination was the "finishing touch" of creation).

Warm-Up

What happens in the movies when you get too close to the screen? Have you ever looked at paintings in a museum or an art gallery? When do you see the picture better, when you get very close to it or when you move away a little? Have you ever watched an artist at work? Did you notice how every once in a while he stops working, moves back a little, looks at it from a distance, examines it from all sides, then goes back to work? Why do you think he does that?

The Problem-Story

On Thursday morning, the class was absorbed in a lesson in American history. Suddenly, as the large clock in front of the room showed fifteen minutes after eleven, the teacher closed her book, passed out papers and announced, "You will now take your final examination in arithmetic." She rolled up the maps which had been covering the blackboard. Now the class could see the writing which had been hidden to this moment—five long, involved problems. "Do the best you can," said the teacher. "The examination will be over at twelve o'clock."

The children began to write hurriedly. Nat wrote his answers and kept looking at the clock. It was now half past eleven. He still had four more questions to answer. He began to write more quickly—adding the long columns, converting the fractions and looking at the clock every few moments. Now it was ten to twelve. His pencil flew faster. The bell rang shrilly. Twelve o'clock. "Put your pencils down," the teacher announced. Nat heaved a sigh of relief. He just managed to finish his last answer.

Monday morning the teacher gave back the corrected test papers. Nat's heart sank when he looked at his paper. There was something wrong in every one of his answers. Some, the teacher had crossed out completely. His mark—30!

When the lunch bell rang and the class filed out of the room, the teacher called Nat over to her. "What happened, Nat?" she asked. "How did you manage to make so many errors?" "I don't know," Nat answered dejectedly. "You made so many foolish mistakes in simple addition. Didn't you check your answers?" "There wasn't time," Nat answered. "But Nat, even if you didn't finish the whole examination, you should have. . . ."

The Enactment

Students are chosen to play the roles of Nat and the teacher. Nat argues that he couldn't possibly have stopped to check his answers, to correct his mistakes in simple addition; that teacher had not allowed enough time for such a long exam; etc. Teacher points out that by not checking his work, the simple mistakes caused complete answers to be wrong; one must always stop to look over his work to check for errors; no matter how short the time, some time must be allotted for evaluating and checking; etc.

CAIN AND ABEL

Genesis, 4:2-10

And Abel was a keeper of sheep, but Cain was a tiller of the ground. And it came to pass, that Cain brought of the fruit of the ground an offering unto the Lord. And Abel, he also brought of the firstlings of his flock and of the fat thereof. And the Lord had respect unto Abel and to his offering; but unto Cain and to his offering He had not respect. And Cain was very wroth and his countenance fell . . . And it came to pass, when they were in the field, that Cain rose up against Abel his brother, and slew him. And the Lord said unto Cain: "Where is Abel thy brother?" And he said: "I know not; am I my brother's keeper?" And He said: "What hast thou done? The voice of thy brother's blood crieth unto me from the ground."

קַיִן וְהֶבֶל

בראשית ד׳, ב׳–י׳

. . . וַיְהִי־הֶבֶל רֹעֵה צֹאן, וְקַיִן הָיָה עֹבֵד אֲדָמָה. וַיְהִי מִקֵּץ יָמִים, וַיָּבֵא קַיִן מִפְּרִי הָאֲדָמָה מִנְחָה לַה׳. וְהֶבֶל הֵבִיא, גַם־הוּא, מִבְּכֹרוֹת צֹאנוֹ וּמֵחֶלְבֵהֶן. וַיִּשַׁע ה׳ אֶל־הֶבֶל וְאֶל־מִנְחָתוֹ. וְאֶל־קַיִן וְאֶל־מִנְחָתוֹ לֹא שָׁעָה. וַיִּחַר לְקַיִן מְאֹד, וַיִּפְּלוּ פָּנָיו. . . . וַיְהִי בִּהְיוֹתָם בַּשָּׂדֶה, וַיָּקָם קַיִן אֶל־הֶבֶל אָחִיו, וַיַּהַרְגֵהוּ. וַיֹּאמֶר ה׳ אֶל־קַיִן: „אֵי הֶבֶל אָחִיךָ?” וַיֹּאמֶר: „לֹא יָדַעְתִּי. הֲשֹׁמֵר אָחִי אָנֹכִי?” וַיֹּאמֶר: „מֶה עָשִׂיתָ? קוֹל דְּמֵי אָחִיךָ צֹעֲקִים אֵלַי מִן־הָאֲדָמָה.”

Values Involved

Jealousy is evil and leads to greater evil. Evil deeds can rarely be hidden; the evil deed itself often testifies against the sinner.

Warm-Up

When I was a little boy I used to resent very much when my parents asked me to wash the dishes instead of telling my sister to do it. Did you ever get into a fight with your brother or sister? Tell us about it. Did it ever happen to you that you appealed to your mother to settle the argument and she told you that you were wrong?

The Problem-Story

Morris and Sol were brothers. Their mother's birthday was coming in two weeks. On an allowance of two dollars per week it is pretty hard to buy school supplies, candy, an occasional movie ticket, and still have enough left over to buy birthday presents. They talked it over and they each decided to make their mother's present themselves. Morris learned how to work with copper while in camp so he made for his mother a beautiful copper dish. However when the dish was finished, he liked it so much that he decided to hang it on the wall of his own room and to make a new one for his mother. The birthday was only two days away so Morris hurried with the work on the second dish so as to get it ready on time. When the dish was almost finished, the tool slipped and made a deep gash in the copper plate. For a moment, Morris debated with himself whether or not he should give the first, the perfect dish to his mother. Finally he decided that his mother wouldn't mind the damage and he wrapped up the second dish for his mother.

Sol decided to paint a landscape. He was quite good at this and he took great pains that the picture should come out perfect in every way. When the picture was finished, he looked it over critically and decided that it was not quite good enough. So he painted a second and a third landscape, until the evening before the birthday came. Then he looked over the paintings, selected the best one and wrapped it as a gift for his mother. He hung the others up in his room.

The morning of the birthday, the boys presented their gifts to their mother. She unwrapped them and, try as she might, she just couldn't help showing her disappointment with Morris' copper dish, knowing that he had kept the perfect one for himself. Morris noticed this and felt hurt.

That afternoon, Morris went into Sol's room and in a fit of jealousy tore up all of Sol's pictures. Mother saw him coming out of Sol's room and, when later Sol came to her, grief-stricken over the torn pictures, she called Morris to her and said . . .

The Enactment

Pupils are chosen to play Sol, Morris and the mother. Sol complains. Mother questions Morris. He denies his guilt. Mother confronts him with the fact that she saw him come out of Sol's room. Morris tries to justify his act by saying his mother was partial. Mother points out to him his selfishness and that one bad act of selfishness led to another bad action—being jealous, which in turn caused him to destroy his brother's property. Denying it only made things worse.

ABRAHAM COMPROMISES FOR PEACE

Genesis, 13:2-13

And Abram was very rich in cattle, in silver, and in gold . . . And Lot also, who went with Abram, had flocks, and herds, and tents. And the land was not able to bear them, that they might dwell together; for their substance was great, so that they could not dwell together. And there was strife between the herd-

אַבְרָהָם רוֹדֵף שָׁלוֹם

בראשית י״ג, ב׳–י״ג

וְאַבְרָם כָּבֵד מְאֹד בַּמִּקְנֶה, בַּכֶּסֶף
וּבַזָּהָב. . . . וְגַם־לְלוֹט, הַהֹלֵךְ אֶת־
אַבְרָם, הָיָה צֹאן־וּבָקָר וְאֹהָלִים.
וְלֹא־נָשָׂא אֹתָם הָאָרֶץ לָשֶׁבֶת יַחְדָּו,
כִּי־הָיָה רְכוּשָׁם רָב. וְלֹא־יָכְלוּ
לָשֶׁבֶת יַחְדָּו. וַיְהִי־רִיב בֵּין רֹעֵי

men of Abram's cattle and the herdmen of Lot's cattle . . . And Abram said unto Lot: "Let there be no strife, I pray thee, between me and thee, and between my herdmen and thy herdmen; for we are brethren. Is not the whole land before thee? Separate thyself, I pray thee, from me; if thou wilt take the left hand, then I will go to the right; or if thou take the right hand, then I will go to the left." And Lot lifted up his eyes, and beheld all the plain of the Jordan, that it was well watered every where, before the Lord destroyed Sodom and Gomorrah, like the garden of the Lord, like the land of Egypt, as thou goest unto Zoar. So Lot chose all the plain of the Jordan; and Lot journeyed east; and they separated themselves the one from the other. Abram dwelt in the Land of Canaan, and Lot dwelt in the cities of the Plain, and moved his tent as far as Sodom.

מִקְנֵה־אַבְרָם, וּבֵין רוֹעֵי מִקְנֵה־לוֹט . . . וַיֹּאמֶר אַבְרָם אֶל־לוֹט: „אַל־נָא תְהִי מְרִיבָה בֵּינִי וּבֵינֶךָ, וּבֵין רֹעַי וּבֵין רֹעֶיךָ, כִּי־אֲנָשִׁים אַחִים אֲנָחְנוּ. הֲלֹא כָל־הָאָרֶץ לְפָנֶיךָ? הִפָּרֶד נָא מֵעָלָי! אִם־הַשְּׂמֹאל – וְאֵימִנָה; וְאִם־הַיָּמִין – וְאַשְׂמְאִילָה". וַיִּשָּׂא־לוֹט אֶת־עֵינָיו, וַיַּרְא אֶת־כָּל־כִּכַּר הַיַּרְדֵּן, כִּי כֻלָּהּ מַשְׁקֶה לִפְנֵי שַׁחֵת ה' אֶת־סְדֹם וְאֶת־עֲמֹרָה, כְּגַן־ה', כְּאֶרֶץ מִצְרַיִם בֹּאֲכָה צֹעַר. וַיִּבְחַר־לוֹ לוֹט אֵת כָּל־כִּכַּר הַיַּרְדֵּן, וַיִּסַּע לוֹט מִקֶּדֶם; וַיִּפָּרְדוּ אִישׁ מֵעַל אָחִיו. אַבְרָם יָשַׁב בְּאֶרֶץ־כְּנָעַן, וְלוֹט יָשַׁב בְּעָרֵי הַכִּכָּר; וַיֶּאֱהַל עַד־סְדֹם.

Values Involved

Love of peace, compromising, sharing.

Warm-Up

Do you think that it is right for someone to ask you to give up something that belongs to you just as much as to him? Did you ever find something of value while walking with some one else? How did you decide who should get it? Tell us about it.

The Problem-Story

It was Barry's birthday and the whole family had come to celebrate. Among the guests was Phil, Barry's cousin who was a half year younger. Excitedly, Barry showed cousin Phil the new English Racer bicycle which he got for his birthday. The house was noisy, full of excitement. The boys kept getting underfoot as mother was trying to serve refreshments to the guests, the adults who stayed on after the birthday party for the children was over. Barry's mother suggested that the boys go over to the nearby park for a while. Both Barry and Phil thought this was a very good idea. "I'll tell you what," Barry said, "we'll ride over by bike. I'll ride my new English Racer and you can use my old bike." "Let me ride your new bike," Phil asked. "Oh no. I just got it. I didn't even try it out." Mother heard the discussion and asked, "What's going on, boys?" I offered to let Phil ride my old bike to the park," said Barry, "but he insists on riding my new one." "I only want to try it out," said Phil. "I'm a guest and he should . . ."

The Enactment

Pupils are chosen to play the roles of Barry, Phil and the mother. Barry argues that he should at least have the first opportunity to ride the new bicycle since it is his present. Phil points out that Barry will have many opportunities to ride it later on and since he is the guest he should be given the chance to try it out. The mother tries to solve the problem. She points out that they are both right. Both have valid arguments for their points of view. One, however, will have to give in, or some compromise will have to be reached. A solution is reached either as a result of the mother's suggestion, an offer of compromise on the part of one of the boys, or as a result of the class discussion following the enactment. They may decide that they "toss for it"; that each ride the new bicycle part way; that, being the host, it is Barry's obligation to give in to Phil in accordance with correct procedure for *Hakhnasat Orhim—hospitality.*

ABRAHAM RESCUES LOT AND THE FIVE KINGS

Genesis, 14:21-23

And the king of Sodom said unto Abram: "Give me the persons and take the goods to thyself." And Abram said to the king of Sodom: "I have lifted up my hand unto the Lord, God Most High, Maker of heaven and earth that I will not take a thread nor a shoe latchet nor aught that is thine, lest thou shouldst say: 'I have made Abram rich.' "

אַבְרָם מַצִּיל אֶת לוֹט

בראשית י״ד, כ״א–כ״ג

וַיֹּאמֶר מֶלֶךְ סְדֹם אֶל אַבְרָם: „תֶּן לִי
הַנֶּפֶשׁ, וְהָרְכֻשׁ קַח לָךְ.״ וַיֹּאמֶר אַבְרָם
אֶל־מֶלֶךְ סְדֹם: „הֲרִמֹתִי יָדִי אֶל־ה׳,
אֵל עֶלְיוֹן, קֹנֵה שָׁמַיִם וָאָרֶץ, אִם־
מִחוּט וְעַד שְׂרוֹךְ־נַעַל, וְאִם־אֶקַּח
מִכָּל־אֲשֶׁר־לָךְ, וְלֹא תֹאמַר: ‚אֲנִי
הֶעֱשַׁרְתִּי אֶת־אַבְרָם.׳״

Values Involved

One should do good, help those in need, because that is part of the obligation of being a human being and not because of expectation of reward, praise, or prestige. The saying has it that "Virtue is its own reward." The satisfaction of having done the right thing is of more lasting value than any material reward.

The Problem-Story

Sam had been saving money to buy a new bicycle. He had a pretty good balloon-tired bike which his parents had bought for him several years ago. But, now he wanted an English Racer. Nearly all the fellows had English Racers. But, his father objected. He told Sam that if the bike he has wasn't good enough for him, Sam would have to buy the Racer himself, out of his own funds.

Fifty dollars is a lot of money. Since September Sam had been putting aside his movie money and whatever else he could save from his allowance. He had also earned a little money by doing some odd jobs. Now it was April. Seven months had gone by since he first began saving. His total capital amounted to only thirty-nine dollars. The weather had turned warm and sunny. Every afternoon the fellows would get on their Racers and take long rides into the country. Sam would chug along on his old bike, struggling up the steep hills which the others took with flying speed. "Wait 'till I get my English Racer," he would think, "then you'll see!" But thirty-nine dollars is still a long way from fifty. The English Racer was still a dream of the future.

Every day, on his way home from school, Sam would go out of his way to pass by the bicycle shop. He would stand at the show window, looking long and admiringly at his dream-bicycle. One day, as he turned away from the window, he noticed a small ladies' handbag lying in the gutter. He picked it up and looked inside. There were about sixty cents in change, an old-fashioned gold pin studded with rubies, and an identification card, giving an address five blocks away.

Sam hurried to the address. He rang the bell and an elderly woman came out. "Are you Mrs. Cantor?" he asked. "Yes," the woman answered. "Did you lose anything?" "I did," the woman replied, her voice rising with excitement, "My handbag . . . I must have dropped it when I carried my bundles from the grocery. Did you find it?" "What was in it?" Sam asked. "Some change, a gold pin with rubies and some papers."

Without a word Sam handed her the pocketbook. "That's it!" Mrs. Cantor called out, excited, delighted. She took out the gold pin and showed it to Sam. "I'm so happy you found it. This pin," she explained, "belonged to my mother. It has been in my family for more than fifty years. It's all I have from my mother and it is very dear to me. Thank you, thank you very much for returning it." Sam said, "You're welcome," and turned to leave. "Wait!" Mrs. Cantor called to him. She went into the house and in a moment she returned holding a ten dollar bill. She held out the money to Sam. "Here," she said, "is your reward for returning my pin." Sam saw visions of himself riding up and down the hills on his English Racer. Now, all he would need is one dollar. That will be easy! "I wish I could give you more," the old woman continued, "but I really can't. You see," she went on, her smile trembling a little, "since my husband died, I have been living on the little that comes in from the insurance company every month." Sam's vision did a quick fade-out. The English Racer would just have to wait! "No, thanks, Mrs. Cantor," he said. He forced himself to smile, although he really felt like crying, thinking about the Racer he almost could have bought. He hurried down the steps, leaving Mrs. Cantor with the ten dollar bill in her hand. Quickly he went home and sat down to do his homework.

Later he told the fellows about what had happened. When Sam's best friend,

Morris, heard how he had refused the ten dollars, he was almost beside himself with anger. "What a sucker!" he cried. "You could have bought the Racer. You earned that ten dollars. It was yours, by right. You sure are a one hundred percent chump!" "What do you mean, 'chump'?" Sam exclaimed indignantly. "She was a poor widow and. . . ."

The Enactment

Students are selected to enact the roles of Sam and Morris. If desired, others may be selected to take the roles of Sam's other friends, some of whom would agree with Morris, some with Sam and some who would be "on the fence." Sam argues, giving his reasons for refusing the reward—the woman's greater need; his obligation to return what wasn't his; etc. Morris argues that Sam didn't have to bring the pin back; he might have left the handbag in the gutter for some one else to bother with it; everybody accepts rewards; etc.

ABRAHAM PLEADS WITH THE LORD FOR SODOM Genesis, 18:23	תְּפִלַּת אַבְרָהָם בראשית י״ח, כ״ג
And Abraham drew near and said: "Wilt Thou indeed sweep away the righteous with the wicked?"	וַיִּגַּשׁ אַבְרָהָם וַיֹּאמַר: ״הַאַף תִּסְפֶּה צַדִּיק עִם־רָשָׁע?״

Values Involved

It is not right to blame or punish a whole group for the evil deeds of some of the group.

Warm-Up

Have you ever come across people who are in the habit of blaming a whole group for the bad things that are done by a few of the group? For example: People who say that all Negroes are gamblers, or all Jews cheat in business. Can you think of other such examples? Has it ever happened to you that you were punished for something someone else in your group did, when the person in charge didn't know who was to blame?

The Problem-Story

The sixth grade class was in the middle of the history lesson when a monitor from the office came in and handed a note to the teacher. The teacher read the note and turned to the class. "Children," she said, "I have to go down to the office for a few minutes. I expect you to be very quiet while I am out of the room. You may read the next few pages in your history books until I return." With this she left the room. For a few seconds there was silence in the room. Everyone was busy reading. Suddenly, from the back of the room, a heavy wad of paper sailed through the air and landed on the back of Phil's head. Phil jumped up with a cry of pain. "Who threw that?" He was answered with a burst of laughter from some of the boys in back of the room. Angrily, Phil grabbed the board eraser that was lying on teacher's desk and threw it at one of the laughing boys. This started a real commotion. Back and forth the eraser flew, thrown by one pupil to the next. Suddenly the door opened. The teacher entered. At the same moment the eraser sailed in her direction catching her on the side of the head.

"Who threw the eraser?" the teacher asked, trying hard to control her anger.

Silence.

"Who threw the eraser?" the teacher asked again.

No one spoke.

"All right. You will all stay in for an hour." With that she turned again to the history lesson.

The class was flabbergasted. Their basketball team was scheduled to play against the seventh grade that afternoon. If they stayed in for an hour, they would not be able to play and the game would be lost by default. Everyone kept looking at David,who was the captain of the team. David hesitated. Teacher didn't look to be in the mood to listen to arguments. But there was the game to be played . . . and anyway . . . why should the whole class suffer? Only a few were involved in the eraser throwing, why punish the whole class? David took a deep breath and raised his hand.

"What is it, David," teacher asked . . .

The Enactment

Students are selected to play the roles of David and the teacher. David asks teacher to reconsider. He gives his arguments: Only a few were at fault; why punish a whole class? Important game; etc. Teacher argues she must have discipline, etc.

Alternate Treatment

Utilizing the same problem story, a different emphasis might be given to the lesson, or the additional value might be treated together with the one indicated, particularly if we emphasize verse 26:

Shall not the Judge of all the earth do justly?	„הֲשֹׁפֵט כָּל־הָאָרֶץ לֹא יַעֲשֶׂה מִשְׁפָּט?"

Values Involved

It is not right to punish a whole group for the evil deeds of some in the group. One in authority should know this and, if he is wrong in the use of his authority, we are obliged to point it out to him—with all due deference. One must not be hesitant to speak out for what is right no matter how important the person who is committing the wrong may be.

Warm-Up

Has it ever happened to you that you got back a test paper and your teacher made a mistake in marking it? What did you do? Should one be afraid to point out a mistake just because the teacher is the one who made it? Supposing the congressman votes for a law which your parents think is wrong, should they let it go, just because he is an important man, or should they protest? Let me tell you a little story along these lines. . . .

ELIEZER AND REBEKAH

Genesis, 24:15-19

And it came to pass, before he had done speaking, that, behold, Rebekah came out . . . with her pitcher upon her shoulder. And the damsel was very fair to look upon . . . and she went down to the fountain, and filled her pitcher, and came up. And the servant ran to meet her, and said: "Give me to drink, I pray thee, a little water of thy pitcher." And she said: "Drink my lord"; and she hastened, and let down her pitcher upon her hand, and gave him drink. And when she had done giving him drink, she said: "I will draw for thy camels also, until they have done drinking."

אֱלִיעֶזֶר וְרִבְקָה

בראשית כ״ד, ט״ו–י״ט

וַיְהִי הוּא טֶרֶם כִּלָּה לְדַבֵּר, וְהִנֵּה רִבְקָה יֹצֵאת, וְכַדָּהּ עַל שִׁכְמָהּ. וְהַנַּעֲרָה טֹבַת מַרְאֶה מְאֹד. וַתֵּרֶד הָעַיְנָה, וַתְּמַלֵּא כַדָּהּ, וַתָּעַל. וַיָּרָץ הָעֶבֶד לִקְרָאתָהּ, וַיֹּאמֶר: „הַגְמִיאִינִי נָא מְעַט מַיִם מִכַּדֵּךְ.״ וַתֹּאמֶר: „שְׁתֵה, אֲדֹנִי.״ וַתְּמַהֵר, וַתֹּרֶד כַּדָּהּ עַל־יָדָהּ, וַתַּשְׁקֵהוּ. וַתְּכַל לְהַשְׁקֹתוֹ וַתֹּאמֶר: „גַּם לִגְמַלֶּיךָ אֶשְׁאָב עַד אִם־כִּלּוּ לִשְׁתֹּת.״

Values Involved

"Thou shalt surely release it (your enemy's fallen animal) with him"—Exodus, 23:5.

שמות כ״ג, ה׳

עָזֹב תַּעֲזֹב עִמּוֹ.

We are obligated to help our fellow man in need. This duty applies not only in the case of our friends and neighbors but also to strangers and, according to the Bible, even to our enemies.

Warm-Up

How many of you belong to the Boy Scouts, Girl Scouts, Cubs, or Brownies? What is meant by the statement in the Scout Oath, that a Scout promises "to help other people at all times"? Would you say this applies only to people you know or to strangers as well? What is meant by the statement that a Scout should do a good deed every day? What good deed were you able to do in the last few days? Would you have done it if it had meant a great deal of inconvenience for you? What if it even exposed you to serious danger?

The Problem-Story

The Pearlman family had spent a lovely day in the country. Now they were driving back home. Father was at the wheel. Mrs. Pearlman and their daughter Hannah were in the front seat next to him. It was late at night. The country road was quite deserted. Not another car was in sight. It was pitch black all around. Only the road ahead unwinded like a wide, gray ribbon, illuminated by the twin beams of the headlights from the Pearlman car. Suddenly Hannah called out, "Look Daddy, someone is signaling up ahead!" Far ahead, at the side of the road, a flashlight beam kept going on and off. "Must be somebody in trouble," mother said. Father kept driving, without slowing up. "Daddy, aren't you going to stop?" Hannah asked. Father didn't answer but instead stepped on the gas a little harder. They were now quite close to the signal light. A man stood at the side of the road, signaling frantically. About twenty-five yards ahead stood a car with the hood up. The Pearlman car came abreast of the stalled car and flashed ahead. "But Daddy! . . ." "We're late," Mr. Pearlman answered. "Who knows who this man is and who is hiding in the car?" said Mrs. Pearlman. "Please, Daddy . . . They need help . . ."

The Enactment

Pupils are selected to play the roles of Father, Mother and Hannah. They enact the situation of Hannah pleading with her father to stop, to turn back and try to help out. It is a deserted road. Who knows when another car may come along? There may be a baby in the car, etc. Father wants to go on. It is very late. He has to be in the office early in the morning. Somebody else will surely come along to help the stalled car. A State Trooper will probably come along shortly. They always patrol the roads, etc. Mother vacillates. Maybe we should stop. Maybe this is just a trick and the people in the car are holdup men. The papers are always writing about such incidents, etc.

JUDAH PLEADS WITH JOSEPH

Genesis, 44:18-34

Then Judah came near unto him and said: "Oh my lord, let thy servant I pray thee, speak. . . . Thy servant became surety for the lad unto my father, saying: 'if I bring him not unto thee, then shall I bear the blame to my father forever.' Now therefore, let thy servant, I pray thee, abide instead of the lad a bondman to my lord; and let the lad go up with his brethren. For how shall I go up to my father, if the lad be not with me? Lest I look upon the evil that shall come to my father."

נְאוּם יְהוּדָה לִפְנֵי יוֹסֵף

בראשית מ״ד, י״ח–ל״ד

וַיִּגַּשׁ אֵלָיו יְהוּדָה וַיֹּאמֶר: ״בִּי אֲדֹנִי, יְדַבֶּר־נָא עַבְדְּךָ דָבָר. . . . עַבְדְּךָ עָרַב אֶת־הַנַּעַר מֵעִם אָבִי לֵאמֹר: אִם־לֹא אֲבִיאֶנּוּ אֵלֶיךָ וְחָטָאתִי לְאָבִי, כָּל הַיָּמִים.׳ וְעַתָּה יֵשֶׁב־נָא עַבְדְּךָ תַּחַת הַנַּעַר עֶבֶד לַאדֹנִי, וְהַנַּעַר יַעַל עִם־אֶחָיו. כִּי־אֵיךְ אֶעֱלֶה אֶל־אָבִי וְהַנַּעַר אֵינֶנּוּ אִתִּי? פֶּן אֶרְאֶה בָרָע אֲשֶׁר יִמְצָא אֶת־אָבִי.״

Values Involved

Responsibility. Every person must be responsible for his own promises and his own acts. We are also responsible for the acts of others who are put in our charge.

Warm-Up

Were you ever a monitor and blamed by the teacher if the class was noisy? Did your parents ever have to pay for a window that you broke? Did it ever happen to any of your friends? Why do you think the parents or the monitor were held to blame?

The Problem-Story

Jane's parents went out to the movies and she was left to mind her eight-year-old brother Michael. About 9 o'clock Jane marched Michael up to his room, saw to it that he undressed and got into bed. She put out the light and went downstairs. All was quiet for a few minutes. Certain that Michael was asleep, Jane telephoned to her friend Rose who lived next door and asked her to come over. In a few minutes Rose came. For ten or fifteen minutes the girls talked about school, their friends, and other subjects. Then Rose suggested that they put on some dance records on the Hi-Fi set. At first Jane hesitated. The Hi-Fi set was her father's pride and joy. She was afraid that perhaps something might go wrong. In the end, she put on a pile of records and switched on the set. For a while the girls just listened to the music. Then they danced several dances. Then they listened some more. Then they got thirsty and the girls went into the kitchen to see what was in the refrigerator. There were plenty of cokes and the girls opened two bottles. In the living room the music kept on playing. Suddenly there was a screeching sound and the music stopped. The girls rushed into the living room. Michael stood near the set. He had come down the stairs and somehow tried to change a record and the phonograph arm slipped and dropped. To her horror Jane saw that the diamond needle had broken. Michael, when told of the damage, became terribly frightened. He began to cry hysterically. Jane told him not to worry, promised him she would take all the blame and finally, after he quieted down, led him upstairs and put him to bed again. When Jane came down, Rose looked at her and grinned. "You sure handled him all right," Rose said. "What else could I do?" Jane answered. "It was a smart idea, promising him you would take the blame. If you hadn't, he would still be crying." "But I do plan to take the blame," Jane answered quietly. "It was my responsibility. I was supposed to take care of Michael and . . ." "But that's absolutely silly," Rose protested. "It was Michael, not you who broke the needle. Some one is going to be punished for it and I don't see why you should stick your neck out . . ."

The Enactment

Students are selected to assume the roles of Jane and Rose. Jane insists that she has to shoulder the blame. Michael was in her charge. If she had watched him nothing would have happened. She had promised to take care of him, etc. Rose argues that it was Michael's fault and he should get the punishment. Her promise to take care of Michael was only to see that no harm comes to him. She isn't even getting regular sitter's fees, etc.

MOSES HELPS JETHRO'S DAUGHTERS

Exodus, 2:16-17

Now the priest of Midian had seven daughters; and they came and drew water and filled the troughs to water their father's flock. And the shepherds came and drove them away, but Moses stood up and helped them, and watered their flock.

מֹשֶׁה מַצִּיל אֶת בְּנוֹת יִתְרוֹ

שמות ב׳, ט״ז–י״ז

וּלְכֹהֵן מִדְיָן שֶׁבַע בָּנוֹת. וַתָּבֹאנָה, וַתִּדְלֶנָה, וַתְּמַלֶּאנָה אֶת־הָרְהָטִים לְהַשְׁקוֹת צֹאן אֲבִיהֶן. וַיָּבֹאוּ הָרֹעִים וַיְגָרְשׁוּם. וַיָּקָם מֹשֶׁה וַיּוֹשִׁעָן, וַיַּשְׁקְ אֶת־צֹאנָם.

Values Involved

We have an obligation to help the oppressed. When we see the strong bully the weak, we must not turn away and say it isn't our affair.

Warm-Up

Did you ever find yourself in a spot where somebody bigger than you was picking on you all the time? Tell us about it. Would you have welcomed help from somebody—your friend, a teacher, an adult?

The Problem-Story

Danny was on his way from the store where he had just bought some eggs for his mother. Suddenly, from around the corner, he heard someone calling frantically for help. Quickly Danny turned the corner. There he saw two fellows of his own age beating up a little ten-year-old kid. "Hey," Danny called out, "why don't you leave the kid alone?" "Why don't you mind your own business?" the others answered as they continued to pummel the little boy. Danny put the bag with the eggs on the sidewalk and sailed into the two boys. Enraged, they let go of the little boy who scurried away, screaming at the top of his lungs. Now they turned their full attention to Danny. Danny was a pretty good fighter but the odds were two to one and before long the odds began to tell. After a few minutes of scuffling, Danny was bleeding from the nose and one of his eyes was closing. In the end he was knocked to the sidewalk. As luck would have it, he fell on the eggs, crushing them. Laughing the two boys walked away.

Danny picked himself up painfully, cleaned off his clothes as best he could and walked home. As he was walking, his friend Joey met him. "Hey Danny, what happened?" Joey asked. Danny told him the story of his encounter with the two bullies. "Well, don't you know enough to get out of the rain?" Joey asked. "Why did you want to take two guys on for?" "I told you," Danny answered, "they were beating up the little kid." "Why don't you mind your own business?" "But it is my business when two guys pick on a kid much smaller than they," Danny replied hotly. "Well if you want to be a big shot . . ."

The Enactment

Pupils are selected for the roles of Danny and Joey. Danny argues that he couldn't keep out of it when there were two against one; we have to help the weak, even at personal risk. Joey is all for "discretion is the better part of valor"; don't look for trouble; don't try to do the impossible; etc.

MOSES AND THE BURNING BUSH

Exodus, 3:4-11

מֹשֶׁה וְהַסְּנֶה

שמות ג׳, ד׳–י״א

God called unto him out of the midst of the bush and said: ". . . behold, the cry of the children of Israel is come unto Me; moreover I have seen the oppres-

וַיִּקְרָא אֵלָיו אֱלֹהִים מִתּוֹךְ הַסְּנֶה,
וַיֹּאמֶר . . . ״הִנֵּה צַעֲקַת בְּנֵי יִשְׂרָאֵל
בָּאָה אֵלָי, וְגַם רָאִיתִי אֶת הַלַּחַץ

sion wherewith the Egyptians oppress them. Come now, therefore, and I will send thee unto Pharaoh, that thou mayest bring forth My people the children of Israel out of Egypt." And Moses said unto God: "Who am I, that I should go unto Pharaoh, and that I should bring forth the children of Israel out of Egypt?"	אֲשֶׁר מִצְרַיִם לֹחֲצִים אֹתָם. וְעַתָּה לְכָה וְאֶשְׁלָחֲךָ אֶל־פַּרְעֹה, וְהוֹצֵא אֶת־עַמִּי בְנֵי־יִשְׂרָאֵל מִמִּצְרָיִם." וַיֹּאמֶר מֹשֶׁה אֶל־הָאֱלֹהִים: "מִי אָנֹכִי כִּי אֵלֵךְ אֶל־פַּרְעֹה, וְכִי אוֹצִיא אֶת־בְּנֵי יִשְׂרָאֵל מִמִּצְרָיִם?"

Values Involved

A person is obliged to forego his own desires for the benefit of the community as a whole. It may happen that an individual is offered an opportunity to act as the savior of many of his brothers at the risk of his own life. Neither a feeling of modesty, nor personal fear should keep him from performing this task.

Warm-Up

How many have ever taken part in a regulation baseball game? Did any of you ever find himself in a spot where he was very anxious for a hit and when his turn came to bat, the captain told him to sacrifice out in order to advance a runner? What do you do on such an occasion? Why? Do any of you have relatives who served in World War II or the Korean War? Do you know of any occasion when they were called upon to volunteer for a particularly dangerous mission? Tell us about it. Do you think he should have volunteered or not? Why? Very often in life we are called upon to decide whether to undertake an unpleasant or a difficult or even dangerous assignment. We could easily get away with it by just refusing. And yet, we undertake these unpleasant or dangerous tasks. Why do we do this? Wouldn't it be wiser to play it safe and refuse to get involved?

The Problem-Story

In Hungary there lived a family by the name of Senesh, that was active in Zionist work. Just before World War II broke out, they realized that there was real danger of war breaking out very soon. In that event, they knew, Hitler would march into Hungary and the lives of all the Jews in that country would be in danger. They were especially worried about their children. What would happen to them if the Nazis came? They were extremely happy, therefore, when their young daughter Hannah, informed them one day that she wanted to go to Palestine with Youth Aliyah, the organization that was rescuing Jewish children from Europe by bringing them to Palestine. They gladly gave their consent for Hannah to go. They planned to join her in Palestine before long. Soon thereafter the war broke out. Within a very short time the Nazis took over Hungary and began to enforce their policy of extermination against the Jews of that country. Many were killed. Many were put in concentration camps. No Jew felt safe. No Jew knew what the next day would bring. Hannah's parents had one consolation—their daughter was safe, living in a *Kibbutz* in Palestine.

One day, the secretary of the *Kibbutz* informed Hannah that a special project was being planned and that she had been requested to appear before the commander of the British Army Intelligence Service. Hannah went and the commander told her the details of the project. A number of Jewish volunteers were needed. They would be flown in army planes to Europe where they were to parachute behind the Nazi lines to organize underground resistance to the Nazis. For the work in each country a native of that country had been selected. Since Hannah was from Hungary and knew the country and the language perfectly, he asked her to volunteer to parachute into Hungary. He was well aware of the dangers. Her chances of success were rather small. If she were caught by the Nazis she would face certain death as a spy. He would like her to think it over, discuss it with her friends at the *Kibbutz* and come back in a few days with her answer.

A small group consisting of the leadership of the *Kibbutz* met that evening and listened to Hannah's report of her interview with the commander. Now the discussion began. What was to be Hannah's answer? If she would undertake this dangerous mission, she would not only be helping to fight the Nazis but may have a chance to arrange an underground movement to smuggle Jews, who were faced with death, out of Hungary to Palestine and safety. On the other hand, was it fair to ask of her and was it wise for her to accept to return to the dangers from which she had only recently been saved when Youth Aliyah brought her from Hungary to Palestine in the nick of time?

The Enactment

Students are selected to play the roles of Hannah; a member of the *Kibbutz* who points out the possible gains and urges her to volunteer; a member of the *Kibbutz* who takes the opposite point of view, underscoring the dangers she would face, the risks involved, the slim chances of success. If the teacher finds it advisable, several pupils may be selected for each point of view.

After the discussion which would follow the enactment, the teacher might point out that the story she told was true. It had actually happened with the great Jewish heroine Hannah Senesh. The teacher might conclude the story of Hannah Senesh—how she undertook the dangerous mission, parachuted into Hungary, worked with the underground resistance, was caught by the Nazis and finally executed. The story of Moses and the burning bush which will now be taught will be imbued with greater emotional vitality in its parallelisms.

CHAPTER 8

Current History

■ Knowing the facts of current history, or current events as it is often called, and examining into their background, their implications, and their possible effect on the welfare of humanity is the daily burden of all who seek to live up to their role of responsible members of society. Learning and understanding the facts and the meaning of *Jewish* current history is the daily onus of all who feel themselves a part of the Jewish people in the context of the talmudic dictum: "*Kol Yisrael areivim zeh bazeh*—All Jews are responsible for one another."

The general news is beamed at us many times each day through a multitude of channels of communication—the newspapers, radio, television, etc. It is often impossible to avoid it. Sports, politics, international news, and news of the arts generally form topics for luncheon conversation, living room discussion, or casual small talk. Even though an individual may have had no formal study of current history while at school he will find himself exposed to the news of the day throughout his life. Even so, current history is generally a part of the curriculum of most schools. The pupils, it is felt, must not only be habituated to reading newspapers but to read them with discrimination and understanding. They must not only be imbued with a continuing lifetime curiosity about the news of the day but must also be sensitized to its inner meaning, to its implications for the general welfare of society and of the individual.

Jewish news, unless it happens to have general implications of major significance, or, at the other end of the pole, unless it is of strictly local interest to be included under the heading of "local news," is not generally reported through the usual communications media. Unlike general current history, Jewish current history, except in its very major manifestations or in the form of local gossip, may remain completely hidden from the consciousness of the average Jew. Unless he moves in certain narrow circles he will not hear about a Peretz anniversary during his luncheon conversation with office colleagues; Israeli politics will not be discussed with business associates; the problems of Jewish education will not be a topic of living room conversation; manifestations of Jewish artistic creativity will not be the subject of casual small talk.

Jewish news must usually be consciously and deliberately sought out in special sources, in places which specialize in purveying news that is of specific Jewish interest. This task is not readily undertaken unless one has strong motivations for keeping abreast with happenings that affect the Jewish people. Evaluating Jewish news and seeing it in proper perspective requires specialized background knowledge and orientation. There are many who have this interest and sensitivity without ever having had formal instruction in Jewish current history. Most people however have neither the curiosity nor the sensitivity unless it be consciously aroused, deliberately developed. Formal study of Jewish current history is extremely helpful in this regard. It familiarizes the student with the sources, helps him to view the news in its proper perspective, habituates him to seek out the news which has special Jewish significance, and sensitizes him to weigh and consider each item for its significance to *K'lal Yisrael* and *Reb Yisrael*—the entire Jewish people and himself as a component of this entity. Thus, whereas study of current history is a useful subject in the general school curriculum it is of prime importance in the Jewish course of study.

Conceding the importance of Jewish current history, the question then arises: how is the subject to be taught? As is true with other subjects, current history too may be taught with many methods, with a variety of techniques. In the pages which follow suggestions will be offered for the use of dramatics as one of the approaches to teaching current history, to be added to the teacher's arsenal of teaching media. Before considering the dramatic techniques themselves, however, some attention to the whys and wherefores of teaching current history as well as the role of communications in general will prove helpful in focusing the teacher's goals in connection with this subject.

■ THE SIGNIFICANCE OF CURRENT HISTORY

It has often been said that an informed public is democracy's strongest safeguard. This is true not only in connection with democracy but with all areas of life that may be affected by the march of events. A public informed of current history has more than once reversed the course of history. Let us consider an actual instance of recent history:

On November 26, 1947, the entire world was breathlessly watching the proceedings of the United Nations General Assembly meeting in Flushing Meadow. The delegates of the World Parliament were considering the Partition Plan for Palestine offered by its Special Committee. Acceptance of the Plan by a two-thirds vote would mean world approval for the establishment of a Jewish state in the ancient homeland after more than nineteen hundred years of exile. Failure to achieve this majority might set back Jewish hopes for many years and would doom hundreds of thousands of refugees to continued homelessness and hopelessness.

As the discussion progressed, as speaker after speaker ascended the rostrum and expressed his government's position, it became apparent that the Partition Plan would be approved with the requisite number of votes. Hopes of the Plan's advocates rose high as the day progressed only to be shattered when, late in the afternoon, Haiti, the Philippines and Greece in quick succession announced their opposition to the Plan. Only an adjournment because of the late hour before a vote could be taken saved the Plan from immediate and imminent defeat. The situation seemed indeed desperate for the hopes of the Jews to re-establish a Jewish state in Palestine.

The news was flashed to the world through all the existing mass communications media. The news galvanized to action the Jews who yearned for a fulfillment of the age-old dream of Return to Zion as well as all those throughout the world who recognized the incontrovertible justice of the Jewish cause. Letters, telegrams, telephone calls and personal visits to the President of the United States demanded support for the Partition Plan. Cables by U.N. delegates to home governments and editorials in newspapers added to the pro-Partition clamor. The people raised their voices, loud and clear, and the heads of government listened. Diplomatic representations were made. New instructions were issued. Three days later, imminent defeat was turned to decisive victory. On November 29, 1947, when the roll call of nations was completed, the Partition Plan was approved. The world had sanctioned the re-establishment of Jewish national existence. A public informed of the facts of current history had acted and changed the course of history!

Time and again we have seen this process in operation. Over and over the stereotyped, bewildered John Q. Public, learning the facts, roars forth, by vote or voice, and changes the course of history. This can only happen in a democracy and it is the very essence of democracy. Awareness—that is the key which unlocks the storehouse within which the kinetic energy of the public is stored. Knowing what goes on, awareness of current issues is the great force that motivates us to action and historic change.

But knowledge of news alone is not enough. We must learn to understand the news in the light of the forces which gave rise to it. We must understand its background and be able to evaluate its possible effects. We must constantly probe, search, and examine the news through the application of criteria which are grounded in democratic, moral, and ethical principles. Only then may thorough knowledge propel to righteous action. Otherwise, knowledge alone may lead only to apathetic acceptance or even wrongful action. We may well become like the character in Balzac's *The Rise and Fall of Cesar Birotteau* who "had caught his opinions like an infection, and he put them into practice without examining into them."

Of course, current history does not always consist of cataclysmic events like the dropping of the atomic bomb on Hiroshima or history-reversing happenings as the U. N. Partition Resolution. Daily, hundreds of items in the news, many very minor indeed, affect the lives of some of us in some measure, and quite often call on us for informed action. The opening of the annual U.J.A. or Federation drive reminds us of our responsibility to our fellows. The report of an address by a speaker at a local meeting may well give us subject for thought or stimulus for self-evaluation. News of a special accomplishment by a neighbor's child—a scholarship won, an award received—propels us to the telephone to offer congratulations and strengthens our feelings of interdependence with our fellows.

This then is the true significance of current history—it is the record of our lives that affects our lives and may in turn be affected by our actions. This too is the basic difference between history and current history: the former tells what has happened and is past changing; the latter informs us of what is happening and is subject to our control. We can only study history. We are able to affect current history.

■ CURRENT HISTORY IN THE CURRICULUM

Jewish educators have recognized the importance of current history study in Jewish education by including it in the curriculum of practically every type of Jewish school. There is at times however a wide gap between including a subject in the curriculum and actually teaching it effectively in the classroom. In many classes the teacher just never gets to it. In others it is taught sporadically and haphazardly. There are a number of reasons for this situation.

The major obstacle to proper teaching of current history would seem to be the lack of time—particularly in the afternoon school. The students usually attend between four and six hours per week. During this limited time the teacher must teach a number of subjects—all of them considered vital to the development of the pupils' Jewish personality. There simply is not enough time to teach all of them properly, according to many teachers who have expressed themselves on this question. The teacher is faced with the unpleasant task of having to make choices. Thus, when current history is placed in competition with such subjects as prayer, language or Jewish observance it just naturally gets "the short end of the stick." For example: The principal of a very large afternoon school which is favorably known for its good educational standards and achievements, reportedly criticized his teachers at a staff meeting for their neglect to teach current events. "This is an important subject," he said, "Every teacher must devote fifteen minutes each month or five minutes each week to teaching current events."

Another difficulty is the fact that current history, by its very nature, must be taught without a textbook. The teacher with limited experience or ability has textbooks as guides and props for teaching many subjects. He has no such help in connection with current history. Every day the news is new—often surprisingly so. To teach it requires a certain amount of originality, ingenuity and inventiveness. Baffled by the lack of a pre-fabricated track to follow, many teachers simply abandon the subject of current history completely and turn their attention to "more basic subjects" for which the lessons have been graded by a "recognized educator," written down and placed between the covers of a textbook.

The lack of a developed methodology is another obstacle to the effective teaching of current history. Because of its peripheral position in the educational structure of the Jewish school little effort has been made to develop proper methods for teaching this subject. Even in those classes where current events is taught from time to time it is done in an haphazard and desultory fashion. The usual procedure is for the students to bring in news items, or the teacher hands selected news items to them, which they read aloud to the class. This may sometimes be followed by a few comments by the teacher, questions about the content of the news item, a bit of discussion, and there the matter ends.

■ DRAMATICS IN TEACHING CURRENT HISTORY

No one method or technique can solve all problems, and dramatics is by no means a cure-all. However, the use of dramatic techniques offers us a solution for some of the problems connected with teaching current history and problems.

Obviously the lack of teaching time is a problem which no method or technique, regardless of how effective or efficient it may be, can completely or even substantially solve. Only a keener awareness of the need and the combined will of the parents and the community can bring pupils into the classroom for more than the four to six hours weekly currently available to the afternoon school and even less to the Sunday school. Fortunately there is a growing tendency to increase the hours of attendance in many supplemental schools.

Nevertheless, despite the admitted difficulties, careful husbanding will enable the teacher to utilize the time that is available in a more effective manner. Some teachers, for example, will find that a brief newscast, prepared outside of class and presented to the class at the close of each session, is an effective and succinct way of keeping the pupils informed of ongoing developments in Jewish life. Others may prefer to pool the time and use it for a more thorough lesson once a week, once in two weeks, or even once a month. The use of dramatic techniques will help the teacher to exploit fully and effectively whatever time is available for this subject.

Dramatics also offers some help to the teacher who flounders and founders without the discipline and support of the textbook. Dramatic techniques follow clearly defined, step-by-step procedures. Consequently they serve to channelize the teaching process along definite lines. The teacher who is at a loss without a predetermined track to follow finds support and confidence in these clear-cut procedures.

In relation to the problem of methodology, dramatics offers real help. Most teachers, in search of stimulating and effective approaches to teaching current history, find that dramatics adds a new dimension to their teaching; that it allows for teaching procedures that are attention-getting, vital, and to a large extent self-motivating.

Whatever has been said about the value of dramatics in connection with history holds true also in the case of current history. Since the elemental characteristic of dramatization is the fact that it recreates characters and situations, it brings a sense of reality and immediacy to the events studied. It helps the pupils to understand the characters who figure in the news and the motivations for their actions. It places the facts in their proper historical perspective so that the students learn not only the factual details of the news but gain an understanding and appreciation of the forces which make and shape the news. The needs of the dramatization stimulate both teacher and pupils to original research into background and history. Above all, dramatization constantly helps to emphasize the relevance of the news as it affects the pupils individually and as members of society.

■ DRAMATICS SEEKS ANSWERS

There are a number of dramatic techniques, some simple, some more complex, that are suitable for teaching current history, which will be considered in detail in this section. These techniques have one common characteristic: we cannot have an effective dramatization of any sort without first finding the answers to certain questions. Basic among these are: What happened? Who was involved? Why? Finding the answers to these questions—both the process and the result—is probably the most important aspect of dramatization in its function as an educative technique. We will consider each of these questions individually.

1. What Happened?

In dramatizing news events we must obviously know what newspapermen call "the story," the facts and details of the news. For example, our dramatization is to deal with:

The opening of the local Federation drive—We should know: When does it begin? Through what function will it be started? How long will it last? What is the goal? What is Federation? How does it serve the community? etc. etc.

Israel to celebrate anniversary—We should know such facts as: When will the celebration begin? Which anniversary? How will it be observed in Israel? In the United States? What will be the central feature of the observance? etc. etc.

New synagogue to be dedicated—Which congregation? Location? When will dedication take place? How will it be dedicated? What are some facts about the new building? Why was it erected? Whom will it serve? How? What is the past history of the congregation? etc., etc.

The major problem for the teacher is where to find the facts. Not all news media deal with Jewish news. In finding the facts, familiarity with the sources is of prime importance.

Sources for General Jewish News

Jewish events that have general interest are usually reported in the general press—particularly of metropolitan centers which have a large Jewish population, such as New York, Philadelphia, Chicago, Los Angeles, etc. In the past the general press gave full coverage to such news as the establishment of the State of Israel, the Sinai Campaign, the capture of Adolph Eichmann, and similar events. A school subscription to an important metropolitan daily newspaper such as *The New York Times* might well be considered in communities with smaller Jewish populations. Placed in the school library and made available to all teachers and students, such a newspaper woud provide information on major Jewish news not generally obtainable in newspapers published in smaller communities.

Sources for Local Jewish News

Jewish news of local interest receives fairly adequate treatment in local general newspapers. Local U.J.A. campaigns, Federation drives, Jewish organizational meetings and events are often more fully reported by small town newspapers than by their counterparts in the metropolis. The various bulletins of synagogues, the community center, local organizations, etc. are also good sources for local Jewish news. The school can usually arrange to be placed on the subscription list of such organizations without too much difficulty. Files of such publications kept in the school library will help materially in obtaining the facts for news dramatizations dealing with local Jewish events.

Sources for Specifically Jewish News

Much of the Jewish news, when it has only specifically Jewish interest and lacks the element of "local news," is often completely ignored by the general press. Furthermore, the general press, when it does report Jewish news, treats it in a detached manner. It does not endow the news reports with the overtones which are of particular interest to Jews alone. Nor can it be expected to do so. The teacher turns to Jewish sources for such news coverage and guides the pupils' attention to these sources in the course of their research.

The Yiddish press is undoubtedly the best source for Jewish news. The teacher who reads and understands Yiddish should make it a practice regularly to read the daily Yiddish press. There the teacher will find not only the news which is neglected by the general press but also articles, comments, and editorials which treat and evaluate the news from the Jewish point of view. In reporting general news, also, the Yiddish press will often stress its implications for specifically Jewish interests. A change in the immigration laws under consideration by the United States Congress will be dealt with in the general press as just another congressional act. The Yiddish press treats it for its effect on Jews—uniting Jewish families, admitting Jewish refugees to America, etc. A cultural exchange program adopted by the U.S. government as reported in the general press may be emphasized for its effect on U.S.–Soviet relations. The Yiddish press will report it for its effect on U.S.–Israel relations as well as for its general stimulus to Jewish culture.

The Anglo-Jewish press also gives thorough coverage to Jewish news events. Regular reading of such newspapers as the *National Jewish Post,* the *American Examiner, London Jewish Chronicle* and a host of other fine Jewish periodicals in English published nationally or locally will provide the facts of Jewish current events particularly for teachers and students who are not able to follow events in the Yiddish press.

Weekly and monthly periodicals in Hebrew, Yiddish and English often deal with Jewish news, either in their articles or in special news columns. The Hebrew weekly *Hadoar, Congress Weekly, The American Zionist, Commentary, Midstream, National Jewish Monthly, The Reconstructionist* and similar publications are good sources for Jewish news.

The Israeli press is another important source. It not only treats Jewish news extensively but provides us with an insight into Israeli reactions to world news and its effect on the Jewish community in general and Israel in particular. Schools will provide an important source for teacher research by placing in the school library one or more such publications. A Hebrew newspaper from Israel such as *Ha-aretz, Davar, Yediot Ahronot,* or *Maariv,* or the English language *Jerusalem Post* is not only a source of Jewish news but a window on Israeli life and culture.

On the children's and young people's level there are magazines such as *World Over, Our Age, Keeping Posted, Jewish Current Events, The Young Judaean, U.S.Y. Bulletins,* etc., which treat Jewish news briefly and in a manner that makes it easily understood by elementary school pupils. Children should be encouraged to subscribe to such publications. Copies of current and back numbers should also be available in the school library. A library subscription to a Hebrew children's newsweekly from Israel such as *Davar Liladim* will be found extremely useful, particularly in day schools and others where the children have a sufficient knowledge of Hebrew to be able to follow the text without too much difficulty.

2. Who Was Involved?

The cast of characters of a news dramatization are obviously the people who made the news: *Yigal Yadin* buys the Dead Sea Scrolls; One hundredth anniversary of *I. L. Peretz* is celebrated; *Ben Gurion* forms new cabinet.

Alongside of the chief protagonist there are usually a number of other characters involved: In addition to Yigal Yadin there functioned in the story about the Scrolls such people as the *Syrian Archbishop, Professor Orlinsky,* etc.; the Peretz anniversary story might well involve people from his background such as his *father* and *mother, characters from his works,* or *modern personalities who arranged the celebration;* an Israeli cabinet crisis might involve not only Ben Gurion but also others prominent in Israeli politics such as the *leader of the opposition, Speaker of the Knesset,* etc.

The students must know at least something about the characters involved in the news—who they are, what they did in the past, their affiliations etc.—in order to understand their actions and portray them with some degree of authenticity. To obtain such information a certain amount of research into the biographical background of the characters, particularly the leading ones, will be necessary.

Sources for Biographical Information

Newspapers maintain "morgues" about most newsworthy personalities. These are files of newspaper clippings of items in which these characters figured in the past. Most newspapers are rather generous in making the "morgue" files available for legitimate research—even by elementary school children. Biographical publications such as *Who's Who* and *Who's Who in Jewish Life* provide background material for most living personalities of some importance. *The Jewish Encyclopedia, The Universal Jewish Encyclopedia* and the Hebrew *Haencyclopedia Haivrit* as well as Jewish history books, biographies, and the like are useful sources of information about historical characters who figure in the news. Such research becomes necessary when the news deals with such items as: an anniversary celebration like the eight hundredth anniversary of Maimonides; an important archeological discovery such as the finding of the Bar Kokhba letters in a cave near the Dead Sea; and the like. The news sometimes deals with characters who died recently. They have not been included in the usual biographical sources for historical characters and are no longer to be found in any current *Who's Who.* If the exact date of their death is known, information about them may be obtained from the obituary published for them in a newspaper on the day of their death or one or two days thereafter. Files of such newspapers may usually be examined in the office of the newspaper. Large central public libraries also often maintain newspaper files going back some years. Such newspapers are also helpful in planning a dramatization which tries to reconstruct the general atmosphere surrounding a certain event. For example:

> In dramatizing the life of Theodore Herzl on the occasion of his anniversary, it might be desirable to reconstruct scenes in Paris on the day that Dreyfus was degraded. Items in newspapers published that day or a day later might be a rich mine of information in this regard.
>
> The newspapers of May 14 and 15, 1948 will give much background detail for a dramatization on the establishment of Israel on the occasion of an anniversary celebration.

3. Why?

This is the chief question which crops up in planning *any* dramatization. It is a constantly recurring question in the process of news dramatization. A proper presentation of the facts calls for highlighting of the reasons for the facts: Why did the Israelis attack Sinai? Why did the cabinet resign? Why are we celebrating Bialik's anniversary? Why was there need for a new synagogue? The answers to such questions are the material which lends vitality to the dramatization and significance to the news.

Interrelation With Other Events

The "Why?" question often goes beyond the search for the immediate and readily apparent reason for an event. It is to be borne in mind that news cannot be completely understood if it is to be seen in isolation—unrelated to other news events. Often incidents occur as a result of seemingly unrelated other events, taking place in distant countries. When Russia withdraws an ambassador from Israel it may be the result of an intensification of hard feelings between Washington and Moscow. Political difficulties in a European country or a revolt in a colonial country may create a need for refuge for Jews of those countries in Israel, which in turn brings about the need for a greater quota in the current U.J.A. drive. The cloak and dagger purchase of the Dead Sea Scrolls must be seen in the light of the hostile relations between the Arab countries and Israel. Consequently it is often necessary to know something about the general world situation in order to understand and dramatize properly a specifically Jewish news item. Thus, in searching for the "Why?" of current Jewish history, the student broadens his understanding of the general world scene and strengthens his appreciation of the interdependence of peoples and people.

Current History in Historical Perspective

Finally, the answer to the "Why?" question which will give reason and meaning to current history often may be seen most clearly in historical perspective. Dramatization is more than a pedantic presentation of facts in dialogue form. It is an emotional re-creation of reality, facts charged with emotional overtones. In searching for the emotional spark we must often go back in history since, in many instances, the news of today has its roots in history and its emotional motivation in an historic process. To illustrate:

Only the historic attachment of the Jews to the Land of Israel can give meaning to the establishment of the State of Israel, and a dramatization of the establishment of the State can hardly ignore the emotionally charged historic baggage which the Jews brought along when they took off on their modern journey into nationhood. The news of the appearance of a new Israeli postage stamp series for the Festivals featuring the "four products" can only be meaningful in the light of an awareness of the ancient rites of offering associated with these products.

News of many so-called every day occurrences is lifted out of the prosaic and given an emotional charge so necessary for a dramatization when the "Why?" is answered by history—when the news of today is viewed in its historical perspective. A new dimension is added to a Federation drive when it is dramatized in the light of the Jewish tradition of helping the needy as expressed in the Bible and practiced in the past. A new meaning is given to a U.J.A. drive when highlighted by the tradition of the *Mitzvah* of *Pidyon Sh'vuyim* as practiced in the ghettoes of Middle and Eastern Europe. The celebration of the anniversary of Sholem Aleichem can hardly be meaningful dramatically or pedagogically without delving, at least a little, into the world of Sholem Aleichem.

Historical perspective is not only a part of the "Why?" of current history. It is its real meaning and its motivating force. Current history must be viewed in this perspective if its teaching is to be more than a marshalling of facts without real understanding of their origins and their implications to current life.

DRAMATICS MOTIVATES SELF-STUDY

Finding the answers to the questions which we have discussed, in addition to providing the soul and substance of the dramatization offers us unusual learning opportunities. It need hardly be pointed out that self-study that is purposeful from the pupils' own point of view, properly guided by an alert teacher, will yield a rich educational harvest. In developing a current history dramatization, while the teacher may make the initial presentation, much of the ensuing research and study is turned over to the students themselves. In this they usually engage willingly, often eagerly, stimulated by the desire to lend vitality and substance to the dramatization. Areas of Jewish life and culture are explored which might otherwise remain foreign territory for the elementary school student. In developing the facts and background of news events, there is a mobility over the entire range of Jewish life and letters which is not usually possible with other subjects. The Bible, Midrash, history, literature, folklore—almost any area of Jewish culture may be tapped to set off the news events in their proper frame. Thus the students come in contact with areas of Jewish culture which might otherwise remain hidden from them.

Furthermore, since the research is voluntarily undertaken to meet the students' own needs which are apparent to them, the result is often better and more thorough learning as well as greater retention than is possible through other class procedures. Also, since much of the learning is done in the course of research, outside of class time, additional time is thus freed for Jewish studies which would not otherwise be available.

HOW TO DRAMATIZE CURRENT HISTORY

By and large, every form of dramatization indicated for history is also suitable for teaching current history. Where already treated in detail, these forms will be merely indicated by reference. Where necessary to clarify their application to teaching current history, examples will be given illustrating their use for this subject. Those techniques which are especially suited to current history, such as *Headline Parade*, will of course be dealt with in greater detail.

Forms of Current History Dramatization

A. NEWSCAST

The newscast is a familiar feature of modern life. News broadcasts are given over the radio or on television many times during the day, at fixed intervals. On some stations the news is presented every hour or half hour. Others open their broadcast day with a newscast and close with a news report. The "eleven o'clock news" every night has become almost a ritual for television stations. The students hear many of these newscasts regularly. Willy-nilly, the newscast is a part of their daily lives.

Jewish news

The newscast of Jewish news might well be made an ongoing event in class life as well. Strictly speaking, the newscast is not a form of dramatization—except that the pupil who is the newscaster assumes a role in which he will usually try to act the part of the newscaster whom he hears on radio or T.V. It is dealt with here because it is a comparatively simple technique and its use often leads to other forms of news presentation that are true dramatic techniques.

A regular feature

An important aspect of the class newscast is that it becomes a regularly recurring feature in the class. It is presented at each class session or once a week, depending on the time available. The teacher decides in advance how often time can be devoted to this activity. Thereafter the schedule is followed with some regularity so that it becomes part of the routine of class life much in the same way as the newscast is part of the routine of life outside the classroom.

Discussion

When a family listens to a news broadcast, discussion usually follows. Similarly, the class newscast is followed by some discussion of the news by the class. In this way, the meaning of certain news items is clarified, problems highlighted, and an opportunity offered for the students to express their personal opinions regarding current questions and problems. In this way, reality is given to the newscast so that the pupils gain the feeling that "it counts" and learn to discover the relevance of current history to their own lives.

Time allocation

The time allotted for the newscast will vary and depend to a great extent on factors such as the total teaching time available, the frequency of the newscast, other forms of current history instruction used, etc. Generally speaking, if the newscast is presented at each class session, two minutes might be devoted to the presentation of the newscast and three to five minutes for discussion. If given once a week, the presentation might take three to five minutes and be divided among several pupils acting as newscasters. Five minutes is then allocated for the discussion.

The newscast is generally presented toward the end of the session. At this time the pupils are usually somewhat tired and welcome this creative activity which their own classmates have planned and in which they all may play a part if they wish it.

The steps

The steps involved in the use of this technique are:

1. Teacher's introduction
2. Selection of Cast
3. Cast Research

4. Preparation of Script
5. Presentation
6. Class Discussion

1. Teacher's Introduction

This is usually necessary the first time the technique is introduced. Thereafter the newscast becomes part of the class routine and a single sentence such as, "We will now have our regular newscast," or "Today's newscaster is Billy Samuels" or "Time for the news" will usually suffice.

The first time the teacher explains the whole idea somewhat as follows:

TEACHER: All of us are familiar with the newscasts on radio or T.V. Even if we are too busy to read the newspapers regularly we can still keep up with the world by listening regularly to the newscasts. Who has recently heard such a newscast?

(Students raise their hands)

All right. Student 1, will tell us just what a newscast is like?

STUDENT 1: A reporter reads news items like John Smith won the election or a plane crashed outside Pittsburgh.

TEACHER: Does any one know where this reporter or newscaster gets his news items?

STUDENT 2: From the papers.

STUDENT 3: From reporters in the field.

STUDENT 4: From the wire services.

TEACHER: He gets the news from all these sources and many others. Then all the items are put together and an editorial committee arranges it, throwing out what is unimportant and keeping the important news items. Then a script is prepared, either by the editorial committee, script writers or the newscaster himself who then reads it on the air. Now, just as the radio and TV stations have regular newscasts of general news, we could have regular newscasts of Jewish news right here in our classroom. We will appoint an editorial committee to prepare the newscast and then one member of the committee will read it in class. How often do you think we should have our Jewish newscasts?

STUDENT 5: Once a week.

STUDENT 6: They have them on the air every day. We should have it every time we come to class.

TEACHER: Suppose we begin by having our newscast once a week. If it works and we can spare the time, we will have it more often.

2. Selecting the Cast

TEACHER: Now, we want to be sure that every one will get a chance to work on the newscasts. There are twenty students in the class so we will divide the class into five editorial committees of four members each.

The teacher divides the class into committees of three to five students each, numbering the committees as First Committee, Second Committee, etc. Knowing the children, the teacher tries to group within each committee those children who will best be able to work together—friends, those who are in the same public school class, those who live near each other, etc. Having selected the committees, the teacher proceeds:

TEACHER: To make sure that every one gets a chance to work on the preparation of newscasts and to be a Newscaster at least once during the term, we will work according to the following plan: First Committee will prepare the newscast for next Thursday. The members of the committee will have a meeting to plan the newscast next Tuesday at which time they will pick a chairman and one to be the Newscaster. For the Thursday after that, Second Committee will prepare the broadcast the same way. For the week after that, Third Committee will do the newscast, and so on, until each committee will have had a chance. Then we will start over again with First Committee but this time with a new chairman and Newscaster until every one in the class will have had a chance at being chairman and Newscaster.

3. *Cast Research*

TEACHER: I have set up a special news section in our school library (*or*, I have arranged a special news section on that little table in the corner of our classroom). There you will find the latest issues of a number of publications that carry Jewish news such as the *National Jewish Post, World Over, Our Age, Keeping Posted, Hadoar Lanoar*, etc. Members of the First Committee will be able to read these in school before or after our session or take them home on loan. I would also advise that you read our local paper and our synagogue bulletin for local Jewish news. As each of you on the committee finds an item which you think should be included in the newscast, write it up briefly in the form in which it should be broadcast. For example, here is an item in today's newspaper. Will you read it aloud Jack, please?

The teacher gives to one of the pupils an item previously selected from that day's newspaper. The pupil reads it aloud.

JACK: Ben-Gurion Spurs Bond Sales in U.S. Washington, September 18—Israel's Prime Minister, David Ben-Gurion, appealed today to American Jews to intensify their support of the drive by which Israel aims in the next ten years to receive and integrate additional hundreds of thousands of immigrants.

In a cablegram to 600 Jewish leaders gathered here he expressed the hope that the expected influx would include brethren from Eastern Europe. This was an obvious reference to Jews behind the Iron Curtain. Since its establishment as a nation in 1948 more than one million Jews have moved to Israel from seventy other countries.

The Ben-Gurion message provided one of the high-lights of the closing session of the National Economic Planning Conference for Israel. The three-day conference, sponsored by the Israel Bond Organization, was held at the Shoreham Hotel.

TEACHER: Thank you, Jack. Now this is an important Jewish news item which should be included in our newscast. But, it's too long and written in difficult

English. The members of the committee will have to re-write it, shorter and simpler. First of course we have to know what it says. Who can tell us?

STUDENT 1: It says that a meeting held in the Shoreham Hotel in Washington was sponsored by the Israel Bond Organization.

TEACHER: Good. What else does it say?

STUDENT 2: Prime Minister Ben-Gurion sent a message to the meeting.

TEACHER: What was in the message?

STUDENT 3: That he hopes American Jews will support Israel.

TEACHER: How?

STUDENT 3: By giving money, I guess.

STUDENT 4: By buying Israeli Bonds.

TEACHER: Ben-Gurion said in the message what the money would be used for. Any one remember?

STUDENT 5: To bring in Jews to Israel.

STUDENT 6: He also said that a million Jews came to Israel since the state was established.

TEACHER: Very good. Now, would any one care to try to tell us how this should be worded for our newscast?

Probably students will volunteer to formulate the newscast. If no one volunteers, the teacher might do it, saying, "Since no one wants to 'bell the cat,' I guess it's up to me. This is just to give you an idea how a news item is to be worded for your newscasts." The teacher then proceeds to give the proposed text. If students do volunteer the following may result:

STUDENT 7: "Washington, September 18—Jewish leaders met in the Shoreham Hotel here for three days to plan how to help Israel. A message was received from Prime Minister Ben-Gurion."

TEACHER: Very good. But, some important details were left out. Who can tell us?

STUDENT 8: We ought to know what was in the message.

STUDENT 9: We should say who sponsored the meeting.

TEACHER: Fine. Would you like to try again, Student 7?

STUDENT 7: O.K. After I say what I have said, I would add this: "In his message the Prime Minister asked for more help to Israel so that more Jewish immigrants could be brought into the country. The Prime Minister pointed out that since the State of Israel was established, more than one million Jews came into the country. The meeting was sponsored by the Israel Bonds Organization."

TEACHER: Excellent! This gives us a good idea how to word news items for our newscasts. Of course, they don't all have to be so long. Usually, the shorter the better. That's about it for today. The First Committee will meet after class next Tuesday to plan the newscast, select the chairman, the Newscaster, and so on. Be sure you read the references and draw up proposed news items. If each member writes up three items that he thinks are important, we should have enough material. In cases where more than one committee member writes up the same item, the one that is shortest and still gives all the facts will get preference. If at all possible, I will try to sit in on your first meeting or at least on part of it.

The Editorial Committee reads the references. Each member prepares at home proposed dispatches. The teacher too keeps abreast of the news and is ready to add suggestions in case important items are omitted during the meeting of the Editorial Committee.

4. Preparation of Script

The teacher attends the first meeting of each committee, if at all possible, in order to guide them in their initial attempt. Thereafter it is best to allow the committees to work on their own. In all cases, however, the teacher will look over the script before it is presented to make sure that frivolous material did not somehow get into it.

At this first meeting a Chairman and a Newscaster are selected. This may be done by vote, by lot, by alphabetical order or other method acceptable to the students. The Chairman presides and the Newscaster writes down the script as each item is agreed upon. The teacher guides the group in the process whenever it becomes necessary. This meeting might proceed somewhat as follows:

TEACHER: Now we have our Chairman and our Newscaster and it's time to begin to prepare our script. Your Chairman will take over the meeting. Your newscaster will write down the news items in the script as you decide on them.

CHAIRMAN: All right, you've all read the news. Now let's go ahead. What should be our first item?

MEMBER 1: I have one: "United Nations, New York—Israel today filed another complaint against Egypt for violations of the Armistice Agreement."

CHAIRMAN: That sounds like a good item. Shall we include it? Fine. Note it down, Newscaster. What's next?

TEACHER: Mr. Chairman.

CHAIRMAN: Yes?

TEACHER: I am afraid that the class won't understand this item without more details. I wonder what the Egyptian violation was, how often they have violated the Armistice in the past, what Israel demands from the UN, and so on. Are these things in the newspaper report?

CHAIRMAN: How about it, Member 1?

MEMBER 1: Yes. It's all there.

TEACHER: Then maybe you ought to turn the item over to your Newscaster so that he can include more details when he prepares the script. Not too much of course. You read the story, Member 1. How would you state it?

MEMBER 1: "United Nations, New York—Israel filed a complaint against Egypt for violation of the Armistice Agreement. An Egyptian armored truck group was surprised by a detachment of Israeli soldiers ten miles inside Israel. The Egyptians opened fire. The Israeli soldiers returned the shooting. Three Israeli soldiers were killed and five wounded. Israel demands the punishment of the Egyptians that are responsible for this violation."

TEACHER: That gives us a good deal more information. I would advise that your Newscaster prepare every item this way—although most items can be a lot briefer. Go ahead, Mr. Chairman.

CHAIRMAN: What's the next item?

MEMBER 2: I have one. "Billy Jacobs will be Bar Mitzvah next Saturday."

CHAIRMAN: What do you say? Shall we include this one?

MEMBER 1: I don't think that belongs in our newscast.
MEMBER 2: Why not? It's news.
MEMBER 1: But it's not important news.
MEMBER 2: It's important to Billy and it's important to me. I'm his friend and so is the rest of the class. And it's Jewish news, isn't it?
CHAIRMAN: What do you say, Mr. ———? Does it go in?
TEACHER: I think it's legitimate Jewish news. Your Newscaster might put all such local items together and give them as the last part of the newscast, introducing them with "And now for the local news."
CHAIRMAN: O.K. What's next?
MEMBER 3: Since I'm the Newscaster is it all right for me to suggest items?
CHAIRMAN: Why not?
MEMBER 3: Well, I have this item: "Amsterdam, Holland—Members of the Netherlands government joined with Jewish leaders to mark the anniversary of the Nazi destruction of the Jewish community of Amsterdam during World War II."
CHAIRMAN: O.K. Note it down. Any others?
TEACHER: You'll have to be careful. You have only three to four minutes for your newscast, so don't put in too much.
CHAIRMAN: I think we ought to get all the suggestions and include everything that's important. Then our Newscaster will put together all the items to make up his script. We'll meet for a couple of minutes just before class on Thursday. If the script is too long, we'll cut out some of the less important items.
TEACHER: That sounds reasonable.
CHAIRMAN: Let's go on then. Are there any other items? O.K. Go ahead read it to ———.

In this way the complete newscast is put together by the Editorial Committee. When more than one member offers the same news item, the committee decides which is the best to be selected. Generally the briefer one is given preference providing it gives all the necessary facts. At times several members submit the same item but each one stresses a different aspect better. It is then possible to take the best of each and combine them into a single dispatch.

When there are no more suggestions, the teacher might offer some if important items have been omitted. Finally all the members turn over their draft-items to the Newscaster. He takes these home and puts them together into a continuous script. Where the members of the committee live near each other, they might get together and do this job co-operatively.

On the day of the newscast, the committee might meet for a few minutes before class to go over the script for final corrections. The Newscaster comes to class a few minutes earlier so that the teacher will have an opportunity to look at the script before it is presented. If the Newscaster can not come early, he sends the script to the teacher with another member of the committee so that the teacher has an opportunity to check the material to be presented.

5. The Presentation

The teacher announces, "We will now have our weekly (daily, monthly) newscast. Today's newcast has been prepared by the First Committee consisting of the following students: ______________. The Chairman is ________ and the Newscaster is ________.

The Chairman and the Newscaster come to the front of the room and the presentation begins. Following is an example of a typical class newscast:

CHAIRMAN: The First Committee presents the Jewish news of the week. Our Newscaster is ________.

NEWSCASTER: Here is a review of the important Jewish news which happened this week:

WASHINGTON, SEPTEMBER 18—Six hundred Jewish leaders from all over the United States held a three-day meeting in the Shoreham Hotel. The meeting was sponsored by the Bonds for Israel Organization to find ways to sell more Israeli Bonds. Prime Minister David Ben-Gurion of Israel sent a special message to the meeting. In this message the Prime Minister said that Israel had taken in more than a million immigrants since the State was established in 1948. He told the Jewish leaders that the money raised from the sale of bonds would make it possible for Israel to take in hundreds of thousands more Jews and provide them with homes and jobs.

UNITED NATIONS, NEW YORK—Israel filed a complaint today against Egypt for violating the Armistice Agreement. According to Israel's complaint, a detachment of Israeli soldiers discovered an Egyptian army armored truck group ten miles inside Israel. The Egyptians began firing on the Israelis and the Israelis returned the fire. Three Israeli soldiers were killed and five wounded. Israel demands that the Egyptians responsible for the violation should be punished.

ATHENS, GREECE—The first school for Jewish children built in Greece since the Nazis destroyed Jewish life in Greece was opened here today. The school was built with the help of the Joint Distribution Committee of America. It is expected that in time 250 Jewish children will receive their elementary general and Jewish education in the school. 80 more children are expected to study in the kindergarten. Of the 75 thousand Jews that lived in Greece before it was conquered by the Nazis, only 10 thousand remained alive. The rest were exterminated by the Nazis. The Jews who now live in Greece look to this school as a sign of their re-born Jewish community.

And now for some local news of Jewish interest:

Billy Jacobs, a member of our class will be Bar Mitzvah next Saturday. Billy is expected not only to chant the *Haftarah* but will also recite a prayer in Hebrew which he wrote himself. His classmates wish Billy the best of everything.

Our local B'nai B'rith chapter has announced that it will have a special Sukkot party for the children of their members and their friends on the first day of *Hol HaMo-ed*. The party will be given in the *Sukkah* of Congregation Adath Israel. This concludes our newscast for today. Next Thursday the newscast will be presented by the Second Editorial Committee. Thank you for your attention.

CHAIRMAN: You have heard the newscast of Jewish news presented by the First Editorial Committee. We now turn over the program to our teacher.

6. Class Discussion

The teacher now takes over the proceedings, stimulating a discussion of the news presented.

TEACHER: That was an excellent presentation of the news. Every member of the First Editorial Committee is to be congratulated for a very fine job.
Now class, which item in the news interested you the most?
STUDENT 1: The item about the Egyptian Armistice violation.
TEACHER: Why?
STUDENT 1: Well, it just goes to show how the Jews in Israel have to be on watch all the time.
TEACHER: That does make things hard for them, doesn't it? How, would you say, can we help them?
STUDENT 2: We can write to our United States delegate in the U.N. to support their complaint.
TEACHER: Don't you think that he would do this anyway, without our letters? After all the Egyptians were ten miles inside Israel. How about it?
STUDENT 3: They might and they might not. Sometimes the U.S. tries to quiet things down by not taking sides.
TEACHER: Do you think this is right?
STUDENT 4: No.
TEACHER: Why?
STUDENT 4: Well, if the guilty parties aren't punished, they will think they can get away with it and do it over again.
TEACHER: How would our writing to our U.N. representative help?
STUDENT 4: Well if our representatives at the U.N. make a mistake, it's up to us to point this out to them. After all, they are *our* representatives and we should let them know how we feel about things.
TEACHER: Very good. What other way can we help the Jews in Israel?
STUDENT 5: With money.
TEACHER: Wasn't there something about that in our newscast?
STUDENT 6: Yes. It was in the story about the Israel Bond meeting in Washington.
TEACHER: What did Prime Minister Ben-Gurion ask American Jews to do?
STUDENT 6: To buy more Israel Bonds.
TEACHER: What, do you think, will Israel do with the money from the bonds?
STUDENT 7: Help new immigrants to come to Israel.
TEACHER: Anything else?
STUDENT 8: Build new homes for them.
STUDENT 9: Establish factories so the immigrants will have jobs.
TEACHER: But why should we in America buy these bonds?
STUDENT 10: To help the Jews in Israel.
TEACHER: But why?
STUDENT 11: Because they are our brothers.

TEACHER: That's very well said. Our sages have said "*Kol Yisrael areivim zeh bazeh*—All Jews are responsible for one another." We have a responsibility to help our fellow Jews wherever they are because, as Student 11 put it so very well, they are our brothers.

Our time is up now, so we will have to cut short our discussion. But we must not let pass one item of local news in which we have a special interest. What is that, class?

CLASS: Billy's Bar Mitzvah!

TEACHER: That's right. We wish Billy every happiness. We are all proud of him, not only because of the fine way he will chant the *Haftarah* and the Hebrew prayer he wrote himself but because Billy has told me that he plans to continue with his Jewish education for many years after his Bar Mitzvah. He plans not only to stay on until his graduation but afterwards he plans to continue in Hebrew high school. Congratulations, Billy.

B. NEWS ANALYSIS

General newscasts are often followed by an analysis of the news. A news analyst takes up one or more of the important items in the news and discusses them in the light of the general world situation, historical background, local political conditions, etc.

After the students have had some experience with the newscasts, the teacher might add the element of news analysis for broadening the students' appreciation and understanding of the news. This may not be feasible in younger classes. But, the older classes will appreciate the added responsibility.

Introducing the Idea

TEACHER: We have had some fine newscasts in the past few weeks. But I know that many of you often wished that you knew a little more about some of the news items. For example, when we discussed the Israel Bonds, I am sure that many of you would have liked to know why we buy bonds instead of giving the money directly. Also a little more about what would be done with the money; what are the chances for large masses of Jews coming to Israel; could we expect Jews to come from the countries behind the Iron Curtain and so on.

In general news broadcasts, this kind of information is supplied by the news analyst. I think the time has come for us to add a news analysis to our newscasts. Next week the Fifth Editorial Committee will prepare the newscast. In addition to choosing a Chairman and a Newscaster, you will also choose a News Analyst. At your editorial committee meeting you will decide what, in your opinion, is the most important item of news. Then your News Analyst will read up about it and prepare an analysis which he will present to us immediately after the newscast and before we begin the general discussion. So that you will have an idea how this is done, I will meet with the News Analyst and help him prepare his analysis this first time.

The following is a variant of this technique: The newscast is presented in the usual manner. During the discussion, the teacher asks the class to decide what, in their opinion, is the most important news item presented. Then the teacher continues:

TEACHER: We are all agreed then, that the opening of the new Jewish school in Athens is the most important news item in today's newscast.

I am sure that many of us would like to know much more about this. Many questions come to our minds such as: Why did it take fifteen years before the school was built? How did the Jews that remained alive manage to save themselves? How is it that they remained in Greece instead of going to Israel as so many Europeans and other Jews did?

In a general newscast the important news items are analyzed by a news analyst who deals with exactly this type of questions. Supposing then one of you becomes our News Analyst, to discuss in detail this item next Tuesday. Our News Analyst will have to read up on the subject and then prepare his analysis. I will help him this first time, so that you will all see how it is done. After that we will select a News Analyst to deal with the news item that interests us most at each Newscast. Now, who will volunteer to be our first News Analyst?

Sometimes there may be difficulty in finding a volunteer the first time. The teacher might then offer to be the first News Analyst in order to give the class an example of what a news analysis is exactly. In younger classes the teacher may explain the function of the News Analyst and then assume that role at the end of each newscast. The students will readily accept the teacher as a participant in their activity.

1. The Presentation

Following is an example of a News Analysis which might be presented by a student:

NEWS ANALYST: The news about the establishment of the Jewish school in Greece, reminds all of us again of the terrible fate of the Jews in most of Europe during the Second World War. From a prosperous Jewish community of 75 thousand, only 10 thousand remained after the war was over. All of them had suffered terribly during the war. They had no food, or clothing. They had lost their homes, their businesses, their jobs. Most of their families had been killed by the Nazis. When the war ended in 1945 the Jews of America brought help to the Jews of Greece. The American Joint Distribution Committee, which gets most of its money from the United Jewish Appeal, brought in food and clothing and medical help. Later the J.D.C. helped them to get jobs and to set up their businesses again. After fifteen years, the Jewish community in Greece was again established and strong enough to undertake to build this new school to take the place of those which the Nazis had destroyed. The J.D.C. helped them with this also, but the Jews of Greece themselves are responsible for it and will keep it up. This story from Athens proves once again that no matter how hard the enemies of the Jews may try, Jewish life can not be destroyed.

The news analysis is often a useful vehicle for the recall of subject matter previously studied. A hypothetical analysis of the news item about the Israeli complaint against Egypt illustrates this:

NEWS ANALYST: The news about Israel's complaint against Egypt reminds us of many other such complaints in the past. Last week, shooting from Syria killed two Israelis who were fishing from their boat on Lake Kinneret in Israel. Ten days ago Arabs came across the Egyptian border at night and set fire to houses in an Israeli *Kibbutz* in the Negev. Still, things have been pretty quiet compared to what was going on before the Sinai Campaign in 1956 when the Israeli Army completely defeated the Egyptian Army. Up to that time Egypt used to train Arabs from Egypt, Syria, and Jordan especially for the job of killing Jews. They were sent into Israel at night. They would set fire to settlements, blow up buildings, kill sleeping Jews. Then they would return across the border under cover of night. Israel kept complaining to the U.N. but the attacks continued every night. Finally Israel decided to stop this once and for all. In a lightning march the Israeli Army occupied the Gaza Strip, the Sinai peninsula, and came right up to the Suez Canal. They were joined by England and France who had their own scores to settle with Egypt for confiscating the Suez Canal. The U.N. saved Egypt that time. It asked Israel, England, and France to get out of Egypt. The three countries obeyed the U.N. which placed its own small army along the borders of Egypt and Israel to see that the Armistice is kept and that no attacks take place. The Egyptians had learned a lesson and for some years things have been pretty quiet. Israel was able to go on with its work of building up the country. Now new attacks from Egypt and Syria have taken place. Israel has filed complaints with the U.N. We may be sure that the U.N. will have to take strong action. The world knows that Israel will not let things like this go on too long. Israel still remembers the years before the Sinai campaign.

The news analysis grows in elaborateness and complexity with the age of the pupils. In a junior high school class, for example, the news analysis of the Armistice violation might well consider the underlying causes which motivated the attacks at this particular time (*fall of 1960, during a Presidential campaign in the U.S.*—possibly the Cold War, Russia's encouragement of Egypt to embarrass the U.S., the dilemma of both candidates in the light of their platforms' assertions of friendship to Israel on the one hand, and the U.S. need for Arab friends and cordial relations with Islamic countries on the other.)

2. Class Discussion

The class discusses the subject matter brought out in the news analysis. This is an important part of the process. By contributing their own ideas to the analysis, the pupils become more absorbed with the presentation, learn the facts more thoroughly, and better retain the details of the presentation. By taking positions, they see the relevance of the news and their own responsibility toward shaping its course. The teacher therefore does not eliminate discussion no matter how pressed for time the class may be. It is far better not to have an analysis at all than to have merely the presentation of the analysis without a follow-up of discussion. At the same time the teacher is careful to guide the discussion so that it keeps to the problem at hand without going off on tangents, and stays within the time limit set for it in the lesson plan, or very close to it. The discussion might proceed somewhat like this:

TEACHER: That was an excellent analysis. I like particularly the way our News Analyst brought in the world situation and its effect on the whole problem. Do you think Russia will support Israel's complaint at the U.N.?

STUDENT 1: Russia will be against Israel.

TEACHER: Why do you say that?

STUDENT 1: Because Russia has been for the Arabs all along.

STUDENT 2: Also, they want to make trouble for America. If they vote for the Arabs and we vote for Israel the Arabs will think Russia is their friend and America their enemy.

TEACHER: What if America should also vote for the Arabs?

STUDENT 3: Then things would be pretty bad for Israel.

TEACHER: Do you think there is a chance of that?

STUDENT 4: Sure. America voted against Israel during the Sinai campaign.

TEACHER: Isn't there a difference?

STUDENT 5: Sure there is. In the Sinai campaign Israel went into Egypt. Now Egypt is making trouble inside Israel. I think they'll vote for Israel.

STUDENT 6: Also, now it's an election year.

TEACHER: What has this to do with it?

STUDENT 6: The candidates wouldn't want to make the Jews angry.

STUDENT 7: I think Kennedy will be elected anyhow. He's the better man and everybody likes him.

STUDENT 8: I know plenty of people who don't like him at all. My father says . . .

TEACHER: Just a moment. Let's not go off on a tangent. We are not discussing the election. We are discussing Israel's complaint against Egypt for Armistice violations.

STUDENT 9: I think America will vote for Israel regardless of the elections because Israel is right and Egypt is wrong in this case.

TEACHER: You are probably right. Especially if our officials realize that Israel is right. Sometimes these things have to be pointed out to them. It is the duty of the citizens of our country to let their officials know how they feel about things. Can any one suggest some ways how we do this?

STUDENT 10: By writing to them and telling them how we feel.

TEACHER: Any other way?

STUDENT 11: By editorials in the newspapers.

STUDENT 12: By the way we vote.

TEACHER: These are all important ways. By letting our officials know what we, the citizens want, we are making sure that things will be done in a democratic way. Only in that way will our representatives be able to speak and act for the people of America.

It is of course obvious that the discussion will vary considerably in different classes. The above example is offered only as a general guide for the teacher, indicating a manner of approach in guiding the discussion.

■ C. THE INTERVIEW

This too is not, strictly speaking, a dramatic technique. It is another way of teaching current history through a reality situation.

A person who is prominent in the news is invited to the class to be interviewed. Naturally only local personalities may be expected to respond to such an invitation. Possibilities are: the new principal; a graduate of the school just entering Hebrew high school; the newly elected president of a local Jewish organization; an official of the local Federation or U.J.A. drive; an actor in a play of Jewish interest about to be presented; an artist about to exhibit or a member of the committee sponsoring the exhibit, etc.

The steps involved are as follows:

1. Teacher's introduction (or motivation)
2. Selection of cast
3. The invitation
4. Correspondents' research
5. The presentation
6. The discussion
7. Follow-up activities

1. Teacher's Introduction

After a newscast the teacher suggests the idea that one of the personalities involved in one of the news items might be invited to come to the class to be interviewed. If the item is not about a particular personality but rather about a community event such as a philanthropic campaign, the dedication of a Jewish communal building, etc., the teacher encourages suggestions by the pupils as to who should be invited as a representative to present the facts about the event.

2. Selecting the Cast

Teacher points out that it might be confusing for the entire class to throw questions at the Subject and suggests that newspaper practice be followed: several students will assume the roles of correspondents. They will prepare questions in advance and will ask them of the Subject during the interview. Since these questions will naturally deal with the matter with which the Subject is involved, the correspondents will have to do some preliminary research so as to prepare questions which will bring forth answers that will give the class the necessary information. Members of the class will also be given a chance to ask questions of their own, after the correspondents will have completed their questioning.

To maintain proper order and to give the subject the proper introduction, a chairman will be necessary. The chairman will have to find out some details about the Subject so as to introduce him properly.

An invitation will have to be mailed to the Subject. A special Invitation Committee will be needed to prepare the letter and send it off.

The correspondents (three or more), the chairman, and the Invitation Committee are selected from student volunteers or appointed by the teacher.

3. *The Invitation*

The Invitation Committee meets after class or during recess and drafts a letter of invitation. The teacher looks over the draft and suggests corrections if necessary. The committee then prepares a neat copy and sends it to the person invited. Following is an example of such a letter of invitation by a student committee:

> Dear Mr. X:
>
> Our class is studying current history. In our class newscast we heard about the beginning of this year's U.J.A. campaign and that you were appointed the chairman.
>
> We want to learn more about the campaign and the work of the U.J.A. We therefore cordially invite you to come to our class on Thursday, October 27th at 4:30 P.M. to be interviewed by our class correspondents. If you are unable to come, please appoint somebody on your committee to come to us.
>
> Please let us know soon so that we can make plans to greet you in our classroom.
>
> Respectfully yours,
>
> For the Invitation Committee
> Class 5
> Beth El Hebrew School

4. *Correspondents' Research*

The teacher suggests sources for research where the correspondents may obtain information about the person to be interviewed, his project, etc.

After several days the correspondents meet and prepare a series of draft questions. Generally the questions will deal with the following areas:

a. Personal information—His position in the community, why he became involved in the project, what he will have to do, what he hopes to accomplish, etc.

b. Information about the project—What the campaign is for (or the exhibit, or the concert, or his work) how long it will last (or where it will take place), the goal, etc.

c. Details of the project—Some questions about past accomplishments, the need for it, future goals, etc.

At the same time the chairman gets some details about the Subject and writes out his introduction.

The teacher looks over the proposed questions as well as the chairman's introduction, offering suggestions for improvements, additions, or deletions when necessary.

5. *The Presentation*

The Subject is seated in front of the class. Near him are the correspondents and the chairman. The chairman introduces the Subject. The correspondents then ask their questions which the Subject answers one at a time. When the correspondents have exhausted their questions, the chairman asks for questions from the rest of the class. The Subject is then given a few moments for a closing statement, the chairman thanks him and the interview is over. Following is an example of the course which an interview with a member of the campaign committee of a local U.J.A. drive might take in a fifth year class:

CHAIRMAN: Fellow classmates: Today we have the privilege of welcoming to our class Mr. X, a member of the campaign committee for the United Jewish Appeal drive in our community. In private life, Mr. X is a well-known lawyer. He has come here to be interviewed about the drive. Mr. X will make an opening statement for a minute and a half before we begin our questioning.

SUBJECT: Thank you for inviting me to your class. I am very happy that you are interested enough in U.J.A. to want to find out more about it. I hope that you will tell your parents some of the things you will learn here about our important work. I also hope that each of you will help U.J.A. personally as much as you are able.

CHAIRMAN: We will now have the questions from our correspondents. We will begin with Correspondent 1.

CORRESPONDENT 1: Mr. X, our chairman told us that you are a lawyer and a member of the Campaign Committee of U.J.A. Will you please tell us, how long have you been working for U.J.A.?

SUBJECT: More than fifteen years.

CORRESPONDENT 1: You are a volunteer, aren't you?

SUBJECT: That's right.

CORRESPONDENT 1: And just what do you do as a member of the Campaign Committee?

SUBJECT: I go out and speak at meetings and fund-raising dinners, telling people about the work of U.J.A. I call people on the telephone asking them to make contributions. Generally I do all I can to help U.J.A. to raise its quota.

CORRESPONDENT 2: Please tell us, what is this year's quota?

SUBJECT: The national quota is $ ——– Of this amount we will have to raise $ ——– in our own community.

CORRESPONDENT 2: What will the money be used for?

SUBJECT: The U.J.A. divides the money it raises among a number of organizations such as the Joint Distribution Committee, the United Israel Appeal and others, whose work it is to help Jews overseas and in America as well.

CORRESPONDENT 3: In what ways are these Jews helped?

SUBJECT: In many ways. Take the United Israel Appeal for instance. It uses its funds to build up the Land of Israel by establishing industries, irrigating desert areas for farming, building homes for new immigrants, and so on.

CORRESPONDENT 3: Are there many new immigrants coming to Israel now?

SUBJECT: It depends on the year. Some years there were many thousands of Jews coming into Israel, some years there were fewer. As soon as the State was established many thousands of refugees who were saved from the Nazis came to Israel. Now it is Jews who are escaping from Arab persecution in North Africa and from some countries behind the Iron Curtain.

CORRESPONDENT 3: Do they all need to be helped?

SUBJECT: Most of them have no homes, no clothes, no one to turn to for help. They have to be brought into Israel, given homes, clothing. They have to be taught a trade or farming. They have to be provided with land, with tools, with many things so that they can live like free men in the State of Israel.

CORRESPONDENT 1: Can you tell us a little about the work of the Joint Distribution Committee?

SUBJECT: The J.D.C. works to help Jews in many countries of the world, outside of Israel. It has helped many Jewish communities in Europe that were destroyed by the Nazis, to become re-established. It has helped Jewish refugees to find homes, get jobs, go into business, regain their health. It maintains schools and supports Jewish education in Europe and in North Africa. Wherever a Jew is in need overseas, the J.D.C. comes to his aid.

CORRESPONDENT 2: Hasn't U.J.A. done anything for the Jews in America?

SUBJECT: Of course it has. U.J.A. money has helped many Jews, refugees from the Nazis, the Iron Curtain and other lands where they were persecuted, to come to America. Here they were helped to settle and establish themselves. U.J.A. has helped Jewish culture and education in America. Above all, it gave us and every Jew in America a chance to help our brothers who are in need and to share in the building of Israel.

CORRESPONDENT 3: You said earlier that you hoped we would help U.J.A. How can we do that?

SUBJECT: U.J.A. is not only for your parents. U.J.A. is for everybody. You can contribute your own money—from your allowance, from what you can earn at odd jobs or from other sources. It doesn't matter how little you give as long as you give as much as you can. You can also tell your parents and friends about the great work of the U.J.A. and the need to help our fellow Jews overseas and in Israel.

CHAIRMAN: Does any one in the class have any questions to ask of Mr. X?

STUDENT 1: I would like to ask a question. What does the U.J.A. do to help Jewish children?

SUBJECT: A great deal. First of all, whenever a Jewish family is helped by U.J.A. the children in the family are naturally helped also. In addition it does many things for children directly. It establishes and maintains homes for children who have lost their families. It maintains schools in Europe and Israel to give children an education and train them to earn a living when they grow up. Many of them have to be fed and clothed and housed as well.

STUDENT 2: Is there a U.J.A. campaign every year?

SUBJECT: Yes.

STUDENT 3: For how many more years do you think U.J.A. campaigns will go on?

SUBJECT: That's hard to say. But you can be sure that as long as there will be Jews anywhere who are in need of our help, the Jews of America will continue to raise funds to help them.

CHAIRMAN: Thank you Mr. X for coming here today and telling us about your important work. We learned a great deal from you. I'm sure we will all do our share for this important cause.

6. The Discussion

After the guest leaves, the teacher leads the class in a brief discussion. The pupils are encouraged to analyze the information they got, to take a position where that is called for, to suggest further areas of usefulness, to explore ways of becoming personally involved in the problem where that is advisable, etc.

7. Follow-Up Activities

At times the interview project ends with the discussion. Often however, follow-up activities are possible which will give the pupils a deeper understanding of the problem, involve them personally, correlate other studies of the curriculum, etc. The teacher is alert to exploit such opportunities for getting the greatest educational benefit out of the interview project. For example:

The U.J.A. interview outlined above provides opportunities for correlating the news lesson with study of sections of the Bible dealing with the obligations to help the needy such as the rules of *leket, shik'hah* and *pe'ah*—the rights of the poor to glean in the fields after the harvesters; study of sections in the prayer book dealing with injunctions to aid the needy such as *Elu d'varim sh'eyn lahem shi-ur;* or in Ethics of the Fathers *(Pirke Avot)* like, "Upon three things the world exists, upon Torah, upon prayer and upon the practice of good deeds"; holiday and Sabbath customs connected with *Tz'dakah* such as giving *Tz'dakah* before candle lighting, giving for the needy on Yom Kippur eve or before the reading of the *Megillah* on Purim, etc. History study might be connected with the news program by asking students to report on methods of helping the needy during the Middle Ages. Compositions might be written comparing ancient forms of helping others in need, such as *pidyon sh'vuyim* (ransoming of captives) with similar modern functions of U.J.A. in rescuing Jews from lands where they are persecuted and oppressed. Stories from Jewish literature dealing with similar practices might be told, read aloud in class, or assigned for home reading, such as, "If Not Higher" by I. L. Peretz, "The Three Deeds" by S. An-sky, the section in *Kiddush Hashem* by Sholom Ash which describes the ransoming of Jewish captives from the Cossacks, etc. An intra-school fund raising campaign on behalf of U.J.A. or *Keren Ami* from which U.J.A. would be a beneficiary might be conducted to give the students an opportunity for personal involvement.

An interview with an artist whose works are about to be exhibited in the community, or with a member of the committe sponsoring the exhibit might stimulate follow-up activities like: study of representative examples of Jewish art by other artists, through reproductions and prints from the teacher's collection or borrowed from a picture collection maintained by some public or school libraries, original examples from their homes brought to class by the pupils, some of the excellent illustrated articles on Jewish Art appearing from time to time in *World Over* Magazine, etc.; a visit to a Jewish museum or to a private collection to view examples of Jewish art; a visit to the synagogue to view and learn about the examples of ritual art such as the ark, the *parokhet* (ark curtain) *M'norah* and similar items; a class visit to the exhibition of the artist who was the subject of the interview; etc.

Similar activities will suggest themselves in connection with many subjects of class interviews. To the extent that time permits, the teacher will stimulate them in order to give added depth and meaning to the pupils' experience with current history.

■ D. PRESS CONFERENCE

This dramatic technique has been dealt with in detail under the same title in the section on "Dramatizing History." For the step by step procedure the reader is referred to that section.

In connection with teaching current history, the teacher will find the Press Conference especially useful for studying news which revolves about an individual. For example: Dr. Selman Waksman is awarded the Nobel prize for his share in the discovery of streptomycin; Dr. Jonas Salk develops anti-polio vaccine; the Israeli Prime Minister re-organizes the cabinet; the President of the United States makes an important statement affecting Jewish interests; an Arab leader like the king of Jordan or the president of the United Arab Republic makes a move or announces a policy decision affecting Israel; a new president is elected by a national or international Jewish organization such as Hadassah, Z.O.A., B'nai B'rith, etc.

By means of the Interview outlined above, the class was able to meet face to face with the subject of the news and learn in detail about him and the event in which he was involved. This may be possible with personalities of local prominence. It is clearly impossible with national or international figures. They are brought before the students by means of the dramatized Press Conference in which a student impersonates them.

The Press Conference is often an outgrowth of a class newscast. At the end of the newscast the class may decide that it would be advisable to learn more about an important news event by dramatizing a press conference with the subject of the item. Students are selected to enact the roles of the Subject, his Advisory Committee, Correspondents who will question the Subject and a Chairman. The role players are given reference materials so that they will learn as much as possible about the Subject, the events in which he is involved, the background, motivations, aims, etc. About a week is permitted to elapse to give the role players an opportunity to do the research, prepare the questions and meet with the teacher for guidance. The enactment takes place during a period regularly scheduled for current history. At least ten minutes of class time are allocated for the Press Conference and the discussion which follows. The following example will illustrate the dramatized Press Conference:

BEN-GURION ANNOUNCES EICHMANN ARREST

CHAIRMAN: During our regular newscast last week we heard that Prime Minister David Ben-Gurion of Israel announced the arrest of the Nazi Adolph Eichmann. Today, by dramatization, we will witness the Press Conference during which this news was given to the world. The role of Ben-Gurion will be played by

———. Our Correspondents are ———. I now present the Prime Minister of Israel, David Ben-Gurion.

BEN-GURION: I have called you, representatives of the press and radio, for an important announcement. We have arrested the man who was directly responsible for the extermination of more than six million Jews during World War II. Adolph Eichmann, who planned and directed the Nazi extermination program is now in an Israeli prison. He will stand trial in an Israeli court for the death of six million Jews.

CORRESPONDENT 1: Mr. Prime Minister, will you tell us please where Eichmann was caught?

BEN-GURION: Eichmann was arrested in a foreign country.

CORRESPONDENT 2: It has been rumored for a long time that Eichmann was hiding out in Argentina. Is this true?

BEN-GURION: It is true that Eichmann escaped from Germany to South America right after the fall of Berlin to the Allied Armies.

CORRESPONDENT 2: Was Eichmann arrested in Argentina?

BEN-GURION: I can not name the country at this time.

CORRESPONDENT 2: How did the Israelis get Eichmann to Israel?

BEN-GURION: When Eichmann was caught he realized that he would have to stand trial for his crimes. He agreed voluntarily to come to Israel.

CORRESPONDENT 1: Who was responsible for his arrest?

BEN-GURION: Millions of Jews lost their dear ones in the Nazi extermination camps. Some had sworn to bring to trial this man who was responsible for the concentration camps, the crematoriums and the gas chambers. For fifteen years they searched for him. Now they finally caught him.

CORRESPONDENT 1: Who directed the search?

BEN-GURION: Tuvia Friedman who directs the work of *Yad Vashem* was of great help in guiding the people who finally caught Eichmann.

CORRESPONDENT 2: What is *Yad Vashem?*

BEN-GURION: It is an organization in Israel which gathers detailed information about the Nazi atrocities against the Jews and about the Nazis who were responsible for them so that the world will not forget our six million martyrs.

CORRESPONDENT 3: Could you tell us a little about your case against Adolph Eichmann?

BEN-GURION: The man Eichmann was the one who planned the whole Nazi extermination program. He organized the concentration camps where Jews from all over Europe were locked up. He ordered that Jews from the countries under Nazi occupation should be deported to these extermination camps, there to be destroyed. Day in and day out thousands of Jews—men, women and little children, were burned and gassed in these horrible camps.

CORRESPONDENT 3: And Adolph Eichmann was the one who was responsible for this?

BEN-GURION: Thousands and hundreds of thousands of German Nazis were responsible for the death of our families. They are all guilty of murder. But Adolph Eichmann was the one who planned it all, the man who gave the orders to kill the Jews, and planned the way this was to be done.

CORRESPONDENT 1: When will his trial take place?

BEN-GURION: In a few months—as soon as all the evidence against him is organized.

CORRESPONDENT 1: Will he be tried in secret or at a public trial?

BEN-GURION: It will be a public trial. Correspondents from all over the world will be given every opportunity to report everything. We want the whole world to know what the Nazis did to our six million martyrs.

CORRESPONDENT 1: Why, Mr. Prime Minister?

BEN-GURION: So that they will see to it that never again will a tyrant be able to repeat what the Nazis have done to us.

CORRESPONDENT 2: Will Eichmann have a lawyer to defend him?

BEN-GURION: Of course! Even a beast like Eichmann is entitled to a fair trial in the State of Israel. He can pick his own lawyer—any one he wants.

CORRESPONDENT 2: Even a German lawyer?

BEN-GURION: Even a German lawyer will be allowed to defend him. If Eichmann wants it, we will give him the best Israeli lawyer to represent him.

CHAIRMAN: Thank you, Correspondents for letting us be present at your Press Conference. Is there any one in the class who would like to ask the Prime Minister a question?

STUDENT 1: I heard that Eichmann was taken out of Argentina on an El Al airplane. Is that true?

BEN-GURION: I can not answer that question.

STUDENT 2: Was Eichmann caught by Irsaeli secret service men?

BEN-GURION: He was caught by Jews from a number of countries. There were Israelis among them.

CHAIRMAN: Thank you Mr. Prime Minister.

■ E. YOU ARE THE WITNESS

This technique is similar to "Witness to History" which is fully discussed in the section on "Dramatizing History." By means of dramatization the class is brought, as it were, into the presence of the news event as if it were just happening.

"You Are the Witness" may be an outgrowth of a newscast in which the event is presented at first in its outlines only. At the end of the newscast the teacher may point out that a given item is of such importance that it would be well if the class could learn more about it. The best way would of course be if the class could actually have been there while it happened. Since that is impossible, the next best thing is to re-create the event by dramatization. The teacher then proceeds to discuss with the class the details of the proposed dramatization, selects the cast and does all the other things suggested under "Witness to History."

"You Are the Witness" may also be used in place of the regular newscast. This will be done especially with news events of major importance which overshadow all others. In that event, the teacher or a student presents the news item to the class in its outline form and then the teacher suggests a "You Are the Witness" dramatization, following the outlined procedure.

This form of dramatization allows for a presentation of many of the details which are usually omitted from a formal news dispatch. It is precisely such details however, many of them quite personal in nature, which enhance the understanding of the meaning and effect of the news event. Furthermore, the dramatization gives the news a sense of immediacy and relevancy which might otherwise be lost for the pupils. Following is an illustration of a "You Are the Witness" treatment of a news item:

THE NEWS ITEM

"Sabbath observers punished for opening stores on Sunday after three day holiday."

YOU ARE THE WITNESS

CHAIRMAN: The Flatbush section of Brooklyn is seething with excitement and anger over what many claim to be a great injustice. Come with me. See what is happening there. Come. You are the witness!

CORRESPONDENT: My name is ______ and I am the correspondent of the New York Times. I am standing on the corner of Avenue J and East 14th Street in Flatbush. There is great excitement here today. In front of a children's wear store a crowd is gathered around a policeman. Let's go over and see what's going on.

MERCHANT 1: But look officer, why do I have to get this summons? It's not fair.

OFFICER: Mister, please. I'm only a policeman. These are my orders. Today is Sunday. You kept your store open on Sunday, so you'll have to go to court.

MERCHANT: But that's not fair!

POLICEMAN: What do you mean it's not fair?

MERCHANT 1: I'm a Sabbath observer.

POLICEMAN: Then why did you keep the store open today? It's the Sabbath. You should observe it. That's the law.

MERCHANT 1: But it's not my Sabbath. I observe Saturday as the Sabbath. I kept my store closed yesterday. Why should I be forced to close for two days?

POLICEMAN: That's the law.

MERCHANT 1: And this week was Rosh Hashanah on Thursday and Friday so my store was closed for three full days. Is it fair to make me close for four full days? How can I make a living this way?

POLICEMAN: Mister, don't tell it to me. Tell it to the judge. Here's your summons. Be in court next Monday.

CORRESPONDENT: Let us talk to the merchant. Excuse me sir, you're the owner of this children's wear store. Aren't you?

MERCHANT 1: I am.

CORRESPONDENT: Why did you open the store today, when the law says you have to close on Sunday?

MERCHANT 1: It's a bad law. Don't we have freedom of religion here?

CORRESPONDENT: What's that to do with it?

MERCHANT 1: Everything! The law says the store should be closed on the Sabbath—fine. But why force a Jew to observe the Sabbath on Sunday? I have the right to follow my religion, and my religion says that my day of rest is on Saturday.

CORRESPONDENT: I see what you mean.

MERCHANT 1: So every week, non-Jewish merchants close one day—on Sunday. I have to close two days—Saturday and Sunday. Now it was Rosh Hashanah and so they say I must be closed four days. In two weeks it will be Sukkot—again four days. How can I stay in business?

CORRESPONDENT: Then why don't you try to have the law changed?

MERCHANT 1: We tried—all of us merchants who are Sabbath observers.

CORRESPONDENT: And what happened?

MERCHANT 1: Nothing happened. Every year a law is introduced in the legislature. It never passes.

MERCHANT 2: That's because nobody cares.

CORRESPONDENT: Who are you mister?

MERCHANT 2: I'm a merchant. That is I was a merchant until I was forced to close my store. I had a shoe store.

CORRESPONDENT: Why did you have to close it?

MERCHANT 2: I couldn't keep going. See—I had a shoe store and a block away a non-Jewish merchant had a shoe store. So Saturdays I'd close my store. My competitor's was open. So I'd see lots of my customers there on Saturdays. O.K. I said to myself. He's open Saturday, on my Sabbath. I'll open Sunday on his Sabbath and things will even out. So I did and right away I got a summons for violating the Sunday closing law.

CORRESPONDENT: Did you go to court?

MERCHANT 2: Sure.

CORRESPONDENT: And what happened?

MERCHANT 2: The judge said "guilty" and I had to pay a fine.

CORRESPONDENT: Didn't you explain things to the judge?

MERCHANT 2: Sure I did. I told him that Saturday and Sunday are the two days when people are home. That's when they can go shopping for shoes. If I have to keep closed every Saturday because my religion says it's my Sabbath and every Sunday because the law says it's the Sabbath, I can't make a living and I'll have to give up my business.

CORRESPONDENT: So what did the judge say?

MERCHANT 2: He said the law is the law and I'd have to pay the fine. The only way out is to change the law. So go fight city hall!

CHAIRMAN: You have witnessed today what happened in the Flatbush section of Brooklyn on Sunday after Rosh Hashanah when Jewish merchants tried to open their stores on Sunday after keeping them closed for three days of holiday and Sabbath. What do you think should happen? Do these merchants deserve help? How can they be helped? You figure this out. You were the witness!

Nearly every dramatization of this type can end with a direct challenge to the class to take a position about the problem raised. If the dramatization deals with an attack on Israel, the students are stimulated to decide on its justification, what course Israel should take, what action they, the students should take, etc. If the news deals with an archeological discovery, the students are encouraged to express opinions on the worthwhileness of the archeologists' effort, to speculate on what light the discovery can shed on the past, etc. A fund raising campaign brings to the fore the problems of how to raise the money, how best to utilize it, what long-range efforts can be undertaken to remedy conditions so that the need will disappear, etc.

This type of current history presentation lends itself especially as a motivation for follow-up activities. Having been "witnesses" to the news, the students can write news reports describing what they have "witnessed." They can also be stimulated to take direct action whenever possible. In the example given here, students might write to their representatives in the legislature to change the Sunday closing law. In a fund raising effort, they participate with their own gifts. The election of a new head of a national organization, the appointment of a new minister in Israel, the award of an international honor to a Jewish scientist, and similar events call for letters of congratulation. The presentation of a Jewish work of art on TV such as *The World of Sholom Aleichem, The Dybbuk* or a special festival program calls for viewing by the students, letter writing to the TV station, writing of reviews, collateral reading, etc. Thus the pupils are not only passive witnesses to current history. They learn to take an active part in it, to become personally involved, and, realizing their personal involvement, they develop a sense of responsibility to shape the news for the common good.

■ F. SOCIO-DRAMA

This dramatic technique is particularly suitable for use in connection with news which has in it some element of controversy. For example: The Israeli Prime Minister repeats his oft-stated demand for a large Jewish immigration from America to Israel. A book appears that is critical of Jewish synagogue life in the suburbs. The New York City Police Commissioner refuses to permit Jewish policemen to take time off during the High Holy Days because of a special need for an augmented police force.

In all situations of this sort it is possible to take a position on either side: The reasons for or against American mass immigration to Israel; the right of the author to describe the facts of Jewish life in the suburbs versus the question of the wisdom of treating intimate problems in public; the need of the community for police protection, set off against the right of the Jewish policemen to worship on their most sacred days.

Socio-drama helps us to bring these controversial aspects to the fore and to search for and often arrive at a solution. The steps in the utilization of this technique have been described in detail under "Socio-Drama for Teaching Bible or *Humash*." Briefly stated it is a creative dramatic technique for use in situations involving social relationships. As applied to current history, students take on roles of people on both sides of controversial subjects in the news. In the enactment they state their positions, bringing out the arguments pro and con. After the enactment the class discusses the arguments and tries to arrive at an acceptable solution.

In teaching current history, the socio-drama is usually motivated by a class newscast. As the class discusses the news item and the controversial subjects come to the fore, the teacher proposes that the controversy be examined by way of a socio-drama in which students will assume roles on either side. To illustrate:

THE NEWS ITEM

"Police Commissioner of New York insists that Jewish policemen remain on duty during High Holy Days because of local emergency situation."

TEACHER: How do you feel about this? Do you think the Commissioner is right?
STUDENT 1: I think he's wrong.
TEACHER: Why?
STUDENT 1: These are the holiest days of the year. He's interfering with the Jews' right to worship according to their religion.
TEACHER: Any one think differently?
STUDENT 2: I do. It's an emergency. A policeman's first responsibility is to protect his city.

Or, the teacher may find that none of the students wants to argue the unpopular position and no one disagrees with the student who was critical of the Police Commissioner. In that event the teacher points out to the students the other side of the problem, somewhat like this:

TEACHER: It's understandable that we Jews should feel this way. But the Police Commissioner gave rather strong reasons for his orders. We may or may not agree, but we should know his reasons.

At this point, the controversy has been brought to the fore and the teacher proposes a socio-drama to make it clear:

TEACHER: Why don't we act out the problem through a socio-drama? One of us will play the role of the Police Commissioner. Three of us can be a delegation of Rabbis from the New York Board of Rabbis that has come to the Commissioner to ask him to change his order.

Students are then selected to play these roles. They are given several minutes to meet outside the room to discuss what they will do. When they return he enactment begins:

RABBI ABRAMS: Mr. Police Commissioner, we are a delegation from the New York Board of Rabbis.
COMMISSIONER: Come in rabbis. What can I do for you?
RABBI ABRAMS: I am Rabbi Abrams, the chairman of this delegation. This is Rabbi Katz and this is Rabbi Cohen.
COMMISSIONER: I am pleased to meet you. Now, to what do I owe this honor?
RABBI ABRAMS: It's about your order that the Jewish policemen will not be able to get time off during the High Holy Days.
COMMISSIONER: That's not my order, Rabbis. My order says that no policemen, Jewish or non-Jewish, can take time off during the present emergency.
RABBI KATZ: But it is the Jewish policemen who are the ones who will suffer.
COMMISSIONER: That is unfortunate. But we do have an emergency on our hands.
RABBI COHEN: But that is interfering with the policemen's right to worship according to their religion.
COMMISSIONER: Not at all, Rabbis. A policeman's duty is to protect his community.
RABBI ABRAMS: But these are the High Holy Days!
COMMISSIONER: What can I do? My job is to see that all the people in our community are safe—Jews and non-Jews, and it has to be carried out by all the policemen, Jews and non-Jews.

RABBI COHEN: Can't you make an exception?

COMMISSIONER: It would be a danger to the community. Look, Rabbi, you wouldn't ask a soldier in war to leave the battlefield on the High Holy Days.

RABBI ABRAMS: Of course not. But this isn't war.

COMMISSIONER: No, but the danger to our community is just as great.

RABBI KATZ: Will all the policemen be required to work on those days?

COMMISSIONER: All, except those who are now on vacation.

RABBI COHEN: Can't you call them in to take the place of the Jewish policemen?

COMMISSIONER: I haven't the right to do that. But I will encourage them to change off with the Jewish officers.

RABBI ABRAMS: But Commissioner, you don't seem to realize what it means for a Jew to have to work on the High Holy Days!

COMMISSIONER: I realize it. I also know my duty to protect all of you and all of our community.

RABBI KATZ: You are an experienced man. You can surely move your men around so as to make it possible for all Jewish police to get the time off.

COMMISSIONER: I'm very sorry. I can not make any distinction between my men on account of their religion. All policemen—Jews and non-Jews must meet their responsibility.

At this point the teacher ends the enactment. The arguments on both sides have been stated and the class is now ready to discuss and evaluate them.

At times the students are not aware of the cross-currents involved in a particular controversy and find themselves unable to enact its protagonists. The teacher might then suggest that the enactment be postponed for a few days while the students do some reading about the matter in references which the teacher gives them.

After the enactment, the students are encouraged to evaluate the content of the play—*not the manner of playing,* but the arguments for and against which have been voiced by the role players. During the discussion the pupils are stimulated to take sides and eventually to try to offer compromise solutions where that is possible or desirable.

As previously stated, this type of enactment is possible with most controversial news items:

"The Premier's statement" might be examined from all sides via a socio-drama of a scene in an American-Jewish home. The son wants to go to Israel and quotes the Premier's statement. His mother takes the view that American Jewry needs its best representatives right in this country for the development of Jewish life here. The father might offer the compromise solution of a year or two of service in Israel by American youth and then a return to this country to apply the experiences gained to American Jewish life.

"The book about the suburbs" may serve as a theme for a socio-drama dealing with an imaginary situation in which the author is autographing copies of his book in a book store. The president of a synagogue in the suburbs comes in with his wife. They examine a copy of the book and express themselves in critical terms about it. The author overhears and walks over to them. He tells them why he wrote the book. He justifies himself on the basis of the need to make Jewish problems public so that they might be properly handled and the evils remedied. The man and his wife argue for the need of being diplomatic about things, of not "washing our linens in public," etc.

Insofar as possible the teacher will use this technique. It is an excellent medium to develop an awareness of the cross-currents at work in Jewish life. It helps the students to understand varying positions and that variety of thought is possible and often desirable. Above all, it helps the students to form the habit of reading the news critically, applying their own judgments, rather than accepting "publicity handouts" as truth and opinions of public figures as proven facts.

■ G. HEADLINE PARADE

This is a form of current history dramatization which allows for the treatment in depth of news items of major significance. The core of the dramatization is a single news item of major significance. It is dramatized in terms of its effect on an identifiable individual. The treatment is personal and emotional. For example, the news item in question might be of a grant by the United States Government to the State of Israel for cultural development and student exchange. Dramatizing this news item, the Headline Parade might tell the story of the effect of this grant on an Israeli young man who is helped to realize his dream to study nuclear physics under a great American professor. This type of treatment of news not only holds the attention of the students but brings about their emotional involvement with the characters and events portrayed.

The element of conflict—usually a basic ingredient of any effective dramatization—is generally an essential aspect of a Headline Parade dramatization. The central character of the dramatization is involved in a struggle to attain a goal. His struggle may be against other individuals, the environment, economic conditions, accepted social mores, or what have you. For example: The Israeli student struggles to obtain an education; the refugee fights against oppression and poverty to obtain his goal of a secure home; the scientist struggles to unlock the secrets of nature, seeking a cure for disease. The news item is dramatized to indicate its effect on the outcome of the individual's conflict. The students who participate in the dramatization as well as those who view it are caught up in the conflict, and become part of it. The struggle of the central character elicits their sympathy and their indentification with his problem. The effect of the news item on the central character affects them also. Thus they vicariously live with the news and within it, making the events a part of their own experience, of their own living memories.

To round out the story and the characters of the dramatization, historical background and related news items are introduced whenever possible. In this manner, each Headline Parade dramatization becomes a complete unit of a current problem set in its proper place in the current scene and within historical perspective.

Class-Created Headline Parade Dramatizations

From many points of view, all too obvious to need elaboration here, it is highly desirable for the class to create its own Headline Parade dramatization of important news. This may be done in a variety of ways: the script may be created during class sessions with the entire class participating; the class may discuss the elements that should be included in the script with the actual script being written outside of class by a committee or one able student; the script may be prepared outside of class with teacher guidance, and presented to the class for the first time in its finished form.

The creation of a *Headline Parade* dramatization during class sessions with the participation of all the students in the class generally involves the following steps:

1. Presentation of the news.
2. Motivating the dramatization.
3. Creating the story skeleton.
4. Background research.
5. Developing the dramatization.
   a. Elaborating the story.
   b. Breaking down the story into scenes.
   c. Determining the characters.
   d. Selecting the cast.
   e. Discussing the first scene.
   f. Enacting the first scene.
   g. Analyzing critically the first scene.
   h. Repeating with the following scenes.
6. Enacting the entire dramatization.
7. Evaluating the dramatization and generalizing.
8. Relating to pupil experiences.

Following is an example of a detailed development of these steps:

1. Presentation of the News

The news item which will become the subject of the Headline Parade is usually first presented to the class as part of the regular newscast. It might also be an isolated item which, because of its importance, is brought to the attention of the class by the teacher, by an individual student, or because it is the subject of general conversation.

At times the news is presented to the class by a student because of his personal involvement with it. For example: The synagogue has arranged a theatre party for a play of Jewish interest such as *The Wall*, Millard Lampell's dramatization of the John Hersey novel about the Warsaw Ghetto. One of the students mentions the fact that his parents took him to see the play. He is encouraged to tell the class something about it. The teacher then points out, directly or by means of class discussion, the importance of keeping alive the memory of the Jewish heroism and martyrdom during the Nazi persecutions; that because of this, the staging of a play such as *The Wall* is important news; that we might try to learn more about this event and the background with which it deals. If the material is at hand, the teacher reads to the class brief excerpts of news items about the presentation, sections of critical reviews, etc.

2. Motivating the Dramatization

If the class has had previous experience with Headline Parade dramatization, very little may be necessary in order to motivate the pupils to do such a dramatization. The suggestion will usually be made by the pupils themselves, or the teacher might initiate it with: "Suppose we do a Headline Parade about this."

If the technique is new to the class, more may be necessary by way of motivation. The teacher stresses the personal aspects of the news—its possible effect on the lives of individuals. The pupils are stimulated to think in personal terms in relation to the news item: "Just imagine if you were a refugee trying to find a new home"; "I wonder how a twelve year old boy in Athens would feel the first time he walked into the new Jewish school building?" "It would be interesting to know when Selman Waksman first realized the wonders of life that exist in a handful of earth." The suggestion is then made: "Suppose we play the story of such a refugee child," "Let's make believe we are such a boy in Athens," "Just imagine it is fifty years ago in the Ukraine and we look in on Selman Waksman when he was just a boy."

Following through with our example of the news item about the opening of the play *The Wall,* the teacher might proceed as follows:

TEACHER: *The Wall* is a play about the life of the Jews in the Warsaw Ghetto. It tells the story of the adults. I wonder how the children lived behind the ghetto wall. Just imagine a ten year old boy or a twelve year old girl. How did they live? Did they go to school? What do you think?

STUDENT 1: They lived in the ghetto a long time. They must have had school.

TEACHER: Do you think they played games in the ghetto?

STUDENT 2: I don't think so. They were probably afraid to go outside.

STUDENT 3: They could have played inside—quiet games, like.

TEACHER: It would be interesting to know. Did they help in getting food? Did they also fight against the Nazis? Suppose we find out. Suppose we play out the stories of two such children in the Warsaw Ghetto.

Having made the suggestion, the teacher proceeds directly to the next step.

3. Creating the Story Skeleton

The teacher and the students together develop in general terms a story line for the dramatization. No attempt is made at bringing out fine details of plot, motivation or characterization. This will be done later, after the pupils have had an opportunity, as a result of research, to learn more about the subject, the period, and the personalities of the news story. In our example, proceeding directly from the suggestion that the class play out the stories of two children in the Warsaw Ghetto, the teacher continues:

TEACHER: What shall we call the boy?

STUDENT 4: Jacob.

TEACHER: That's a good Jewish name. What about our twelve year old girl?

STUDENT 5: Let's call her Miriam.

TEACHER: Fine. Now who do you think Jacob and Miriam should be? Neighbors? Brother and sister? Strangers who meet in the ghetto for the first time?

STUDENT 6: I think it would be good to make them brother and sister.

TEACHER: Why?

STUDENT 6: If they are brother and sister they would tell each other things that strangers would not. In that way we would find out things about their private lives.

TEACHER: Any one think differently?

STUDENT 7: I think they ought to be friends and not relatives.

TEACHER: Why?

STUDENT 7: In that way we will find out about the lives of two families and not only one.

TEACHER: How about their being total strangers? Any one like that idea? No? Let's see then—how many want to make them brother and sister? How many want them to be neighbors? I see that most of you would rather have them be neighbors. Fine. Now, let's go on with our story. What will we tell about Jacob and Miriam?

STUDENT 8: We will tell about their life under the Nazis.

STUDENT 9: We will tell how bad things were for them.

TEACHER: Should we tell about the fight against the Nazis?

STUDENT 10: Of course. That's the whole idea.

TEACHER: Do Miriam and Jacob take part in the fight?

STUDENT 11: Sure. They could be carrying ammunition. They could be messengers. They could do a lot.

TEACHER: That gives us the general idea of the story. It will go something like this: Jacob and Miriam are neighbors in Warsaw. They live under Nazi occupation. Life is pretty bad for them and for all the Jews in Warsaw. Finally the Jews revolt against the Nazis. Jacob and Miriam help in the fight. In the end . . . Well, we can figure out the end later.

4. Background Research

After the general story line has been developed, the pupils are guided to a realization that they need additional information before they can decide on the details of their story.

TEACHER: How shall we begin our dramatization?

STUDENT 1: Let's begin as the Nazis capture Warsaw.

STUDENT 2: We should start before the Nazis come.

TEACHER: Why?

STUDENT 3: So that we can show the difference of how nice things were for them before and how bad after the Nazis came.

TEACHER: That sounds reasonable. How do you think things were after the Nazis came?

STUDENT 3: Bad.

TEACHER: In what ways?

STUDENT 3: Lots of ways. The Nazis killed Jews. The Jews had no food. They were beaten. And other things like . . .

TEACHER: Like what?

STUDENT 3: Well . . . I don't know. . . .

TEACHER: I see. How about good things? Did they have parties in the Ghetto? Did they have schools? Did they go to shows? Do you think that's important for us to know for our story?

STUDENT 4: Sure it's important. But how should we know these things?

TEACHER: Well, there are books that describe Jewish life under the Nazis in Warsaw. What about the revolt? When did it start? Why did the Jews revolt? I see we have a lot to find out before we can continue making up our story of Jacob and Miriam.

The pupils now see for themselves the need for research if they are to go on with the project. At this point the teacher suggests sources for research to broaden their knowledge:

TEACHER: I see that we can't go on further at this time. Suppose we first try to find out a little more about Jewish life in Warsaw under the Nazis and then continue making up our story? If you will look in *The Jewish People,* Book III by Deborah Pessin, you will find the story of the Warsaw Ghetto told briefly and interestingly. It begins on page 283 and ends on page 286. Read it during the next few days and then, next Thursday we will continue with our story.

5. Developing the Dramatization

After the pupils have had an opportunity to do the background research the teacher proceeds to develop with them the details of the story and its dramatization. This might be done in the course of a single session lasting from twenty minutes to a half hour if the subject is not too complex. Often more time will be needed and the project will be continued for several sessions. In that event, the teacher is careful not to let too much time elapse between sessions. To do so would be to court a cooling down of interest. Also, a good deal of time would be wasted because of the need to go over much of the same ground at each session to refresh the pupils' memories.

In developing the dramatization the teacher may follow one of two courses of action: 1) The entire story is developed in full. It is then divided into segments of action or scenes. Each scene is separately dramatized. Then the scenes are put together and the entire dramatization is enacted. 2) The story is developed in general terms. Following this, the first segment or scene is fully developed and dramatized. Thereafter, the story of the second segment is developed in detail and dramatized. This continues until the entire story is created and dramatized, scene by scene. Thereafter, all the segments are put together and enacted as a complete unit. Here then are the steps in developing the dramatization of a Headline Parade:

a. Elaborating the Story

The teacher guides the pupils in the creation of the story, using leading questions, judiciously placed suggestions, etc. The teacher is careful not to impose a preconceived story on the pupils. It is to be the pupils' creation, developed by them under the teacher's stimulation. However, when there is a lag, the teacher does not hesitate to offer suggestions and even give direct help when absolutely necessary. But, when the well-springs of pupil creativity begin to flow once again, the teacher quickly retires to his original role of guide, allowing the students to carry on with the story development.

In our current example of *The Wall,* we are assuming that the teacher has followed course 1, developing the entire story before proceeding to dramatize any part of it. The story, as elaborated by the class after proper research, might be as follows:

BEHIND THE GHETTO WALL

THE STORY

Jacob, a boy of ten and Miriam, a girl of twelve, live next door to each other in an apartment house in Warsaw. Jacob likes Miriam very much because she often tells him stories which she has read in the school library books. Miriam speaks Polish very well, having learned it in school. Jacob speaks Polish only haltingly since he studies in a *Heder* where Polish is not taught. He does know *Humash* (Bible in Hebrew) and *Talmud* and is considered a good student.

Miriam's father is a physician and has an important post in Warsaw's greatest hospital. Jacob's father is a leather merchant.

One day, Jacob and Miriam are seated on the stoop of their apartment house. They talk about the war which everybody says is sure to come. They are both worried about the Nazis. They heard so much about their cruelty to Jews. Miriam, to put Jacob at ease, begins to tell him a story. They hear the sound of planes and bombs dropping. The Nazis are attacking. Miriam takes Jacob's hand and together they run off to the bomb shelter.

It is now October 1940. We are in Jacob's house. Jacob's father and mother discuss the situation in Warsaw. The Nazis have captured the city. They have put up a brick wall dividing the Jewish section from the non-Jewish. Jacob's father Reb Moshe, has had to give up his business. He has been conscripted for forced labor. Now, just before dawn, he goes off for work in a Nazi military shoe factory. He gets no pay but will get a ration of bread and potatoes at night. Jacob wakes. He is fed some left-overs. Miriam comes for him. She no longer goes to the Polish school. She and Jacob study together in the Jewish school organized by the Jews in the ghetto.

It is a few months later. In Miriam's house we meet her father, Dr. Joseph Balin and her mother Mania Balin. He has been hidden out by the Jews of the ghetto. He is one of the few doctors left and they need him. He is busy day and night at his task and is very discouraged. There are no medicines. There is great overcrowding, etc. Jacob comes in. He is worried. That morning both his parents were ordered to be at the Recruiting Place along with several thousand other Jews. They were to be taken to a factory outside of Warsaw for work. They have not returned. Mania Balin calms him down. Two Jewish girls, Malkah and Rachel come in and tell that news has come from the Nazis that the people who were sent for work that morning would remain at the factory for some time and that the Jewish community has been ordered to deliver each day several thousand new workers. At the same time, those who are too weak to work, older people, and children whould be transported to villages far from Warsaw. However, the girls have information that the Nazis are operating an extermination camp at Treblinka, not far from Warsaw, and that's where the transports are being sent.

It is spring 1943. Every day thousands have been transported to Treblinka. Other thousands are dying from disease. Only 40 thousand are left from the original 450 thousand Jews in the Warsaw Ghetto. At the Balin home Miriam is practicing the *Mah Nishtanah* for the *Seder* that night. Shooting begins outside. The revolt has started. Mania Balin wants to hide the children. They refuse. They want to take part in the struggle. Dr. Balin agrees with the children. All must share in the fight against the Nazis.

It is a corner near the wall. Miriam has been sent with a message outside to try to bring help from the Poles. Now Rachel and Isaac, a young ghetto fighter, are waiting for her to return. Jacob comes with a message that the Nazis are coming in with tanks. They are needed to defend a bunker. Jacob says he will stay and watch for Miriam. They leave. Miriam comes. She has come through a sewer pipe. She tells Jacob that the Poles were very nice but will not help. They claim they cannot spare arms and ammunition. All they could give were six pistols. The Jews will have to fight alone.

It is forty-two days since the revolt started. Jacob meets Miriam among the ruins. They think everyone is dead. Dr. Balin comes. He urges Miriam and Jacob to try to get out through the sewers. It is their duty to try to live, to get to Palestine where they will help to build a Jewish homeland where Jews will no longer have to be afraid of persecution. Also, they are to tell to the world how the Jews of the Warsaw Ghetto died fighting tyranny. The children leave. The father goes back to fight to the last.

Under careful guidance and stimulation by the teacher the story has been developed by the pupils in full detail. Every suggestion by a student has been carefully considered. Many have been discarded for one reason or another. A great many more have been accepted and made a part of the story. The final product is a mosaic of student ideas with minor "assists" by the teacher.

In the course of the story development, the teacher has guided the process so that the final result consists of a plot that is built up from fairly well-defined blocks of action which will fall easily into a series of scenes. Characters of the story are clear-cut and identifiable. In that manner, the task of converting the story into a dramatization becomes less difficult than it might be if the story were more diffused and the characters more vague.

Steps b,c,d,e,f,g,h

These are the steps involved in converting the story in to a dramatization. They have been treated in detail in steps 5 *through 12* of *Direct Dramatization* in the chapter *Dramatizing History*. The reader is referred to that section for particulars in the creative dramatization process.

The *Headline Parade* type dramatization differs somewhat from *Direct Dramatization* in that it utilizes a less formal approach. In actual practice it comes much closer to the *Living Newspaper* format than to the conventional stage play since it utilizes every possible technique which will advance the action and story. The *Headline Parade* quite often employs a Narrator to clarify and tie the elements of the story together. Charts, graphs and even slides and films are included, if they help to build up the background of the dramatization or supply needed information. The test for the inclusion of any medium is: a) Is it necessary for clarity or does it add to our knowledge? b) Does it help to advance the action of the dramatization? If it meets either of these two tests it must meet still one more before it can be accepted within the fold of the dramatization, namely: that it help to intensify the emotional impact or, at the very least, that it does not weaken it.

6. Enacting the Entire Dramatization

After all scenes have been fully developed individually, they are put together and enacted as a complete dramatization. It is at this point that such elements as opening and closing announcements and narration are added to the script. When practical, recorded music or songs sung by a class chorus are included for mood or as bridges between scenes.

All along there has been no attempt to reduce any of the dramatization to writing. Each enactment has been improvised on the basis of the plot for each scene which was developed in class discussion. The enactment of the entire dramatization follows the same line—the dialogue being created impromptu by the pupils as they play out the dramatization. By now they have had sufficient experience with the scenes individually so as to enable them to present a fairly smooth dramatization. Even so, it will not be of auditorium quality. But that is not our purpose. In developing this Headline Parade dramatization of a unit stimulated by a current news item, the *process* is of major value and not the final result. Of course, we always aim for quality. But our real aim here has been to teach through dramatization, to provide the pupils with an opportunity for participation and indentification with the subject through emotional involvement. This we have done. The simple and at times halting dramatization which has resulted from the class efforts is a cause for great satisfaction. It was born out of a creative process involving teacher and pupils working together toward a common objective. The immediate didactic goals which it has helped to reach are readily apparent. Equally important, though less easily noticed, are the effects which this undertaking may have on the thinking, feelings, and future acts of the students. The teacher is satisfied with that. Once the dramatization has been enacted in its entirety, no further effort is usually made to polish it, to write it down, to present it before an audience as a finished production.

Since the dramatization is a free improvisation, it is to be expected that each group of players will do it differently. The plot development and dialogue will differ, often radically, with each group dealing with the same subject or even with the same basic story. The Headline Parade dramatization stimulated by the news of the opening of the play *The Wall* must therefore be seen in this light. It is offered here by way of example of what might be achieved with an older elementary school or junior high school class that has had previous experience with dramatization and is under the guidance of an experienced teacher. Younger classes or those with little experience will, of course, achieve much less in the final result—although probably just as much as the others during the process of creation. Here then is the dramatization:

BEHIND THE GHETTO WALL

THE DRAMATIZATION

MUSIC *(We hear the singing of the opening section of "Ani Ma'amin." After a few lines the singing grows softer until we hear it only as a background to the dialogue.)*

VOICE: Headline Parade!

ANNOUNCER: Today's headlines are tomorrow's history!

MUSIC *(Bring up the volume of the music for one line, then fade and continue as background.)*

ANNOUNCER: The students of class . . . . present Headline Parade, a dramatized review of Jewish current news and life. Today's presentation—"Behind the Ghetto Wall."

MUSIC *(Up strong to a finish)*

VOICE: New York City—The play *The Wall,* a dramatization by Millard Lampell of the famous book by John Hersey opened here to very good notices by the Broadway critics. The play, like the book upon which it is based, deals with the life of the Jews in the Warsaw Ghetto and their revolt against the Nazis in World War II.

MUSIC *(One half of the class sings softly "Ani Ma'amin," while the other half of the class recites in unison the English translation of the song.)*

CLASS:

I believe with perfect faith
In the coming of the Messiah.
And though he tarries
I shall await him daily
And believe in his coming.

NARRATOR: *Ani Ma'amin*—with this song on their lips millions of Jews died at the hands of the Nazis. With this song to give them courage, the Jews of Warsaw fought and died behind the Ghetto walls. Their heroism is remembered in this new play, *The Wall.* Today, we too remember the heroism of the Jewish children behind the Ghetto wall—we remember particularly Jacob and Miriam. It is September, 1939. Jacob is only eight years old and Miriam is ten. They are seated on the stoop of the apartment house in Warsaw where they live.

JACOB: Miriam . . .

MIRIAM: Yes, Jacob?

JACOB: Why didn't you write to me all summer?

MIRIAM: I don't know. I was busy, I guess.

JACOB: What did you do in the country?

MIRIAM: Lots of things. I went swimming and berry picking and for walks in the woods. And you Jacob?

JACOB: I stayed in Warsaw.
MIRIAM: I know. But what did you do?
JACOB: I went to *Heder.* We don't get a vacation in *Heder* like you do in the Polish school. I began to study *Gemarah* last month.
MIRIAM: That's nice. I'm so glad.
JACOB: Are you?
MIRIAM: Sure. *(Slight pause)* Jacob . . .
JACOB: Huh?
MIRIAM: What's *Gemarah?*
JACOB: Don't you know? It's the laws and other things that the Sages made up, explaining the Bible.
MIRIAM: Is it hard?
JACOB: Sure. It's not even in Hebrew. The *Gemarah* is mostly in Aramaic. That's a very hard language.
MIRIAM: Is it harder than French? I study French in school.
JACOB: It's much harder than French.
MIRIAM: How do you know? You never studied French. How do you know it's harder?
JACOB: Because only big boys study *Gemarah* and anybody can study French—even girls.
MIRIAM: Smarty!
JACOB: Well it's true. *(Pause)* Miriam . . .
MIRIAM: Yes?
JACOB: They say there's going to be a war.
MIRIAM: I know.
JACOB: They say Hitler will come to Warsaw if a war starts.
MIRIAM: No he won't. The Polish army is strong. They won't let the Nazis march into Poland.
JACOB: What'll we do if . . . ?
MIRIAM: If what?
JACOB: If Hitler comes to Warsaw . . . I mean . . . we Jews . . . what'll we do?
MIRIAM: I told you, the Nazis won't come to Warsaw. They can't.
JACOB: My father went to buy leather this morning at the Polish tannery. He got into an argument about the price with the Polish salesman and he said to my father, "Just you wait! Next month Hitler's armies will come to Warsaw. Then he'll kill all the Jews." Will he, Miriam?
MIRIAM: Of course not.
JACOB: But the salesman said . . .
MIRIAM: So he said. What of it? My father hears this kind of talk in the hospital all the time. He doesn't pay it any mind. He says they talk that way just because they're jealous of him because he's the head doctor in Warsaw's biggest hospital.
JACOB: I'm scared, Miriam.
MIRIAM: There's nothing to be scared of. I told you. Listen Jacob. I read a new book last week. Want to hear the story?
JACOB: Sure. All summer there was nobody to tell me stories.
MIRIAM: Well, I'm back now. It's a wonderful book. It's about this knight Ivanhoe and this Jewish girl Rebecca and it all takes place, long, long ago.
JACOB: How long ago?

MIRIAM: Hundreds and hundreds of years ago, maybe a thousand years.
JACOB: That's not so long ago. The *Hanukah* story took place much before that.
MIRIAM: All right. So it did. Anyway, this Jewish merchant, Isaac of York has a very beautiful daughter by the name of Rebecca and once, when Isaac and his daughter were . . .
JACOB: Miriam! Listen!
MIRIAM: Sounds like a lot of bees.
JACOB: It's airplanes! Look! Hundreds of them!
MIRIAM: They've got Swastikas on them!
JACOB: They're Nazi planes! Hitler's coming to Warsaw, Miriam! Look over there!
MIRIAM: They're dropping bombs! All over! Come inside Jacob! Down the bomb shelter! Quick! Give me your hand! Let's run Jacob!
NARRATOR: After the planes and the bombs came the German tanks. Hitler's Panzer divisions spread out all over Poland and within a few days, Poland was in the hands of the Nazis. A year has gone by. Now it is October 1940. In Jacob's home his father, Reb Moshe the leather merchant, is talking to his wife Leah, Jacob's mother.
MOSHE: I'm not the only one, Leah.
LEAH: I know, Moshe.
MOSHE: Every Jewish merchant in Warsaw has lost his business to the Nazis. I'm no exception.
LEAH: But they promised to pay when they first took your stock of leather.
MOSHE: They promised lots of things. What can we do? We're in their hands.
LEAH: Don't I know it! I just can't understand how they can be this way. Why during the last war we were glad that Warsaw was under the Germans. They were real gentlemen, then—they paid for everything they took, they treated the Jews very nicely, they . . .
MOSHE: That was during the last war. This is a different war. These are different Germans. These are Nazis, Leah.
LEAH: But to put us in a ghetto! Why, it's almost as bad as the Middle Ages.
MOSHE: Worse. In the Middle Ages the Jews could at least earn a living. They were protected a little bit. Now—they put up a wall around us. They pushed four hundred and fifty thousand Jews behind this wall. We are not allowed to move outside the wall except to go for forced labor . . .
LEAH: Moshe . . . We're forgetting. It's time.
MOSHE: Already?
LEAH: It will be dawn soon.
MOSHE: I better go. The Nazis warned us to be at the Conscription Place before sunrise.
LEAH: Are there many at the shoe factory where you work?
MOSHE: About twelve hundred of us. We're lucky they took us for forced labor. The others—they just disappear.
LEAH: Where do they take them, Moshe?
MOSHE: Who knows? The Nazis say they take them to villages far from Warsaw where they do farm work. Who knows if that's true? They're loaded on trucks and off they go, and we never hear about them again.
LEAH: And if they refuse to go?
MOSHE: Refuse? You're joking, Leah!

LEAH: Joking? Bella refused.

MOSHE: And where's Bella today? Dead. Shot through the head by a Nazi soldier.

LEAH: She's better off.

MOSHE: No, Leah. She's not better off. We are forced to labor for the Nazis. We are kept like animals behind the ghetto wall. We never have enough to eat. But we are better off than Bella. We are alive and while we live we can hope that all this will end, that some day the wall around us will be broken down and we will be free again.

MIRIAM: *(Enters)* Reb Moshe.

MOSHE: Yes, Miriam?

MIRIAM: They're almost all at the Conscription Place. It's getting late.

MOSHE: Thank you, Miriam. Good bye, Leah *(Calls)* Good bye, Jacob.

JACOB: *(Enters)* Good bye, pappa.

LEAH: Maybe they'll give you some potatoes tonight.

MOSHE: Who knows? Good bye. *(He leaves)*

JACOB: You ready Miriam?

MIRIAM: Yes.

LEAH: You like your new school, Miriam?

MIRIAM: It's all right.

LEAH: But it's not as good as the Polish school you used to go to, is it?

MIRIAM: We're lucky to have what we've got.

LEAH: If the Nazis knew that we have this school in the Ghetto, they'd close it up, one, two, three.

JACOB: But who's going to tell them? Mamma . . .

LEAH: Yes, Jacob?

JACOB: What's for breakfast?

LEAH: Well . . . There's some bread . . . and there's half of a potato left over from last night.

JACOB: Left over?

LEAH: Well . . .

JACOB: That was your supper, Mamma.

LEAH: I wasn't hungry. Take it now. Go on. You'll be late for school.

NARRATOR: A crust of bread and half of a potato for breakfast. Forced labor. Disease. Overcrowding. But life goes on behind the Ghetto wall. Under the very noses of the Nazis the Jews have organized schools . . . theatres . . . they publish newspapers, give concerts and lectures. Meanwhile the terror grows. Hundreds are shot every day for breaking the slightest of the rules proclaimed by the Nazis, or for no reason at all. Months go by. Now disease is all over the overcrowded Ghetto. Miriam's father Dr. Joseph Balin works eighteen and twenty hours a day trying to heal the sick.

MANIA: Joseph, what good is it?

JOSEPH: I'm a doctor, Mania.

MANIA: But you have nothing to fight with. How can you heal without medicines, without anything at all?

JOSEPH: I can give them hope.

MANIA: Hope for what? To be shot the next day by a Nazi who doesn't like the way they look, or walk, or bow down?

JOSEPH: The Nazis won't last forever. A day will come when . . .

MANIA: I know, a day will come when we will be free again. I've heard that before.

JOSEPH: You must believe it, Mania.

MANIA: But if you don't get some rest, Joseph, you will not live to see that day. Please, Joseph . . .

JOSEPH: Mania, listen to me. Our neighbors have been hiding me out because I am a doctor, because I am needed to help the sick. There's only a handful of us to treat many thousands. They have provided us with food. They see to it that I am not dragged off for forced labor . . .

MANIA: You'd be better off.

JOSEPH: You don't really mean that, Mania.

MANIA: No I don't. But I am so worried about you.

MIRIAM: *(Enters)* Hello Pappa. You're home?

JOSEPH: Just for a few minutes.

MIRIAM: Mamma, did you see Jacob?

MANIA: No, Miriam. Wasn't he in school with you?

MIRIAM: He was. But when we came home he didn't find his mother and father. He ran off to look for them. *(Jacob enters)* Oh, here you are.

JACOB: Mrs. Balin, I can't find my mother or father.

MANIA: They'll be all right, Jacob.

JACOB: This morning they were ordered to come to the Recruiting Place. I went along. There were a few thousand Jews there. The Nazis told them they were taking them to work in a factory outside Warsaw. They're not back yet.

MANIA: They'll be back, Jacob. Don't worry.

JACOB: But it's so late at night. Dr. Balin, do you think that the Nazis will . . .

JOSEPH: I don't think anything will happen to them, Jacob. They're both healthy. The Nazis don't harm the healthy Jews. They need them to work in their factories.

JACOB: I'm scared, doctor.

MANIA: There's nothing to be scared of. Have you had your supper, Jacob?

MIRIAM: He didn't, Mamma.

MANIA: Here, Jacob . . . Some cooked lima beans.

JACOB: Oh, no . . .

MANIA: Come on, no nonsense now. Sit down over here and eat.

MALKAH: *(Enters, followed by Rachel)* Dr. Balin!

JOSEPH: What is it, Malkah?

MALKAH: My brother Michael is very sick, doctor.

JOSEPH: I'll come right away.

RACHEL: Have you heard about the transports, doctor?

JOSEPH: Something new, Rachel?

RACHEL: You know the people that were taken this morning to the factories outside Warsaw?

JOSEPH: Rachel! Another time!

JACOB: What about them? *(Silence)* What about them, Rachel?

RACHEL: The Nazis sent us word that they won't come back tonight. They'll keep them at the factory.

JACOB: I knew it!

MANIA: It's all right, Jacob. Nothing will happen to your parents.

RACHEL: Better he should know the truth! They ordered us to deliver thousands of new workers every morning.

JOSEPH: As long as they need us for work, we're all right.

MALKAH: But can we believe them? They also ordered that we deliver all the old people, the children and the sick. They'll be loaded on transports and . . .

JOSEPH: In heaven's name, what for?

RACHEL: They say they want to move them to villages outside Warsaw, far away.

MALKAH: That's what they say. But we have our own ways of finding out. We found out the truth, Dr. Balin.

RACHEL: They're not taking them to distant villages. They bring the transports only a few miles out of Warsaw, Dr. Balin—to Treblinka.

JOSEPH: But why should they . . . ?

RACHEL: To make good on what they promised us all along—to exterminate us—every single Jew in Warsaw.

MANIA: What will we do about it?

JOSEPH: What can we do?

MANIA: We can refuse to be led like sheep to the slaughter. We can fight for our lives.

JOSEPH: Fight? With what? We have no arms. We have no ammunition.

MANIA: We can fight them with stones, with bricks, with our bare hands . . .

JOSEPH: Mania, Mania . . . This is foolish talk.

MANIA: All right, Dr. Joseph Balin, what would you do?

JOSEPH: Wait.

MANIA: For what?

JOSEPH: For help to come from the outside—from the Poles, from the Allies . . .

MANIA: What do they care about us? What is it to them if four hundred and fifty thousand Jews of the Warsaw Ghetto live or die?

JOSEPH: Mania, please . . . You're frightening the children.

MANIA: The Nazis have done that already. Nothing can frighten them any more.

NARRATOR: Mania, Dr. Balin's wife, saw what was coming. Every day the transports rolled out of Warsaw, loaded with Jews. The Jews never came back. Treblinka with its gas chambers, with its crematoriums was the last stop. The Jews that remained behind the Ghetto wall tried to continue their lives somehow—They still had their schools, but now there were fewer and fewer pupils. They continued to give plays—but the audiences kept growing smaller. Their newspapers now had much fewer readers. In October 1940 there were 450 thousand Jews in the ghetto. Now it was Spring, 1943.

MANIA: Well, Dr. Balin? Your work is getting easier. Not as many patients as you used to have, eh doctor?

JOSEPH: Please, Mania, don't talk this way.

MANIA: Why not? How many Jews are left now in Warsaw? Less than 40 thousand. What happened to the other four hundred and ten thousand? What happened to my grandfather, to your aunts and uncles, to their children?

JOSEPH: Mania, please . . . The Allies are defeating the Germans on every front. Before long they'll . . .

MANIA: Before long we will all be dead.

JOSEPH: Mania, please. Tonight is Passover. Let's try to make of it a happy holiday—for the children's sake.

MANIA: All right, Joseph. I'll try.

JOSEPH: The committees have been hoarding flour for months. There is enough now for Matzos—every family got one Matzo for the Seder. *(He holds out Matzo)* Look!

JACOB: *(Enters with Miriam)* Hello, Dr. Balin—Mrs. Balin.

MIRIAM: Hello.

JOSEPH: Ready for the Seder, children?

MIRIAM: Look pappa! They gave it to us in school. Bitter herbs!

MANIA: That's one thing we have enough of—bitterness.

JOSEPH: You know the questions, Miriam?

MIRIAM: Perfectly. *(She begins to chant) Mah nishtanoh halayloh hazeh mikol haleylos?* Why is this night different from all other nights?
(She is interrupted by a sound of shooting)
What's that?

MANIA: Shooting. Jews are dying again. They always do. Why should this night be different?

RACHEL: *(Enters)* Dr. Balin! Dr. Balin!

JOSEPH: What's wrong, Rachel?

RACHEL: Wrong, doctor? Everything is right at last. We are fighting the Nazis at last.

JOSEPH: Fighting the . . . ? Who's fighting?

RACHEL: The Jews of Warsaw—all of us—you doctor, your wife Mania . . . It has started. The Jews of the Warsaw Ghetto are celebrating Passover tonight, doctor! We're celebrating our festival of freedom by fighting for our freedom . . .

JOSEPH: How can we? We have no arms . . .

RACHEL: We have a few guns . . . We have some home-made bombs. Maybe the Poles from outside the wall will help us. Mania—you've been assigned to bunker number five. Doctor, you'll be needed right away—urgently. Come.

JOSEPH: What about the children?

MANIA: You stay here, children. If it gets very bad, hide in the cellar.

MIRIAM: We're not hiding, Mamma.

JACOB: We're not hiding, Mrs. Balin. We will fight too.

MANIA: But children . . .

JOSEPH: The children are right, Mania. It is their fight too.

RACHEL: We can use everybody. Jacob can be a messenger to go from bunker to bunker with orders. Miriam—you speak Polish well, don't you?

MIRIAM: You will never tell me from a Polish girl.

RACHEL: That's what I told Tsivyah.

JOSEPH: Tsivyah?

RACHEL: One of our commanders.

JOSEPH: A girl?

RACHEL: Yes, doctor. When the Nazis kill us they treat us all alike. When we fight them at last, we're all alike too. Tsivyah has a special task for you, Miriam.

MIRIAM: All right.

RACHEL: You will go through an underground tunnel and get outside the wall.

MANIA: That's very dangerous. The Nazis will catch her.

RACHEL: We hope they won't. If Miriam succeeds, our revolt may succeed also.

MIRIAM: What do I do?

RACHEL: You will get outside the wall. You will go to the leader of the Polish Underground. You will tell him that the Jews of the Ghetto have revolted against the Nazis. That we beg them to join our fight now. If we strike against the Germans inside and outside we may win our fight.

MIRIAM: Will they believe me?

RACHEL: We will give you a password. They'll believe.

JOSEPH: Will they join our fight?

RACHEL: We hope so. If they refuse, ask them to send us at least arms and ammunition.

MANIA: Miriam . . .

MIRIAM: Yes, Mamma?

MANIA: It's very dangerous.

MIRIAM: I know, Mamma.

MANIA: She doesn't have to go, Rachel, if she doesn't want to, does she?

RACHEL: She doesn't *have* to go. This is an assignment for a volunteer.

MANIA: You hear that, Miriam?

MIRIAM: I want to go, Mamma. I'm a Jew too, Mamma.

MANIA: I'm glad, Miriam. I'm glad my daughter knows how to be a proud Jew. You'll be careful, Miriam?

MIRIAM: I'll be careful, Mamma.

RACHEL: Come. It's time.

NARRATOR: Miriam went out to the world of clean streets and gardens and bright shops that was Polish Warsaw outside the Ghetto wall. Inside the Ghetto the Jews fought desperately against the Nazis. They attacked armored tanks with bare hands. They destroyed the tanks and died fighting, with joy in their hearts that their death served some purpose . . . Every night Rachel and Isaac, another ghetto fighter, waited in the shadows near the wall, waited for Miriam to come back.

ISAAC: Do you think she'll come tonight, Rachel?

RACHEL: She's been gone five days, Isaac.

ISAAC: There has been no sign that the Poles will join our fight.

RACHEL: We can't tell. When Miriam returns . . .

ISAAC: If she returns.

RACHEL: She's a smart girl. She knows how to take care of herself.

JACOB: *(Whispers)* Pstt. . . . Rachel . . .

RACHEL: Here we are, Jacob.

JACOB: You'd better get back to the bunker—both of you.

ISAAC: What happened?

JACOB: The Nazis are coming into the ghetto with a whole batch of tanks. Every fighter is needed. Tsivyah sent for you.

RACHEL: What about Miriam?

JACOB: I'll wait for her.

ISAAC: All right. Let's go, Rachel.

JACOB: *(Remains alone. Starts to whistle the melody of "Ani Ma'amin")*

MIRIAM: *(Enters quietly, calls softly)* Jacob . . .

JACOB: Miriam! How did you get through?

MIRIAM: The sewer pipe.
JACOB: What did they say?
MIRIAM: The Poles? They said we were very brave—but foolish.
JACOB: What do you mean?
MIRIAM: They don't think we should fight the Nazis now. It's too soon, they say.
JACOB: Too soon? We waited while more than four hundred thousand Jews from the Warsaw Ghetto were killed.
MIRIAM: I told them that. They said we must wait.
JACOB: For what? Until the last Jew in the Ghetto is dead?
MIRIAM: I asked them that. Yes, they said—if necessary.
JACOB: Did you tell them what Tsivyah said, what all of us say, that we won't let ourselves be slaughtered any longer without putting up a fight, that we are not sheep or cattle?
MIRIAM: I told them.
JACOB: And still . . . ?
MIRIAM: They smiled. They were polite. They fed me well. They understood how we feel, they said.
JACOB: But they won't join our fight.
MIRIAM: No. They won't fight with us against the Nazis.
JACOB: Will they give us arms?
MIRIAM: They said they must save their arms for later.
JACOB: For later? Isn't it later now?
MIRIAM: They gave me six pistols.
JACOB: That's all?
MIRIAM: That's all.
JACOB: Well . . . Let's go then. Even six pistols . . . The Germans are coming in tonight with lots of tanks. Our fighters will make good use of the six pistols.
NARRATOR: For forty-two days the uneven fight in the Ghetto went on—human flesh and blood against armored tanks. Men and women and children, weak from hunger and disease, against the best of Germany's trained soldiers. Every Ghetto fighter that died, sold his life dearly. The Germans had to destroy every house, every bunker, until the Warsaw Ghetto was one great mass of ruins. Now, after forty-two days, the revolt was over. Some of the fighters were captured, some escaped through the sewers. Most of the forty thousand were dead. While the Nazis were blowing up the last remaining houses, Dr. Joseph Balin met with Jacob and Miriam among the ruins.
JOSEPH: You know the way Miriam.
MIRIAM: I know the way, Pappa.
JOSEPH: You'll keep an eye on her, Jacob?
JACOB: Of course, doctor.
JOSEPH: When you get to the other side, go to the address I told you. Dr. Kowalski was one of my students. He will hide you. After the war, you must try to get to Palestine.
MIRIAM: Must we go, Pappa?
JOSEPH: You must. Mamma is dead. All the others are dead. Some one must remain to carry on the life of the Balins.
MIRIAM: But you're staying.
JOSEPH: Please, Miriam. You must get to Palestine. You and Jacob will help build

a homeland there where Jews will never again be slaughtered and shot, gassed and burned just because they are Jews. And you have a duty—both of you.

JACOB: A duty, doctor?

JOSEPH: Yes, a duty, to live, to get out, to tell the world all that happened here, all that happened behind the wall of the Warsaw Ghetto. Let the world hear and know and be ashamed and never let this happen again.

JACOB: I see what you mean, doctor.

JOSEPH: Then go, quickly. I too must go now.

MIRIAM: Where to, Pappa?

JOSEPH: Where the Nazi soldiers are blowing up our last bunker. I still have three bullets left.

MIRIAM: Come with us.

JOSEPH: I'd be caught before I was three steps outside the wall. They'd recognize me for a Jew.

MIRIAM: Try, Pappa.

JOSEPH: It's no use Miriam. It wouldn't work. Besides, Mamma is here. I want to stay where she died. Good bye, children. *(He leaves).*

MIRIAM: Pappa! *(Softly)* Good bye, Pappa.

JACOB: Come, Miriam, you lead the way.

MIRIAM: All right, Jacob.

JACOB: He wanted us to tell the world.

MIRIAM: We'll tell the world.

JACOB: Miriam. . . .

MIRIAM: Yes?

JACOB: Remember how you used to tell me stories—before the war?

MIRIAM: I remember.

JACOB: Do you think that someday, long after this war is over another Miriam will tell another Jacob the story of what happened here, behind the Warsaw Ghetto Wall?

MIRIAM: They'd better tell it and keep on telling it and telling it. They must remember Rachel and Malkah and Isaac and your father and mother and my Mamma and Pappa. They must remember them!

NARRATOR: We must remember them! That's the only way we can make sure that the ghettos and the gas chambers will not be built again. We must keep on telling their story and remember them!

MUSIC: *(Half the class sings a few lines of "Ani Ma'amin," while the other half recites in unison)*

CLASS:

I believe with perfect faith
In the coming of the Messiah.
And though he tarries,
I shall await him daily
And believe in his coming.

VOICE: The Headline Parade passes by!

ANNOUNCER: You have been listening to Headline Parade, a dramatization of the highlights of Jewish current news and life. Today you heard the story of "Behind the Ghetto Wall." The headlines of today are the history of tomorrow!

If the dramatization is used for teaching purposes only, the teacher proceeds directly to the next step—evaluating the dramatization and generalizing—as soon as the entire dramatization has been enacted as a complete unit. The dramatization itself has served its purpose. The only continued existence it has is in the pupils' memories and in their storehouse of experience.

At times the teacher and the class may want to present their *Headline Parade* dramatization before another class or as part of an assembly program for the entire school. In that event, more polishing of the enactment will be necessary.

For the audience, the process of creation is of no importance. For them only the final product, the presentation itself, has interest and meaning. The teacher may prefer that the script be presented orally, as an improvised dramatization. In that event, several rehearsals, repeating the entire script, will be necessary so that the role players are fluent enough to present a smoothly flowing dramatization.

At times the teacher may find it more advisable to have the final script written down. A committee of students is selected to write the script outside of class. It is then read aloud to the class. The pupils make suggestions for corrections. The final version is written or typed in enough copies to make one available for each participating student. The dramatization is then presented as a simulated radio broadcast—the participants reading their lines from the script. This procedure has advantages in that it eliminates a number of rehearsals and gives assurance that there will not be embarrassing halts during the presentation. Even so, one rehearsal is needed with the final version of the script so that the role players will read their lines smoothly and effectively.

As indicated earlier, the teacher may decide that the time can not be spared to develop a *Headline Parade* script by means of pupil improvisation during class sessions. In that event the class, in the course of discussion, develops the story and treatment in its general outlines. Thereafter the actual script is written outside of class by a committee or one able student. If this course is followed, the teacher looks over the finished product and makes suggestions for improvements and revisions where necessary. Thereafter copies are made of the final script. The procedure which follows is exactly the same as that which will be indicated later for utilizing a published *Headline Parade* script—copies are distributed in class, roles are assigned, students read their parts from script, etc.

7. Evaluating the Material and Generalizing

As usual the teacher begins with words of praise for the pupils and then proceeds to stimulate a discussion about the *content* of the dramatization. In our current example, the discussion would deal with the justification of Dr. Balin in demanding that the children save themselves, the compelling reason for the revolt despite the certain knowledge of ultimate defeat, etc. Thereafter the class would explore such problems as the importance of preserving the memory of the Ghetto Revolt, the inspiration which the Warsaw fight gave to the fighters for Israeli independence, the constant need for watchfulness against the rise of new tyrants, etc.

8. Relating to Pupil Experiences

Whenever possible the teacher tries to help the students to see a relationship between the news, its dramatization and their own lives. In our current dramatization, some of the pupils may have had first hand experiences, their relatives may have been involved, etc. They are encouraged to share reminiscences with the class. Following this they are helped to see democracy as a bulwark against a repetition of such horror, the role of the State of Israel as the home for the unwanted and oppressed, etc. Through discussion they are guided to see what role they can play in the preservation of democracy, the building of the State of Israel, the prevention of a recurrence of such horrors, etc.

Sometimes a follow-up activity is possible. Here, the pupils may decide to plant trees in Israel in memory of those who died behind the ghetto wall; issue a memorial magazine of poems, stories, and articles about the ghetto fighters; set up an exhibit of objects connected with the vanished world of Jewish Eastern Europe, etc.

The Published Headline Parade Dramatization

Generally speaking, it is greatly to be preferred that the class create its own Headline Parade dramatization. However on occasion, the published Headline Parade script might be utilized to good advantage, particularly when the pressures of the time schedule do not permit the development of an original story and dramatization in connection with an important news event.

The published Headline Parade dramatization of current history was originally conceived as a classroom aid. More than forty such dramatizations were written by this author and published by the Jewish Education Committee of New York since 1945. New Headline Parade dramatizations are published from time to time. The teacher might find it worthwhile to keep informed about their intermittent appearance.

Even when not used in the class as a teaching tool, they have their use as a reference source in which the material is presented in an organized fashion.

Although Headline Parade scripts have been widely used in the assembly, they are specifically designed for use as a classroom teaching tool. When the published Headline Parade script is used for this purpose, the teacher is careful not to succumb to the temptation of making of it a "production piece." No attempt is made at memorizing parts or staging action and movements.

The teacher introduces the subject in a few words, referring to the news item which is the theme of the dramatization. Copies of the script are then distributed to all the students in the class. Students are assigned to assume the different roles. The script is then read aloud. From time to time parts are changed off during the reading so as to give as many pupils as possible an opportunity to assume roles in the dramatization. Interruptions are avoided although the teacher may occasionally stop the reading when absolutely necessary for a *brief* clarification of an obscure point. After the reading of the script a discussion serves to fill in any information which may still be needed for a clear understanding of the news, to evaluate the news, and to allow the students opportunities to express points of view in connection with controversial problems. Usual classroom techniques such as research, reports, scrap books, etc. may be used to supplement the dramatization.

Often it is desirable to heighten the dramatic impact of the news in order to achieve a stronger emotional involvement by the pupils. In that event the Headline Parade script is presented in the form of a simulated radio broadcast. After the usual introduction the teacher proposes the presentation of the Headline Parade script.

Students are selected for the roles. They are then given copies of the script to read over at home so as to become familiar with it. They are advised to read their parts aloud several times. In this manner they will be sufficiently familiar with the lines to read them smoothly, with understanding and with some degree of interpretation. Several days later the script is enacted before the class. The front of the room is the "Radio Studio." The role-players read their lines aloud from the script. One of the students serves as "sound technician" playing the indicated incidental music on a portable phonograph. The music may of course be omitted altogether if necessary. The usual discussion follows the presentation.

Following are examples of several published Headline Parade dramatizations:

YOUTH ALIYAH

The News

In 1954 there appeared the following news item: "World Jewish Child's Day to mark the twentieth anniversary of Youth Aliyah." The article then went on to tell how many young people were saved by Youth Aliyah, from what countries they came, how they were integrated into Israeli life, etc.

This news item seemed important enough to warrant the more difficult and complex Headline Parade treatment. Given in its bare outlines, as part of a newscast, the student would learn that this is an anniversary of a rescue organization which saved many young people and integrated them into Israeli life. However, if dramatized in personal terms, the great role which Youth Aliyah has played in current Jewish life would receive its proper emotional emphasis. Furthermore, by means of a Headline Parade dramatization, the details of Youth Aliyah—its origins, its plan of operation, its effect on children's lives—could be brought out clearly and naturally. Thus the students would learn and assimilate the news as an important segment of Jewish life and not merely as an isolated news event.

Another factor which gave this item added importance was the fact that anniversaries come again and again. In 1954 it was the twentieth anniversary. In 1959 it would be the twenty-fifth, and so on. At each anniversary, the figures might change somewhat but the basic facts would remain the same; the memory of the dramatization would give rise to a clear image in the minds of the students whenever they would once again hear a reference to Youth Aliyah.

The Dramatization

The Headline Parade dramatization* tells the story of Hasdai, a Youth Aliyah child who runs away from the discipline of his Youth Aliyah village. While in the forest, he meets two of the first Youth Aliyah graduates. In trying to make Hasdai see the value of his Youth Aliyah training, they bring out for him—and for the

* "Fifteen Minutes in the Forest" by Samuel J. Citron, Copyright February, 1954 by the Jewish Education Committee of New York.

students who are doing or witnessing the dramatization—the whole story of Youth Aliyah.

The following is the script:

MUSIC *(A few measures of "Anu Ni'yeh Ha-ri-sho-nim," played forte. Music is then faded down and played softly as background.)*

VOICE: Headline Parade!

ANNOUNCER: Today's headlines are tomorrow's history!

MUSIC *(Bring up the volume of the music for a few measures, then fade and continue playing softly as background.)*

ANNOUNCER: The students of Class ______ (*or,* the members of the Dramatic Group) of ______ School present Headline Parade, a dramatized review of Jewish current news, written by Samuel J. Citron.

MUSIC *(Up strong to a finish)*

VOICE: * World Jewish Child's Day will be celebrated in America this year on April 4th. The celebration will take on added meaning since 1954 marks the 20th Anniversary of Youth Aliyah.

NARRATOR: Twenty years and sixty four thousand lives! Sixty four thousand children saved from Hitler's gas chambers, from Iraqui pogroms, from North African slums! Sixty four thousand children cared for, trained, and educated by Youth Aliyah! Sixty four thousand boys and girls growing up, healthy and strong, joining the ranks of the *Halutzim,* the pioneers, bringing life to the Land of Israel, bringing strength to the people of Israel.

VOICE: This is the story of two of these boys and a girl, of Hasdai and Hannah and Yaacov and fifteen minutes in the forest which bridged the space of twenty years.

MUSIC *(Play softly as background.)*

YAACOV: The years do fly don't they?
It hardly seems so long ago.
I was fifteen then and Hasdai wasn't even born.

MUSIC *(Bring up the volume of the music for a few measures, then fade and continue playing softly as background.)*

YAACOV: I walked with Hannah through the forest and my mind kept wandering back these 20 years . . . There were 43 of us on the SS Martha when she docked at Haifa that February 19, 1934 . . . We were the first—the first youth immigration group, the first of the Youth Aliyah to arrive from Germany. . . .

MUSIC *(Bring up the volume of the music for a few measures then fade and continue playing softly as background.)*

YAACOV: The images of the past crowded in as Hannah and I walked between the even rows of trees in the forest . . . What did they call us then? "Brands plucked out of the fire!" Only that day I didn't feel much like a firebrand. I sang with the others to keep from crying . . . I was too old to cry . . . but mother was in Germany and I was alone. . . .

MUSIC *(Bring up the volume of the music for a few measures then fade and continue playing softly as background.)*

YAACOV: The sun shone through the leaves and dappled the forest floor with patches of gold. My memories kept going back, back for 20 years . . . They who waited on the dock called out their greetings. We acknowledged their greetings with

* Make date and figures current.

song and I sang with the rest, louder than the rest . . . louder . . . for I was too old to cry for my mother . . .

MUSIC *(Out)*

YAACOV: The crack of breaking wood suddenly wiped out this long ago remembrance. It brought me up short, startled . . . then angry . . .

MUSIC *(Two chords)*

YAACOV: Hey there! Stop that!

Can you imagine it? Here we were nursing along every tree in the forest like a baby. . . .

Hey there! What do you think you're doing?

HASDAI: Nothing.

YAACOV: What do you mean, "nothing"? You're breaking branches from that tree!

HASDAI: What's it to you?

YAACOV: Well, I like that! Here! You stop that!

HASDAI: Why don't you mind your own business?

YAACOV: Stop it, I tell you!

HASDAI: You let go of me! Let go of me!

HANNAH: Let him be, Yaacov!

YAACOV: He's destroying that tree, Hannah.

HANNAH: Easy, Yaacov . . . What's your name, boy?

HASDAI: Hasdai.

HANNAH: You mustn't break branches from a living tree, Hasdai.

HASDAI: I was only breaking off one branch—for a walking staff.

HANNAH: Even so. It hurts the tree.

HASDAI: Hurts?

HANNAH: Yes, Hasdai. Hurts. A tree is a living thing. When you break off its branches, you destroy its life. In time it withers and dies. You understand, Hasdai?

HASDAI: Yes, *G'veret.*

HANNAH: Hannah.

HASDAI: Hannah . . . I'm sorry, Hannah, I didn't know . . .

YAACOV: Hannah had a way with children, even with tough kids. Hasdai looked to be plenty tough.

HANNAH: Are you going on a trip, Hasdai?

HASDAI: Why?

HANNAH: I was just wondering . . . You need a walking staff. You're from Eddie Cantor Children's Village, aren't you?

HASDAI: Huh?

HANNAH: Aren't you?

HASDAI: What's it to you?

HANNAH: I like to know where my friends come from. Yaacov and I come from Maaleh Ha-hami-shah—you know—the *Kibbutz* right nearby. You are from the Youth Aliyah Village, aren't you?

HASDAI: Yes.

YAACOV: See . . . ? I told you Hannah had a way with kids!

HANNAH: Why are you running away?

HASDAI: Who said I was running away?

HANNAH: Don't you like it at the Village?

HASDAI: It's all right.
HANNAH: Don't you like the food, or going to school?
HASDAI: The food's all right. I like school.
HANNAH: Do the other children bother you?
HASDAI: I get along.
HANNAH: But you're running away. Why?
HASDAI: I'm no *fellah*, that's why! They can't make me work the ground like a *fellah*. Farming is for Arab peasants, for *fellahin!*
HANNAH: So you're running away . . .
HASDAI: Yes.
HANNAH: I see . . .
YAACOV: We were in a hurry and this needed time. But this was important. Hannah sat down on the flat rock at the base of the tree whose broken branch hung down limply. She indicated a place beside her.
HANNAH: Come here, Hasdai. Sit down here. Now, tell me, do I look like an Arab peasant woman?
HASDAI: O no, *G'veret!*
HANNAH: Hannah. . . .
HASDAI: O no, Hannah!
HANNAH: How about Yaacov here? He's my husband. Does he look like a *fellah*, like an Arab peasant?
HASDAI: No, Hannah.
HANNAH: Yet we work on the land, both of us.
HASDAI: Both of you . . .
HANNAH: Yes, Hasdai. We're farmers, Yaacov and I.
HASDAI: In Morocco where I come from, only the *fellahin*. . . .
HANNAH: That was in Morocco. This is Israel, Hasdai . . . Where were you going with your walking staff?
HASDAI: Back home.
HANNAH: To Morocco?
HASDAI: You're making fun of me.
HANNAH: I'm sorry, Hasdai. I didn't mean to. Where is home?
HASDAI: Hartuv.
HANNAH: The *Ma'abarah?*
HASDAI: Yes.
HANNAH: The tin huts, the mud, the filth? Hasdai!
HASDAI: My mother is there . . . my older brothers. . . .
YAACOV: What could one say to that?

The *Ma'abarot* are only temporary camps to which new immigrants are sent until more decent homes could be provided for them. Rows and rows of tin huts and tents stretching along unpaved streets . . . filthy . . . overcrowded . . . To Hasdai the *Ma'abarah* was home. His mother was there. . . .

HANNAH: And your father?
HASDAI: My father is dead.
HANNAH: I'm sorry.
HASDAI: He was killed when the mob attacked the Jewish quarter . . . two years ago . . . in Morocco. . . .
HANNAH: What does your mother do?

HASDAI: Nothing. She's waiting.
HANNAH: And your brothers?
HASDAI: They're waiting too.
HANNAH: For what?
HASDAI: I don't know. Until the government gives them something to do, I suppose. The government man promised. I really don't know.
HANNAH: And what will you do if you go back? You'll also wait?
HASDAI: I suppose so.
HANNAH: Yaacov. . . .
YAACOV: Yes, Hannah?
HANNAH: Tell him, Yaacov . . . Tell him about this tree whose branch he was breaking. Tell him about this forest. Tell him about farming. Tell him about us.
YAACOV: Why, Hannah?
HANNAH: Hasdai is today and we are of yesterday. Yesterday must teach today and you were with the first. Tell him, Yaacov.
YAACOV: I leaned against the tall cypress and I told of long ago, back in 1933 when I was 14 and Recha Freier, the great woman who first thought of saving the young, came to my mother in Berlin.
FREIER: Frau Levin, your son, Yaacov asked me to speak to you.
LEVIN: About what, Frau Freier?
FREIER: He wants to join the group of boys and girls that is being trained for emigration to Palestine.
LEVIN: I told him my answer already. Definitely no.
FREIER: But why, Frau Levin?
LEVIN: Why? Because this is his home.
FREIER: The Germans don't seem to think so.
LEVIN: The Nazis are not Germany.
FREIER: No? Yet they threw your husband out of the hospital which he organized.
LEVIN: If we could all leave Germany together, it would be different. We could come back in a year or two, when things changed.
FREIER: Can you leave?
LEVIN: Of course not. The Nazis would strip us of everything we owned before they would permit us to leave Germany.
FREIER: At least you would be alive.
LEVIN: You're exaggerating, Frau Freier.
FREIER: I sincerely hope so. Many of us don't think so at all. We see Hitler fanning the flames of hate against the Jews. Before long we will be caught up in the flames. He will destroy us all. We must at least pluck some brands out of the fire. We must at least save some of our young!
LEVIN: But why to Palestine?
FREIER: Because that is the only place they will truly be able to call home.
LEVIN: What will they do there?
FREIER: Grow! Study!
LEVIN: Study for what?
FREIER: To be farmers, mainly.
LEVIN: Yaacov a farmer? Whatever are you talking about?
FREIER: Why not?

LEVIN: Yaacov was going to be a doctor.

FREIER: Was, Frau Levin. Isn't that so?

LEVIN: Well. . . .

FREIER: But they threw him out of school, long, long before he could even begin his medical studies, just as they threw your husband out of the hospital to which he gave the best years of his life. Isn't that so, Frau Levin?

LEVIN: Yes, Frau Freier.

FREIER: Germany does not want Jewish doctors. Germany does not want Jews at all. Palestine needs young men and women who will bring life to its neglected soil, who will build homes for themselves and the hundreds of thousands of Jews returning home, who will come after them.

LEVIN: My Yaacov knows nothing about farming.

FREIER: We will teach him. We are forming our first group of young people now. Will you let Yaacov join?

LEVIN: I don't know. . . . Palestine is so far. . . .

FREIER: Far enough to be safe from the Nazis. Will you let Yaacov join?

LEVIN: He's only fourteen. Who will take care of him?

FREIER: The Zionist groups abroad have formed a special organization for the care and training of our young people. Youth Aliyah they call it. Will you let Yaacov . . . ?

LEVIN: Another organization . . . I don't know . . . He's my only child. . . .

FREIER: Henrietta Szold will be with Youth Aliyah.

LEVIN: Henrietta Szold of Hadassah?

FREIER: Yes. She will direct Youth Aliyah in Palestine. Will you let Yaacov join?

LEVIN: He's all I have. No organization could . . . But to entrust him to Henrietta Szold . . . Let Yaacov join your group.

MUSIC *(A few measures played as a bridge)*

HASDAI: That was long ago?

YAACOV: Before you were born, Hasdai. More than twenty years ago.

HASDAI: You liked farming?

YAACOV: Not at first. I wasn't used to handling a spade and a hoe. My hands blistered and my back ached all the time. The months passed and my hands calloused and the backache was gone and work became joy.

HASDAI: Joy?

YAACOV: Yes.

HASDAI: Digging?

YAACOV: And planting and watching things sprout and grow . . . Then we were ready. Then there were the good byes. By now conditions had gotten much worse for the Jews in Germany. Now Mother was happy that I would be given a chance in Palestine. She gave me along a two years' supply of clothes and I promised to write every day. There were the tears and embraces. There was the long journey on the ship and the docking at Haifa . . .

HASDAI: Our ship docked at Haifa also. Six months ago. When did you come?

YAACOV: February 19, 1934.

HASDAI: Twenty years!

YAACOV: Yes, Hasdai. Twenty years. We were the first to come.

HASDAI: With Youth Aliyah—the same as in Eddie Cantor Village?

YAACOV: Yes. Only then we were very few—forty-three boys and girls.

HASDAI: Were you happy to get there?
YAACOV: Happy? We sang the songs of Zion as the ship pulled in to the dock. We tried to sing away the loneliness, the homesickness, the fear of this strange life that was to come. We sang and tried to hold back the tears . . .
HASDAI: I know.
YAACOV: Sure. I walked down the gangplank at last. I walked right up to a little lady in black who waited for us, for each one of us . . . embracing me . . .
SZOLD: Welcome home, Yaacov.
YAACOV: Thank you.
SZOLD: The trucks will be here in a few minutes to bring you to your new home. In the meantime you'd better go inside the shed. You'll catch cold.
YAACOV: Will I be able to be together with my friends?
SZOLD: Of course. Now go inside. Your lips are blue.
YAACOV: You sound just like my mother.
SZOLD: Do I?
YAACOV: She always worried I'd catch cold when my lips changed color.
SZOLD: Well, now . . . remarkable, isn't it?
YAACOV: I suppose all mothers are the same.
SZOLD: I suppose so.
YAACOV: I used to be annoyed when mother worried about me.
SZOLD: Were you now?
YAACOV: I was younger then. I didn't know. I'm fifteen now.
SZOLD: Now you know . . .
YAACOV: Now I know.
SZOLD: You miss your mother, don't you?
YAACOV: Very much.
SZOLD: You'll go to a settlement. You'll live with *Madrihim,* your counsellors who will teach you and guide you. You'll learn and work and grow. You'll make a place for yourself and in time maybe you'll send for your parents . . .
YAACOV: You think so?
SZOLD: I hope so . . . You'd better go inside now. There's stationery on the desk. You might write your mother that you arrived safely. Go on now . . .
YAACOV: I bet your grandchildren think a lot of. . . .
SZOLD: I never married, Yaacov.
YAACOV: I'm so sorry.
SZOLD: Sorry? Look! Forty three of my children just came home to me. You, Yaacov and all the rest of you of Youth Aliyah—all of you are dear to me as if you were my very own.
YAACOV: You're very sweet . . . Thank you Miss . . .
SZOLD: Szold. Henrietta Szold.
MUSIC *(A few measures played as a bridge)*
YAACOV: We saw her often after that day. She wanted to know how we got along in our studies. She asked about our families in the old country. She helped us plan for our lives in this new land.
HASDAI: I heard about Henrietta Szold. They told us about her in our history class.
YAACOV: They'll be telling about her in history classes until the end of time. She who never had children of her own became the mother of sixty-four thousand

children who were saved through Youth Aliyah. Of course that took a long time—almost twenty years.

HASDAI: Were you in Youth Aliyah too, Hannah?

HANNAH: Yes, I came with the Teheran Children in 1942.

HASDAI: Will you tell me about it?

HANNAH: Another time. Now the telling is for Yaacov.

HASDAI: Did they make you work very hard?

YAACOV: Make us? We were eager to prepare for what lay ahead. For two years we trained—four hours a day for study, four hours a day for work on the farm. The evenings were spent in reading, choral singing, dramatics and other activities . . .

HASDAI: Sounds nice.

YAACOV: It was nice.

HASDAI: And after the two years were over?

YAACOV: A group of us were given land and we established our own settlement. When Maale Ha-hamisha was established we settled here.

HASDAI: I saw Ma'aleh Ha-hamishah on my way to the children's village. It's nice.

YAACOV: It's beautiful.

HASDAI: What about your mother? Did she ever come here?

YAACOV: No, Hasdai. When I finally established a home to which I could bring her, it was too late.

HASDAI: I'm so sorry. I guess I'm lucky. My mother is in Israel. She'll be able to come live with me as soon as I establish a home for us.

HANNAH: Where, Hasdai?

HASDAI: In a *Kibbutz,* I suppose.

HANNAH: When?

HASDAI: When I finish my training in the Eddie Cantor Youth Aliyah Village.

HANNAH: Why, Hasdai! Aren't you going back to Hartuv?

HASDAI: Now what would I be doing in the *Ma'abarah?* You know, of all the things on the farm I like chickens best.

HANNAH: Do you now?

HASDAI: When I finish my training, I will see to it that we have lots of chickens on our *Kibbutz.* Maybe they'll let me take care of them.

HANNAH: Maybe . . .

HASDAI: You wait and see, our *Kibbutz* will be the finest in all Israel!

YAACOV: As nice as Ma'ale Ha-hamisha?

HASDAI: Nicer! Of course we probably won't have a nice forest like this one near our *Kibbutz.* You're lucky!

YAACOV: Lucky? No Hasdai. We planted every tree in this forest ourselves. This tall cypress, Hasdai, I planted as a young sapling. That one there, Hannah planted. We watered them and cared for them and helped them grow . . .

HASDAI: That's why you were so angry when I. . . .

YAACOV: That and because trees are living things and because this forest reminds all of us of our mothers, having been planted in memory of the mother of all of us in Youth Aliyah.

HASDAI: I didn't know . . .

YAACOV: Of course you didn't. But now you do know. This is Henrietta Szold Forest.

HASDAI: And I broke a branch from a tree here . . .

HANNAH: Never mind, Hasdai. You didn't know. In time to come you too will plant trees in forests to be named in memory of the leaders of Youth Aliyah who have passed on or in honor of those who are still with us—Hans Beit, Moshe Kol, Chanoch Reinhold, David Umanski, Bertha Schoolman . . .
HASDAI: If you don't mind.
HANNAH: Yes?
HASDAI: I'd like to go now. It's getting late.
HANNAH: Sure, Hasdai.
HASDAI: Today we're transplanting tomatoes. I want to get back in time.
YAACOV: Transplanting tomatoes? Why Hasdai, isn't that farming?
HASDAI: Sure!
YAACOV: Isn't that work for *fellahin?*
HASDAI: That's in Morocco. Here in Israel everybody has to help build the homeland.
YAACOV: Well now!
HASDAI: Well, *Shalom!* I gotta go now.
HANNAH: Do you mind if we walk along with you?
HASDAI: Are you going my way?
HANNAH: Yes, all the way. They are short of *Madrichim,* of counsellors, in the Eddie Cantor Children's Village. Yaacov and I will be *Madrichim* for a while.
HASDAI: Mine, maybe?
HANNAH: Maybe . . .
MUSIC *(Up strong to a finish)*
VOICE: The Headline Parade passes by!

The Headline Parade treatment is especially suitable for dramatizing an event involving an outstanding individual. By means of this dramatic technique it is possible not only to emphasize the immediate event but to present the biographical background of the subject. In that manner the students learn to know intimately many details about the life and character of the figure in the news. They also often learn to realize how events in the early life of the subject shaped his character and affected his actions.

This type of re-creation of biographical background is particularly useful in the case of individuals who figure in a news event that is of general interest and derives its Jewish character from the fact that the subject happens to be a Jew. Research into his background often discloses specifically Jewish influences which have a direct bearing on the subject's acts—influences which highlight Jewish values and ways of life which might profitably be brought to the attention of the pupils.

The Headline Parade script "The Fruit of the Earth" * illustrates this. The news item told how Dr. Selman Waksman was awarded the Nobel Prize for medicine for his contribution in the discovery of streptomycin. Selman Waksman is a Jew and Jews were justly proud of his contribution to the art of healing. However, his discovery for which he was honored and which was the subject of the news report was of a general nature without any specific Jewish significance. To dramatize this would add very little to the sum total of the pupils' *Jewish* knowledge or attitudes. Further search revealed many details of Dr. Waksman's early life which

* The Fruit of the Earth by Samuel J. Citron, revised edition, Copyright March, 1953 by the Jewish Education Committee of New York.

emphasized the specifically Jewish influences which impelled him to his life work. Much of this came out in reports and articles about him published in the Yiddish and Anglo-Jewish press. A personal interview with Dr. Waksman confirmed this and added further detail. The following script was the result:

THE FRUIT OF THE EARTH

MUSIC *(A few measures of "Anu- ni'yeh Ha-ri-sho-nim," played forte. Music is faded and played softly as background)*

VOICE: Headline Parade!

ANNOUNCER: Today's headlines are tomorrow's history!

MUSIC *(Bring up the volume of the music for a few measures, then fade and continue playing softly as background)*

ANNOUNCER: The students of Class ——— (*or* the members of the Dramatic Group) of ——— School, present Headline Parade, a dramatized review of Jewish current news, written by Samuel J. Citron.

MUSIC *(Up strong to a finish)*

NARRATOR: She stood with the rest of the crowd, waiting outside of Stockholm's Symphony Hall.

EVA: How much longer, Daddy?

HELLSTROM: Only a little while.

NARRATOR: With her left hand, Eva clutched the hand of her father, Swedish engineer, Bertil Hellstrom.

EVA: Will he be coming out this way?

NARRATOR: In her right hand, little Eva Hellstrom clutched a bouquet of five red carnations.

EVA: How will I know who he is?

NARRATOR: Five red carnations.

HELLSTROM: He is gray and has a mustache and wears glasses. I'll point him out to you. Now, will you remember what to say, Eva?

EVA: Yes, Daddy. I'll walk up to him.

HELLSTROM: Yes . . . ?

EVA: And hand him the flowers.

HELLSTROM: Don't forget to curtsey.

EVA: I'll curtsey and hand him the flowers.

HELLSTROM: And what will you say?

EVA: I'll say, "Here are five red carnations. . . ."

HELLSTROM: Go on . . .

EVA: "One carnation for each . . . for each . . ."

HELLSTROM: *(Prompting her)* "For each year . . ."

EVA: "For each year of my life!"

HELLSTROM: Good girl, Eva!

NARRATOR: Within the great Symphony Hall were gathered royalty and diplomats, socialites and scientists.

MUSIC *(A few measures played as a bridge, then fade and continue playing softly as background)*

NARRATOR: It was December 10th, 1952. Before that glittering crowd, King Gustaf Adolph of Sweden was awarding the Nobel prizes to the world's outstanding creative geniuses. One by one, the physicists and chemists, the writers and statesmen, were led forth to receive their awards. Now Professor A. Wallgren, one of Sweden's great medical authorities, led forth a gray-haired man and presented him to the king.

WALLGREN: Your Majesty, I have the honor to present this year's winner of the Nobel Prize for medicine, one of the greatest benefactors of humanity, the discoverer of streptomycin, Dr. Selman A. Waksman of the United States of America.

NARRATOR: Dr. Selman Waksman, the gray-haired man with mustache and glasses for whom little Eva Hellstrom was waiting with her five red carnations.

MUSIC *(Up forte for a few measures and out)*

NARRATOR: It's a far cry from Stockholm's Symphony Hall to the little town of Novaia Priluka in the Ukraine. There, Selman Waksman was born in 1888. There, like other little Jewish boys, he first learned to read the *Siddur* and at the age of five began to study the *Humash.*

REBBI: Go on, Selman, repeat, "*B'reshis*—In the beginning."

WAKSMAN: *(As five year old)* "*B'reshis*—In the beginning."

REBBI: "*Boro Elohim*—God created"

WAKSMAN: "*Boro Elohim*—God created"

REBBI: "*Es Hashomayim ve-es ho-oretz*—The heavens and the earth"

WAKSMAN: "*Es hashomayim ve-es. . . .*"

NARRATOR: He repeated the words of the Bible after his teacher.
He learned the Biblical story of the creation of the heavens
And the earth
And the planets
And the stars
And the seas
And life!
This he learned from his teacher
Like all other five year old Jewish boys in Priluka.
Unlike other Jewish boys of five, Selman wanted to know more—much more!

WAKSMAN: Grandma. . . .

GRANDMA: Yes, Zolminiu?

WAKSMAN: In *humash* today, the Rebbi said . . .

GRANDMA: Yes . . . ?

WAKSMAN: That God made a man from the earth.

GRANDMA: That's right.

WAKSMAN: And made him live.

GRANDMA: Uh hu. . . . Here, Zolminiu, hold on to these bills while I make a note on the door in chalk concerning my accounts.

WAKSMAN: Sure, Grandma. Did God make animals live also?

GRANDMA: He made the animals live.

WAKSMAN: And fish?

GRANDMA: And fish.
WAKSMAN: And bugs?
GRANDMA: And bugs.
WAKSMAN: *(Awed)* Golly. . . .
NARRATOR: Grandma Hava was a wonderful woman. She answered all of Selman's questions for which she knew the answers. Selman asked lots of questions. The older he got, the more questions he asked and the harder they were to answer.
WAKSMAN: Mamma . . .
FRADIA: Yes, Selman?
WAKSMAN: What makes people sick?
FRADIA: I suppose if they go out in the cold without an overcoat they catch cold, or something.
WAKSMAN: It isn't cold now, Mamma.
FRADIA: No. It's midsummer.
WAKSMAN: David got sick yesterday.
FRADIA: Maybe he got his feet wet, or drank cold water too fast or something. I'm sure I don't know.
NARRATOR: Now even Mamma, who was a learned woman, didn't know the answers to Selman's questions.
WAKSMAN: What makes people get sick?
What makes them well?
What makes them live?
MUSIC *(A few measures played as a bridge)*
GRANDMA: Fradia . . .
FRADIA: Yes, Mamma?
GRANDMA: Zolman is becoming too much for me.
FRADIA: Mother! I thought you liked our Zolminiu.
GRANDMA: Like him? I love him, but he's becoming too much for me. His questions are just—well—maybe you'd better send him to Odessa to study at a Gymnasium.
FRADIA: What of his Jewish studies?
GRANDMA: He's past fifteen now. He's been studying the *Torah* and the *Talmud* for more than eight years now. He knows enough to continue on his own—with some help from a rabbi or a . . .
FRADIA: The Gymnasium is expensive, Mamma.
GRANDMA: We are not poor people, Fradia. I've done well in my business. Of what good is my money if I can't help my favorite grandson learn the answers to his many questions?
NARRATOR: Selman went to Odessa. He studied with good teachers and presented himself for examinations to the Russian Gymnasium. He studied languages and sciences and mathematics. He found answers to many a question and many a new question arose in his searching mind, for, at the base of it all there was one great question . . .
WAKSMAN: Mother, I cannot stop now. I must go on to study at the university.
FRADIA: But, Selman, no Russian university will admit you.
WAKSMAN: I know that, Mother. I haven't forgotten that there is little room for Jews in Russian universities. I plan to go to Switzerland.

FRADIA: But why, Selman? You finished the eight classes at the Gymnasium. You have now a better education than most here in Priluka. Why not come into the business? You are almost twenty-two. You'll be wanting to get married soon.

WAKSMAN: Marriage will wait until I finish my studies. I tell you I must go on with my studies.

FRADIA: I suppose you have to find the answer to some more questions.

WAKSMAN: Yes, Mamma.

FRADIA: What is it this time?

WAKSMAN: The same as ever. The question that is basic to all my other questions. I want to know what makes people sick and what makes them well again. What makes the plants grow? What makes all living beings eat and breathe? In short—I want to understand the processes of life and the very nature of life itself.

FRADIA: I guess you weren't cut out to be a coppersmith like your grandfather, or a merchant like your mother. Men have been asking your questions since time began. Maybe you will be lucky enough to find some of the answers. Go to Switzerland—if you must.

NARRATOR: But Selman Waksman never did get to Switzerland. His mother soon died. Relatives from America urged him to come here. There were great universities in the New World where eligible students were admitted without regard to their religion. On his cousin's farm in New Jersey, Selman Waksman filled out his application for admission to Columbia University's College of Physicians and Surgeons.

MENDEL: Selman where were you?

WAKSMAN: At the postoffice.

MENDEL: Any word?

WAKSMAN: Not yet.

MENDEL: Well, maybe tomorrow.

WAKSMAN: I wonder.

MENDEL: Selman . . .

WAKSMAN: Yes?

MENDEL: Why don't you go over to Rutgers University?

WAKSMAN: What for?

MENDEL: There's Dr. Jacob Lipman. He's the Dean of the College of Agriculture at Rutgers.

WAKSMAN: But I don't want to study agriculture. I want to study medical sciences.

MENDEL: Still, you might talk to Dr. Lipman. What harm would there be in your talking to him while you're waiting to hear from Columbia.

WAKSMAN: I suppose it can't do any harm. I'll go over to see Dr. Lipman tomorrow.

MUSIC *(A few measures played as a bridge)*

LIPMAN: Now, tell me, Mr. Waksman, why do you want to study medicine?

WAKSMAN: Because I want to find the answer to questions which have been troubling me since my earliest childhood.

LIPMAN: Namely?

WAKSMAN: I want to study the processes of life, Dr. Lipman.

LIPMAN: Human life?

WAKSMAN: Just—life.

LIPMAN: So Mr. Waksman! Look here. I dip my hand into this flower pot. Now look here—what do you see?

WAKSMAN: A handful of soil.

LIPMAN: Is that all, Mr. Waksman?

WAKSMAN: What else?

LIPMAN: Life, Mr. Waksman. This handful of soil is teeming with life—plants, animals, living beings which your eye cannot see. Some the microscope will reveal. Others are too tiny to be seen by even the most powerful microscope.

WAKSMAN: I never knew . . .

LIPMAN: They are born, they feed, they grow and they die while giving birth to others of their kind. They feed on vegetable matter and on each other. Some, there are, that make this earth fruitful. Others, there are, who destroy it. There are enough of the processes of life going on in this handful of soil for a lifetime of study. Now, tell me, Mr. Waksman, do you really want to go to Columbia?

WAKSMAN: If you will have me as a student, Dr. Lipman, I'd like to come here, to Rutgers.

NARRATOR: Rutgers provided a scholarship to young Waksman. Rutgers provided a chance to earn twenty cents an hour to the student with the many questions. Rutgers provided teachers who inspired him to study and to search.

MUSIC *(A few measures played as a bridge)*

NARRATOR: After graduation from Rutgers he went to California for his PH.D. On August 5th, 1916 he married Deborah Mitnik, who had also come to America from Priluka, in the Ukraine. Then he returned to Rutgers, to teach and to do research.

BOBILE: Selman, I brought you your dinner.

WAKSMAN: Thanks, Bobile.

BOBILE: What's in those cartons?

WAKSMAN: Soil.

BOBILE: You're working on them?

WAKSMAN: Yes.

BOBILE: Doing what?

WAKSMAN: Look. This first one—tomatoes would grow beautifully in this soil. In the soil of the second carton, the plants would come up spindly and after a while they would die altogether.

BOBILE: Why is that, Selman?

WAKSMAN: Different microbes. In the first, the microbes feed on the vegetable matter in the soil and give off substances on which the tomato plant could feed and grow. The second doesn't have the desirable microbes.

BOBILE: And I always thought that microbes are harmful beings.

WAKSMAN: There are those that are harmful. But, for every harmful microbe there are thousands that are good, without whom life could not go on. Enough now. Come, let's eat, Bobile.

NARRATOR: Bobile—Yiddish for "Little Granny"—Selman Waksman's pet name for his wife. To this day he calls her so. To this day she shares his problems and his triumphs.

MUSIC *(A few measures played as a bridge)*

NARRATOR: Dr. Waksman continued to search and seek and try to solve the mysteries of the life with which the soil is forever teeming. He was seeking to develop strains of microbes which would improve the soil and help it bring forth better crops. But while searching, a tremendous thought flashed through his brain—a thought which held out the promise of a life giving gift for mankind.

WAKSMAN: Bobile, you know what actinomycetes are, don't you?

BOBILE: Of course. I've heard enough of them. Haven't you named one after your mother and another one after me?

WAKSMAN: Well then—as you know, they are typical organisms which live in the soil. They are a bit more developed than bacteria and a bit less developed than fungi. Is that clear?

BOBILE: Not exactly.

WAKSMAN: It doesn't matter. At any rate, these organisms, when they come in contact with bacteria, tend to destroy them.

BOBILE: Does that do harm to the soil in which they are found?

WAKSMAN: We are not sure, Bobile! But you are learning well!

BOBILE: It's about time, don't you think? After being married to you for nearly twenty-three years . . .

WAKSMAN: That is true—come next week.

BOBILE: Now, why are you telling me about these microbes? Is there anything special about them?

WAKSMAN: I'm not sure, but, I was sort of wondering . . . Look, Bobile, there are many different kinds of actinomycetes. Some are harmful to one type of bacteria and some to others. Now, isn't it possible that we may find some that are harmful to bacteria that cause human and animal diseases?

BOBILE: Such as . . . ?

WAKSMAN: Such as typhus or plague, meningitis or tuberculosis. Where's my hat, Bobile?

BOBILE: Over there, on the chair. Where are you going?

WAKSMAN: To the laboratory. I must talk this over with the director and with my assistants.

BOBILE: But your dinner!

WAKSMAN: I'll be back later.

NARRATOR: The few minutes stretched into many hours while Dr Waksman outlined his idea to the Director of his Institution and to his various assistants. Then came many months of endless experiments. Systematically, Dr. Waksman and his assistants tested cultures of ten thousand microbes.

MUSIC *(A few measures played as a bridge)*

NARRATOR: Ten thousand! Each one was separately tested. None served the purpose. Doggedly the team of scientists continued their search. Then, late one night the researchers crowded around a group of test tubes.

WAKSMAN: It looks as if this is it, Schatz.

SCHATZ: There's no doubt about it, Dr. Waksman.

WAKSMAN: Let's try it on this one.

SCHATZ: Tubercle baccile?

WAKSMAN: Yes, Schatz. The culture in this test tube is teeming with tubercle baccile. They are constantly multiplying and growing more numerous.

SCHATZ: We can see it quite clearly under the microscope.

WAKSMAN: Now here is a culture of the same baccile. However, we've added some of the chemical substance which we got from our soil bacteria. Now look . . .

SCHATZ: The baccile have stopped growing.

WAKSMAN: Yes, they have stopped growing.

NARRATOR: Were the lips of Dr. Selman A. Waksman whispering a blessing?

WAKSMAN: *Baruch ata Hashem* . . .

NARRATOR: Blessed art Thou O Lord our God, King of the Universe who bringest forth the fruit of the earth.

MUSIC *(A few measures played as a bridge)*

NARRATOR: In 1944, Dr. Waksman announced to the world about the substance he had discovered with the help of Mr. Schatz and Miss Bugie, which would go a long way toward curing tuberculosis, meningitis and other ailments. He called it streptomycin. Drug companies began to produce streptomycin. They paid royalties for the right to produce it. The professor might have become a very wealthy man. However, he had other plans. Bobile agreed and Dr. Waksman sought an interview with the President of Rutgers University.

WAKSMAN: Mr. President, in a short time our royalites from streptomycin have mounted tremendously.

PRESIDENT: Even after you and your assistants get their share?

WAKSMAN: Even then. The royalties now amount to about one million five hundred thousand dollars.

PRESIDENT: That's quite a sum.

WAKSMAN: Yes, much more than any of us will ever need. I should like to suggest that ninety percent of the royalties be retained by Rutgers University.

PRESIDENT: That is quite a generous sum.

WAKSMAN: Rutgers has been generous to me. It gave me my education. It provided me with the possibilities to do my research.

PRESIDENT: But, in time, the royalties will amount to many millions of dollars.

WAKSMAN: Good. We will build an Institute for the study of microbes. We will try to attract the best scientists to come here so that they can do research to improve our soils to grow more food; to find other substances to cure man's diseases; to keep on searching for the secrets of life for a better life for mankind.

MUSIC *(A few measures played as a bridge)*

NARRATOR: Now, eight years after the discovery of streptomycin, Dr. Selman A. Waksman was given the world's greatest award, the Nobel Prize, for its discovery. *(Pause)* in Symphony Hall, the king of Sweden gives the coveted prize to the former Talmud student from Priluka.

MUSIC *(A few measures played as a bridge)*

NARRATOR: Outside the hall, wait little Eva Hellstrom and her father, engineer Bertil Hellstrom. The ceremonies are over. The scientists, the writers, the diplomats, the scholars are filing out. Now comes the gray-haired man from Rutgers with the mustache and eye-glasses and engineer Hellstrom nudges his daughter . . .

HELLSTROM: Now, Eva! There he is! Don't forget to curtsey!

EVA: Mr. Waksman . . .

WAKSMAN: Yes, little girl?

EVA: Here are five red carnations. One carnation for each . . . for each . . . Daddy! I forgot!

HELLSTROM: For each year. . . .

EVA: One carnation for each year of my life!

HELLSTROM: Good girl!

WAKSMAN: Thank you very much, but what does all this mean?

EVA: I don't know.

HELLSTROM: This is my daughter, Eva, Dr. Waksman. Five years ago she was stricken with meningitis. The doctors had already given up hope when the news of your discovery of streptomycin reached us. The drug was rushed to the hospital and saved her life.

WAKSMAN: I see . . .

HELLSTROM: And so these red carnations—five—one for each year my daughter has lived so far as a result of your discovery.

MUSIC *(Played softly as background)*

NARRATOR: The earth gave forth her fruit to him who knew how to search out her secrets. And the fruit of the earth brings healing and hope of her new life to those who once despaired of life.

MUSIC *(Up strong to a finish)*

VOICE: The Headline Parade passes by!

MUSIC *(A few measures of "Anu Ni'yeh Ha-ri-sho-nim" played forte, then fade and continue playing softly during final announcement.)*

ANNOUNCER: You have been listening to Headline Parade, a dramatization of the highlights of Jewish current news. The following students of class ______ *(or,* the following members of the Dramatic Group) participated in the program. *(Give the names of the students taking part.)* The entire program was directed by ______. The headlines of today are the history of tomorrow!

MUSIC *(Up forte to a finish)*

■ USING PUBLISHED HEADLINE PARADE SCRIPTS

Examination of the published Headline Parade dramatizations will reveal that many of them may be used, with minor changes, to teach news events of a recurring nature. For example:

> *Fifteen Minutes in the Forest*—This script was published in 1954 on the occasion of Youth Aliyah's twentieth anniversary. It may continue to be used each year to highlight the news of the current World Jewish Child's Day observance. Only minor changes in the statistics are necessary to bring the script up to date.

> *Herzl Comes Home*—This dramatization was written in 1949 on the occasion of the re-interrment of Herzl's body near Jerusalem. Since the script includes much biographical detail about Theodore Herzl it had widespread use in 1960 on the occasion of the one hundredth anniversary of the birth of Herzl. It is regularly used on the occasion of the annual observance of his death on the twentieth of Tamuz.

> *Father of Hassidism*—Was written in 1950 on the occasion of the two hundred and fiftieth birthday of Rabbi Israel Baal Shem Tov. In 1960 many news items dealt with the observance of the two hundredth anniversary of the death of

the Baal Shem. Teachers once again found the script useful for teaching this aspect of current history.

Eliezer Ben Yehudah was written in 1950. It continues to be used every year in connection with the observance of Hebrew month.

Israel published in 1951 is used annually in connection with the observance of Israel Independence Day.

■ IN CONCLUSION

Obviously, none of the suggestions for teaching current history offered here can be followed on the basis of "five minutes a week or fifteen minutes a month." The approaches indicated call for time. They demand teaching in depth—concentrating on small segments of Jewish life and teaching them from many aspects. It will be recognized however that these approaches deserve the time and the effort involved. Such teaching goes far beyond the immediate subject. It allows for free range over many areas of Jewish knowledge and Jewish life. It opens up vistas for the pupil, helping him to see that what he studies is important, that it *counts.* It helps him to understand how much of the Jewish present has come out of the Jewish past. Above all, it speaks directly to the mind and emotions of every individual student, fixing his role as part of the human race and the Community of Israel, indicating for him the course he must follow—the deeds he must perform to meet his responsibilities to himself and his fellow men.

Indexes

General Index

Index of Dramatizations Given as Examples

5. Language Teaching

6. Socio-Drama in Teaching Bible or *Humash*

7. Story Dramatization

United Synagogue Commission on Jewish Education

Jack J. Cohen
CHAIRMAN

Louis L. Ruffman
VICE-CHAIRMAN

Harry Malin
SECRETARY

Hyman Chanover
Elias Charry
Samuel Chiel
Josiah Derby
Samuel Dinin
Samuel H. Dresner
Azriel Eisenberg
George Ende
Sylvia C. Ettenberg
Myron M. Fenster
Henry R. Goldberg

Martin Goldstein
Simon Greenberg
A. Hillel Henkin
Ario S. Hyams
Adina Katzoff
William B. Lakritz
Alter F. Landesman
Arthur H. Neulander
Elliot Schwartz
Samuel Sussman
Alfred Weisel

EX-OFFICIO

Seymour Fox
Wolfe Kelman
Abraham E. Millgram
Samuel Schafler
Bernard Segal

Committee on Textbook Publications

Henry R. Goldberg
CHAIRMAN

Samuel Schafler
SECRETARY

Barnet Cohen
Josiah Derby
Morris S. Goodblatt
Solomon Grayzel
Isidore S. Meyer
Abraham E. Millgram
Saul Teplitz

FUNDERBURG LIBRARY
MANCHESTER COLLEGE

296.68
C498d